AMERICA'S LONGEST RUN

HABS No. PA-1487-8

THE PENNSYLVANIA STATE UNIVERSITY PRESS, UNIVERSITY PARK, PENNSYLVANIA

America's Longest Run is made possible through the support of Phoebe W. Haas Charitable Trust "A," the William Penn Foundation, and the Walnut Street Theatre.

Frontispiece: The earliest known photograph of the Walnut Street Theatre (see fig. 12).

A KEYSTONE BOOK®

A Keystone Book is so designated to distinguish it from the typical scholarly monograph that a university press publishes. It is a book intended to serve the citizens of Pennsylvania by educating them and others, in an entertaining way, about aspects of the history, culture, society, and environment of the state as part of the Middle Atlantic region.

Library of Congress Cataloging-in-Publication Data

Davis, Andrew, 1952–
America's longest run : a history of the Walnut Street Theatre / Andrew Davis.
p. cm.
Summary: "Traces the history of the Walnut Street Theatre in Philadelphia from its founding in 1809. Documents the productions and players at the theater, and the difficulties it has faced from economic crises, changing tastes, and competition from new media"—Provided by publisher.
Includes bibliographical references and index.
ISBN 978-0-271-03578-9 (cloth : alk. paper)
ISBN 978-0-271-03053-1 (pbk. : alk. paper)
1. Walnut Street Theatre (Philadelphia, Pa.)—History.
I. Title.

PN2277.P52W352 2010
792.09748'11—dc22
2009036142

Printed in the United States of America
Published by The Pennsylvania State University Press,
University Park, PA 16802-1003

The Pennsylvania State University Press is a member of the Association of American University Presses.

It is the policy of The Pennsylvania State University Press to use acid-free paper. Publications on uncoated stock satisfy the minimum requirements of American National Standard for Information Sciences—Permanence of Paper for Printed Library Material, ANSI Z39.48–1992.

This book is dedicated to the memory of

DOPHIE HAAS AND ESTHER KLEIN

CONTENTS

ILLUSTRATIONS

fig. 1 The current exterior of Walnut Street Theatre.

AMERICA'S OLDEST THEATRE

It is easy to overlook the building that stands on the northeast corner of Ninth and Walnut streets in Philadelphia's central city. In a city full of historic buildings, there is little to draw your attention to this particular structure. Its marble façade and Greek columns make it look more like a bank than a theatre. But this is the Walnut Street Theatre, America's oldest and—Philadelphians will tell you—most distinguished theatre. This building has served the city of Philadelphia for more than two hundred years. A bronze marker, placed there by the Pennsylvania Historical and Museum Commission, announces the Walnut as "the oldest playhouse in continuous use in the English-speaking world." That is reaching a bit. The Walnut is certainly the oldest theatre in the United States, and it predates any of the London theatres: Covent Garden dates back to 1856, rebuilt after a fire, and Drury Lane was constructed in 1812 after a similar disaster. The honor of the oldest operating theatre in the English-speaking world rightly belongs to the Theatre Royal in Bristol, England, which has been standing since 1766. The basis for the claim that the Walnut is oldest playhouse "in continuous use" is that the Theatre Royal was shuttered for most of World War II. By that measure, the Walnut has been in continuous use only since the Great Depression, for it too was dark for several years.

Whether the Walnut is older than Bristol's Theatre Royal is a small matter. The Walnut Street Theatre's significance is secure. The Walnut has been at or near the center of American theatrical activity since Thomas Jefferson was president of the United States. While there have been seasons when the Walnut was dark, it has been serving the people of Philadelphia as an entertainment center for more than two hundred years. That is no mean accomplishment, particularly when you consider its origins. The Walnut was not a particularly prestigious theatre. It was not built as a theatre at all. The arena that opened on February 2, 1809, was announced as the New Circus. There was no stage, merely a sawdust ring, with three tiers of boxes surrounding it, in the style of European circuses. It was a temporary arena, built to house an equestrian show whenever the circus was in town. This was before the circus tent came into use, when circuses played in wooden arenas in various cities where they appeared. The Walnut—or what would become the Walnut—was one of several structures built by Victor Pepin and Jean Breschard in Boston, New York, Baltimore, and Philadelphia. The others were made of wood and were torn down within a few years. Philadelphia fire regulations required that it be built of brick. And so it lasted.

The building that now occupies the lot at Ninth and Walnut streets bears little resemblance to the arena constructed on the western periphery of the city back in 1809. The original building had a plain brick façade and a peaked roof. Its most striking feature was an immense dome that rose some eighty feet into the air. Topped by a flagpole, it was the tallest structure in the city. The dome was removed in 1820 to improve acoustics, while the Greek revival façade along Walnut Street comes from an 1828 renovation.

From the beginning, the Walnut was a populist house. The fashionable set patronized the Chestnut Street Theatre (spelled Chesnut in those days), located diagonally across from Independence Hall, on Chestnut just west of Sixth. Built in 1794, the Chestnut was the most elegant and palatial theatre in the United States. Philadelphians were justifiably proud of the Chestnut and its acting company, which rivaled anything New York City had to offer. The theatre's managers amassed the largest library of music and plays and the largest collection of costumes this side of the Atlantic Ocean, and it contributed to Philadelphia's status as "the Athens of the United States."

At the Walnut, on the other hand, they stabled horses. Circus was *the* popular entertainment of the time. There was no vaudeville or burlesque or musical comedy or minstrelsy. All of these entertainment forms developed out of the early American circus, and eventually all of them would play at the Walnut. The circus appealed to the less sophisticated set, and the emphasis at the Walnut was on entertainment and spectacle. Even when a stage was added at one end of the equestrian ring, the Olympic, as it was then called, was best known for grand historic spectacles and hippodramas—melodramas that featured action on horseback. The public flocked to see these attractions, particularly when they featured a patriotic theme.

Why should the people's theatre survive, when other, more prestigious theatres did not? Luck had something to do with it. Fire claimed many of the early theatres. In an era when the stage was lit by oil or gas lamps, there was always the danger that an open flame might catch a piece of wardrobe or curtain. If this happened during a performance, the loss of life could be catastrophic. As frightened theatergoers stampeded to the exits, people were more likely to be trampled to death than overcome by smoke and flame. The night the Walnut offered its first legitimate theatrical production—January 1, 1812—word arrived from Virginia that just such a tragedy had occurred at the Richmond Theatre. Seventy-two people lost their lives in the crush to escape the burning building. The governor of Virginia was among the dead.

Such a horrific loss of life never occurred at a Philadelphia theatre, but fire claimed many of the early theatres. Philadelphia historians Thomas Scharf and Thompson Westcott estimated that one of every three theatres built in Philadelphia between 1799 and 1871 was destroyed by fire.[1] Fire ripped through Ricketts's Circus on a cold December night in 1799, destroying the first circus building in America. The Chestnut Street Theatre went up in flames under suspicious circumstances in 1820. The acting company moved over to the Olympic Theatre, christening it the Walnut Street Theatre. In 1824 a fire swept through Vauxhall Gardens, an open-air theatre at Broad and Walnut, where the public could imbibe refreshments and enjoy variety entertainment. Some of this public, which had enjoyed too many of these refreshments, set fire to a hot-air balloon that was supposed to ascend into the sky that day. The National Theatre, located at Chestnut and Ninth, went up in flames on another day of celebration—July 4, 1854. Gilmore's Auditorium, two doors east of the Walnut, burned down four times between 1863 and 1892. Nine firemen were killed during the 1867 fire when the walls collapsed.

Those that were not destroyed by fire fell victim to the wrecker's ball. The Southwark Theatre was taken down in 1913. The fact that it was the oldest surviving theatre building in North America was not enough to save it. Built in 1766, the Southwark served the people of Philadelphia for fifty years. The Southwark had not been used for theatrical performances since 1817. A fire partially destroyed the building in 1821, making it unusable as a performance space. It was rebuilt as a hayloft and for many years housed a distillery. Another great historic building, the Arch Street Theatre, was razed in 1936. It was one of half a dozen historic theatres that yielded to the wrecker's ball during the Great Depression. At the time of its demolition, the Arch was the second-oldest theatre in America, dating from 1828.

The Walnut Street Theatre was set to be demolished several times during the course of two centuries of operation. The first time was in 1827, but the owners decided to renovate instead. Plans were made to construct a fashionable new building on the lot in 1920, but zoning laws would have reduced the size of the theatre that could be built. There was thought of tearing it down in 1956, when it was being run as a tryout house by the Shubert Organization. The Shuberts had run into antitrust problems; a federal judge had ordered them to divest themselves of some of their properties, and they decided that the Walnut had to go. Only the intervention of the wife of the theatre's manager saved it from the wrecking ball.

Until the 1960s, no one paid much attention to preserving historic theatres in the United States. Older theatres were considered something of an embarrassment. They have a way of looking dowdy a few decades after they were built, as paint peels, upholstery fades, and ideas of what is stylish and chic change. We might preserve historic sites like Independence Hall or the elegant homes of the nation's founding fathers. But theatres, despite the glamour attached to them, were treated more like factories. They were judged by utilitarian standards, and when their usefulness ended they were abandoned or torn down. That the Walnut has remained standing for so many years, through wars and economic downturns, is a testament to its usefulness.

By 1964 people had begun to appreciate the historic nature of the Walnut. That year, the Interior Department declared the Walnut a National Landmark. This meant, among other things, that the original structure was protected. By that time, however, there was very little of the original structure left to protect. All that remained were three of the outside walls. The roof and the interior of the building were renovated sometime between 1820 and 1920. Owners were still free to make changes to the interior, and in 1970 they gutted the inside to give it a modern, up-to-date look.

It is not the architecture that gives the Walnut Street Theatre its historical significance, however, but the events and productions that have taken place within its walls. Like the Civil War battlefields that are hallowed by the lives of soldiers that were lost there, the Walnut is hallowed by the men and women who have given their lives to the theatre.

Most of the great figures in American theatre appeared at the Walnut in the nineteenth century—Edwin Forrest, Junius Brutus Booth, Charlotte Cushman, Edwin Booth, Joseph Jefferson, Mrs. Drew, Richard Mansfield, Minnie Maddern Fiske—most of them returned season after season. Popular entertainers also appeared—General Tom Thumb, Harrigan and Hart, Lotta Crabtree, Buffalo Bill Cody, and Lillian Russell, among others. European stars were booked into the Walnut during their American tours—Edmund Kean, Charles and Fanny Kemble, Rachel, Lola Montez, Tommaso Salvini, and Lillie Langtry.

The twentieth century brought such distinguished stage stars as the Barrymores, Eva Le Gallienne, Walter Hampden, Alfred Lunt and Lynne Fontanne, Dame Judith Anderson, Maurice Evans, Helen Hayes, Jessica Tandy and Hume Cronyn, Ossie Davis and Ruby Dee. Many of the stars we remember today made their names in film. Lillian and Dorothy Gish, William S. Hart, Gloria Swanson, Douglas Fairbanks, Will Rogers, W. C. Fields, Mae

West, Edward G. Robinson, James Cagney, the Marx Brothers, Boris Karloff, Claudette Colbert, Henry Fonda, Kirk Douglas, Marlon Brando, David Niven, Sidney Poitier, Jack Lemmon, Jane Fonda, Robert Redford, and Gene Hackman are just a few of the Hollywood celebrities who have graced the Walnut's stage. Some of them appeared at the Walnut before they became stars; others returned to the stage after successful Hollywood careers.

Every kind of performing art has been represented at the Walnut—comedians like Pigmeat Markham, Lily Tomlin, and Bill Cosby; dancers like Ruth St. Denis, Martha Graham, Alvin Ailey, and Twyla Tharp; magicians from Blackstone to Penn and Teller; mimes from Marcel Marceau to Mummenschanz. Sports figures like heavyweight champion James J. Corbett and tennis great Big Bill Tilden have graced the Walnut's stage. So have presidents—Jimmy Carter and Gerald Ford held their first debate at the Walnut during the 1976 presidential election campaign. The Walnut has been host to writers like Bernard Malamud, newscasters like Mike Wallace, opera singers like Jessye Norman, activists like Yippie leader Jerry Rubin, rock icons like Sting.

While it may be gratifying to note the famous actors who have stood on the stage of the Walnut Street Theatre, much of the story of the Walnut has been carried forward by far less notable names. One of these is "Pop" Reed, the stagehand who lit the gas jets before every performance for nearly fifty years and who, on his death, bequeathed his skull to the theatre. The managers also figure prominently, among them Francis Courtney Wemyss, E. A. Marshall, and Mrs. M. Augusta Garrettson, who ran the Walnut for several years. There is John Sleeper Clarke, who purchased the Walnut with his brother-in-law, Edwin Booth, and later bought him out. These men and women spent a good portion of their careers and often their life savings in the ever-risky profession of producing live theatre.

The Walnut's story is a classic American success story. Built by immigrants who came to America to seek their fortune, the Walnut adapted to the ever-changing tastes and desires of the theatergoing public. Today, the Walnut boasts of being the largest subscription theatre in the United States. It has not been an easy journey. Over the years it has suffered many setbacks due to economic downturns and competition from new media. The Walnut's owners and managers lost their shirts—and sometimes their entire wardrobes—when the economy or changing tastes turned against them. Through it all, an entrepreneurial spirit has prevailed—each time one manager failed, there were always people waiting to try their hand at running the theatre.

This book chronicles the struggles and triumphs of the men and women who have made the Walnut run. While this is the story of a single theatre, it is also the history of the American stage. The Walnut is uniquely situated. Because Philadelphia is located so close to New York City, the fortunes of the Walnut have been closely tied to what was happening on Broadway. For nearly three decades it was a tryout house for Broadway-bound shows. At the same time, it shared the problems and concerns of theatres in the rest of the country, booking shows out of New York, adapting to competition from movies, and moving into the nonprofit world.

The way theatre is produced—and consumed—has changed dramatically over the past two hundred years. When the Walnut opened, theatres operated as stock companies, employing a resident corps of actors who put on a different show every night of the week. This system was replaced by the star system, with the leading European and American actors coming in, and local actors taking on supporting roles. Technology affected how theatre was produced; new technology radically changed theatre practice. Advances in lighting altered acting styles and allowed new scenic effects. The growth of railroads had an even greater impact, allowing producers to ship a full show, complete with sets and wardrobe, across the country. The Walnut, like most theatres outside New York, became a rental house for touring productions. Circuits were organized at the end of the nineteenth century to streamline distribution, and the Walnut was taken over by the Syndicate, a group of powerful producers who controlled theatrical distribution nationwide. Their power faded only with the introduction of movies, which devastated the theatre industry. New owners coped with this new challenge in any way they could, mounting trashy potboilers to lure customers away from nickelodeons. The Walnut entered its most difficult era during the Great Depression, as the owners tried every means of keeping the theatre open, offering movies, burlesque, and Yiddish theatre before briefly becoming the home of the Federal Theatre Project.

The Walnut enjoyed what many consider its golden age during World War II, when it was purchased by the Shubert Organization and became a tryout house for Broadway-bound shows. *A Streetcar Named Desire* had its tryout run at the Walnut before moving on to Broadway. Several other important shows debuted at the Walnut, including *The Diary of Anne Frank* and *A Raisin in the Sun*. With its fortunes so closely tied to Broadway, however, the Walnut fell on hard times in the 1960s, as Broadway began to decline. Recognizing that legitimate theatre—like other arts—could survive only with support from government and foundation sources, a group of civic leaders raised money to buy and restore the old building and converted the Walnut into a nonprofit performing arts center. Again there were difficulties. The civic leaders had no experience running a theatre and ran a deficit year after year, which was picked up by the William Penn Foundation. With the arrival of Bernard Havard in 1982, and the decision to become a producing house again, the Walnut found its purpose.

Today, the Walnut is one of the most successful regional theatres in the country. More than 350,000 people attend a show at the Walnut each year. Fifty-seven thousand people have season subscriptions—more than any other theatre in the United States. The Walnut mounts five mainstage productions each year and five second-stage or studio theatre productions. It also operates a theatre school and a community outreach program. While it is tempting to see this as the culmination of the story, in fact, the history of the Walnut Street Theatre will continue to be written as long as someone arrives each day to light the lights.

THE BEGINNINGS OF THEATRE IN PHILADELPHIA, 1682–1809

Theatre had no place in the ideal society William Penn envisioned for the city on the banks of the Delaware River. "How many plays did Jesus Christ and his apostles recreate themselves at?" he demanded in *No Cross, No Crown*. "What poets, romances, comedies, and the like did the apostles and saints make or use to pass away their time?" In Penn's view, such amusements distracted people from the more important duty of preparing their souls for the hereafter. Pennsylvania was to be a "free, just and industrious colony," offering a haven and a livelihood for ingenious spirits of all faiths and social classes. Amusements "excited people to rudeness, cruelty, looseness and irreligion" and were incompatible with a city based on brotherly love.[1]

Such attitudes were widespread in the American colonies. Commercial amusements like the theatre, circus, and other entertainments were considered a waste of time. Traveling players were viewed with suspicion, seen by many as unsettled and untrustworthy vagabonds. At best, those who earned their livelihoods through such activities were seen as frittering away their lives. At worst, they were viewed as an immoral and dissolute lot. Restoration theatre, with its portrayal of marital infidelity and flirtation, was seen as especially licentious. Disapproval was strongest in New England, where the Puritan church held sway, but there was a good deal of suspicion wherever traveling entertainers appeared, and Quaker leaders also spoke out against the pernicious effects of the theatre. Stage plays smacked too much of the aristocracy in the view of many Protestant settlers in America. Like many others, William Penn had a distaste for the rich trappings and loose morals of the aristocracy, which had been returned to power in England after the Puritan commonwealth of Oliver Cromwell came to an end.

When Penn drafted the first *Frame of Government of Pennsylvania* in 1682, he explicitly prohibited theatrical productions, subjecting violators to a twenty-shilling fine or ten days' imprisonment at hard labor.[2] The British monarchy took a different view of theatrical activity. The Crown regularly reviewed the legislation coming out of the colonies and set aside the statute against the theatre in 1683. The Pennsylvania Assembly continued to pass laws against stage plays, masques, and revels, which the British Crown reversed. In 1700 the Assembly passed an Act Against Riots, Rioters, and Riotous Sports, Plays and Games, which was revoked in 1705. The following year a new prohibition was enacted, which was overturned in 1709. Yet another statute was enacted in 1711 and repealed two years later.[3] No other prohibitions were attempted until 1759, but antitheatre bias remained strong in Philadelphia, not just among the Quakers but among Presbyterians and various German Calvinist groups as well.

ITINERANT SHOWMEN AND TRAVELING ENTERTAINMENTS

Theatrical productions were rare in the colonies before the middle of the eighteenth century. There are only scattered indications of plays being staged. In 1699 and 1702 one Richard Hunter petitioned the governor of New York for a license to present plays. Though permission was granted, there is no evidence that any performances took place. In 1714 a play titled *Androboros, a Biographical Farce in Three Acts*, which satirized local political figures, was published in New York, but it was never produced. In 1716 a playhouse was built in Williamsburg, Virginia, the first in the English colonies. There is some evidence that plays were produced there, but it was eventually converted to other uses.[4]

Generally, the population was too sparse and too spread out to sustain a regular company of professional players. In 1700 the population of Philadelphia was roughly two thousand—too small to support a resident theatre company. Travel between the colonies was slow and arduous. A single dirt road connected most communities, and in wet weather roads became impassable. Under the best conditions it took three days to travel overland from Philadelphia to New York in the early 1700s, another four to get to Boston. Sustaining an entire theatre company on the road would be difficult.

Professional theatrical activity, where it occurred, was largely in the hands of individuals. One of the more common amusements during the colonial period was the exhibition of trained or exotic animals. Such exhibitions probably go back to times when a hunter would bring a tame bear into town and exhibit it at frontier taverns or village commons, passing the hat in order to buy food and drink. Sailors picked up pet monkeys on their overseas travels, which they showed off in the ports they visited. By the early eighteenth century, large exotic animals were being brought to America. The first lion was exhibited in 1716, a camel was brought over in 1721, and a polar bear captured in Greenland was on view in 1733.[5] In 1796 a sea captain named Jacob Crowninshield purchased a three-year-old female elephant in Bengal for $450 and brought it into New York City. A Philadelphian identified only as Mr. Owen bought the elephant for $10,000 and began traveling with it up and down the Atlantic seaboard. For the next twenty-five years Owen toured the elephant as far south as Savannah, Georgia, and as far north as Newburyport, Massachusetts.[6]

These creatures excited great curiosity. There were, of course, no zoos, and no public museums or other collections of animals. Such exhibitions could be justified as educational and scientific, thereby circumventing the laws against amusements. Devout colonists could be enticed into paying money to see one of the animals mentioned in the Bible. Animals were usually exhibited individually, but in 1781 a menagerie featuring "birds, reptiles, snakes and quadrupeds" was advertised.[7]

Itinerant showmen were common during the colonial period, performing many of the same tricks common in European festivals. Tightrope walkers, acrobats and leapers, and animal trainers exhibited their skills, often taking advantage of local fairs, court sittings, election days, and other public events that drew people together. John Durang described the gathering at one such harvest fair. "The market place is furnish'd with every description of fineries with some useful as well as ornamental goods by settle merchants from Philad'a and Baltimore; all kinds of diversions going on during the whole day, the taverns crowded: in every room a fiddle, and dancing, bottles of wine on the table; showfolks with their signs out, hand organs and trumpits to invite the people to see poppet shows, wire dancing, slight of hand."[8]

The earliest report of such a showman in Philadelphia dates to 1723, when one set up a stage just south of the city limits, putting on a program that featured jokes and tricks. The General Assembly tried to get the governor, Sir William Keith, to prohibit the performance. Instead, he announced that he intended to go see it. The following year, the showman returned with a program that featured a seven-year-old girl "who danced and capered upon a strait roap, to the wonder of all spectators," with humor provided by "your old friend Pickle Herring," a traditional German clown character.[9] Handbills advertised "the New Booth on Society Hill," just south of the city on South Street. No description of the theatre building is available, but it suggests one of the booth theatres that were often set up at European fairs. These were little more than a raised platform—planks laid across the tops of barrels—enclosed by a canvas or a temporary wooden structure.[10]

With no permanent theatre buildings, itinerant showmen often made use of inn yards and other public locations. In 1727 a lion was exhibited in Water Street. A marvelous cat, "having one head, eight legs, two tails and from the breast down two bodies," was advertised in 1737. In 1739 a mechanical contrivance of moving figures was exhibited at Clark's Tavern.[11] Marionettes were exhibited at "at the Sign of the Coach-and-Horses, against the State House, in Chestnut Street" in 1742. The following year, a "Magick Lanthorn" show was advertised at Joseph Barber's "at the Temple Bar in Second Street."[12]

THE BEGINNINGS OF THE PROFESSIONAL THEATRE IN AMERICA

The first professional actors' company did not appear in America until 1749, when a company led by Walter Murray and Thomas Kean arrived in Philadelphia. The origin of the troupe is unknown, but it probably came from England by way of the West Indies. In August 1749 this company staged Joseph Addison's tragedy *Cato* in a warehouse space owned by William Plumstead on Water Street. The troupe remained in Philadelphia until February 1750, when the actors were forced out by pressure from the community. They moved on to New York, where they settled in for two seasons, performing a repertory of five plays and three afterpieces.[13] An evening's entertainment of the time typically featured a one-act farce called an afterpiece, which followed the main production. Murray and Kean then moved to Williamsburg, Virginia, and toured other towns in Virginia and Maryland for several years before fading from the scene.

The first permanent theatre company in America was organized in 1752 by William Hallam, a small-time theatrical manager in London. He persuaded his brother, Lewis Hallam, to take his wife and three children to the New World to form the nucleus of a company that would tour the colonies. Theatre at this time was often a family business. The difficulties of touring, with its lengthy separations, meant that actors toured with their spouses. It was not unusual for touring players to bring the entire family. Children gained stage experience in bit parts, and many took up the trade. The Hallams were the first of many important acting families that would shape the history the American stage.

This "Company of Comedians from London," as the troupe billed itself, was organized like a typical provincial English company of the period. The actors were not paid but received shares in the company, dividing up box office receipts. The Hallam troupe had twelve members, and each actor was given a share, with several shares set aside for the backers. Each actor specialized in a "line" of parts, playing more or less the same roles in various productions.

These lines were standard roles in English plays of the time. Lewis Hallam, in addition to being the manager of the troupe, was the low comedian, playing broad comic characters. Mrs. Hallam was the leading lady. She was paired with a Mr. Clarkson, the leading man, but sometimes played opposite Mr. Rigby, the leading tragedian and light comedian. Supporting the leading man was Mr. Singleton, a juvenile who specialized in playing young lovers and fine gentlemen. Mr. Malone was the heavy, playing villainous roles and middle-aged men. Mr. Herbert, Mr. Adcock, and Mr. Winnel had minor roles. Two of the men brought along their wives; Mrs. Clarkson and Mrs. Rigby were both used in supporting roles. Miss Palmer was cast as the soubrette, playing saucy ladies' maids. The Hallam children were put to work in minor walk-on roles.[14]

The Hallam troupe set sail for America in the spring of 1752 on a ship called *Charming Sally.* During the forty-two-day crossing—considered a very quick passage in the age of sail—they rehearsed their plays on the quarterdeck. The repertoire was mostly stock pieces popular with London audiences and consisted of some two dozen plays, including five works by Shakespeare, three Restoration dramas, and fifteen works by the leading playwrights of the day—including five by George Farquhar, three by Nicholas Rowe, and two by Colley Cibber.[15]

The *Charming Sally* landed in Yorktown on June 2, 1752, and the company proceeded to Williamsburg, then the capital of Virginia. Lewis Hallam applied to the governor of the colony for permission to perform and was denied. The Murray-Kean company had performed in Williamsburg the previous year and had run up considerable debts and engaged in "loose behavior." Hallam managed to persuade the citizenry of his troupe's responsibility, and the governor eventually gave his permission. The Company of Comedians moved into Williamsburg's playhouse and began refurbishing it.

They opened on September 15, 1752, presenting *The Merchant of Venice.* The part of Shylock was played by a Mr. Malone, Portia by Mrs. Hallam, and the comic role of Launcelot Gobbo by Mr. Hallam. Lewis Hallam Jr., who was only twelve at the time, made his first stage appearance.[16] He was seized with stage fright and had to leave the stage. Despite this inauspicious beginning, he would go on to have an important career as an actor and theatrical manager. The Company of Comedians gave regular performances in Williamsburg for the next nine months, performing every Monday, Wednesday, and Friday evening.

In the summer of 1753 they departed for New York, where they appeared from September 17, 1753, to March 18, 1754. During their New York run, Hallam was approached by "several gentlemen from Philadelphia" who encouraged them to come to that city, then the largest in the colonies. After some difficulty, Hallam received permission to put on twenty-four performances, on the condition that the repertory contain "nothing indecent or immoral." They used the same warehouse that William Plumstead had made available to Thomas Kean and Walter Murray two years before. On April 15 they debuted with Nicholas Rowe's *The Fair Penitent*, followed by an afterpiece by David Garrick titled *Miss in Her Teens*.[17]

After a two-month run in Philadelphia, the Hallam Company moved on to Charleston, South Carolina, then sailed for Jamaica. Their plans were disrupted by the death of Lewis Hallam. The activities of the Hallam troupe in Jamaica are uncertain, but four years later Mrs. Hallam returned to America, married to an energetic theatrical manager named David Douglass, who had combined his company with the Hallam troupe. At eighteen, Lewis Hallam Jr. was now the company's leading man. During the winter of 1758 the company played in New York at a theatre Douglass built. By spring the company was back in Philadelphia, where they played for six months, presenting eighty plays.[18]

In 1759 Douglass constructed the Society Hill Theatre, a modest frame building on the south side of Cedar Street (now South Street), just outside the city limits. This was a common tactic, which put the troupe outside the jurisdiction of the Quaker-dominated Assembly. The theatre was used for only six months, when organized opposition by the press and clergy stopped its use for theatrical purposes.[19] The company continued to tour the larger cities along the Atlantic coast—New York, Philadelphia, Annapolis, Newport, and Charleston—in playhouses that Douglass constructed.

Anti-British feeling was growing in the colonies, and a company of English actors was becoming increasingly suspect. In the early 1760s Douglass decided to change the name of his troupe from the London Company to the American Company. For several years the American Company toured primarily in Virginia and South Carolina, where there was less antitheatre sentiment.[20]

THE SOUTHWARK THEATRE

Returning to Philadelphia in 1766 for the first time in several years, Douglass constructed the first permanent theatre building in North America. The Southwark Theatre was built at the intersection of Fourth and what is now South Street, just outside the city limits. It had the outward look of a church, with a belfry set in the middle of a steeply sloped roof. The foundation and first floor were of brick and the second floor of wood frame construction painted red, a typical color for colonial theatres. The building was ninety-five feet long and fifty feet wide and held about eight hundred people.[21] The building was famous for its ugliness, uncomfortable seating, and poor sight lines. The roof leaked, and in the winter audiences had to bring small stoves to keep warm. The stage was lit by plain oil lamps without glass. Large, square wooden pillars that supported the upper tier and the roof blocked the audience's view of the stage. Despite these problems, the Southwark was the most important theatre in Philadelphia for the next thirty years, and was occasionally used by touring companies as late as 1817. In 1821 a fire partially destroyed the building, and it was rebuilt as a hayloft, then taken over by a distillery, which occupied the building until the early twentieth century.

At this point the American Company consisted of some two dozen actors and featured an orchestra. During the opening season, the company played three nights a week—again on Monday, Wednesday, and Friday. Forty-two different plays were produced during the first season, in addition to farces and musical entertainments. The more popular plays would be performed two or three times.[22] The price of admission was seven shillings and six pence for box seats, five shillings for the pit, and three shillings for the gallery. Doors opened at four o'clock for a six o'clock curtain. Since seats were not reserved, it was common for more affluent Philadelphians to send their servants to claim their seats in the boxes or pit. The repertoire featured the best of the British theatre, and during the course of a season included thirty-five to forty different plays, with farces, short comedies, musical plays, and pantomimes as well.[23]

It was in the Southwark Theatre, on April 24, 1767, that the American Company staged the first production of a play written by an American—*The Prince of Parthia*. Thomas Godfrey, a Philadelphian, had died several years before, and Douglass staged it at the urging of several of Godfrey's friends. It does not seem to have been successful, for there is no record of a second performance. The same year, a student from Princeton identified only as Mr. Grenville joined the company, deserting college for a life on the stage—becoming the first American-born player.[24]

The American Company went to New York, where it built a replica of the Southwark, the John Street Theatre. The troupe returned to Philadelphia in the winters of 1768 and 1769 and did not return after that until 1772, spending the intervening years touring the South. During the winter of 1772–73 the players performed the second original American drama, *The Conquest of Canada, or The Siege of Quebec*, a spectacular production that featured artillery, boats, and soldiers from the local militia. The company returned in the winter of 1773, but during that run Mrs. Douglass died, and the company left the city.[25]

THEATRE DURING THE REVOLUTION

As the American Company was preparing to return to Philadelphia in the fall of 1774, the Continental Congress, meeting in Philadelphia, passed a resolution discouraging "every species of extravagance and dissipation, especially all horseracing, and all kinds of gaming, cock-fighting, exhibition of shews, plays and other expensive diversions and entertainments."[26] The American Company, which was then preparing for its 1774–75 season, took the cue and disbanded. David Douglass took most of the company to Jamaica, where the actors remained for the duration of the American Revolution.

With the American Company gone, no professional theatre productions were presented during the Revolution, but both British and American troops put on amateur productions. After British troops captured Philadelphia in the fall of 1777, British officers organized a company composed of officers and soldiers' wives and reopened the Southwark Theatre for plays. They put on thirteen performances at the theatre between January 19 and May 19, 1778.

A leader of this effort was Major John André, who would later be hanged as a spy for his involvement with Benedict Arnold. A talented artist, André painted the drops, including a landscape "presenting a distant champagne country and a winding rivulet" that remained in the Southwark until it burned in 1821.[27] His story became the subject of a tragedy by William Dunlap, titled *André*. It is reported that years later one of the drops painted by Major André was used in a performance of the play depicting his death.

American troops presented two plays at Valley Forge in the spring of 1778. George Washington attended a performance of *Cato*, a poetic tragedy by Joseph Addison about the Roman statesman who resisted tyrannical rulers. It was a great favorite with Americans during the Revolution and the early years of the Republic.

The Americans drove the British from Philadelphia in the summer of 1778, and some of the troops took over the Southwark Theatre and began offering performances themselves. In October, however, the Continental Congress—asserting that theatrical entertainments diverted the minds of the people from the defense of their country and protection of their liberties—passed a resolution declaring "that any person holding an office under the United States who shall act, promote, attend or encourage such plays, shall be deemed unworthy to hold such office and shall be accordingly dismissed." Those who built a playhouse or caused one to be built would be fined $500.[28]

THE OLD AMERICAN COMPANY AND ITS COMPETITORS

General Cornwallis surrendered to American forces in Yorktown in October 1781, ending the fight for American independence. A few months later, John Henry, a member of the American Company, was back in Philadelphia petitioning authorities for permission to present a dramatic offering titled

"A Lecture on Heads." He was unsuccessful. Lewis Hallam Jr. returned to the city early in 1784, reopening the Southwark Theatre with a series of programs billed as "lectures," "moral dialogues," and "pantomimical fables" in the hope of getting around the ban on theatrical performances. The ruse only served to anger the opposition, and the company was forced to move to New York.

John Henry returned to Philadelphia in late 1785 with several members of the American Company, joining forces with Hallam a few months later. Lewis Hallam campaigned to have the Philadelphia Assembly repeal the ban against theatrical activity, arguing that the stage served to "support scenes of morality." Restrictions on theatrical performances remained in place in Philadelphia until 1789, and the Old American Company, as the troupe was now called, continued to disguise their plays as lectures, concerts, and moral dialogues. The company alternated between the Southwark Theatre in Philadelphia and the John Street Theatre in New York, playing shorter engagements in Baltimore, Richmond, Charleston, and other smaller cities.

In 1790 the capitol of the United States moved to Philadelphia. George Washington took up residence in the city in the fall. With the seat of government located in the city, Philadelphia was becoming more cosmopolitan, and attitudes against the theatre began to loosen. The new president was a great fan of the theatre and regularly attended performances at the Southwark. "When Gen'l Washington visited the theatre, the east stage box was decorated with the United States coat of arms over the box," John Durang recalled. "Mr. Wignell, dress'd in black and powdered, with two silver candlesticks would wait at the box door to receive him and light him to his seat. A guard of soldiers where [*sic*] in attendance on the occasion, one soldier at each stage door, four placet [*sic*] in the gallery, with the assistance of our high constable Mr. Carlisle, a man of gigantic make."[29] Such pomp did much to soften public attitudes and helped to legitimize the theatre.

The increasing population led to increased competition. In 1785 two troupes were formed by disaffected members of the Old American Company. These new companies had only limited success and soon folded. In 1791, however, Thomas Wignell, the principal comedian of the troupe, quit and formed a partnership with Alexander Reinagle, a Philadelphia musician, and the two of them established a company that would dominate Philadelphia for the next several decades.

Wignell returned to England to recruit actors for the new theatrical company. He came back with "a numorous [*sic*] company of good actors together with an extensive wardrobe and library of dramatic and musical books."[30] At the time, the Old American Company had pretty much settled in New York, playing occasionally at the Southwark Theatre until it quit the city for good in 1794. Wignell and Reinagle put together what would become the premiere company of actors of the early Republic.

THE CHESTNUT STREET THEATRE

Wignell and Reinagle began work in 1791 on a theatre on Chestnut Street, just west of Sixth Street. Originally referred to as the New Theatre, it became better known as the Chestnut Street Theatre. Modeled on the Theatre Royal at Bath, England, the new theatre was the largest and most elegant theatre constructed in America up to that time. Built to seat twelve to fourteen hundred people, it was made of brick and sat on a lot 90 by 134 feet located diagonally across the street from the statehouse buildings that include Independence Hall.[31]

While the theatre was being constructed, Wignell made use of the time by returning to England and securing several actors from Britain, along with "a front drop, an extensive and brilliant wardrobe and music."[32] Wignell and Reinagle had to delay the opening of the New Theatre because of a yellow fever epidemic that struck the city in the summer of 1793. Such epidemics caused severe hardship for theatres, since spectators stayed away from crowds, and those who could afford to left the cities entirely. By the winter of 1793–94, the yellow fever had abated, and the New Theatre opened on February 17, 1794, with an opera, *The Castle of Andalusia*, followed by an afterpiece titled *Who's the Dupe?*

The interior of the Chestnut Street Theatre was more impressive than the exterior. The auditorium was painted gray with a gold design. It had three tiers of fifteen boxes each, forming a horseshoe shape. Gilt railings on the third row of boxes added a touch of elegance, and the interior walls of the boxes were covered with red wallpaper. A small shuttered window at the rear of each box could be opened for ventilation. Each box held eight people on two rows of benches. The pit was raked from the first tier of boxes down to the orchestra pit. Thirteen rows of benches were set up in the pit and held around four hundred people. The auditorium was lit by small chandeliers placed in every other box. The stage was lit by oil lamps, which could be lowered for night scenes.[33]

Wignell traveled periodically to England to pick up new scripts, sheet music, and actors for the Philadelphia company. In 1796 he returned with three actors who would play an important role in the making of American drama. Thomas A. Cooper was only twenty when he arrived in America. He had made a spectacular debut at Covent Garden in *Hamlet*, but he failed to get more London engagements and was enticed into coming to America, where he became the leading tragedian of his era. Cooper remained at the Chestnut Street Theatre only a short time before moving to New York for better roles, and was one of the first English-born actors to become a citizen of the new United States. William Warren specialized in playing comic old men but was better known as a theatre manager, taking over for Thomas Wignell as head of the Chestnut Street Theatre. Mrs. Ann Merry was one of the most popular actresses of the British stage, and she became a favorite with Philadelphia audiences as well. Slim, feminine, and gifted with a melodious voice, she was lauded as "the most perfect actress America has seen." She married Thomas Wignell and, after his death, went on to marry William Warren, helping him manage the Chestnut Street Theatre until her death in 1808.

THE CIRCUS

Competition for this new company came not from other theatre troupes but from the circus. Although some histories trace the circus back to the Roman era, it is simply the term "circus" that survives from ancient times. In the late eighteenth century the circus was a relatively new creation. The first modern circus was established in England in 1768, when a retired British cavalry officer named Philip Astley built a riding school on the outskirts of London. He began staging open-air demonstrations of trick riding, and the events proved so popular that he began charging admission, using the profits to enclose the ring. He soon added several acts to support his own—a rope walker, a clown, a strong man, acrobats, an educated horse, and a band.

In Philadelphia, a riding master identified as Mr. Faulks appeared in 1771, performing feats on horseback. According to one account, "He mounts a single horse, standing upon the Saddle, and rides him, playing on the French Horn. Second. He mounts two Horses, with one Foot in each Horse's Stirrup, putting them into full speed, and mounts out of them to the tops of the Saddle at the same Pace. . . . He concludes His Performance by riding a single Horse in full speed, dismounting and mounting many times, and will on that Stretch dismount fairly, with both Feet on the Ground, vault clear over the Horse, back again, and mount on the near Side."[34]

Another equestrian, Jacob Bates, appeared in Philadelphia the following year, giving a display of comic riding he called "the Taylor riding to Brentford." A classic equestrian routine, the "tailor act" involves a man with no apparent knowledge of horses who needs one in order to keep an appointment. The horse, or in some cases a mule, is highly trained, and as the tailor tries to mount it, the horse sits, lies down, bucks, and eventually chases the tailor offstage. The routine, which pits an ignorant man against a smart animal, has remained extremely popular throughout the history of the circus and is occasionally revived today.

After the Revolution, Thomas Poole erected a "menage" in Philadelphia and began giving performances. Shows took place on Tuesday and Friday afternoons at four, weather permitting, which suggests that this was an uncovered arena. Billing himself as the first American to perform feats of horsemanship, Poole would mount a horse running at full speed and, standing on the saddle, perform various feats, among them drinking a glass of wine without spilling it, firing a pistol, leaping over a bar, and throwing up an orange and catching it on the point of a fork. The show also featured an educated horse and a clown who entertained the audience between the acts. Poole concluded the performance with "the Taylor riding to Brentford."[35]

The first performer in America to bill his show as a circus was John Bill Ricketts, a Scotsman who opened a riding school at Twelfth and Market streets in Philadelphia in 1792. Ricketts had been a pupil of Charles Hughes, who operated the Royal Circus in London in competition with Astley. Ricketts's first circus, which referred to the building, *not* the performance, was an open-air wooden structure that sat eight hundred spectators. A riding ring was set within a solid fence, which was painted and decorated and divided into boxes and a pit, with benches for seating.[36] He began giving public performances on April 22, 1793. Among those attending the first performance were George and Martha Washington.

Ricketts, performing on his horse, Cornplanter, was the star attraction. Standing on the saddle of his moving horse, he leaped over a ribbon stretched across his path, landing again in the saddle. He hung from the horse by one leg, letting his hat brush against the ground. And he rode with one foot on each of two horses. The show also featured a ropewalker, a clown, and several other equestrians. Ricketts appeared there until midsummer, when he took the troupe to New York City. When cold weather set in, the troupe went south to Charleston, returning to Philadelphia in September 1794.

Ricketts gradually introduced new tricks and entertainments. Eventually the program featured riding, tightrope dancing, tumbling, clowning, and dramatic entertainment. A grand entry featuring a procession was added, and this evolved into a costumed spectacle in which the horses circled, moved by twos, waltzed, and so on.[37]

In 1795 Ricketts replaced his original open-air arena with a larger, enclosed amphitheatre, located at Sixth and Chestnut streets, just opposite the Chestnut Street Theatre (still called the New Theatre). The new arena, which was billed alternately as Ricketts's New Amphitheatre and the New Pantheon, was a circular structure, ninety-seven feet in diameter, with eighteen-foot walls that supported a conical roof. The amphitheatre held twelve hundred people. Seating was arranged in a horseshoe shape, and there was a stage at one end of the arena. The equestrian ring was located in the center of the arena, and a stage at one end, with room for an orchestra situated between the ring and the stage. The Pantheon opened on October 19, 1795, and for the next four years provided stiff competition for the actors at the Chestnut.

There was no sharp distinction between circus and theatre at this time. Both forms of entertainment competed for the same audience and borrowed freely from each other. Circus troupes staged farces and pantomimes as part of the evening's entertainment. Theatrical productions incorporated variety acts, acrobatics, and feats of strength between the acts of a play. Wignell and Reinagle added an acrobat to their company, while French pantomimists helped strengthen the musical and dancing programs. To avoid head-on competition, the circus and the theatre generally alternated nights. Ricketts performed on Tuesday, Thursday, and Saturday, while Wignell and Reinagle presented productions at the New Theatre on Monday, Wednesday, and Friday.

Both companies faced additional competition when a Swedish circus entrepreneur, Philip Lailson, arrived in Philadelphia in 1797. Lailson built an immense arena on Fifth Street, the dome of which rose ninety feet in the air, where he presented circus acts, pantomimes, farces, and "comic ballads."[38] He was unable to sustain these efforts, however, and within a year he sold off his amphitheatre and returned to Europe. A few months later, the dome of the circus collapsed.

In 1799 Ricketts suffered a series of devastating setbacks. Sometime that year, his circus in New York City burned. Then, on December 17, 1799—the night the news arrived in Philadelphia of George Washington's death at Mount Vernon—Ricketts's Pantheon burned to the ground. Ricketts was set to close the show that night with a new pantomime called "Don Juan, or The Libertine Destroyed," the last scene of which represented "the Infernal Regions with a view of the mouth of Hell." The hellfire was said to have set the amphitheatre ablaze, but the fire was probably caused by a candle a carpenter left burning in a storage room before the pantomime began.[39] The audience left the amphitheatre with no loss of life, and the performers were able to rescue the horses, the wardrobe, and most of the scenery.

Ricketts tried appearing in what remained of Lailson's Amphitheatre but closed after three weeks. Hoping that the West Indies might prove more profitable, he outfitted a ship with stalls for horses, loaded it with lumber for the construction of a new arena, and sailed to the Caribbean. His ship was seized en route by French privateers, who sold off the horses and the lumber. Disheartened, Ricketts sailed for England. His bad luck held—the ship was lost at sea, and John Bill Ricketts was never heard from again.[40]

With Ricketts out of the picture, Wignell and Reinagle had a virtual lock on theatrical activity in Philadelphia. The Southwark Theatre was only occasionally used for productions. John Durang, a dancer and gymnast who had performed with Ricketts, opened for a couple of weeks in the spring of 1800, featuring performances on slack wire and gymnastic stunts, music, and recitations. During the summer he staged a pantomime called *Harlequin Mariner, The Recruiting Officer,* and a farcical afterpiece, *Botheration.* Later that summer, another pair of actors played one night at the Southwark with a festival of songs and recitations, and a buffoon named Prigmore came in with a "theatrical medley" of variety acts.[41] Generally, however, the Southwark remained dark, for the major theatre companies stayed out of one another's territories.

Four companies dominated the American theatre at the turn of the century. The Old American Company, now headed by John Hodgkinson and William Dunlap, was centered in New York City, housed in a splendid new facility, the Park Theatre, built in 1799. In Boston, the Federal Street Theatre was struggling to get established. The southern states were dominated by John Joseph Sollee, who was headquartered in Charleston, South Carolina. Wignell and Reinagle dominated the mid-Atlantic states, touring Baltimore and Annapolis during the summer and wintering in Philadelphia.[42] When the nation's capital shifted from Philadelphia to Washington, D.C., in 1800, they opened a theatre in a converted hotel that was dubbed the National Theatre. It was soon replaced by a new building on Pennsylvania Avenue, and the Philadelphia company performed there regularly during the summer.

All of these theatres operated as stock companies, much like the summer stock companies of today, with the same group of actors appearing in different productions. Wignell and Reinagle staged roughly a hundred productions each year, counting both plays and afterpieces. Most plays ran for a single night, although especially popular productions might run for two or three.[43] English drama still dominated—there were few American playwrights of any note. Thomas Wignell made annual trips to England to secure new scripts and sheet music for their productions, while Alexander Reinagle composed incidental music and overtures, and led a twenty-piece orchestra from his seat at the piano.

In January 1803 Wignell married his leading actress, Mrs. Anne Brunton Merry. He died only a month later, when a puncture wound he received during medical treatment became infected. Mrs. Merry then became co-owner of the company. She turned the managerial duties over to William Warren and William B. Wood, who became "acting managers." Three years later she married William Warren, who became co-owner of the Chestnut Street

Theatre when Mrs. Merry passed away in 1808. After Alexander Reinagle's passing in 1809, William Wood bought an interest in the theatre.

Warren and Wood continued the practices that Thomas Wignell had established. Warren traveled to England periodically to secure scripts of the latest London successes and to entice actors to seek their fortune in America. The two men would dominate Philadelphia theatre for the next twenty years, and the company they built was considered the finest troupe of actors in North America. Although theatre people were not entirely respectable by the standards of the day, by the early part of the nineteenth century the theatre had established itself as an integral part of the cultural life of Philadelphia. Enterprising actors and managers had succeeded in overcoming religious prejudices against plays and players, in no small measure through the patronage of George Washington. Even so, the cultural legitimacy of theatre was by no means secure. Theatre managers faced threats from many sources—among them competition from a circus soon to be built at the corner of Walnut and Ninth.

CIRCUS AND SPECTACLE AT THE WALNUT STREET THEATRE, 1809–1820

The winter of 1807–8 was not the most opportune time for starting a new theatrical venture. Philadelphia was entering an economic recession brought about in large part by an embargo passed in December 1807. The European powers were engaged in the Napoleonic Wars, and the principal belligerents, England and France, tried to prevent neutral ships from trading with the enemy. In 1806, American shippers began to suffer losses from both sides. The president of the young Republic, Thomas Jefferson, fought back by declaring an economic boycott. Hoping to force the warring powers to accept America's rights as a neutral nation, the embargo tied American shipping to home ports. The embargo hit Philadelphia particularly hard, since its economy depended heavily on trade. For eight years, from the beginning of the embargo in 1807 until the end of the War of 1812 (1812–15), ships remained in port.

Nevertheless, in the winter of 1807, a French circus company led by Victor Pepin and Jean Breschard set sail for America. There had been no circuses in America since Ricketts had sailed away to his death eight years earlier. Pepin and Breschard had been encouraged to come to America by the Spanish consul in Philadelphia, Don Luis de Onis. Don Luis had seen them perform in Europe, and he encouraged them to build an amphitheatre in Philadelphia for riding demonstrations. He began to make arrangements to purchase land for that purpose on the northeast corner of Ninth and Walnut streets. Pepin and Breschard would build similar arenas in the major cities in the northeastern United States and appear for part of the year at each of them. The circus tent had not come into use, and circuses typically played in permanent structures in large urban areas.

PEPIN AND BRESCHARD

Victor A. Pepin was born on March 8, 1780, in Albany, New York, to parents of French descent, and was taken to France as a young boy.[1] There are no images of Pepin, but one observer described him as "small in stature, having a dark complexion and very black hair and eyes."[2] A highly skilled rider, Pepin had been a French cavalry officer and learned horsemanship in the military. In his chronicle of early Philadelphia theatre, Charles Durang recalled that "Pepin was a dashing rider, executing surprising leaps over an illuminated gallery, without that eternal dodging of the object, over which the rider leaps, which we witness now-a-days . . . . We have not seen a more dextrous or sure equestrian since Pepin."

His partner, Jean Baptiste Casmiere Breschard, was a native of France. He specialized in what is now referred to as Roman standing riding, balancing on the backs of two horses, and doubled as the comedian of the troupe. "Breschard was a model of a performer," reported Charles Durang. "He looked like a genteel comedian attired for the polished drawing-room. He was truly a picture, when dressed in his superb gold-laced Spanish uniform, white cassimere small-clothes, silk stockings, neat pumps and gold shoe buckles, going through his exercises on two horses."[3] The company also included Mrs. Breschard, who leapt a horse over several bars and hogsheads; eleven-year-old Master Diego, who performed acrobatic maneuvers with hoops; and a "Young African," who danced to the hornpipe while riding on horseback.

Pepin and Breschard arrived in Plymouth, Massachusetts, late in 1807.[4] They planned to build their first arena in Boston, but when they petitioned the city council, local clergymen objected that such entertainment was "too frivolous for these sober times," and their request was denied. Instead, they built an amphitheatre on the outskirts of the city, opening in Charlestown on December 19, 1807. Advertising themselves as the "First Riding Masters of the Academies of Paris," they played in Charlestown until the following May. They proceeded to New York City, where an open amphitheatre was constructed for them on the corner of Broadway and Anthony streets, near the southern tip of Manhattan. The circus opened in New York on June 2, 1808, and the company remained there until the end of the year, closing their run with a performance on New Year's Day 1809.[4] Then it was on to Philadelphia, where a piece of property on the corner of Walnut and Ninth streets was waiting for them.

THE NEW CIRCUS ON WALNUT STREET

The land chosen for this new enterprise was located on the western edge of the city. It lay across the street from the row house where the Spanish consul

fig. 2 Circuses of the period were equestrian shows with four basic acts: hurdle riding, two-horse riding, leaps, and vaults. A skilled rider could leap between several horses.

lived. Don Luis is said to have made the arrangements for the purchase and construction of the theatre. The land was bought from a merchant named John Brown for $11,058 and ran for 96 feet on Walnut Street and 120 along Ninth. They signed the deed on October 4, 1808. Charles Durang believed that work probably began the previous March. It was undertaken by Joseph Randall, a master craftsman and carpenter with his own company.

The building took up most of the property and was made of brick. "The dimensions, eighty feet on Walnut by one hundred feet on Ninth Street. Within, it was circular, seventy-five feet in diameter, including the seats, and fifty-four feet including the area of the riding course. Every office connected with the circus was under this roof," James Mease reported in *The Picture of Philadelphia*. The building stood three stories high, with a peaked roof facing Walnut Street. Three doors provided public access to the theatre lobby from the Walnut Street side. Toward the rear of the building, a wide door led from Ninth Street into a carriage house, providing access to the backstage area, which was equipped with stables. The most striking architectural element was a large dome that covered the riding ring. "The dome over the ring was an immense affair," reported Charles Durang. "It had from the pit the appearance of being some eighty feet in height, and looked very oriental and magnificently imposing."[5] The dome was topped by a flagpole that reached ninety-six feet into the air, making it the tallest structure in the city.

The interior was similar to European circuses. A riding ring occupied the center of the building, with a raked area for the audience behind a waist-high wooden fence. There were three levels of seating, and posts set at intervals around the fence supported the upper tiers. On the ground floor, on the level of the equestrian ring, was the "pit." Those occupying the pit probably sat on benches. Above the level of the pit was a tier of "boxes," which were partitioned off from one another. The boxes had simple ornamentation and held three to five seats each, offering the more affluent members of the audience privacy and distinction. At the very top was a balcony with open seating, known as the "gallery," where the cheapest seats could be had. Admission to the boxes was one dollar, to the pit, seventy-five cents, and to the gallery, fifty cents.

THE OPENING OF THE "NEW CIRCUS"

Pepin and Breschard made their debut on a Thursday night, February 2, 1809. Newspaper announcements billed it simply as the "New Circus." Charles Durang recalled that "their company was numerous, their stud of horses was thoroughly broken and composed of splendid animals. Their wardrobe was new, costly and indeed the best thing of its kind that had been seen in this country."[6] Pepin and Breschard's show opened with military exercises on horseback, as eight members of the company, Pepin, Breschard, Cayetano Mariotini, and Messrs. Codet, Segne, Clavery, Palli, and Alexander guided their horses in various formations. This was undoubtedly choreographed to music, for there was a band connected with the show.

Circuses of this period were equestrian shows. As circus historian Stuart Thayer observes, there were four basic types of equestrian acts in the early 1800s: hurdle riding, two-horse riding, leaps, and vaults. In hurdle riding, the rider takes the horse over fences or other objects. It was well suited for sidesaddle riding and became a feminine specialty. For two-horse riding, the rider stood with one foot on the back of two horses, holding onto their reins. A skilled rider could add a third or a fourth slightly ahead of them. Leaps were done on horseback, usually on a saddled horse. "Objects were placed in his path which the horse would run under causing the rider to leap into the air, alighting again in the saddle," Thayer writes. "Canes, poles, strips of cloth were common hurdles and it became a mark of excellence to clear broader and broader banners. Balloons (i.e. hoops filled with paper) and hogsheads [i.e., large casks] were also used in this type of act. Outstanding practitioners could leap a hurdle at the same time the horse leaped a barrier, a test of ability of the first order." Finally, there were vaults, which could be done either from the ground or on horseback. "A vaulting rider was one who stood on his head, jumped from horse to ground, to horse again, leaped over the horse as it cantered the circle and did acrobatics in which the moving horse was a platform. From this specialty came the art of somersaulting from horse to ground, from ground to horse and finally, in the 1840's, a somersault on the animal's back, the zenith of vaulting riding."[7]

The less experienced performers appeared during the first half of the program, and each act would last up to twenty minutes. Mr. Segne, a pupil of Pepin and Breschard, performed several comic attitudes on horseback and concluded his act by vaulting over his horse. Mr. Codet followed with tricks on horseback; he too vaulted over his horse. Master Diego performed various feats with hoops. Cayetano Mariotini finished off the first half with vaultings on horseback and "several singular tricks with a glove, hat, etc." Mr. Cayetano, as he was billed, concluded the first half with a comic riding act, "French Taylor in London," undoubtedly a version of the classic "Taylor's Ride to Brentford."

The second half featured the stars of the show—Messrs. Pepin and Breschard, along with an educated black stallion named Conqueror. Breschard opened the second act with the comic scene of a Canadian peasant. This is sometimes called a flying wardrobe act and it is still seen in circuses. It features a rustic character planted in the audience who insists on performing a stunt in the ring. After a series of awkward maneuvers, he throws off layer upon layer of coats, vests, and trousers, revealing himself to be in a costume of the circus equestrian. Breschard's act featured exercises with hoops and culminated with leaps over a ribbon. Next, Conqueror was brought out. The horse was trained to retrieve a handkerchief, gun, basket, chair, and other objects, as instructed, and finished off the routine by sitting down at a table for a small repast with his trainer. Victor Pepin followed, performing various forms of leaping, jumping over ribbons, and landing on the back of his horse. He concluded his act by jumping through a barrel—a trick he claimed had "never been attempted by any person but himself in America." Finally, Jean Breschard returned, balancing on two horses while juggling oranges and apples and catching them on forks. He finished off his act with a pyramid, carrying Master Diego on his head while standing on two horses. The finale of the program featured a fireworks display, with an "undaunted horse calmly wrapt in flames."[8] The entire show probably lasted from two and a half to three hours.

THE FIRST SEASON

Pepin and Breschard's company performed on Tuesday, Thursday, and Saturday nights, alternating nights with the acting company at the Chestnut Street Theatre, which appeared on Monday, Wednesday, Friday, and Saturday evenings. Performances began at 6:30, with doors opening at 5:00. The lineup remained more or less the same from one week to the next. Sometimes they altered the running order, and periodically they introduced new specialties. Mr. Cayetano alternated the French Taylor act with another comic scene, *Madame Angot*, in which he portrayed a woman taking her first riding lesson.

On February 21 the managers announced that a grand ball would be held at the circus in honor of George Washington's birthday. They had installed a wooden floor in the center of the arena. "They have spared no pains or expense to have the Circus fitted up in an elegant style, and handsomely illuminated," the announcement read.[9] The equestrians performed a shortened program before the dance, which began at eight o'clock. For the first time, Madame Breschard appeared on the program, leaping over hurdles, executing various attitudes on horseback, and concluding her act by riding her horse at full speed through two hogsheads.

Other acts were introduced periodically to add novelty to the program. On April 3 Pepin and Breschard announced that the circus had engaged Mr. Victorian and Mr. Menial as tumblers and tightrope walkers. Mr. Menial took over the role as clown in the scene of the tailor, while Mr. Victorian vaulted over twelve men, topping off this feat by repeating it over six horses. The following performance he performed on the slack wire. Over the course of the month, Victorian added new tricks on the tightrope, leaping over ribbons, dancing a hornpipe, and eating a meal while seated on a chair balanced in the center of the tightrope.

At the end of April, Pepin and Breschard announced the engagement of Mr. Manfredi and his two daughters, Miss Miniguina and Miss Catherine, as rope dancers. The two young ladies danced on the tightrope "with the modesty and decorum which ladies of the first distinction may have a right to expect." Their father danced the hornpipe "with all the steps and countersteps, according to measure of music, as if he was on the floor."[10]

On April 26, 1809, the company introduced its first full-length dramatic piece, a pantomime on horseback of *Don Quixote de la Mancha*. It starred a Mr. Grain as Don Quixote and featured Victor Pepin as Sancho Panza. The pantomime bore almost no resemblance to Cervantes's story but was an excuse for battles and buffoonery. The combination of theatrical and equestrian drama seems to have been a success, for the company revived *Don Quixote* twice that season and included it in their repertoire in following seasons. They had less success with a second pantomime, *Tartarian Princess*, which they staged on June 3, for it had only one performance and did not remain in the repertoire.

The season finished off with a series of benefit performances for various members of the company. Such benefits were common practice in the early American theatre. On those nights, all the proceeds, above and beyond the fixed management costs, went to the actor so "benefited." The actors receiving the benefit could program the evening in any way they wished. Such benefits were held at the end of the season both to increase business at the end of the run and to provide the actors with additional funds to get them through the summer hiatus.

TOURS OF PEPIN AND BRESCHARD, 1809–1811

Pepin and Breschard concluded their season on June 5, 1809, and set out on their summer tour. Their first stop was Lancaster, Pennsylvania, where they appeared at an agricultural fair. By July 1 they had moved on to New York, where they remained until late August. On September 3 the company returned to Boston. Things must not have gone well there, for they closed after only a month and never returned to that city. On October 23 they were back in Philadelphia, announcing their fall run. They remained there through the end of November, when the acting company at the Chestnut Street Theatre returned for its winter season. Then it was south to Baltimore, where Pepin and Breschard had recently built an arena.

The two circus men now had permanent facilities in each of the major cities in the Northeast. Over the next two years they operated as a circuit. The circus typically played in Philadelphia from early October through December, went south to Baltimore for the first few months of the year, returned north for the agricultural fair in Lancaster, and moved to New York for a summer engagement, returning to Philadelphia in the fall.[11] During their absences from Philadelphia, the amphitheatre on Walnut Street remained dark.

Although the circus was primarily an equestrian show, some theatrical fare was introduced, most of it limited to simple slapstick farces. One such routine was *Brothers Millers*, which was sometimes billed as *The Miller and the Coalman*. It featured two men—a miller, dressed entirely in white and carrying a sack of flour, and a coalman, outfitted in a black costume and carrying a sack of coal dust. One of them accidentally leaves a smudge on the other. So, of course, the other retaliates, leaving a smudge. From there the action builds, as each man takes revenge on the other until they have emptied the contents of their respective sacks on each other. In the end, it is impossible to tell the two apart.[12]

Early in 1811, Pepin and Breschard made the decision to offer theatrical fare. There was a recession going on, and the decision was probably a response to a falloff in circus attendance. On February 1 they purchased an additional piece of land from John Brown, just north of the circus, for $6,250, increasing the size of the property to 96 by 140 feet. In the fall, they used the property as collateral for a $1,700 loan. On their tours, Pepin and Breschard began introducing more dramatic elements into their show—closing with such afterpieces as *The Fashionable Barber, The Scheming Milliners, The Brazen Mask, Harlequin Statue, The Village Lawyer,* and others. These are mostly standard farces that served as afterpieces for theatrical productions.[13]

THE OLYMPIC THEATRE

Pepin and Breschard would normally have opened in Philadelphia in the fall of 1811. Instead, they spent the season in Baltimore, while the Walnut Street facility was being remodeled. A young, British-born architect living in Philadelphia, William Strickland, was put in charge of making it suitable for theatrical productions. The plan was to add a stage on the north side of the building. Builders broke through the back wall of the existing structure and built an extension to the new property line, approximately twenty feet back. The back wall of the original building can still be seen in the backstage area of the Walnut Street Theatre.

The riding ring remained as it was. The stage was fifty-four feet across, the same size as the riding ring, and was raised to the level of the boxes, which were reconstructed so that they intersected the stage. Between the riding ring and the stage was an orchestra pit, on either side of which was a doorway allowing riders to enter the ring from beneath the stage. A corridor behind the boxes provided access to them, and on that floor there were rooms for refreshments. A portion of the gallery level was given over to a second tier of boxes.[14]

Pepin and Breschard entered into an agreement with two actor-managers, John Dwyer and Donald McKenzie, to put together an acting company. Neither Dwyer nor McKenzie was well suited to managing a theatre company. The Irish-born Dwyer was said to be "impulsive to a fault," and McKenzie, a Scot, was "phlegmatically prejudiced."[15] McKenzie had been a member of the Chestnut Street company and had not left on the best of terms. He brought several disaffected members of the Chestnut Street company with him.

The combined acting and circus companies appeared together in Baltimore and moved north to Philadelphia for a grand opening on New Year's Day 1812. The house, now named the Olympic Theatre, opened with Richard Brinsley Sheridan's comedy *The Rivals*. The play starred Mrs. Wilmot as the sentimentally romantic Lydia Languish, determined to marry for love, and Mr. Dwyer as the dashing and aristocratic Captain Jack Absolute, who pretends to be impoverished in order to woo her. Comic relief was provided by Mrs. Melmoth as Mrs. Malaprop, determined to marry Lydia off to the rustic squire Bob Acres, played by the company's low comedian, Mr. Smalley. The evening opened with "a grand display of horsemanship." More horsemanship was featured between the main production and the afterpiece, a musical farce titled *The Poor Soldier*.

The opening of the new Olympic Theatre was marred by news that had reached Philadelphia of a devastating theatre fire in Richmond, Virginia. On December 26 the Richmond Theatre was packed with more than six hundred people for the final performance of the season, a benefit for the leader of the company, Alexander Placide. The main production had concluded and the afterpiece had just begun when an open flame from a chandelier set the scenery on fire. There were not enough exits, and the fire spread quickly, trapping many. Seventy-two people lost their lives; many of the bodies were burned beyond recognition. The governor of Virginia, George W. Smith, was among those who died.

The Philadelphia papers published the grim details as news trickled in. "The event cast a gloom over the country and its amusements for some time," wrote Charles Durang, "and militated materially against the interests of the drama everywhere."[16] In an era when theatres were lit by open flames, the threat of fire was very real. Those who opposed the theatre on moral grounds looked on the Richmond Theatre fire as divine judgment against the immorality of the theatre. Theatre managers tried to assure their patrons of adequate means of escape. But the fire hurt theatre attendance everywhere. "It seemed to create a perfect panic," William B. Wood recalled, "which deterred the largest portion of the audience for a long time from venturing into a crowd, either theatrical or other."[17]

Despite the shocking news from Richmond, the combined company at the Olympic Theatre drew respectable audiences. They did so by playing to the public's growing taste for spectacle and melodrama. The melodramatic formula is familiar to us today, but it was still a novelty in 1812. It features a virtuous hero or heroine who is hounded by a dynamic villain motivated to do evil. The hero or heroine faces a series of seemingly insurmountable threats, until the final act, when the heroine is rescued and justice is meted out. The action is easily understood, emotions are uncomplicated, and the characters are familiar stock types. Because the outcome is preordained and there is little in the way of character development, suspense has to be maintained by ingenious plot twists. Dramatists resorted to mystery, surprise, and sensationalism to keep the audience involved. Important events all take place on stage and frequently involve such elaborate spectacles as battles, floods, and earthquakes.

Melodrama was well suited to the Walnut Street Theatre, still known then as the Olympic. In serious drama, the suspense grows out of the internal conflicts of the leading character and is communicated through the dialogue. The Olympic, with its immense dome, made such dialogue difficult. Equipped with a large stage and a riding ring, the Olympic Theatre was ideally suited to the large-scale spectacles that were popular features of the melodramas of this period.

The first of these spectacles was *The Escape of Adelina, or The Robbers of the Pyrenees,* which premiered on January 20, 1812. The production seems to have been quite successful, for it ran through four performances and was revived twice in response to public demand. This play commenced with a beautiful view of Count Almaviva's castle and featured a ballet solo by a child prodigy, Master Whale. There were combats featuring real horses on the stage, with Victor Pepin cast as the Captain of the Banditi and Jean Breschard as the hero, Don Alonzo.

Even more familiar plays were produced with an eye toward spectacle. On February 3 *The Winter's Tale* premiered at the Olympic, the first time this Shakespeare play was performed in Philadelphia. The managers announced that they had "spared neither pains or expense" to render it worthy of the "support of the publick of Philadelphia." They had added an entirely new scene "representing a Royal Court of Justice for the trial of the Queen in which will seem to be assembled thousands of spectators." These "improvements" on the Bard were by no means unusual for the time. David Garrick, Colley Cibber, and other playwrights produced adaptations of Shakespeare's plays, often altering the endings of tragedies to make them more pleasing to audiences. Some of these adaptations, like Garrick's *Katherine and Petruchio,* proved more popular than the originals.

The Olympic Theatre offered eighteen plays that had never been seen before in Philadelphia. This was an unusually large number of premieres that necessarily required considerable rehearsal time. These included two patriotic spectacles, *The Taking of Yorktown* and *American Generosity and Moorish Ingratitude*, both by local writers, and *Marmion, or The Battle of Flodden Field*, by James Nelson Barker. Most of the productions were pantomimes and farces that had proved themselves on the London stage. The theatre was open four nights a week and offered a different show each night. The emphasis on melodramatic spectacle in the spring of 1812 seems to have drawn a large portion of the audience away from the Chestnut Street Theatre—at least temporarily. The next season would prove to be quite another matter.

THE WAR OF 1812 AND THE END OF A PARTNERSHIP

Pepin and Breschard concluded their first dramatic season on May 15, 1812, and divided up the equestrian troupe. Breschard headed to New York City, while Pepin played in York, Pennsylvania, during the fair. That summer, hostilities between the United States and England, which had been building for years, finally broke out. On June 18, 1812, Congress declared war on Britain. Pepin returned to Philadelphia for a brief run, appearing at the Olympic from June 29 to July 4, but reportedly closed without paying his company.[18] Breschard returned to Philadelphia on September 25 and, in partnership with William Twaits, presented a new equestrian drama, *Timour the Tartar.*[19] On October 8 Breschard and Twaits put on a patriotic piece, *Philadelphia Volunteers, or Who's Afraid?* Despite their best efforts, audiences were sparse and this play closed on October 15.[20]

The Olympic was not the only theatre facing difficulties. War dampened attendance everywhere. But Pepin and Breschard had gone heavily into debt to convert their circus into a theatre, and creditors were pressing. Their property was seized by the sheriff for nonpayment of debts and was to be auctioned off on February 5, 1813. There were no buyers for the property, however, and the theatre fell into the hands of the lien holder, a flour merchant named James Clemson.[21]

The theatre remained dark until the end of the summer, when Pepin and Breschard returned. They resumed their policy of offering equestrian acts and short comic afterpieces. But the war continued to occupy the minds of most Philadelphians. On September 24 news reached the city of Oliver Hazard Perry's victory over the British fleet on Lake Erie. This was the battle in which Perry uttered the famous line, "We have met the enemy and they are ours." There were victory celebrations in the streets, and the entire city was lit up at night. Pepin and Breschard prepared a patriotic battle spectacle. On October 10 they announced a "grand display of the Gallant Commodore Perry's glorious victory on Lake Erie."

The appeal to Philadelphians' patriotic fervor seems to have drawn the audiences Pepin and Breschard needed. The production was repeated for the next two nights and reprised a week later. Similar heroic pantomimes followed. On October 29 they featured a pantomime of *General Proctor's Defeat by General Harrison,* which marked William Henry Harrison's victory in the

Battle of the Thames, near Detroit, on October 5. The production was revived three times. On November 17, *Fall of York, or Death of General Pike* honored the American victory over the British in Toronto that had taken place the previous spring. Pepin and Breschard played one more night at the Olympic Theatre, closing the season on December 2, 1813. It was the last time the two men would appear together in Philadelphia, and the last time Jean Breschard would perform in the city.

The circus moved on to Baltimore for its regular winter run. Given the threat of war and a blockade of eastern ports by British ships, the circus managers began to look westward. Pepin, Breschard, and Cayetano took the circus to Pittsburgh in the spring of 1814, the first circus to appear west of the Appalachians. The company had moved to Cincinnati by June 11. Back in Philadelphia, the war was drawing ever closer. On August 25, 1814, news reached the city that British forces had defeated the Americans outside Washington, D.C., and had burned the Capitol. They were moving north, and Philadelphians began to make preparations for the defense of the city. On September 12 word came that British troops were closing in on Baltimore. British gunships bombarded Fort McHenry for twenty-five hours, the attack that inspired Francis Scott Key to compose the poem "The Star-Spangled Banner." In the morning, the flag was still flying, and British troops had returned to their ships.

Given the very real threat of military action, Pepin and Breschard chose not to return to Philadelphia. Cayetano Mariotini remained in Cincinnati over the winter of 1814–15, with a troupe of apprentices. Pepin and Breschard headed south to Charleston, South Carolina, with the rest of the company, where they began appearing in November 1814. The southern states were less directly affected by the war, in part because their exports of cotton were so important to British mills. This was the last engagement for Pepin and Breschard. Breschard took part of the company south to Savannah, Georgia, while Pepin remained in Charleston until January 3, 1815. Pepin sailed for Europe with several members of the company and did not return until 1816. Breschard did not accompany him, for he was appearing with his wife in Boston on January 14, 1815. There is no further record of his presence in the United States until 1817, when he was listed as an acrobat in theatres in Charleston and Savannah in the early months of that year. After that, Jean Breschard disappears from the historical record.[22]

With Pepin and Breschard out of the picture, nobody made regular use of the Olympic Theatre. A troupe of rope dancers, Vilallave and Company, played there in late September and early October 1814. Around Christmastime, another company of wire walkers, Perez and Company, occupied the space. The Olympic was not particularly well suited to such productions. It was built for large-scale spectacles, and by 1814 there were better venues for variety entertainment. Two pleasure gardens had been constructed in the previous years that offered entertainment during the summer months. The Columbian Garden on Market Street opened in July 1813 as an outdoor place of amusement. Vauxhall Gardens, named after a similar entertainment venue in London, was opened the following year at the northeast corner of Broad and Walnut streets.[23] Both featured tree-lined walkways, ornamental shrubbery, and outdoor stages, where concerts and other performances were given during the summer.

On November 29, 1814, the Olympic Theatre was again offered up for sale and was sold at public auction. It was purchased by a local attorney, Charles Bird, who came up with the winning bid of $12,650. The house remained vacant until January 17, 1814, when a troupe announcing itself as the Theatrical Commonwealth took over the theatre for a two-month run. The Commonwealth had been organized by William Twaits the previous spring. He was rebelling against the growing power of the managers of the Chestnut Street Theatre in Philadelphia and the Park Theatre in New York. This was undoubtedly a response to moves the managers took to exclude the actors from a share of the theatre's profits—a practice that had prevailed since colonial times. Twaits appealed to other working people to support his efforts. But, as Durang recorded, "Its efforts, however just and meritorious, met with little assistance from our republican play-goers, from whom a sympathetic response was fondly anticipated."[24] Twaits was ill with asthma. When he died later that year, so did the Theatrical Commonwealth.

The Olympic continued to be rented out for an eclectic mix of performances. Sleight-of-hand conjuring was announced for six nights, and there was a concert on May 30, 1815.[25] On June 14, 1815, a historical play called *Yankee Chronology, or The Tars of Columbia* was staged—an adaptation by William Dunlap of his tragedy *André*. But there was no company to occupy the space on any steady basis until Victor Pepin returned from Europe.

PEPIN AND HIS PARTNERS, 1816–1818

In August 1816 Pepin was back in Philadelphia, refitting and reopening the Olympic with "a company that included Mr. Menial, Master Peter Coty, the horses Mentor and Palafox and a new face, Mr. Garcia." Pepin had difficulty keeping the theatre open and supplemented his income by offering riding lessons and training and stabling horses. In November, however, help came in the form of an English circus company, headed by James West.

Pepin engaged West on November 28 for a series of twelve nights. "James West and his company made a great sensation here, and their business was tremendous. The Olympic was crowded nightly to its very extent, and the old Chestnut street theatre felt the sudden opposition seriously," Charles Durang recalled.[26] The highlight of the season was a production, on December 16, 1816, of *Timour the Tartar*. The play—a melodrama by Matthew Gregory "Monk" Lewis—had previously been staged at both the Chestnut and the Olympic, but James West was the first to fully explore the dramatic possibilities of horsemanship. "The true hippodrama," A. H. Saxon explains in *Enter Foot and Horse*, "is literally a play in which trained horses are considered as actors, with business, often leading actions, of their own to perform." West's horses were trained not just to execute spectacular feats but to perform dramatic actions. They could rear and kick on cue or lie down and play dead. Audiences were astounded when a horse "staggered onstage, fell down, and lifted her head to give her master one last kiss before dying."[27]

Timour the Tartar was one of the first plays to take full advantage of the melodramatic possibilities of the men and horses. Philadelphia audiences had never seen anything like it. "The manner with which they did their pantomime business, their combats, &c., took our audience by surprise," wrote Charles Durang. "Ramparts were scaled by the horses, breaches were dashed into, and a great variety of new business was introduced. The horses were taught to imitate the agonies of death, and they did so in a manner which was astonishing. In the last scene, where *Zorilda*, mounted on her splendid white charger, ran up the stupendous cataract to the very height of the stage, the feat really astounded the audience. Perhaps no event in our theatrical annals ever produced so intense an excitement as that last scene. The people in the pit and boxes arose with a simultaneous impulse to their feet, and, with canes, hands and wild screams, kept the house in one uproar of shouts for at least five minutes. The next day the success of the piece was the general topic of conversation."[28]

After Christmas 1817, Pepin and West went their separate ways. Pepin opened in Baltimore, while West remained at the Olympic for two more weeks. West then moved on to New York City, where he presented *Timour the Tartar* at the Park Theatre. Pepin returned to Philadelphia for a two-week summer season of riding and farcical pieces. He joined up with James West for the fall season at the Olympic beginning October 2, 1817. The combined company continued to present the melodramatic equestrian spectacles that had worked so well the previous season. Not wishing to go head to head with the Chestnut Street Theatre, they concluded their Philadelphia performances on November 29, when the Chestnut commenced its season. James West had now secured enough money to produce his own shows, and he began to tour separately.

In the spring of 1818, Victor Pepin entered into a partnership with James H. Caldwell and James Entwisle. Caldwell and Entwisle managed theatres in Alexandria, Virginia, and the District of Columbia, but they wanted to produce spectacles of the kind that James West was presenting so successfully. Needing both horses and men who could ride them, Caldwell and Entwisle naturally allied themselves with the leading riders of the day. In April they announced their partnership with Victor Pepin. "During the season, it is the intention to produce, in a style of splendor and magnificence never equaled in this, and which, they presume has not been surpassed in any other theatres several spectacle melodramas, in which all the horses will be actively employed," local newspapers announced.[29] Among the pieces promised were *Marmion*, *Tekeli*, *Forty Thieves*, and *Lodoiska*—all popular melodramas that could be enhanced by equestrian spectacle.

Things did not go well in the partnership, however. Charles Durang reported that "Messrs. Caldwell and Entwisle did not move in harmony, even before they joined Pepin in management. The stage company was split into factions; the salaries were not regularly paid; an invidious line of demarcation was drawn between the stage performers and the equestrians."[30] On June 6, 1818, Caldwell withdrew from the management, and the theatrical department dissolved. Caldwell went on to establish theatres in New Orleans and operated the first theatre circuit along the Mississippi and Ohio rivers.

Victor Pepin now entered into a partnership with James Entwisle to reopen the Olympic in the fall. Entwisle left for England with funds to engage new performers and procure new pieces. Pepin put together a corporation of stockholders to purchase the Olympic Theatre and to make necessary improvements to the property. On October 21, 1818, Pepin purchased the theatre from Charles Bird for $34,000. He immediately turned the premises over to William Meredith, an attorney; Dr. Rodman Coxe; and Frederick Ravesies, a merchant, for the same amount. The three men established a declaration of trust, and the property was held on behalf of a group of 115 merchants and professional and cultural leaders known as the Proprietors of the Walnut Street Theatre. This corporation of stockholders would operate the theatre for the next thirty years.

With the property now secured, "the period approached for the opening of the winter campaign, but no Mr. Entwisle came with reinforcements, nor, indeed was any communication of any kind received from him," wrote Charles Durang. "However, the Olympic corps, dramatic and equestrian, took the field early in the autumn, as it was agreed upon before Mr. Entwisle left Philadelphia, and a part of a stage company had been duly engaged." Pepin opened the season on November 4, 1818, with a show that relied primarily on circus acts. In late November the company revived *Timour the Tartar* for a week. Entwisle finally returned late in the year, "and all the novelty he procured of any description was the new farce of *Rendezvous*."[31] Entwisle's mission to England was a decided failure. The dramatic company closed on

February 19, 1819. Pepin continued with circus acts for another month, closing with a benefit for himself on Monday, March 22.

VICTOR PEPIN'S LAST YEARS

This was the last time Victor Pepin was associated with the theatre he had built. Pepin took his troupe to New York City and then to Newburyport, Massachusetts, whence, on October 28, 1819, he sailed to the West Indies. He remained in the Caribbean until the summer of 1821, when he began appearing in Pensacola, Florida. He moved on to New Orleans in November, venturing up the Mississippi to Natchez, then returning to New Orleans to close the season. During the winter of 1822–23 he formed a partnership with a Mr. Barnet, and they began touring as Pepin and Barnet, traveling up the Mississippi River by steamboat in 1823 and appearing in Natchez, St. Louis, and Louisville before settling into Lexington, Kentucky, for the winter in an arena they constructed there. When the weather improved, Pepin and Barnet visited various cities in the Ohio River valley—Louisville, Cincinnati, and Pittsburgh—after which they parted company. By December 1824, Pepin was once again in Louisville.[32]

Pepin continued to offer equestrian entertainment in a new arena in Louisville, touring various cities on the Ohio and Mississippi rivers during the warmer months. In June 1826 Victor Pepin's wife, Martha, filed for divorce. She still lived in Philadelphia, and she and her husband had clearly been separated for some time. According to testimony, Pepin did not supply her with enough money to live on and was engaged in an adulterous affair with a lady employed as a circus rider. Martha Pepin was granted a divorce in February 1827 and remarried shortly thereafter.[33] On February 17, 1827, Victor Pepin gave his last known circus performance—a benefit for victims of a recent fire in Alexandria, Virginia.[34] He retired from the circus business and spent the rest of his life in Louisville.

Pepin returned to Philadelphia only once after that, in 1831. Charles Durang reported that he arrived in the city poor and friendless, looking for an opportunity to give riding lessons. The managers of the Arch Street Theatre, recognizing his contribution to Philadelphia theatre, tendered him a benefit on February 18, 1831. Junius Brutus Booth was among those who appeared in his honor.[35] Pepin did work briefly as a riding instructor in Baltimore in 1831 and was given a benefit in Louisville by Fogg & Stickney in 1837. He died in 1845 and is buried in New Albany, Indiana, across the Ohio River from Louisville.[36] His grave remained unmarked until February 2000, when his descendents arranged for a headstone.

The real monument to the life and career of Victor Pepin is the building that still stands on the northeast corner of Ninth and Walnut streets. Although the Walnut Street Theatre looks quite different than it did when circus and spectacles were staged within its walls, its subsequent history was shaped by the fact that it was built for equestrian shows. Equipped with stables and a riding ring, the Walnut Street Theatre became Philadelphia's principal venue for popular entertainment, and in particular large-scale spectacle. In 1809, when the Walnut Street Theatre was built, it was largely the affluent who patronized the theatre, and prestige houses like the Chestnut Street Theatre catered to the tastes of this class. The circus, and the entertainments that grew out of it, appealed to a broader and less sophisticated public. Victor Pepin catered to the tastes of this audience by producing equestrian spectacles, patriotic plays, and melodramas. As such, Pepin belongs in the ranks of showmen like P. T. Barnum, Buffalo Bill Cody, Florenz Ziegfeld, and Billy Rose, who produced exciting, large-scale theatrical productions aimed at popular tastes. Although he will never be as familiar as the impresarios who followed him, Pepin was the first to push the bounds of the circus, introducing dramatic elements into equestrian demonstrations. Such parts would continue to be important as the Walnut was gradually transformed into a legitimate theatre.

THE ERA OF THE ENGLISH STAR, 1820–1829

The equestrians at the Olympic never seriously challenged the supremacy of the Chestnut Street Theatre. Old Drury, as the Chestnut was affectionately called, was a cultural institution on a par with an opera or symphony orchestra today. It had the support and patronage of Philadelphia's best families. The managers of the Chestnut—William Warren and William B. Wood—catered to the upper-class desire to make Philadelphia an important cultural center. Although they suffered setbacks due to war or economic recession, William B. Wood found that by 1820, "we were by this time firstly fixed in the public estimation, and were in a train of systematic operation, and of regular and certain profits."[1] Victor Pepin had wisely avoided going head to head with the dramatic corps, choosing to open during the early fall and closing when the Chestnut Street Theatre began its season. With Pepin out of the picture after 1819, no one was eager to challenge the Chestnut, and the Walnut Street Theatre remained dark for more than a year.

Warren and Wood operated theatres in Philadelphia, Baltimore, and Washington, shifting their company from one to another. The Chestnut was their flagship theatre, and they returned there during the lucrative winter season. They benefited by the stock system that prevailed at the time. They relied not on expensive stars but on a resident company of players who appeared in all the productions. The acting company they put together was considered the best in America. Their repertoire was a mixture of established pieces and a handful of new plays, mostly recent successes from London. The theatre was open four nights a week—typically Monday, Wednesday, Friday, and Saturday—with a different production each night. The actors were not highly paid, but they could count on regular employment. Some, like Joseph

Jefferson, the beloved comedian of the troupe, stayed with the company for decades. Jefferson never achieved the level of celebrity of the grandson who shared his name, but he was able to support a large family on his earnings as an actor. Most of his children followed him into the profession.

With a virtual monopoly on theatrical fare in Philadelphia, Warren and Wood were able to pursue a long-term strategy for success. They marshaled their resources, plowing their profits back into the theatre, investing heavily in wardrobe, scenery, and stage machinery, much of which was imported from Europe. They regularly sent representatives to England to procure scripts and sheet music from the latest London successes, and they had the largest dramatic library in the Americas. Fortunes have a way of changing very quickly in the theatre, however. The change in Warren and Wood's fortunes can be traced to the night of April 2, 1820. That night, the Chestnut Street Theatre burned to the ground.

THE FIRE AND ITS AFTERMATH

The Chestnut Street Theatre company was playing in Baltimore when William Wood received word that a fire had swept through the Chestnut. The company had closed in Philadelphia a week before, and had just opened its season in Baltimore. Wood and Warren hurried back to Philadelphia to survey the damage, arriving in time "to witness the last wall topple to the ground," Wood recalled. The devastation was complete; smoking ruins were all that was left. The only items rescued from the smoldering rubbish pile were a mirror from the green room, a model ship, and the prompter's clock. The rest—the scenery, lights, library, and costumes acquired over a quarter-century—were gone.

"The loss was very great, as the property had been liberally augmented and improved through a long series of years," Wood recalled. "The most irretrievable part, was the splendid English scenery, presented to Wignell in 1793 by Richards, Hodges and Rooker, artists of the first reputation in their day. The wardrobe was of great extent, including the whole of the dresses from Lord Barrymore's theatre, as well as those from a French establishment recently purchased. The library and music were of an extent and value unknown to any other American theatre. Two grand pianos, costing 100 guineas each, a noble organ, used in the *Castle Spectre*, and other chapel scenes, and models of scenery and machinery, imported at a large cost, swelled the sum of our misfortune."[2]

Worst of all, the holdings were uninsured. There had been a rash of such fires in Philadelphia, and insurers were reluctant to cover theatres. Warren and Wood were still looking for insurance coverage when the Chestnut went up in flames. Rumor had it that the fire was purposely set. William Wood did not think it likely, since the fire had started in a highly visible spot across the street from a fire company. An arsonist would have had access to much less noticeable spots, and Wood concluded that a spark had probably started it. In any case, no one was ever charged with arson.

CONVERTING A CIRCUS

The Walnut Street Theatre had remained unoccupied since Victor Pepin left the city more than a year before, and the stockholders offered the facility to Warren and Wood, who accepted immediately. Before the building could be occupied, however, it had to be completely refurbished. "The house having been originally constructed only with a view to circus purposes, and subsequently imperfectly changed to dramatic uses, required expensive improvements in every part," Wood explained. "The performers' dressing-rooms, the green-room, and indeed nearly every portion of the building needed alteration."[3] William Strickland, one of Philadelphia's leading architects, was put in charge of the renovation. The landmark feature of the circus—its immense dome—was taken down to improve the acoustics. The stage was brought forward, while the riding ring was taken out and replaced with seating. Lobbies and boxes were redecorated. In response to what had happened to the Chestnut Street Theatre, new fire exits were installed on Ninth Street.

The theatre opened on Monday, November 10, 1820, with a production of *Wild Oats,* followed by an operatic afterpiece, *The Agreeable Surprise.* For the first time, the theatre bore the name by which it is still known—the Walnut Street Theatre. The house on opening night was respectable but not up to the usual level of the Chestnut Street house. Audiences who supported the Chestnut Street Theatre did not like the new facility on Walnut Street. The association of the circus with lower-class pleasures offended the sensibilities of the more fastidious patrons. The proprietors tried to assure them that they would not have to rub elbows with these less reputable types. Playbills promised that "a large and convenient new door has been opened on Ninth street, by which the audience of the pit may leave the theatre without meeting the other part of the audience."[4]

If the facilities were less than ideal, the productions at the Walnut Street Theatre that season were unsurpassed. The season of 1820–21 was one of the most impressive in the history of the American stage. Within two months of its opening, three of the most important actors of the nineteenth century would make their debut at the Walnut Street Theatre. A young Philadelphian who was to have a profound impact on American drama, Edwin Forrest, made his professional stage debut. Thomas A. Cooper, the leading American actor of the time, appeared for the first time at the Walnut. In early 1821, the great English actor Edmund Kean also made a triumphal appearance.

EDWIN FORREST'S DEBUT

Edwin Forrest was only fourteen when he appeared at the Walnut Street Theatre on November 27, 1820. Born and raised in Philadelphia, Forrest would soon rise to stardom, but he was unknown in 1820, billed simply as a "young gentleman of Philadelphia." He appeared as Young Norval in John Home's tragedy *Douglas*, a favorite debut role for young actors. A local newspaper identified the young actor by name in its review. "The chief object of attraction was a youth of this city, of about fifteen, of the name of Forrest, who made his debut in young Norval. . . . Of the performance of young Norval, we must say that it was uncommon in the performance by such a youth, as it was extraordinary in just conception and the exemption from the idea of artifice, such as is common in the most practiced players. . . . We trust that this young gentleman will find the patronage to which his extraordinary ripeness of faculty and his modest deportment entitle him."[5]

The receipts for Forrest's performance amounted to $319.75—a respectable sum for an unknown actor, and Forrest was invited to reprise the role the next Saturday, December 2. He returned again on December 29, to play Frederick in *Lovers' Vows*, a comedy by the popular German playwright August von Kotzebue. On January 6 the theatre held a benefit for the young actor; he played Octavian in George Colman's *The Mountaineers*. Receipts for that night were only $215, but the applause was hearty and the critical response flattering. It confirmed to Forrest that he had a future on the stage.

THOMAS A. COOPER

On December 15, 1820, Thomas Abthorpe Cooper made his first appearance at the Walnut Street Theatre. At forty-four, Cooper was the leading actor of the American stage. Born in England, he had made his American stage debut at the Chestnut Street Theatre on December 9, 1796, in *Macbeth*. Sensing that he would be relegated to minor roles, Cooper broke his contract and joined the company at the Park Theatre in New York City. He quickly established himself as the leading tragedian there, and later managed the theatre. In 1814 Cooper resigned from the management of the Park to devote himself

fig. 3 Edwin Forrest made his Walnut Street Theatre debut on November 27, 1820. The Philadelphia native would quickly rise to stardom.

exclusively to acting. He became the first legitimate American star, touring towns and cities up and down the eastern seaboard.

Cooper opened in a new play, *Virginius, or The Liberation of Rome,* a tragedy by the Irish playwright Sheridan Knowles. Written in blank verse, *Virginius* tells the story of a Roman father who is driven to murder his daughter in order to save her from the lust of the emperor. Cooper had premiered the play at the Holliday Theatre in Baltimore. It would become one of his most critically acclaimed roles and became a popular vehicle for many other actors. Cooper remained at the Walnut Street Theatre until December 23, reprising *Virginius* twice and also appearing in *Macbeth, Hamlet,* and *Richard III.*

Edwin Forrest's debut, a few weeks before Cooper's, prompted comparisons between the two actors, and the young actor sought out the older man's advice. According to Forrest's biographer, Richard Moody, "Cooper cautioned him against putting too much stock in his first flashes of success; a young actor must learn his art step by step. The old man may have been alerting him to the need for diligent and devoted study; Forrest thought that he was advising him to backtrack and begin as a super. He could not endure such nonsense. He got up and walked out."[6] Despite this early disagreement, Cooper was a major influence on Forrest, and the two tragedians had great respect for each other. Although neither actor ordinarily shared billing with another star, they often appeared together, alternating in the roles of Iago and Othello.

EDMUND KEAN

Both Forrest and Cooper were eclipsed during the winter of 1820–21 by the arrival of Edmund Kean. Kean was truly a phenomenon. A touring provincial player from an impoverished background, Kean had made his London debut in 1814, and his portrayal of Shylock had taken the city by storm. Kean did not look the part of the tragic hero. He was relatively short in stature and by no means handsome, but he was a powerful presence onstage. "Kean's whole style, mode, elocution, stage business, dressing, his diminutive figure, his frequent pauses, his deep repose, which was suddenly disturbed by irresistible bursts of terrific passion, took the audience by surprise," Charles Durang observed. "Quick transitions of voice distinguished him, with now and then a salient point, as leaping from a deep abstraction to catch the conclusion, ere it departed from its conception."[7] It is this quality that led Samuel Taylor Coleridge to remark that watching Kean perform was "like reading Shakespeare by flashed of lightning."

Kean was one of those rare talents who changed the acting traditions of an era. Before Kean, stage acting was measured, dignified, refined. Kean challenged the formal, declamatory style that had dominated until then, bringing powerful emotions to his depiction of Shakespeare's tragic heroes. "He penetrated and incorporated himself with the characters he represented until he possessed them so completely that they possessed him, and their performance was no simulation, but revelation," wrote Edwin Forrest's biographer, W. R. Alger. "His playing was the manifestation of inspired intuition, infallibly true and irresistibly sensational. It came not from the surface of his brain, but from the very centers of his nervous system, and suggested something portentous, preternatural, supernal, that blinded and stunned the beholders, appalled the imagination, and chilled their blood."[8] This passionate approach to acting was in keeping with the romantic movement that was then taking hold in literature and art, and it deeply influenced the actors who would follow, including the young Edwin Forrest, who attended all of Kean's performances at the Walnut Street Theatre.

Kean had been brought to America by Stephen Price, the ambitious manager of New York's fashionable Park Theatre. He made his debut at the Anthony Street Theatre in New York on November 29, 1820, and played there through December 26. The next stop on his American tour was Philadelphia, where he opened a sixteen-day engagement at the Walnut Street Theatre on January 8, 1821, with a performance as Shakespeare's Richard III, one of his signature roles. The audience witnessed a power rarely seen on the stage before. "His Richard was full of fiery energy," Durang recalled. "He never flagged from the first word till his last extraordinary gaze on Richmond. During his dying speech, the expression which accompanied it; for natural intenseness and terror of aspect, may be denominated the sublime of tragic passion. There was no exaggeration about it; so truthful was it, that it was touching to behold."[9]

The curtain fell to rapturous applause. Although some critics disparaged Kean's passionate acting style, Philadelphians were eager to judge for themselves, and the excitement built throughout the week. On Wednesday, January 10, Kean played Othello, and on Friday he appeared as Shylock in *The Merchant of Venice*, finishing out the week with *Hamlet*. The following week he reprised his performance in *Richard III* and acted the title role in *Brutus*, a neoclassical tragedy written especially for Kean by the American playwright John Howard Payne. He appeared as Sir Giles Overreach in Philip Massinger's *A New Way to Pay Old Debts* and finished off the week with a benefit performance of *Macbeth*. Kean remained for two more weeks, playing several new plays—*Rule a Wife and Have a Wife*, *Bertram*, and *Town and Country*—returning to the classics—*King Lear*, *Othello*, and *The Merchant of Venice*—for his last week. He closed the run on February 3 with George Colman's *The Iron Chest*.

Kean's effect on Philadelphia audiences was tremendous, and his appearances at the Walnut Street Theatre introduced the custom of bringing out the actor for a curtain call, a practice that the theatre's manager found ludicrous. "The absurdity of dragging out before the curtain a deceased Hamlet, Macbeth or Richard in an exhausted state, merely to make a bow, or probably worse, to attempt an asthmatic address in defiance of all good taste, and solely for the gratification of a few unthinking partisans, or a few lovers of noise and tumult, is one which we date with us from this time," wrote William Wood.[10] Today the curtain call is standard practice, but it was introduced at the Walnut during Kean's tour.

If Kean's acting was electrifying, his offstage behavior was often out of control. Kean was a serious alcoholic who preferred the company of wastrels in

fig. 4 Edmund Kean in Shakespeare's *Richard III.*

the taverns he frequented to his well-to-do admirers at the theatre. He seemed to go out of his way to alienate his supporters. Reports of Kean's arrogant and dissolute behavior had made their way from London to America, but during his first run at the Walnut, William Wood found him "a mild, unassuming and cheerful man, wholly free from every affectation of superiority of dictation."[11] There was a marked change in his behavior on his return engagement, April 9–18, 1821. On the closing night of the run, Kean appeared as Jaffier in Thomas Otway's tragedy *Venice Preserved*, but "soon fell into eccentric contrasts, doing strange things, so palpably nonsensical that the audience, especially the box portion, began to wince, and, at length, to express disapprobation more decidedly, so that the disapproval could not be mistaken," according to Durang. "At length hisses came from the boxes, and groans, with 'Off!' 'Off!' from every part of the house came tumbling down like an avalanche."[12]

When the catcalls subsided enough for him to be heard, Kean addressed the audience, calling them cowards and scoundrels. This enraged the crowd even more, and Kean was forced to make a hasty exit. The afterpiece was hastily put up, but the audience would not let the actors proceed. They were hissed and pelted with apples, oranges, and other missiles, until they too were forced off the stage. When an audience member sitting in one of the stage boxes tried to defend Kean, members of the crowd climbed into the box and threw him and his companions onto the stage. "This riotous behavior brought the performance to a sudden close," Wood recalled, "and the melée in the front was brought to an end by the forethought or presence of the lamplighter, in blowing out the lights, which drove out the belligerents, who were now fully satisfied with their caterwaulings, groans, hisses, and other horrible demonstrations of savage conduct."[13]

Such tumultuous behavior on the part of the audience was not at all unusual in the early nineteenth century. Audience members could be vocal in their appreciation of their favorite players, and just as vocal in their disfavor. Periodically riots would break out at the theatre. Americans were sensitive to any perceived slights by Europeans, who they believed were arrogant and disdainful of Americans, and the theatre was one arena in which class resentments were acted out. Periodic outbreaks of violence contributed to the low regard in which the theatre was held, and kept many women from attending. Most observers blamed Kean for goading the crowd with his insensitive and self-centered remarks. He would replay the scene during his return visit to Boston by refusing to perform one night because the audience was too small. Newspapers across the country lambasted him for his arrogance, turning most Americans against him.

THE 1821–1822 SEASON

During the summer months, Warren and Wood played regular engagements in Baltimore and Washington, returning to the Walnut for two weeks in July. They opened their second season at the Walnut on October 13, 1821. The 1821–22 season was by no means as impressive as the previous one. There were no stars of the magnitude of Edmund Kean to draw people to the theatre. The grandest attraction was a deputation of Indian chiefs who attended the theatre on December 19 and 22. The most notable performance of the season was a benefit for the Orphan Asylum, which was destroyed by fire on January 24, 1822, killing twenty-three of the children; the benefit was held at the Walnut four days later. The outpouring of public support surprised even William Wood. "Attached to the theatre as I have been for 47 years, this is the only instance I ever witnessed of a *full house*," he remarked. "On this memorable night every seat was occupied, from the orchestra to the remotest part of the gallery."[14] More than $1,700 was collected to assist the orphans. On most nights, receipts were between $100 and $500.

Several days later, on February 2, Edwin Forrest made his only appearance at the Walnut Street Theatre that season, playing the part of Zaphna in *Mahomet*. "I played on [that] evening better than ever I did before," he wrote his brother, William. "After the murder of my father, repeated bravos rose from all quarters. Last scene, bravos again."[15] The cheers kept up, so that the afterpiece had to be suspended, as the audience demanded that Forrest be offered another engagement. Wood agreed, but when the young man appeared at the theatre the following week, Wood had changed his mind. Forrest was unable to secure any further performances in Philadelphia, and in the fall of 1822 he joined a troupe touring the western states. He would remain in the west for the next three years, developing his craft. When he returned to the East Coast three years later, the public took even greater notice.

Other notable productions of the 1821–22 season included a new play by Philadelphia-born Mordecai M. Noah, *Marion, or The Hero of Lake George*, a story of the American Revolution. Noah had produced a number of patriotic plays, but he discovered that he could not support himself through writing and gave it up, ending a promising writing career. Poor copyright protection hampered the development of American drama. On March 1, 1822, Rossini's opera *The Barber of Seville* was staged at the Walnut, the first time the opera had been put on in Philadelphia. It starred a popular English tenor, Thomas Philipps, who was the big attraction that season. On March 22 the managers engaged a live elephant for a production of *Forty Thieves*. It was advertised as "the largest animal of the kind ever exhibited in America, superbly caparisoned, with Riders, &c. in the Asiatic style."[16] Unfortunately, the elephant failed to draw much of an audience. The season closed on April 23, 1822, with a performance of *The Spy, or The Tale of Neutral Ground*, a play based on James Fenimore Cooper's novel of the same name.

PRICE AND SIMPSON'S CIRCUS

The company and much of the audience were unhappy with the facilities at the Walnut Street Theatre. Business had fallen off from the year before.

Morale was low. The stockholders of the Chestnut decided to rebuild the theatre on its original site at Sixth and Chestnut streets, and construction of the new facility began during the summer of 1822. While the work progressed, the Walnut Street Theatre was converted back into an amphitheatre for equestrian performances. The seats were torn out of the pit area to make room for a riding ring.

The new lessees of the Walnut were Stephen Price and Edmund Simpson, managers of the prestigious Park Theatre in New York City. They had just purchased James West's equestrian troupe. West had been appearing in New York, and his equestrian dramas had been drawing audiences away from the Park Theatre. Price and Simpson wanted to buy him out, but West turned them down. So they hatched a scheme to trick the circus man into selling to them. They circulated a rumor that they were about to build an arena for their own equestrian shows, and went so far as to have a model built and exhibited in the lobby of their theatre. They hired one of West's riders, Sam Tatnall, and employed him in breaking horses in a vacant lot behind the theatre. The ruse worked, for West gave up his stable of horses, along with his leases to amphitheatres in New York, Philadelphia, Washington, Charleston, and Savannah, and retired to London. Most of West's performers remained with the circus, now being managed by Sam Tatnall, an apparent reward for his role in deceiving his boss. They opened at the Walnut, now renamed the Olympic, on September 9, 1822. The company offered circus acts, along with the hippodramas that West had made popular, staging *The Tiger Horde*, *The Secret Mine*, *Timour the Tartar*, *Blue Beard*, *Tekeli*, and *Lodoiska*, all of which played to excellent houses.

On October 16, 1822, the circus announced a new feature; a rider named James Hunter, from Astley's Circus in London, would ride "without saddle or bridle."[17] It was the first bareback riding act ever presented in America. Hunter was a small, unprepossessing man with "a regular Cockney face," but the impression he made was tremendous. "We well remember when the prancing steed on which Hunter was to perform was first brought into the ring, naked—without any accoutrements at all—the grooms vainly restraining the 'Fair Virginia's' wild energies," Charles Durang recalled. "The wild and odd appearance of the animal, springing and bounding on her *entrée*, struck the audience with something like awe. The rider entered, and quietly bowed to a general reception . . . mounted on the bare back of the Mazeppa-like steed, and, at a furious gallop, struck attitudes, executing the various feats with ease and grace, the hitherto silent but intense curiosity burst forth in crashes of tumultuous applause. The enthusiasm, the shouts of approbation and loud huzzas, with other Babel noises, defies all reasonable description."[18]

In taking over James West's circus, Price and Simpson not only eliminated competition to the Park Street Theatre but put new pressure on the management of the Chestnut. Philadelphia was very much the equal in New York as a theatrical and cultural center, and the New York managers now had a presence in both cities. The Walnut (still called the Olympic) now became the center for organized opposition in Philadelphia. Following Victor Pepin's strategy, Price and Simpson closed their season a few days before Warren and Wood opened their rebuilt Chestnut Street Theatre on December 2, 1822.

Warren and Wood were given a ten-year lease on the new building. But they now faced competition from a pair of theatre managers as experienced as themselves. Increasingly, they found themselves turning to their competitors for attractions for their theatre. Following the success of Edmund Kean, Stephen Price began to bring over other British stars in earnest. He found that he could tempt them to come to New York with the promise of high salaries. To recoup the costs, he arranged for them to tour other American cities, taking a percentage of the proceeds for himself. William Wood soon realized the ill effect that this reliance on imported British talent would have on the Chestnut Theatre. The English stars were guaranteed a set appearance fee. Although they attracted crowds, the house was unable to make a profit because of the exorbitant fees the actors charged. Wood, however, had little say in the matter. The stockholders who subsidized the building of the new theatre were exerting new authority. Drawn as much by the glamour of the theatre as by the investment possibilities, they insisted that these stars be booked, whatever the cost.

What had been a trickle before Kean's arrival now became a flood, as Price introduced a steady stream of English actors, singers, and comedians to American audiences. Among the first to come over was the English comedian Charles Matthews. A talented mimic, Matthews was especially famous for his one-man entertainments, in which he told anecdotes, delivered monologues, sang songs, and impersonated various characters. He remained in America only a short time, but he influenced American comedians, like James H. Hackett, who began creating their own comic Yankee characters.

When the Walnut, still called the Olympic, opened for its second season on August 30, 1823, Joseph Cowell had replaced Sam Tatnall as manager of the circus. Unlike his predecessor, Cowell came from a theatrical rather than a circus background. He guided the circus through its most successful years; James Hunter's bareback riding remained the principal attraction. Cowell introduced other novelty acts. Master Whittaker, a child of ten, performed on the trampoline, "throwing somersets through hoops, over garters, and a number of horses." A spotted horse called General Jackson did various tricks on command. Slack-rope performer James Stoker joined the company, performing an act in which he appeared to hang himself. "It looked terrific—truly horrible!" Charles Durang remarked. "We recollect the sensation his hanging first produced on the audience. Several ladies fainted, and the men trembled. This was enough to make excitement out of doors, and crowds ran to see a sight which disgusted many."[19]

Cowell combined acts like these with equestrian dramas, repeating successes from earlier years and adding such pieces as *Blood Red Knight, or The Fatal Bridge; The Coronation of Henry V;* and *El Hyder, or Love and Bravery.* The circus remained in Philadelphia until December 1, 1823, when Cowell divided the company and sent one half to Boston and the other half to Savannah. The two companies joined up in New York for a summer run, then returned to Philadelphia on August 30, 1824.

The great public event of the 1824–25 season was the arrival of the Marquis de Lafayette, who was touring the United States. September 28 was appointed for his reception in Philadelphia. The streets of the city were brilliantly illuminated, and an emblematical transparency was projected on the front of the circus. Lafayette was escorted into the city by two troops of cavalry in a carriage drawn by six cream-colored horses. That night, the dance director, Mr. Parker, staged a new ballet titled *The Brave Frenchman, or The Female Restored to Liberty.* The highlight of the ballet was "a fancy nosegay dance" by his two daughters, ages four and five, in which they spelled out the words Lafayette. The marquis remained in the city a week, during which time there were receptions, balls, and other festivities in his honor. On Friday, October 1, the circus staged a patriotic drama called *La Fayette, or The Castle of Olmutz.*

Another popular spectacle, William Moncrieff's *The Cataract of the Ganges,* premiered during the week of October 18, 1824. It featured many striking effects, including a torrent of real water that spilled onto the stage during the final climactic scene. The season ended December 1, 1824, with *Cataract of the Ganges,* and again the equestrian and dramatic companies split up. The two contingents were reunited in Philadelphia on May 6, 1825, for a three-week run. They reopened on August 29, 1825. The highlight of the season was a pantomime, *The Talking Bird,* which opened on October 17 and featured scene changes and effects typical of the pantomimes being presented at Sadler's Wells in London by the great clown Joseph Grimaldi. Audiences filled the house most of the season.

The circus began to decline in 1826, when Cowell lost most of the company's horses during a fierce storm at sea en route to Charleston, South Carolina. The animals had been stabled on deck, and a number of horses were drowned when the sea washed over them. Others were killed or badly hurt by falling spars, and were cast overboard.[20] Cowell was able to secure new horses for an opening in Philadelphia on August 7, 1826, but the circus never recovered. On September 19, Edmond Simpson announced that his circus business was for sale. No one seemed interested. At the end of the 1826 season, Joseph Cowell left the circus to become the stage manager at the Chestnut Street Theatre.

THE PHILADELPHIA THEATRE

Warren and Wood had grown increasingly estranged. Wood did not like the new reliance on expensive stars. Concerned that the stockholders were exerting too much influence and that the Chestnut was becoming "a mere tributary to New York," he resigned from the management of the company, leaving William Warren as sole owner.[21] Joseph Cowell was hired as manager of the Chestnut but remained only one season. In May 1827 he bought a half-interest in Price and Simpson's circus and opened at the Olympic for a summer run that lasted from May 28 through July 25. That summer, Cowell decided to separate the equestrian company from the dramatic corps and sent the circus on tour. The theatre was closed and the ring once again replaced with seating. From that point on, the Walnut Street Theatre would be devoted to legitimate drama, as Price and Cowell entered into direct competition with the Chestnut.

The new season began on August 29, 1827. The Walnut Street house now bore yet another name—the Philadelphia Theatre. "New dramas of a spectacular nature were produced," Durang reported. "Troupes of new actors and actresses were brought from England, and a band of accomplished musicians from the continent of Europe."[22] Two new stars were brought in who would appear regularly over the years. On September 3, Thomas S. Hamblin opened a run in which he appeared in the title roles in *Macbeth*, *Pizzaro*, *William Tell*, *Virginius*, and *Othello*, and as Jaffier in *Venice Preserved*. Born in England in 1800, Hamblin was already an important figure when he made his American stage debut in October 1825. He chose to remain in America, where he became best known as the manager of the Bowery Theatre in New York, which he ran in partnership with James H. Hackett from 1830 until his death in 1853. They popularized a working-class theatre that emphasized blood and thunder.

Also making his first appearance at the Philadelphia Theatre was Junius Brutus Booth, the father of the famous acting clan that included three sons—Junius II, Edwin, and John Wilkes Booth—and a daughter, Asia Booth. The elder Booth played on September 6 and 8, 1827, and returned for a six-night engagement beginning September 19. Unlike most of the British stars, Junius Brutus Booth was a virtual unknown in America when he arrived in 1821, but he quickly established himself as a favorite with American audiences. Booth bore a passing resemblance to Edmund Kean, and he suffered from the comparison, often being accused of being simply an imitator of Kean. Supporting him on September 26, in a performance of *Richard III*, was seven-year-old Louisa Lane, making her stage debut. The daughter of actors, Louisa Lane became a child star, taking on adult roles at the age of twelve and playing opposite the leading actors of the day. Many years later, under her married name, Mrs. John Drew, she became a major figure in the Philadelphia theatre, as both an actress and a theatrical manager. Thomas A. Cooper also made an appearance on October 22. He was about to depart for England, where he hoped to make his mark with London audiences, and this was a farewell tour. The season closed on November 3, with Cooper appearing in *Venice Preserved* alongside Thomas Hamblin.

The Philadelphia Theatre reopened on May 1, 1828, for a brief season. Joseph Cowell was now in partnership with Junius Brutus Booth. The performances met with general success, as reduced ticket prices attracted audiences away from the Chestnut Street Theatre. While the Chestnut was popular with more patrician crowds, the Walnut "enjoyed the smiles of the working man."[23] Pleased with the size of the houses, the stockholders of the theatre granted Cowell a ten-year lease on the building and authorized its complete renovation.

RENOVATING THE WALNUT

During the summer of 1827 the building was entirely remodeled, based on the designs of John Haviland, one of the leading architects in the city. The walls of the old circus remained, but the theatre was redone, inside and out. The plain brick front was covered over in stucco and marble. The most dramatic new feature was a Greek-influenced colonnade along the Walnut Street entrance. Four doors provided access to the theatre, each separated by two Doric columns that stood on a marble slab, and between the columns a Greek lamp was placed. The columns supported a "bold architrave entabulature" that extended across the entire length of the building, separating the first and second floors. The entabulature, or mantle, was decorated by a cast-iron wreath set above each of the columns and a *guilloche*, a decorative border of intertwining iron bands. The old interior was taken out. A new wall of stone, some two feet thick, was built within the old exterior walls to relieve pressure on them. Iron columns supported three tiers of boxes. Part of the third tier was given over to open gallery seating. Sight lines were improved by angling the stage boxes so that every part of the theatre had an unimpeded view of the stage.

While these renovations were under way, another theatre was under construction on the corner of Sixth and Arch streets. The erection of yet another competing theatre gave Cowell second thoughts about operating the Walnut.

fig. 5 A portrait of Junius Brutus Booth.

He was convinced, he wrote later, that "Philadelphia would not or could not support more than one establishment of this sort; and the one the public would most probably select, in despite of my popularity, would most likely be the new one, and I began to tremble for the consequences."[24] The proprietors of the Tremont Theatre in Boston offered him the opportunity to manage their theatre. Viewing the prospects of competing with two other theatres in Philadelphia as dubious, he left the city for Boston.

THE COMPETITION HEATS UP

William B. Wood was enticed into running the new Arch Street Theatre. Why he agreed to do so is uncertain. In his autobiography, he claimed that he believed the Walnut Street Theatre was to be demolished. It was probably lingering animosity toward William Warren, who had control of the Chestnut, that led him to this rash and ultimately self-destructive act. In any case, the two partners now engaged in a fierce rivalry. Wood opened the Arch Street Theatre on October 1, 1828. Warren leased the Chestnut to a French opera company until he was ready to open his own season. Once he returned in mid-November, the competition heated up further. Both houses spent heavily on visiting stars, while cutting ticket prices.

Wood hired the British star James W. Wallack to appear at the Arch for an unheard-of fee of $200 a night. Although Wallack was a guaranteed draw, his exorbitant salary meant that Wood could not meet expenses, even if he filled the house every night. The stockholders, however, were anxious to establish the new house and agreed to Wallack's terms, even if it meant digging into their own pockets. Warren tried to counter by bringing in Edwin Forrest on the same nights. Forrest demanded the same $200 Wallack was making, however, and Warren passed. While Wallack attracted good houses during his run at the Arch Street Theatre in December, the receipts did not cover expenses. When the stockholders refused to make good on their promise, Wood angrily withdrew from managing, and the Arch closed in the middle of Wallack's engagement, on December 29, 1828.

Having triumphed over his former partner, William Warren decided that he had had enough. Tired of the competition and the exorbitant sums demanded by touring stars, he announced his farewell benefit for December 30, 1828. New management planned to reopen the Walnut Street house, which would mean that three theatres were competing for the same audience. Warren would remain with the Chestnut Street Theatre as an actor, but he was turning over all management responsibilities to his stage manager, Francis Wemyss, and Wemyss's new partner, Lewis T. Pratt. For $2,000 in cash and a promise of $3,000 a year, they would have the use of theatrical properties in Philadelphia, Baltimore, and Washington.

BLAKE AND INSLEE

The Walnut Street Theatre had remained dark through the fall of 1828. In December, William R. Blake, a member of the Arch company, and his partner, John A. Inslee, announced that they were taking over the theatre. Inslee was reputed to have a lot of money, being part owner of a fashionable hotel on Chestnut Street. With confidence that the project would be properly funded, Blake put together a strong cast that included Thomas S. Hamblin, Henry Wallack, and Jane Placide. The theatre opened on the evening of January 1,

1829, once again under the name the Walnut Street Theatre, with a performance of a comedy called *Honey Moon* and a farcical afterpiece, *The Lottery Ticket*. The opening night audience got the first sight of the new interior. It had been completely transformed, and "all were astonished at the sight of so beautiful a theatre, created as if by magic, out of the old circus."[25]

The new managers spent freely on new attractions. On January 6 they announced M. and Mme. Charles Ronzi Vestris, who performed their *grand pas de deux* between the play and the afterpiece. Local papers cautioned that "no ladies could visit the theatre to witness such an exhibition," but the novelty and elegance of the dancers overcame any sense of propriety. Francis Wemyss reported that "a Vestris mania resulted, pervading all orders of society, filling the theatre nightly."[26] Two days later they produced a dramatic sketch by a Philadelphia playwright titled *The Glorious Eighth of January*. It commemorated Andrew Jackson's victory at the Battle of New Orleans in the War of 1812. Jackson had just been elected president and was to be sworn into office in March. Then, the following Monday, January 12, 1829, Edwin Forrest made a much anticipated return to the Walnut.

EDWIN FORREST RETURNS TO THE WALNUT

Edwin Forrest was only twenty-two when he returned to the Walnut Street Theatre, but he was coming back a star. The young actor had spent several years touring the western territories, first as a member of a touring company that worked the Ohio River valley, floating from town to town via flatboat. Later, he joined James H. Caldwell's company in New Orleans and spent two seasons there. Forrest returned east in 1825, joining a stock company at the Pearl Street Theatre in Albany, New York, where he had the opportunity to act opposite Edmund Kean. Forrest took supporting roles, playing Iago to Kean's Othello, Richmond to his Richard III. It was a unique opportunity to observe Kean's technique, and Forrest incorporated much of what he saw into his own style—the "impulsive displays of passion, the fiery spurts of eloquence which 'made the pit tremble,' the realistic bursts of physical movement."[27] Kean also took note of the young American actor, predicting his rise to greatness.

Forrest's break came in the summer of 1826. He was not yet twenty-one when he played Othello at a benefit performance at the Park Theatre on June 23. It was a daring move, typical of Forrest. Kean had recently done the role, and his performance was fresh in people's minds. While Forrest's performance fell short of the Englishman's, critics judged it "superior to any in this country except Kean."[28] Forrest was quickly signed on as a member of the stock company of the new, three-thousand-seat Bowery Theatre and was promoted as the principal attraction against the British actors at the Park.[29]

Forrest was engaged for three nights at the Walnut in January 1829. He opened in *Damon and Pythias*, playing Damon opposite Henry Wallack as Pythias. His appearance was cheered by the hometown audience. "We believe no performance upon the Philadelphia stage has been marked with such uniform excellence," a reviewer for the *United States Gazette* exulted. He followed this up two nights later with Hamlet, a role he had only recently added to his repertoire. Although his performance was not faultless, the reviewer judged it "the best Hamlet we ever saw." On the sixteenth he performed in Sheridan Knowles's *William Tell, or The Hero of Switzerland*. He concluded his engagement on Monday, January 19, in John Howard Payne's *Brutus, or The Fall of Tarquin*.

Although some critics dismissed Forrest as unlettered and coarse in his acting style, his talent and charisma put him in the same ranks as the leading English tragedians. Blessed with rugged good looks and a powerful voice, Forrest had built himself up through daily exercise. His muscled body contrasted sharply with the slight, even diminutive, bodies of the leading English actors of the period, Edmund Kean and William Macready. He was best as a representative of the common man who stood up against powerful tyrants. He was most successful in strenuous, heroic roles, often choosing to portray leaders who challenged authority and tyranny. Forrest was a truly heroic figure, and Philadelphians were especially proud of their hometown boy.

MORE EXPENSIVE ATTRACTIONS AT THE WALNUT

Blake and Inslee continued to pack the Walnut Street Theatre with expensive attractions. On January 20 they brought in James H. Hackett, a comedian who was gaining renown for his portrayals of local characters. He premiered in a new play, *John Bull at Home, or Jonathan in England*, in which he introduced a comic Yankee character, Solomon Swap. Hackett was the first of many comedians to represent the stage Yankee. On the twenty-third he appeared in *The Comedy of Errors* as one of the Dromios—apparently the first time this Shakespearean comedy had been performed in Philadelphia. Observers remarked on how perfectly Hackett imitated the other Dromio, played by John Barnes.

On January 21 the managers brought in an entire *corps de ballet*. The French company was said to be excellent at pantomime, and they made their first appearance in a comic production called *La Marriage, or Love Protected by Folly*. William B. Wood joined the company toward the end of the month, making his debut with the French corps as Don Felix in the comedy *The Won-*

der. Edwin Forrest returned to play King Lear on January 24, appearing opposite Thomas S. Hamblin. Forrest received a benefit on the twenty-eighth, appearing in *Macbeth* alongside Louisa Lane.

Although these attractions guaranteed full houses, the costs were enormous. Blake and Inslee were paying for the visiting stars, an entire *corps de ballet,* and a specialty dance team, as well as maintaining a high-priced stock company. "Vast sums had been received," Charles Durang reported, "but a most expensive company and the stars had absorbed the moneys so received. No assets were left but unbalanced ledger sheets and protested notes." By the middle of February, the quality had begun to decline. "The leading talent had receded—the attractions lessened—fashion vacated the box seats, and the theatrical horizon was darkened with black clouds," Charles Durang wrote. "The 'salary day' became uncertain. A feud of a violent nature arose between Inslee and Blake. The cabinet councils were in discord—managers' notes at a discount."[30] Blake and Inslee kept the season going until April 14, when the partnership dissolved amid much acrimony.

COLLAPSE OF THE THEATRE

As experienced managers like Joseph Cowell and William B. Wood anticipated, the city could not sustain three competing theatres. The fierce competition forced managers to pay premium prices for stars who could bring audiences into their theatres. While the stars drew people in unprecedented numbers, their salary demands made it impossible for the theatres to turn a profit. The managers hurt themselves by engaging in a bitter competition, reducing ticket prices and bidding against each other for talented actors and stage managers, with the predictable result that all three Philadelphia theatres failed.

The Walnut and the Arch closed their doors during the winter of 1828–29. At the Chestnut, Pratt and Wemyss struggled along until the end of May, but they too were forced to close. This was the most devastating blow, at least for William Warren and William B. Wood. As long as Warren held the lease on the Chestnut Street Theatre, he retained certain rights to the property and its holdings. But by transferring the lease to Wemyss and Pratt, he had unwittingly given up those rights. The terms of the lease being unfulfilled, the stockholders took possession of the theatre and its contents. Sets and costumes were auctioned off by the sheriff for a fraction of their value. William Warren, who had looked forward to a comfortable retirement supported by the leases on the Chestnut, was forced to go back to work. At sixty-two, he was no longer up to starting over. He aged perceptibly and died within three years. Wood, too, depended on continued income from the Chestnut, based on his agreement with Warren. But because the agreement was verbal, it could not be enforced, and he too was left financially devastated. "There had been a complete debacle, or breaking up of everything that had been," he wrote. "I never became lessee again, nor very permanently connected with any theatre as a stock actor. Permanence belongs now to nothing except failure, disorder and bankruptcy."

The collapse of the three leading theatres in Philadelphia marked a major change in the history of the American theatre. Power passed out of the hands of theatre managers like Warren and Wood and into the hands of touring stars. Audiences were eager to see the leading names of the London stage but could not be enticed into theatres otherwise. Stock companies in Philadelphia and other cities increasingly acted as supporting players to the stars coming from New York City. New York now emerged as the theatrical center of the United States, while Philadelphia increasingly became—as William Wood had feared—a "mere tributary" of the New York stage. America was entering a new era, symbolized by the election of Andrew Jackson to the presidency. As William Wood observed, "The vitality of the theatre neither was nor can be destroyed, but its action was irregular, spasmodic and disordered."[31] New entrepreneurs were eager to try their luck in the glamorous but risky world of theatrical production.

THE WALNUT IN THE AGE OF JACKSON, 1829–1840

On March 15, 1829—one day after William Rufus Blake and John Inslee closed the doors on the Walnut Street Theatre—a new president was sworn into office. Andrew Jackson's inauguration marked a major change in American politics, a period remembered as the Jacksonian era. Celebrated as the hero who defeated the British in the Battle of New Orleans, Jackson won the election of 1828 in a landslide, carrying the Philadelphia vote by a wide margin. His populist message resonated with an electorate eager to show that America was the equal of Europe.

The egalitarian ideals of the young Republic were still looked down on by the aristocratic society of London and Paris, who viewed Americans as socially and culturally backward. The democratic idea that a society could be governed by the people was still radical. While the United States had proved itself militarily and commercially, the new nation had yet to produce any artists or writers equal to Europe's leading lights.

The American theatre was still an extension of the British stage when Andrew Jackson took office. The leading actors—even those who had moved permanently to America—were all born and trained in London. British plays and playwrights predominated. America had produced several playwrights of note—Mordecai Noah, William Dunlap, and James N. Barker stand out—but they could not support themselves through their writing, and most returned to more lucrative pursuits. Copyright laws worked against the development of American drama. British copyrights were not enforced in the United States, so theatre managers were able to stage British plays without paying royalties to the writers. When local plays were produced, playwrights received only the proceeds from a single night's benefit for their work—hardly enough to support them.

Americans of all social classes were eager to see American life and American values represented on the stage, although different groups had distinct ideas of what American drama should be. Elite audiences, those who paid for private boxes at the theatre, favored plays that would demonstrate that American audiences had as much taste and sophistication as those in London. They tended to support literary works, primarily neoclassical verse dramas like those being produced in England. The public who occupied the pit and the upper galleries wanted to see a different kind of drama—one that captured the vitality of the young nation. They favored productions that depicted patriotic sentiment and local character types. These two groups patronized the same houses, and managers catered to the needs of both. But as the number of theatres increased, the classes increasingly became segregated in different theatres. The Chestnut Street Theatre, still the most prestigious house in Philadelphia, catered to elite audiences, while the Walnut and Arch theatres were more popularly priced.

CHAPMAN AND GREENE

New management took over the Walnut Street Theatre on May 26, 1829. John Greene and Samuel Chapman were young actor-managers eager to try their hand at running a prestigious house in Philadelphia. Greene was a native Philadelphian who specialized in comic Irish characters. The creative force behind the enterprise was British-born Sam Chapman, a member of a close-knit theatrical family that had come to America two years before. The lessons of the previous year were not lost on them. Chapman and Greene organized their company as a theatrical commonwealth, paying their actors very little but allowing them to share in the profits of the company. With the failure of both the Arch and the Chestnut in the winter and spring of 1829, Chapman and Greene were able to put together a large and talented cast that included Joseph Jefferson, his son John and daughter Elizabeth, Clara Fisher, Joseph Cowell, and several members of the Chapman family. Also joining the company were William Wood and William Warren, now reduced to being stock actors. With this cast, Chapman and Greene organized a season that did not rely on touring stars but made the most of old melodramas, comedies, and farces. It was successful enough that they were granted the lease for the fall season.

During the break, Samuel Chapman married Elizabeth Jefferson, and the two honeymooned in Niagara Falls. Several stars were on hand to get the season off to a good start, and the theatre opened to good business. Clara Fisher appeared for the first week. Thomas S. Hamblin joined her on September 17, appearing as Romeo to Fisher's Juliet. Junius Brutus Booth appeared for three nights on September 23–25. A wire walker, Herr Cline, appeared between the main production and the afterpiece, performing various feats on the "elastic cord." His act culminated in an ascension from the stage to the gallery on a wire. His brother André, billed as "the German Hercules," performed gymnastic exercises with coach wheels and ladders, and balanced a wooden beam fifteen feet long.

The highlight of the fall season was a production of *Faustus,* which premiered on December 12, 1829. Chapman discovered that the Arch Street Theatre was preparing its own version of the play and sent his orchestra leader, John Clements, to observe the rehearsals, jotting down the music and words. His carpenters and scene painters copied the sets. Chapman was able to mount his production of *Faustus* before the Arch production was ready, completely stealing their thunder. The show ran through the Christmas season. On January 16, 1830, another spectacle was premiered, a historical drama titled *Pocahontas, or The Settlers of Virginia,* written by George Washington Custis. The Walnut suddenly closed on January 22, and the management dissolved amid accusations of financial impropriety. John Greene withdrew from management of the company, and this theatrical commonwealth was brought to an end.

SAMUEL AND WILLIAM CHAPMAN

Samuel Chapman reopened a month later in partnership with his twin brother, William. Sam Chapman's talents in staging melodrama and producing elaborate stage effects soon became apparent. He put together a number of original productions that dramatized local events. On March 23 he brought out a parody of *Faustus* titled *Dr. Foster from Philadelphia,* about a local schoolmaster who conjures the devil. Written by John Clements, it proved quite popular, particularly when a fire eater, Mr. Hart, was cast as one of the demons. *Gasperoni, or The Roman Bandit,* which debuted on April 19, dramatized the exploits of an outlaw then terrorizing the Italian states. The final scene depicted the conflagration of the outlaws' lair, in which the heroine, played by Mrs. Flynn, "is seen clinging to a beam, which falls with a tremendous crash." Durang noted that "the audience was nearly choked with sulphur and dense volumes of smoke, and . . . Mrs. Flynn was nearly killed in the fall."[1]

Samuel Chapman penned another melodrama, *The Mail Robbers, or The Punishment of Crime,* which related the events and prosecution of a trio of bandits who robbed the local mail coach and were even then on trial for their lives. It premiered on May 10, 1830. The next night, Chapman, who played the part of the lead bandit, became ill and had to be taken home. He died several days later. Accounts differ as to the cause of his death, but according to Charles Durang, Chapman "took a ride out to the scene of the robbery, the better to regulate the action of a piece he was preparing on the subject, was thrown from his horse, and slightly grazed his shoulder. He had to wear that night a suit of brass armour, and the weather being excessively hot, he wore it next to his skin, which increased the excoriation; and it was supposed the verdegris [i.e., the patina] had poisoned the wound."[2]

The loss of such a talent cannot be overstated. "Poor Chapman!" Francis Wemyss declared. "He was a man of varied talent, of much literary knowledge, and an universal favourite: with all his faults, the stage 'could have better spared a better man.' Had he lived, he would have produced an entire revolution in the minor drama of America; with his death, ceased the prosperity of the theatre."[3] Sam Chapman's funeral was one of the biggest Philadelphia had ever seen.

THE CHAPMAN FAMILY

William Chapman tried to keep the enterprise going with the assistance of other family members, but they were not up to the task. They kept the theatre open through the summer, relying on touring stars and curiosities to attract audiences. Junius Brutus Booth appeared for several performances beginning May 29, and Mary Ann Duff was brought in on June 11. They revived *Dr. Foster;* engaged Calvin Edson, "the Living Skeleton," on June 17; and advertised the appearance of an elephant and her calf onstage on June 21. The season continued until August 4, with benefits for various members of the company.

For the fall season, the Chapmans brought in a new musical director, Mr. Taylor, from the Italian Opera House in London, and a new orchestra leader. The attempt to develop an audience for English opera did not work. They were more successful with spectacles like *Slaves in Barbary, or The Bombardment of Algiers,* which opened in October with extensive scenery and machinery, costumes, fireworks, and other spectacular effects. By all accounts, it was a good season with a talented company, but the managers were unable to meet the payroll, and they closed in the middle of December. When spring came, the Chapman family set out for Pittsburgh. There they built the first floating theatre—a flatboat on which they drifted down the Ohio and Mississippi rivers, giving shows along the way. After several years the family had saved enough money to buy a steamboat, which they equipped with a stage, auditorium, and living quarters, that allowed them to travel up and down the rivers giving performances. It was the first showboat.[4]

With the Chapmans gone, the Walnut was briefly reopened as a circus. Jeremiah Fogg and Samuel P. Stickney's troupe had a two-week run beginning in late March. Later that spring the theatre was taken over by a trio of managers—Robert C. Maywood, H. H. Rowbotham, and Lewis T. Pratt—calling themselves Maywood and Company. Robert Maywood was a well-educated Scot with good London contacts and a solid reputation as a Shakespearean actor. He made his first appearance in America at the Park Theatre in 1819, playing the title role in *Richard III.* His partners both had previous experience managing theatres in the city. They opened for a summer season on May 9, 1831.

That summer, the Chestnut Street Theatre also became available, and the partners quickly snapped up the lease. Maywood and Company now controlled two of the principal theatres in Philadelphia. The Walnut Street Theatre was once again renovated and opened for the fall season on August 27, 1831. *The Marriage of Figaro* was produced at the Walnut on September 5, 1831—in a rather doctored version. Durang indicates that "Mozart's chief music was left out, and there were substituted six or eight songs of a popular kind." The season closed on October 15, and the company was transferred to the Chestnut Street house.

By controlling both houses, Robert Maywood and his partners were able to limit the competition that had been so ruinous for so many Philadelphia managers. For a time they tried operating both theatres simultaneously, using the same company at both houses but playing alternate nights in each one. This did not sit too well with the public, which was not eager to pay twice as much at the Chestnut to see the same cast that had just played at the Walnut. Maywood and Company finally hit on a workable strategy of playing part of the season at one house and part at the other—the Chestnut being occupied during the more lucrative winter season and the Walnut functioning primarily as a summer theatre. This arrangement proved very effective. Philadelphia theatre entered a period of success and stability that it had not enjoyed since Warren and Wood's day. "It was a coveted restoration of a profession thought to be 'past praying for,'" Durang wrote, "and those only who saw its tribulations can truly appreciate its critical straits and dire calamities."[5]

COMPETITION AT THE ARCH STREET THEATRE

Maywood and Company's principal competition came from the Arch Street Theatre, which had been taken over in 1831 by Edwin Forrest's brother, William, in partnership with William Duffy and William Jones. Forrest and his partners tried to promote American talent. The principal draw at the Arch was, not surprisingly, Edwin Forrest, who vigorously promoted American drama and dramatists. He shared the nativist sentiments of the audience, and catered to them.

In 1828 Forrest announced a competition for "the best tragedy, in five acts, of which the hero, or principal character, shall be an aboriginal of this country." The winner was a romantic historical drama entitled *Metamora, or The Last of the Wampanoags*, about the Indian chief who led the Indians against white settlers in King Philip's War. The play was written by John Augustus Stone and became a regular part of Forrest's repertoire.

Forrest continued to create opportunities for American playwrights by promoting such competitions, which yielded several plays over the next few years. *Caius Marius*, by Richard Penn Smith, premiered at the Arch on January 21, 1831. *The Gladiator*, by Robert Montgomery Bird, opened on September 26, 1831, at the Park Street Theatre and gave Forrest one of his most popular roles—that of Spartacus, who led a slave revolt against the Romans. Another play by John Augustus Stone, *The Ancient Briton*, won Forrest's competition the following year and premiered at the Arch Street Theatre in 1833, but played only one performance. *The Broker of Bogota*, also by Bird, premiered on February 12, 1834, at the Bowery Theatre. The most successful of these productions allowed Forrest to play the powerful defender of the working man against the machinations of a powerful tyrant. They made Forrest extremely popular with the audience in the pit.

It was Forrest who profited most from these plays, for beyond the initial prize money, the playwright received nothing, in spite of the fact that Forrest kept the plays in his repertoire for decades. The competitions did encourage American dramatists to write new plays, and other actors followed Forrest's lead in offering prizes. Forrest has been criticized for profiting in this way, but given that there was no copyright protection for stage plays, it was a practical arrangement.

Maywood and Company were eager to improve the quality of the productions at both the Chestnut and the Walnut. Maywood's preference was for European stars and European productions that appealed to the fashionable element in Philadelphia society. The better class of people had stopped patronizing the theatre. But as the quality of the dramas improved, "the respectable and learned again approached their temple, and lent their aid to emblazon its desecrated fame, and to add new laurels to dramatic literature," Durang reported. Robert Maywood's extensive links with London and solid reputation as a Shakespearean actor put him in a good position to produce high-quality attractions. He tried to buck the trend toward presenting native fare and appealed to an elite audience with highbrow productions featuring European actors. Maywood and Company also introduced Italian opera to the city, although they often presented abridged versions of the originals.

Maywood and his partners "cared very little about American feeling, and had all the London stock actors of the two national theatres at their disposal, as fast as they could cross the Atlantic," Durang reported.[6] Stephen Price also continued to lure English stars to Philadelphia by offering high salaries. After appearing at the Park Theatre in New York, they usually made their next appearance in Philadelphia. John Sinclair, a vocalist from Covent Garden, was introduced with much fanfare in the opera *Rob Roy*. Several weeks later, a thirteen-year-old prodigy, Master Burke, was engaged to play such roles as Shylock and Richard III. He was followed by Charles Kean, the twenty-year-old son of Edmund Kean.

THE KEMBLES

The most widely anticipated stars of the era were the Kembles, who arrived in Philadelphia in October 1832. Charles Kemble was the younger brother of John Philip Kemble and Sarah Siddons, the most respected actors of the day. A talented comedian in sophisticated comedies, Charles Kemble never achieved the fame of his siblings. He had, however, managed London's prestigious Covent Garden Theatre for a number of years. Accompanying him on this tour was his daughter Frances, better known as Fanny. At twenty-three, Fanny Kemble was a beauty, and a skilled actress in her own right. She had made her stage debut three years earlier at Covent Garden as Juliet, to high acclaim. Charles made his Philadelphia debut at the Chestnut Street Theatre in *Hamlet* on October 10. Two days later Fanny appeared as Bianca in Reverend H. H. Milman's tragedy *Fazio,* one of her signature roles. On Monday, October 14, father and daughter played opposite each other in *Romeo and Juliet* and "drew the largest audience in numbers and fashion since Cooke's great benefit, when all the front and second seats of the upper boxes were taken."[7] They remained at the Chestnut until November 3 and returned to Philadelphia in January 1833. This time they played at the Walnut, opening on January 25 in *Macbeth* and playing through February 4. Hundreds had to be turned away from Fanny's benefit on the night of February 1.

It was Fanny Kemble who captured the hearts of the American public, and her father "did wisely to act as a foil to his daughter's excellence." It was said that the Kembles single-handedly revived the fortunes of the American theatre during their tour of the United States. This may be an overstatement, but their performances certainly brought the respectable elite back into the theatre. Wemyss wrote, "That she revived the prostrate fortunes of the drama

fig. 6 This painting of Fanny Kemble, depicted here as Julia in Sheridan Knowles's *The Hunchback* by the renowned Philadelphia artist Thomas Sully, was painted in 1833.

in the United States, admits not of a doubt; her popularity, and the name of Kemble, made the theatres once more a fashionable place of amusement."[8] Most important, Fanny made it acceptable for women to attend the theatre. Her grace and obvious breeding improved the image of all actresses.

The Kembles remained in America for two years, during which time Fanny was actively courted by a rich Philadelphian named Pierce Butler. She eventually agreed to marry him, but only after they had secured enough money to provide for her father's retirement. The Kembles returned to the Walnut Street Theatre on May 26, 1834, for their farewell engagement, closing on June 6. The following day, Fanny Kemble married Pierce Butler at Christ's Church in Philadelphia, and shortly afterward she retired from the stage.

THE GROWING POPULARITY OF NATIVE TYPES

Most of the stars who played the Chestnut also appeared at the Walnut Street Theatre, usually on a return engagement in the spring or summer. The summer months tended to be a time for lighter fare. Most plays depicted life in Europe, but American audiences were especially interested in seeing local characters portrayed on the stage. The most popular, and most problematic, of these native characters was a blackface character called Jim Crow, created by Thomas Dartmouth "Daddy" Rice, who made his first East Coast appearance at the Walnut Street Theatre on July 21, 1832. At the time, he was little known in the East. Born in New York, Rice had spent several years performing in towns along the Ohio River. In one of these western towns he encountered a crippled black stable hand who performed a curious dance. Rice appropriated the song and dance and began performing it between the main attraction and the afterpiece. "The roars of laughter with which his extravaganza of Jim Crow . . . was received, his excellent acting as well as singing, soon induced offers from managers, which filled his pockets and their treasury. He was for a time the 'lion' of the minor theatres," noted theatre manager Francis Wemyss.[9]

Rice was not the first white man to work in blackface, but his Jim Crow dance proved to be spectacularly popular with white audiences and brought him international celebrity. This renown was still ahead of him when he first appeared at the Walnut. "When he arrived from the West he was destitute of all pecuniary means. He stated his case to the management, whose sympathies gave him an opportunity to appear and to sing his 'Jim Crow,' which at once relieved his wants, and, indeed, relieved the treasury's wants subsequently," Durang wrote.[10] Soon audiences in America and England were singing the ditty that Rice had learned from the black stable hand: "Wheel about, turn about, do jes so, / An' ebery time I wheel about, I jump Jim Crow."

Today, such portrayals are understood to be offensive and demeaning, but blackface entertainment arose at a time when comic representations of every ethnic and racial group were in vogue. Dialect humor was popular, and American audiences were eager to see depictions of Americans; comedians obliged them with portrayals of backwoodsmen, riverboat men, urban dandies, and fast-talking Yankee types. Blackface characters were merely one "type" among many. One of the most popular was the stage Yankee. James H.

Hackett had created the first Yankee character in the late 1820s, basing it on a Yorkshire character by the English comedian Charles Matthews. Another of the leading Yankee delineators was George H. "Yankee" Hill, who made his first appearance at the Walnut on February 22, 1833. Two days later he shared a bill with T. D. Rice, and he performed at a benefit for Rice on February 27. Both men returned regularly to play the Walnut after that.

A third strain in America's emerging comic tradition was the Irish comedian. The comic Irishman had been a fixture of the English stage, and Irish comedians were coming over to perform in America as well. The most renowned was Tyrone Power, the great-grandfather of the Hollywood star. Power made his Philadelphia debut at the Walnut Street Theatre on September 14, 1833, as Sir Patrick in *The Irish Ambassador* and O'Rourke in *The Irish Tutor,* a comic afterpiece. He became a great favorite with American audiences and returned for two more tours. His *Impressions of America* is a valuable record of America in the Jacksonian era. Sadly, on his return to England after his third tour, in 1841, his ship was lost at sea.

These three figures—the African American, the Yankee, and the Irishman—figure very prominently in American stage comedy. All were rustic types looked down on, even despised, by more respectable Americans. On the stage, however, they were celebrated. If the elites supported European stars to demonstrate their own taste and sophistication, the audiences in the pit and in the gallery reveled in the lowbrow. It satisfied their desire to see local characters and life lampooned on the stage and on some level appealed to their need to feel superior. Clown figures defined by racial and regional characteristics allowed them to do that, expressing the deep ambivalence characteristic of the comic genre.

F. C. WEMYSS AND THE AMERICAN THEATRE

The balance of power in Philadelphia changed quite suddenly when, on March 3, 1834, William Forrest died. His partner, William Duffy, kept the Arch Street Theatre going on his own for a short while but gave up the lease when it expired at the end of July. Maywood and Company quickly snapped it up, relinquishing control over the Walnut Street Theatre, which was taken over by Francis Courtney Wemyss. Wemyss had been a fixture in Philadelphia theatre since 1822, when he came over from England to join Warren and Wood's company at the Chestnut Street Theatre. He specialized in light comedy roles and made a dashing figure both on and off the stage with his easy, refined demeanor and expensive wardrobe. Moving into the management end of the business, "Wemyss speedily established himself professionally and socially, becoming the co-mate and centre of our then rising youthful literary circles, so that he soon became affiliated in our society," as Durang put it.[11] For a while Wemyss helped William Warren run the Chestnut Street Theatre, taking it over entirely in 1829 in a failed partnership with Lewis Pratt. In 1833 Wemyss decided to try his luck in Pittsburgh and put together a stock company there. The company proved to be too large for the settlement, and when the Walnut Street Theatre became available in the summer of 1834, Wemyss closed the deal. Rent was set at $4,150 per year. Paying $1,000 in advance, he returned to Pittsburgh and closed the season there, returning with the dramatic corps to occupy the Walnut in the fall of 1834.[12]

While Maywood and Company continued to rely on European stars, Wemyss took a different tack, relying less on touring stars and emphasizing "blood-and-thunder" spectacles. The money he saved in star salaries could be put to use in spectacular scenic effects. Wemyss played to his audience's nationalistic sentiments. He rechristened the Walnut the American Theatre and redecorated the auditorium with a gaudy patriotic theme. "A large sum of money had been expended on the decorations, which represented celebrated events in American history, from the Declaration of Independence to the closing of the late war following the glorious battle of New Orleans," Durang explained. "Each tier of boxes was decorated with paintings representing some celebrated battle in the history of the United States. Around the dress circle were placed medallions of the heads of all the presidents, around the second tier the heads of celebrated generals, and around the third tier the heads of naval heroes. Between each medallion and its corresponding painting was a large gold star, the whole forming a pink ground—a most novel and beautiful interior."

The finishing touch was a giant eagle—eighteen feet wide and six feet high—that was placed over the proscenium on Washington's birthday in 1835. "We never shall forget the 'fuss and feathers' that the conveyance of this eagle caused," recalled Charles Durang. "From the shop in Kensington, where it was carved, to the Walnut Street Theatre, it was carried in a large wagon drawn by six horses, preceded by a band of music, with a large 'star-spangled banner' flying over it, with about a thousand persons of all ages and conditions following."[13] The eagle motif was reproduced in the broadsides for the American Theatre during this time. The eagle clutches in its talons a ribbon that reads "Walnut Street."

THE STOCK COMPANY

Wemyss was fortunate in already having a stock company, made up of twenty-two actors, equally split between men and women. He simply shifted his operations from Pittsburgh to Philadelphia, opening the American Theatre on December 22, 1834, with an established favorite, *Wild Oats*, and an afterpiece titled *The Dumb Belle*.

The most renowned member of the troupe was Mary Ann Duff. At forty, she was considered the most talented dramatic actress in America. Her fame had been eclipsed by Fanny Kemble, but she remained a charismatic presence on the stage, and she was tapped to play opposite the touring stars that periodically performed at the Walnut. The leading actress of the company was her daughter, Miss Mary Duff, then twenty-four. Although she lacked her mother's emotive power, she had charm and presence that served her well as an ingénue. She was often paired with British-born John Sefton, an up-and-coming light comedian. The pair first acted together in *The Golden Farmer* on December 24, 1834. Sefton played the part of a cockney pickpocket named Jemmy Twitcher, a part he made famous. "Sefton's spare figure and peculiar aspect made up this character almost without the aid of the so-called 'making up.' And when he uttered the well-known reply to rebukes of his thievish propensities, 'Vell, vot of it?' the laughter and applause were irresistible," Durang wrote.[14] Sefton built his career on this character, playing it more than a hundred times.

As Arthur Herman Wilson has pointed out, "In a day when visiting stars often came to a distant theatre to play leads in their own individual repertoires with which they were completely familiar, the members of the stock companies seldom played the character of Hamlet, Othello, Lear and other great tragic roles. Comedy, then, frequently became the province of the stock-players during the intervals when the great and near great were in absentia." Wemyss's company was well supplied with comic talent. "The Misses Anderson, Charnock, [Alexina] Fisher, and [Eliza] Riddle frequently alternated with Mary Duff," Wilson wrote, "and the Messrs. [E. S.] Connor, [Thomas S.] Hadaway, and J. G. Porter with J. Sefton."[15] All had their individual specialties. Thomas S. Hadaway was the low comedian. E. N. Thayer was an all-round comic actor, performing both genteel and eccentric comedy. E. S. Connor was primarily used in dramatic and melodramatic roles. Mr. and Mrs. Kent, Mr. and Mrs. Knight, and Mr. and Mrs. Muzzy took on the supporting roles of parents, friends, and relatives of the young lovers. Wemyss also appeared onstage in supporting roles, as did his stage manager, William Barrymore.

THEATRICAL SPECTACLE

Having functioned for several years as a summer theatre, the Walnut was generally considered a "half-price house," and Wemyss "saw, very wisely, that he never could run counter to old-fashioned prejudice and make his theatre the legitimate or fashionable seat of dramatic amusement," as Durang put it. "Having a theatre so admirably adapted to melodramatic performances, Wemyss very properly dedicated his house to scenic spectacle, in which his active corps could excel." Wemyss and his company produced a series of spectacular melodramas in rapid succession.

On January 28, 1835, Wemyss's company premiered *Zanthe*, a romantic drama based on the tragedy *Hernani*—"one of the most splendid pageants that ever was presented in any theatre in America," in Durang's view.[16] Wemyss hired a full military brass band for the production, along with six drummers and 130 extras. The procession was lit by wax candles and red, blue, and green fires. The spectacle filled the house for eighteen successive nights. Although he never recouped his expenses, Wemyss was pleased, recalling in his memoirs that "it gave the Walnut Street Theatre a reputation for spectacle which has served it for capital ever since."[17] Other productions were mounted that season with the same sense of spectacle—*Tom and Jerry* was revived on February 9, and *The Last Days of Pompeii* premiered on March 23.

Pompeii showed the difficulties that could arise with the complicated scenic effects Wemyss and Barrymore were trying to produce. The final scene, of course, required the volcanic eruption of Mount Vesuvius. The stage crew had prepared an avalanche of burning liquid lava that would cover the stage. On opening night, the fuse that set off the pyrotechnics became disconnected and "went fizzing about to the eye of the spectators in a most ridiculous manner." The audience burst out laughing, and the curtain was brought down. William Barrymore, anxious that the audience see the effect he had worked so hard on, seized a flame, ran to the magazine where the pyrotechnics were arranged, and ignited them. As the fireworks went off, Barrymore called for the curtain to be raised. The stagehand responsible for the curtain had already left his post, assuming he was done for the evening. Barrymore got to the curtain and raised it himself, but the last charge had been set off. The curtain came up on the exhausted fires of Vesuvius as smoke billowed out over the audience. The sight was greeted with laughter and hisses. Barrymore was so mortified by the failure of his effect that he ran out of the theatre and was not seen for two days. The scenic effects must have continued to cause problems, for the play was withdrawn after only a week.

The 1834–35 season at the Walnut ended on Saturday, April 11, 1835. Durang says of this season that it "was one of an extraordinary character. Much deserved praise was due to Wemyss for his enterprise and consequent success. The Chestnut was a powerful opponent, and there was a vast number of powerful foreign stars and new dramas to contend with. It was a remarkable era in stage annals, as it brought forth much native talent in every department—actors and actresses, great scenic artistes, musical ability and stage mechanism."[18]

In the fall of 1835 Wemyss instituted an ambitious policy of debuting a new show each week. "I laid out a plan from which I never departed, to produce a new piece every Saturday night, and the steady perseverance in this plan, first gave the Walnut Street Theatre one night in the week, on which the manager could depend upon a good house by very moderate exertion," he wrote.[19] Although this policy was not strictly adhered to, on most Saturdays a new comedy or melodrama was introduced. Wemyss premiered an astounding fifty-six new plays during the 1835–36 season. This meant that the actors were constantly rehearsing new roles. Charles Durang, who was Wemyss's stage manager that season, recalled that it "made my labors, with that of the company, very onerous and incessant."[20]

The plays that debuted that season were forgettable, with one exception. On December 7, 1835, Wemyss premiered a new play by Philadelphia playwright Robert T. Conrad called *Jack Cade, or The Noble Yeoman*, a historical tragedy based on Wat Tyler's rebellion in England in 1381. Conrad wrote the play for Augustus A. Addams, a young tragedian whom many expected to vie with Edwin Forrest for stardom. But Addams was too drunk to go on. The role was turned over to another actor in the company, David Ingersoll, who went on two nights later. The play had only a short run, but several years later, with Wemyss's encouragement, Conrad revised it for Edwin Forrest, who made Jack Cade one of his signature roles.

In January a juggler and plate spinner named Signor Vivalla was booked for a week. More notable was Vivalla's manager, twenty-five-year-old Phineas T. Barnum, who was just beginning his career as a showman. Barnum demonstrated a flair for generating publicity when he promoted a rivalry between Vivalla and a local juggler named J. B. Roberts, offering a $1,000 reward to anyone who could duplicate Vivalla's tricks. The two men rehearsed together and the competition was such a huge draw that he repeated it in several other cities.

Wemyss continued to stage elaborate spectacles. Most of these were set in far-off realms, which offered the set painters and costume designers the opportunity for imaginative and unusual creations. On February 29, 1836, Wemyss adapted the Old Testament story of Esther for an elaborate pageant titled *The Jewess*, which had "no other merit than its picturesque accessories; its Egyptian and Assyrian scenery."[21] The climactic scene featured a procession led by the allegorical figure of Time, wielding his scythe, followed by a group of twenty girls scattering flowers before two hundred extras outfitted in costumes representing the various nations of the world. A platform—the earliest evidence of a runway in any American theatre—was laid over the pit, and the procession emerged from the back of the house, passed through the audience on an eight-foot-wide platform onto the stage, and disappeared behind the scenery. The scenery was raised, and all two hundred–plus extras were in position for the following scene.

Other such productions followed with more or less success. Wemyss opened the 1836–37 season with a magical tale set in China, *The Bronze Horse, or The Spell of the Cloud King*, a "show of scenery, dresses, games, religious ceremonies" of the Orient.[22] *La Fitte, or The Pirate's Home*, which opened on October 28, 1836, was a romantic depiction of the pirate chieftain Jean Lafitte and his exploits during the War of 1812. *Thalaba, or The Burning Sword*, which opened on February 20, 1837, was set in Arabia and featured an enchanted cavern, Arabian tombs, and the fortress of the sultan. Such elaborate spectacles gave the Walnut a reputation for scenic pieces that Wemyss was proud to say were superior even to those of the Bowery Theatre in New York. But this kind of extravagance was about to come to an end.

THE PANIC OF 1837

Throughout the 1830s America had enjoyed a robust economy, fueled by easy credit and western expansion. In his second term as president, however, Andrew Jackson had withdrawn government assets from the Bank of the United States and distributed them to various state banks. Each bank issued its own notes rather than rely on a national currency. People began to demand hard currency, or specie, and many hoarded coins, creating an artificial scarcity. When the federal government suddenly announced the suspension of payments in silver in May 1837, the economy collapsed. Credit suddenly tightened, prices shot up, and there was a run on the banks. Fears that the government would default on its debts were widespread. The nation was about to enter the worst economic recession in its history, one that would last for the next six years.

Wemyss's lease on the Walnut expired that summer, and he hoped to make some improvements to the property. In particular, he wanted to replace the oil-burning lighting equipment with gas. The City of Philadelphia had recently finished a municipal gasworks and was laying pipes under the city. Gas offered superior safety, brilliance, and flexibility over the whale-oil lamps then in place. Gas had been introduced at the Chestnut Street Theatre as far back as 1816. But it was still experimental back then, the gas had to be manufactured from coal on the premises, and the fumes gave off a foul odor if the building was not properly ventilated. When the Chestnut Street Theatre was rebuilt after the fire of 1820, the decision was made to return to oil lamps. Maywood and Company were installing gas lamps at the Chestnut, and Wemyss applied to the stockholders of the Walnut about doing the same. Given the economic troubles the country was experiencing, the stockholders were reticent about spending money on such improvements and insisted that they would install gas lamps only on the condition that they receive a $1,000 advance on the rent.

Wemyss's relationship with the stockholders began to take a decided downturn. He approached them again about renting out the theatre to a British equestrian, Thomas T. Cooke. Cooke's circus drew the same audience that Wemyss depended on for his spectacles, and he was not anxious to go head to head with it. He preferred to turn the Walnut over to Cooke for a fall run, keeping his troupe in Pittsburgh. The stockholders, however, seeing an opportunity to squeeze some extra profits for themselves, demanded an extra $2,000 from Cooke for the privilege. Cooke rejected the offer and had a new arena built on Chestnut Street, just below Ninth, where he began appearing on August 28, 1837. Wemyss delayed opening the fall season until November 15, keeping his company in Pittsburgh, while the Walnut was being fitted with gas fixtures. Cooke closed shortly thereafter and took his company to Baltimore. There, on the night of February 3, the theatre caught fire, and Cooke lost everything. He returned at the end of the season to perform at the Walnut, and this time the stockholders relented. Cooke played at the Walnut from April 2 to May 5, 1838, premiering several new works, including *Mazeppa*, which ran for seventeen consecutive nights. The most significant result of Cooke's run in Philadelphia was that the city now had yet another performance space—one that was suitable for spectacle, and only a block away from the Walnut. "This permission a year before would have saved Wemyss much pecuniary loss, and would have prevented, of course, the building of the circus, which proved so formidable a rival to the Walnut street house," Durang concluded.[23]

Wemyss reopened the Walnut on June 23, 1838, for what would be its longest season ever. The season started slowly; houses were poor during the hot summer months. In August, Wemyss tried an experiment, staging a pageant called *The Coronation of Queen Victoria*. The young monarch had recently ascended to the English throne, and local papers were filled with details about the pomp and majesty of her coronation. There was some question as to whether the Walnut's largely working-class audience would stand for this, given their antiaristocratic prejudices. But Durang reported that the show drew large crowds and that "the pit and upper tier audience, which had abandoned the Walnut street house, again returned to witness this royal English pageant." Instead of taking offense at the playing of the English national anthem, the audience eagerly joined in singing "God Save the Queen."

Wemyss now returned to the star system. The Chestnut had the pick of foreign stars, but Wemyss could count on T. D. Rice, "Yankee" Hill, Junius Brutus Booth, and other American stars. He also noted that Edwin Forrest's name did not appear on the roster for the Chestnut. Wemyss was able to secure him for the

Walnut, and on October 15 Edwin Forrest made his first appearance at the Walnut Street Theatre in nine years. His last appearance had been in January 1829, when he had extracted $200 a night from Blake and Inslee. Forrest had played in his hometown regularly since then, but primarily at the Arch Street Theatre, supporting his brother, William. Since William's death he had spent several years in Europe, first on vacation and later as an actor. On his opening night at the Walnut, Forrest played *Othello*. The critics proclaimed it a masterly performance. He followed it up with *Damon and Pythias* on the sixteenth, *Lady of Lyons* on the seventeenth, and *Macbeth* on the eighteenth. *Metamora* ran for two successive nights on October 19 and 20. His engagement was extended, and he reprised *Metamora* and *Lady of Lyons* and introduced *The Gladiator* and *Richard III*.

Opera was proving to be a successful draw over at the Chestnut, and Wemyss decided to take it on. With Forrest's help he was able to secure the rights to *Amilie, or The Love Test*, a new romantic opera doing well with New York audiences. It was produced with much fanfare on November 19 and played for twelve nights. Forrest returned for a seven-night engagement beginning December 3. On January 30, 1839, *Titus Andronicus* was debuted. It was the first time this bloody Shakespeare tragedy was tried in Philadelphia. The play was altered considerably by actor-playwright Nathaniel H. Bannister in such a way that it "excluded the horrors with infinite skill, yet preserved all the interest of the drama," in Durang's words.

A THEATRE TRANSFORMED

Tensions continued to grow between Wemyss and the Walnut's stockholders. When Wemyss signed a lease for the 1839–40 season, the board announced that the stockholders would henceforth be in charge of admission prices. They wanted to raise the price of admission to the pit. This seems to be unusual, since the stockholders had no financial interest here. The price increase may have been designed to get rid of the more unruly element in the audience. In any case, Wemyss resisted. The economy was not good, and Wemyss accurately predicted that raising ticket prices would severely reduce attendance. The president of the board, Henry G. Freeman, demanded that Wemyss comply with the terms or vacate the theatre. Wemyss was forced to accept the conditions, for he had already finalized contracts for the stars who would appear. He would have cause to regret it.

The season of 1838–39 officially came to a close on Saturday, September 14, 1839. Wemyss announced that the theatre would reopen the following Monday, completely refurbished. The crew worked over the weekend to transform the theatre. Wemyss's scenic artist had prepared the new decorations on canvas, so that they could be tacked over the front boxes and the proscenium in a matter of hours. The renovation was completed within forty-eight hours. On Monday night, Durang reported, the auditorium was "newly painted, seats recovered, every department apparently renewed, and all points even to mouldings regilt and burnished."[24] The curtain had to be delayed just half an hour. The transformation had the effect Wemyss had hoped for. The audience was struck with wonder that such a transformation could be produced so quickly. "So like magic did this appear that it was three nights before the audience could be assured that such a thing had been accomplished," Wemyss recalled.[25]

EDWIN FORREST RETURNS AS RICHELIEU

The opening night of the 1839–40 season featured Edwin Forrest in *Virginius*, and he followed it with several standard works in his repertoire—*The Gladiator, Damon and Pythias, Metamora*, and *Othello*. On September 24 he appeared in a new play by Edward Bulwer-Lytton, *Richelieu, or The Conspiracy*. Forrest had debuted the play earlier in the month in New York. It would become one of his finest roles, and one of the most popular dramatic vehicles of the nineteenth century. Forrest had invested a lot of money in costuming the show, and the New York press had remarked favorably on the elegance and authenticity of the wardrobe. Wemyss was intent on making his sets equally sumptuous and spared no expense. "The room of the Cardinal was splendidly painted and decorated with the heavy arras of gold tissue figures of that luxurious age, and heavy, unwieldy arms. . . . The gardens of the Louvre were taken from the facsimiles of the proper period. The Bastille and its corridors were painted from accurate views," Durang reported.[26] Forrest was so impressed with the production values that he offered to perform one night for free as a special benefit for the theatre.

Wemyss was equally impressed with Forrest's interpretation of the Machiavellian cardinal. Thirty years later he could vividly recall Forrest's performance. "Of Mr. Forrest's performance of this part I can scarcely find words to speak in terms of sufficient praise; it was one of those masterly efforts of genius that sets criticism at defiance; full of beauties, full of faults; but an endeavor to analyze the latter would lead . . . [to] the discovery of a flash of genius so brilliant as to make you doubt the correctness of your judgment, and pronounce the fault you had determined to expose, a necessary foil to the excellent effect which followed."

Forrest had evidently devoted little time to studying the character of Richelieu, but he used the performance "to polish his crude ideas of the author as chance might direct." Forrest portrayed Richelieu as a doddering old man, which Wemyss recognized as an old stage trick that gave greater effect to any powerful expression of emotion. That great outburst of passion, when it came at the end of the fourth act, "was equal to any of Edmund Kean's best efforts, of a similar nature; taking his audience by surprise, and charging onward, until their admiration broke forth into an involuntary acknowledgment of his excellence, continuing several seconds after the fall of the curtain hid the actor from their view."[27] Every great dramatic actor, from William Macready to Edwin Booth, attempted the role. Wemyss judged Forrest's portrayal, as hastily put together as it was, the best representation he ever saw.

WEMYSS'S LAST SEASON AT THE WALNUT

Despite its excellence, *Richelieu* lost money. Certainly the extravagance of the production played a role. But to a large extent it was the result of increased ticket prices, which kept much of the audience away, just as Wemyss had predicted. The country was still in an economic depression brought about by the Panic of 1837, which affected the theatre especially. As a popularly priced house, the Walnut relied on filling the pit. On January 25, 1840, the board gave Wemyss permission to lower ticket prices, but by then it was too late, according to A. H. Wilson. "The pit could not be coaxed back. In 114 nights, he lost six thousand dollars. In the whole season of 261 nights, 155 produced less than half the amount of the nightly expenses necessary to keep the doors open. Wemyss, from that time forth, never recovered himself."

The year 1840 marked a distinct change in the history of the Philadelphia theatre; that year, both Wemyss and Maywood took their leave of the stage. On December 30, 1839, Robert Maywood announced his retirement from the firm of Maywood and Company, asserting that he had "exhausted his energies, his purse, and all the talent of both hemispheres, in the service of the public." Or so he said. Durang pointed out that "Maywood had become very unpopular, principally because he was himself a mass of foreign prejudices against our 'native graces.'"[28] Francis Wemyss was having difficulties, too, mostly with the Walnut's Board of Agents. He offered to take the lease for 1840–41 if the stockholders would not require any payment in advance, and if they would be satisfied with receiving $200 a week. He also insisted on a number of improvements to the property, but he was never answered. In July 1840 Wemyss withdrew from the Walnut, taking most of the company over to the Arch Street Theatre. A new pair of managers—William Dinneford and E. A. Marshall—were eager to try their hand at running the theatre.

Wemyss immediately ran into problems at the Arch. "My resources had been crippled by my last season in Walnut Street; the aid of my friends taxed to the utmost, to enable me to prepare for a campaign," he admitted.[29] The season lasted all of two weeks. On September 18 Wemyss announced to the company that he could no longer keep the theatre open. They moved on to Baltimore, where he began managing the Front Street Theatre. But Wemyss did no better there. Shortly after Thanksgiving he was back at the Arch Street Theatre. Yankee Hill and Junius Brutus Booth were there to support him, but to no avail. Wemyss struggled on for two more months but was forced to close in early February.

Creditors were well aware of his financial difficulties, and several had him arrested for nonpayment of debts. To keep himself out of debtor's prison, Wemyss applied for bankruptcy protection. His property was seized and the assets were sold to pay his creditors. "My large establishments were completely broken up. Philadelphia, Baltimore, and Pittsburgh Theatres, all passed from my hands—my property disposed of under the sheriff's hammer, at a time when real estate would hardly be taken as a gift—ruining me, without aiding my creditors. A theatrical wardrobe, the most extensive in the United States, which ten thousand dollars could not replace, sold for one hundred and thirty-six dollars!!" he lamented. "April, 1841, found me without one cent, crushed, heart-broken and degraded in my own estimation, by the white-washing process I had been compelled to undergo."

It was the last time Francis Wemyss would operate a theatre on his own. He remained active in the theatre for the rest of his life, but he never again ran a playhouse. Perhaps this was just as well, for he had lost his confidence. "Difficulties which previous to this epoch in my life, I gloried in surmounting, have been suffered to master me. My energy of character, which gave me nerve to face any emergency, seems to have deserted me," he confessed.[30]

Once again, the twin demons of economic downturn and cutthroat competition wreaked havoc with the theatrical community. Robert Maywood and Francis Wemyss, who had defined the theatrical scene in Philadelphia in the 1830s, were out of the business. It would be up to the next generation of producers to make their mark. They were already there—William E. Burton was in charge of the new National Theatre, while over at the Walnut, E. A. Marshall was making his mark. In his hands, the Walnut Street Theatre would become the prestige house in the city, and Philadelphia managers would make their first forays into New York City.

THE MARSHALL ERA, 1840–1849

Four first-class theatres competed in Philadelphia as the fall 1840–41 season got under way. Francis Wemyss was struggling at the Arch Street Theatre. Lewis T. Pratt took over the Chestnut, employing William B. Wood as his stage manager. An ambitious newcomer, William E. Burton, leased Cooke's Circus on Chestnut Street and converted it into a theatrical house, which he renamed the National Theatre. The Walnut was in the hands of another pair of newcomers, E. A. Marshall and William Dinneford.

Ethelbert A. Marshall did not come from a theatrical background. He began his career as a printer and publisher in Providence, Rhode Island, but left in 1838 to get involved in theatrical management and speculation. He devoted himself to the financial end of the business, leaving the artistic decisions to others. Marshall's success came from his ability to employ capable stage managers. Stage managers of the time functioned much as directors do today. They were responsible for selecting the plays, engaging the performers, and rehearsing the company.

Marshall's partner in the venture was an old theatrical hand, William Dinneford, a handsome and charismatic Englishman who had been managing theatres for nearly two decades. Dinneford was first associated with the Walnut in 1823, when he joined the theatrical company associated with Price and Simpson's Circus. He took over management responsibilities in 1826. After that he managed several New York theatres, including the Bowery.

Marshall and Dinneford's company was said to be strong, but the productions that season were not particularly remarkable, mostly tried and true comedies. Comedies tended to work better during times of economic uncertainty, and the strategy of presenting old favorites without bringing in outside stars allowed Marshall and Dinneford to reduce ticket prices. The season opened on October 14, and in November the two managers began bringing in stars. The first to appear was a curious figure who went by the name Signor Hervio Nano. Nano was, in reality, an American named Harvey Leach. Born with stunted legs, he made a career of playing nonhuman characters.[1] With his powerful arms, he was able to perform remarkable feats of strength and agility. His signature piece was *The Gnome Fly*, in which he impersonated a gnome, a baboon, and a fly. Nano must have been a good draw, for he remained at the Walnut for three weeks and returned numerous times over the next several years.

Familiar stars followed. Yankee Hill and T. D. Rice appeared in early December, along with Herr Cline on the tightrope. Junius Brutus Booth was brought in during Christmas week. Several new pieces were produced after the first of the year: *Norman Leslie*, an adaptation of a popular novel by Theodore Faye; *The Carpenter of Rouen;* a local burlesque titled *Philadelphia as It Is*, and a new farce called *P.P.P.P.* By spring Marshall and Dinneford were ready to try their hand at more elaborate productions. *Rookwood, or Richard Turpin the Wonderful Highwayman* ran for fifteen consecutive nights, beginning March 13. Durang judged it "a thrilling drama." Marshall and Dinneford revived equestrian dramas, bringing in horses from Raymond and Waring's circus to mount *Cataract of the Ganges* and other equine dramas. J. R. Scott and E. S. Connor both made starring appearances later that spring, and Hervio Nano returned to close the season on July 5, 1841.

E. A. MARSHALL TAKES CONTROL

The partnership between Marshall and Dinneford did not hold up. William Dinneford lived well and, according to Durang, his expenses often outran the profits at his theatres. Both men applied to the stockholders of the Walnut for a new lease. Marshall won, and Dinneford moved over to the Arch Street Theatre. E. A. Marshall became the sole lessee of the Walnut Street Theatre and remained in the position for the next sixteen years. Under his charge, the Walnut experienced a stability it had never before enjoyed.

Although he was an important figure in Philadelphia and, eventually, New York theatre, little has been written about E. A. Marshall. He was a quiet, unassuming man who did not draw attention to himself. Charles Durang described him as "a man of strong perceptions, ready tact in business, and of quiet social relations, having all the honorable principles of a man of business."[2] He remained very much in the background, allowing more experienced theatre people to make the artistic decisions.

Marshall brought in Thomas Flynn to stage manage. The English-born comedian had previously managed the Bowery Theatre in New York and was a close friend of Junius Brutus Booth. Marshall and Flynn opened the theatre after the summer hiatus with a romantic drama titled *The Water Queen, or The Sprites of Donau*. The play was a fairy spectacle, popular at the time, patched together from scenes from other such productions. The climax of the piece was a grand scenic effect of a "transparent sea" that employed five thousand jets of water and six thousand jets of liquid fire. The narrative was poorly thought out, and most of the audience left the theatre before the grand finale. *The Water Queen* was notable, however, for introducing Edward Loomis Davenport into the company. At twenty-five, E. L. Davenport had not achieved the renown that he would later earn, but he already showed the versatility that distinguished his acting style; he could play both tragic and comic roles. Edwin Forrest was among those who regarded him as the best actor in America.

Junius Brutus Booth returned on September 11, co-starring with James W. Wallack Jr., the second generation of that illustrious acting family to take to the boards. Booth and Wallack played opposite each other in *Richard III, King Lear, Othello*, and several other productions. Yankee Hill returned in October with his Yankee characters. Hervio Nano was back in the *Demon Fire Fly*. Several new musical pieces were produced. A nautical drama, *Blue Jackets, or United States Service*, premiered on September 10. It featured dances by a *corps de ballet* that also performed "Amazonian evolutions with boarding pikes, cutlasses, etc." On September 18, *Giovanni in Philadelphia, or Life in the City* set the Don Juan story in Philadelphia. *The Naiad Queen*, a mythological drama, was produced soon thereafter. The spectacle, the playbill reported, "had been months in preparations, and upwards of four thousand dollars had been expended in its stupendous production."[3]

The highlight of the season came on November 6, 1841, when Marshall presented *London Assurance*, a new play by a talented young Irish playwright named Dion Boucicault. The play had had a spectacular debut in London and is one of the few comedies from the period that endures. Modeled on the Restoration comedies popular with audiences, *London Assurance* tells the story of a foppish aristocrat, Sir Harcourt Courtly, whose attempt to woo an heiress is thwarted by his own son. The production was most notable in that it used a box set rather than the wing-and-drop scenery common at the time. This gave the audience the experience of looking through the fourth wall into a real house. The Philadelphia production featured "a display of carpets, cushions, pianos, candelabras, chairs, tables, flower-pots, and statues—all real," according to Francis Wemyss.[4] Charles Durang was impressed that the furniture was "the very kind used in the dwellings of such persons as the characters are intended to represent—no mere stage frippery covered with Dutch metal in imitation of gilt, but the bona fide articles in every sense of the word."[5] *London Assurance* played nightly for two weeks and was revived periodically after that. It was such a success that the Walnut and its major competitor, the National Theatre, both presented the play.

WILLIAM E. BURTON AND THE NATIONAL THEATRE

Marshall's principal competition came from the National and its ambitious manager, William E. Burton. Durang characterized Burton this way: "He was restless, ambitious, and of very jealous impulses. Fertile in genius, irresistible in enterprise, of great perceptive faculties, he seemed to conceive only to give immediate birth to his rapid conceptions."[6] Like Marshall, Burton began in the printing trade, but he left in 1825 to pursue a stage career. He came to America from his native England in 1834, making his debut as an actor at the Arch Street Theatre. He was a member of several companies before leasing the National in 1840. Burton specialized in low comedy roles and was reputed to be the funniest man in America. As a manager, however, he was known as a dogged competitor, often putting on the same shows as the other theatres. Marshall and Burton pursued different strategies in theatre management. While Marshall relied on touring stars to draw audiences, Burton was committed to reviving the stock system, employing a small corps of talented performers who appeared in all the productions.

Both Burton and Marshall would use the profits from their Philadelphia operations to move into the New York market. Burton was the first to venture into the nation's theatrical center. In January 1842 he took the lease on the National Theatre in New York, moving his company there in April. F. C. Wemyss joined him as stage manager. A fire destroyed the theatre less than two months later, consuming the scenery and costumes for a lavish production of *The Naiad Queen*, along with Burton's personal wardrobe, books, and manuscripts. Forced back to Philadelphia, Burton reopened the National Theatre on August 21 for the fall season.

Marshall was more cautious. The economy had not improved, and theatres in Philadelphia and New York were struggling to stay afloat. The Walnut was one of the few that remained solvent. Marshall fell back on popular entertainments to draw people into his theatre. On February 7, 1842, he engaged Turner's Celebrated Equestrian Troupe. A moveable ring was set up on the stage for demonstrations of riding, tightrope walking, and tumbling. The highlight of the circus was Timothy Turner's back somersault atop a moving horse. It was one of the earliest flips done entirely on horseback, although it was probably done on a pad affixed to the horse.[7] The circus advertised a Negro "extravaganza"—a song-and-dance act in the parlance of the time—a precursor to the minstrel shows that would soon become popular.

There were more "imitative negro performances" by Master Diamond, James Sanford, and Richard Myers, beginning June 10. At the end of June, Herr Driesbach, "the celebrated tamer of lions, panthers, leopards, &c.," began a run of eight nights in a piece called *Mungo Park*, which had been written especially to display Driesbach's trained felines. E. L. Davenport played an intrepid African explorer. This kind of spectacle helped the Walnut through a very difficult period. Despite economic hardship, "the Walnut seemed to float best through this turbulent sea of hard times," in the words of Arthur Herman Wilson. Other theatres were not so fortunate. During the summer of 1842, Lewis T. Pratt was forced to declare bankruptcy, ending his tenure at the Chestnut.

THE FIRST WOMEN MANAGERS

With the Chestnut Street Theatre once again vacant, its owners were searching for a new lessee. They approached Robert Maywood, who declined to return but proposed his daughter, Mary Elizabeth Maywood, instead. The owners accepted, knowing that her father would be guiding the effort. E. A. Marshall also needed a new stage manager to replace Thomas Flynn, whose deceitfulness and intrigue had alienated his boss. Observing that the Chestnut was "under a petticoat dynasty," Marshall offered the position to a talented young actress named Charlotte Cushman.

At twenty-six, Cushman was gaining a considerable reputation. Within a few years she would be heralded as the finest actress America had ever produced. She was in no way a traditional leading lady. Tall and ruggedly built, with a pronounced jaw, wide-set eyes, and angular features, Cushman was, even by her own account, homely. But there was no denying her presence onstage. "I played Rolla with her [in *Pizarro*]; and she was, even then, the best Elvira, I ever saw," wrote the English actor George Vandenhoff, who played opposite Cushman that fall. "The power of her scorn and the terrible earnestness of her revenge, were immense. Her greatest part, fearfully natural, dreadfully intense, horribly real, was Nancy Sykes, in the dramatic version of *Oliver Twist;* it is too true; it was painful, this actual presentation of Dickens's poor, abandoned, abused, murdered, outcast of the streets; a tigress, with a touch, and but one, of woman's almost deadened nature, blotted, and trampled under foot by man's cruelty and sin."[8]

With Cushman as the leading lady and E. L. Davenport in supporting roles, Marshall had an extraordinary company and was able to attract other talented stars. Edwin Forrest arrived on October 17, 1842, for a three-week run, playing opposite Cushman in *Macbeth* and in various other roles. The comedian Henry Placide was booked, and there was an all-star cast of *London Assurance* the week of November 11 that featured Placide, Mr. and Mrs. John Brougham, and Charlotte Cushman. At Christmastime the company presented an original pantomime, *The Black Raven of the Tombs*, based on a German legend. It featured the usual grand tableaux, transformation scenes, and original music. In the spring, Raymond, Ogden and Company's equestrian troupe was brought in to provide "bold, graceful and daring feats of horsemanship, unsurpassed voltiguers, rope dancers, classical posturers and pantomimists." Among the other touring stars were Junius Brutus Booth, Yankee Hill, William E. Burton, and Dan Marble.

Charlotte Cushman had a powerful, even masculine presence onstage. Modern scholars generally agree that Cushman was a lesbian, although such things were never spoken about openly in Cushman's day. She became especially renowned for her "breeches roles." It was not unusual for actresses to play male characters, as there were a limited number of great dramatic roles for women. In Cushman's case, however, male roles suited her better than female ones. The most famous of these was Romeo, which was not considered a great role at the time; most male stars chose to play Mercutio. Cushman took on the role for the first time at the Walnut in the spring of 1843 at a benefit for E. A. Marshall, playing opposite her sister Susan as Juliet. The lesbian implications delighted some members of the audience and disturbed others. George Vandenhoff, who played Mercutio, recalled, "She looks neither man nor woman in the part,—or both; and her passion is equally epicene in form. Whatever her talents in other parts, I never yet heard any human being, that had seen her Romeo, who did not speak of it with a painful expression of countenance, 'more in sorrow than in anger.'"[9] Not all critics found her performance so disturbing. It would be her Romeo that drew the praise of London some years later and established her as an international star. Many hailed Cushman as the finest Romeo of her era.

Cushman lasted only one season as stage manager. It was, Durang concluded, "a most extraordinary season of great duration, marked by prodigious exertion in producing the first stars of the day, and a rapid succession of new pieces and other extra novelties of an unprecedented character."[10] Nevertheless, Marshall replaced her with a more experienced stage manager, William Rufus Blake, for the 1843–44 season. This was the same William Blake who had run the theatre briefly in 1829 with John Inslee. A heavyset comedian who specialized in old man roles, he turned primarily to managing. At one time or another he operated the Bowery, the Franklin and the Olympic theatres in New York, and the Tremont Theatre in Boston. Cush-

fig. 7 Charlotte Cushman (*left*), depicted here in her most famous role as the title male character in *Romeo and Juliet*. Her sister Susan played her love interest in the production. Image courtesy of the Theatre Collection, Free Library of Philadelphia. Painted by Thomas Sully in 1833.

man was given the position of acting manager, but this was clearly a demotion for the talented actress.

SPECULATIONS AT THE CHESTNUT

Elizabeth Maywood's management of the Chestnut had not been very successful, and by the fall of 1843 it was again empty. This time, E. A. Marshall took control of the house. Despite the failure of several managers, the Chestnut was still considered the premier house in Philadelphia, and Marshall was eager to produce more prestigious fare. In late October the great English actor William C. Macready arrived in Philadelphia. Macready was considered the finest actor in England, the legitimate successor to John Philip Kemble and Edmund Kean. A fastidious intellectual, Macready researched his characters in great detail and was very concerned with improving the professionalism of the theatre. He always resented the low esteem in which actors were held, and he had no patience for second-rate talent. Macready opened at the Chestnut on October 23 in *Macbeth*, and Marshall brought the Walnut's company over to the Chestnut to support him. Charlotte Cushman played Lady Macbeth, one of her great roles. She continued to star opposite Macready, playing Gertrude to his Hamlet, and Beatrice to his Benedick in *Much Ado About Nothing*. Macready was impressed by Cushman's talent but considered her technique crude and undisciplined. He urged her to travel to London and gain some experience working with an English company. When her contract at the Walnut expired the following summer, Cushman followed his advice.

Macready remained in Philadelphia until November 8, 1843. Cushman and the rest of the company continued at the Chestnut until the end of the year. During this time the Walnut was rented out to Nathan Howe's Circus, which presented horsemanship, acrobatics, vaulting, and tumbling. The circus remained at the Walnut until the acting company returned at the end of the year. Among those appearing was twenty-year-old Dan Rice, who would go on to become America's first great circus clown and the model for Uncle Sam. He appeared in bills for November 17–18, singing his "popular comicalities."

Marshall's management of the Chestnut did not go well. He tried to create an audience for English opera there but lost heavily. It was the lighter fare at the Walnut that drew the public. The company returned to the Walnut on December 30, 1843, at which time *The Bohemians, or The Rogues of Paris* was brought out with spectacular scenic depictions of Paris. A grand romantic spectacle of *Sleeping Beauty* premiered on January 8. *The Black Raven of the Tombs* was revived in February, and the patriotic naval drama *Naval Glory, or Decatur's Triumph* played a week in March. Rufus Blake was considered especially good at staging spectacles. Junius Brutus Booth came in on January 18. William E. Burton was engaged for six nights beginning April 10. He played with William B. Wood, the old manager of the Chestnut.

Marshall gave up the lease on the Chestnut but kept the Walnut Street Theatre open through the summer. Business that spring was hurt by rioting that broke out in early May in the working-class neighborhood of Kensington. Native-born workers resented the influx of unskilled Irish immigrants willing to work for minimal wages. Violence resumed in the summer, when fighting broke out following July 4th celebrations. The militia had to be called in, and it was three days before peace was restored. The rioting left fifteen people dead and more than fifty wounded.

The Walnut continued to succeed with spectacles and extravaganzas. On July 4, 1844, *Beauty and the Beast* was staged there for the first time in the city. It featured "magnificent new scenery, music, dresses, dances, tableaux, magical changes and novel effects," as Durang reported. *The Black Raven of the Tombs* was revived. On July 20 a patriotic drama written by James Rees, *Washington, or The Hero of Valley Forge*, presented the career of the Father of His Country. On July 29 a grand pantomimic spectacle titled *Munchausen, or The Sorcerer of the Green Isle* premiered and continued to play through August 12. "There was no end to the new scenery, machinery, new dresses, trophies, banners &c., &c.," Durang commented. "It was full of tricks, transformations, tableaux, processions, dances, choruses, illusions and funny effects."[11]

That summer, William E. Burton returned to theatrical management, taking over the lease on the Arch Street Theatre, where he began staging "burlettas," farcical musicals that featured popular songs. Lewis T. Pratt returned to the Chestnut, bringing Francis Wemyss in as his stage manager. Welch and Company took over the National and converted it back into a circus venue. For Marshall and Blake, it was a period of rebuilding. The two most talented cast members left the company: E. L. Davenport set off to try his luck in New York, while Charlotte Cushman took William Macready's advice and left for London in the fall. Both would win acclaim.

Edwin Forrest returned for the first time in two years to open the fall season at the Walnut. The most impressive production that fall was *Putnam, or The Iron Son of '76*, a patriotic Revolutionary War drama, which opened on September 21, 1844, and ran steadily through October 28. The theatre closed for a night and then reopened with the premiere of *Knights of the Dark Ages*, which ran for two weeks. *Bohemian Girl* was brought out on December 18 and ran through the end of the year. A traditional English pantomime, *Harlequin and the Silver Tower*, opened after Christmas and ran into early January. The theatre was given over to opera in January, and late that month *Old Hearts and Young Hearts* was produced.

MRS. MOWATT AND *FASHION*

The highlight of the spring season was the production of Anna Cora Mowatt's new comedy, *Fashion, or Life in New York*. The play, which depicted the social pretensions of ambitious New Yorkers, premiered at the Park Theatre in New York on March 24 and was an immediate hit. Its run of twenty performances was a record for the time. E. A. Marshall purchased the rights to the play and produced it at the Walnut on April 16. Mrs. Mowatt attended the premiere. She and her party were seated in a private box and provided with a satin playbill. The play was staged "in the most magnificent style in regard to the furniture and appointments, and Mrs. Mowatt thought that the scenic arrangements, with the accessories, surpassed the original production of the piece at the Park Theatre," Durang reported.[12]

Anna Cora Mowatt was an extraordinary figure. Born into wealth and privilege, she began her theatrical career when her husband became disabled. With no background in the theatre, she took to writing for the stage and giving dramatic readings. Her society friends shunned her. Mrs. Mowatt used the success of *Fashion* as a springboard for her own acting career. With only ten days of training and one rehearsal with her company, she made her debut in Edward Bulwer-Lytton's melodrama *The Lady of Lyons,* playing the starring role of Pauline. Following her debut at the Park Theatre in New York, she played seven nights at the Walnut, beginning June 23, in six different plays, including *Fashion.* The response was tremendous. She had real acting talent, and her story caught the imagination of the public.

REBUILDING THE COMPANY

The economy was beginning to improve, and with business increasing, E. A. Marshall was able to persuade the Walnut's stockholders to make much-needed improvements to the building. "The scenery had been entirely renewed. New stock scenes, streets, landscapes, chambers, palace saloons, castles, Gothic interiors and exteriors, had been painted," wrote Durang. The dress circle lobby was enlarged, and new carpeting and wallpaper were installed. The proscenium was redesigned with a likeness of Washington encircled by a gold wreath topped off with an American eagle, which had become the Walnut's emblem. The ceiling was painted with allegorical figures representing Europe, Asia, Africa, and the Americas.

It was less easy to replace the company, many of whom were taking advantage of new opportunities provided by an improving economy. The company, Charles Durang noted, "had been materially denuded of its leading actresses. The Misses Charlotte and Susan Cushman had withdrawn; Mrs. Thayer and daughter had also gone over to Burton; and E. Forrest, one of the regular mammoth attractions of the theatre, had gone to London, whither the Cushmans had also wended their way."

Forrest's absence provided an opening for several younger actors. James W. Wallack Jr. opened the fall season on October 1, 1845, playing a series of tragic roles. He had been a stock actor but was now touring as a star, performing with his wife. A local teacher of elocution, identified as Mr. J. Fest, made his stage debut in *Hamlet* on October 15 and created a stir. James E. Murdoch followed on November 3, finally getting the kind of attention he deserved. His performance of Benedick in *Much Ado About Nothing* was especially well received. The Philadelphia-born Murdoch became a special favorite with local audiences, and his Hamlet was unsurpassed at the time. Murdoch remained active on the stage until 1889, appearing regularly at the Walnut.

During the spring, Marshall and Blake brought out a number of spectacular pieces. An operatic drama, *The Enchantress,* had a two-week run beginning in late January and was revived several times during the season. On March 19, 1846, Francis Wemyss, who had fallen on hard times, was given a complimentary benefit. "Broken in fortune through unsuccessful managerial exertions, and advancing in years, his numerous friends and once professional patrons tendered him, in his adversity, this testimonial of their respect for him as an actor and a gentleman," Durang recalled.[13]

Toward the end of the 1846 season, President James K. Polk declared war on Mexico. Volunteers began joining up. Patriotic dramas were popular during the summer season, including *Campaign of the Rio Grande,* depicting General Zachary Taylor's Mexican campaign. The 1846–47 season was a good one, possibly as a result of the war. As the economy continued to improve, English stars began to cross the Atlantic. A bidding war for this talent ensued, which Marshall seems to have won. John Collins, an Irish singer and comedian, appeared on September 7. Mr. and Mrs. Charles Kean followed, making their first appearance in seven years. Anna Cora Mowatt also put in an appearance, along with her new co-star, E. L. Davenport. They were setting off on their own European tour.

Edwin Forrest arrived on October 19. It was his first engagement in Philadelphia since his troubled tour of England, where he had been savaged by the London press. Forrest was bitter and blamed his rival, William Macready, for turning the critics against him. The controversy had been played up in the American press, and "a kind of national feeling had sprung up in his behalf," according to Charles Durang. "This feeling, now pervading the Union, elicited a most enthusiastic reception in every city that [Forrest] played in, and so continued for a lengthened time."[14] Forrest's reception at the Walnut did much to restore his confidence.

Two actors long associated with the Walnut made their final appearances during the 1846–47 season. On November 18, William B. Wood received a farewell benefit, appearing on the stage for the last time. At seventy years of age, he was still active with various stock companies. He performed with his daughter in *The Maid of Croissy, or The Last of the Old Guard,* an appropriately titled piece for the aged manager. Wood lived until 1861, turning his attention to writing his memoirs, which were published in 1856. Also making his final appearance at the Walnut was Junius Brutus Booth, who played for a week in April 1847. Booth remained active in the theatre, appearing periodically in Philadelphia, but he no longer played at the Walnut. Booth died in 1852 while on tour.

The Walnut remained open for the entire summer of 1847. In July it was occupied by an Italian opera company that arrived from Havana. They performed a new opera by Donizetti, *Linda di Chamounix*, and *Ernani*, a work by Giuseppe Verdi, then largely unknown in America. They remained until August 7, whereupon Marshall's company took over. Marshall continued to indulge his interest in operatic performance. The Seguin troupe came in for two weeks in October with English opera. Edwin Forrest played for three weeks in November with his standard repertoire. More opera followed. Mr. Collins, the Irish tenor, returned in December, while Madame Anna Bishop, an English vocalist, brought her company in to finish up the year.

Profits were now rolling in, and E. A. Marshall began to look for new opportunities. In January 1848 he made a move into the New York market, going into partnership with Colonel Alvah Mann, a circus impresario, at the Broadway Theatre, the largest theatre in New York up to that time. Located at Broadway and Anthony Street in lower Manhattan, it seated forty-five hundred people. William Rufus Blake joined him as stage manager. In the fall of 1848 Colonel Mann withdrew from the Broadway and returned to the circus. On December 15, 1848, the Park Theatre burned to the ground, leaving the one-year-old Broadway Theatre as the leading venue for English stars. Philadelphia managers controlled the two prestige houses of the period.

Peter Richings took over stage-managing duties at the Walnut in the spring of 1848. Richings was an old theatrical hand. Born in London in 1797, he came to America in 1821. He was a member of the company at the Park Street Theatre for sixteen years, before leaving to assist William E. Burton at the National Theatre in Philadelphia as stage manager. When Burton's efforts failed, Richings joined the Walnut as a stock actor, before moving into management at the Holliday Theatre in Baltimore.

Nothing terrifically notable happened during the 1848 spring and summer season. James W. Wallack Jr. and his wife played at the Walnut in early January. Julia Dean made her first appearance there in February. Only seventeen, Dean had grown up in an acting family and had toured the towns along the Mississippi River. She made her New York debut at age fifteen and was an overnight sensation. Among the more unusual stars to play at the Walnut were the Heron Children, billed as "Lilliputian histrionics." The three children, Agnes, Joseph, and Mary Ann Heron, occupied the Walnut for some time in March. A ballet company arrived the same month. Monsieur Monplaisir's troupe of dancers appeared in June.

Mose's Visit to Philadelphia, a local drama about Mose the Bowery B'hoy (said to evoke an Irish pronunciation of "boy"), played during the closing week of the season. The character of the fireman had debuted in a piece called *A Glance at New York* at Mitchell's Olympic, based on the types often seen in volunteer fire companies of the time. Francis S. Chanfrau captured the fireman's style and attitude with the plug hat, red shirt, turned-up trousers, and "soap locks," and it depicted the underworld life that appealed to the "Bowery B'hoys." William E. Burton had produced a version titled *A Glance at Philadelphia* earlier in the month, and this was the Walnut's response. Peter Richings took on the role of Mose.

Competition between the Philadelphia theatres was strong. The Arch was open and there was opera at the Chestnut. Welch's Circus had taken over the old National, and Peale's Museum was offering theatrical productions. They would be joined by yet another museum theatre, the Athenaeum. Museums were popular places for offering theatrical fare, able to entice people who were suspicious of the theatre by offering "moral entertainments" in their "lecture rooms."

Marshall and Richings opened the fall 1848–49 season at the Walnut on August 28 with an original comedy, *The Millionaire.* The afterpiece that night was an old farce, *No! No! No! The Millionaire* was a success, poking fun at high society, and played through September 2. Another new play, *John Saville of Haysted,* premiered on the fourth. On September 25 an English opera company, the Seguin Opera Troupe, played for two weeks. On October 9, the Ravel Family returned, performing Spanish dances, pantomimes, and so on, and remained through October 18. They were followed on November 1 by the Monplaisir Operatic Ballet, a troupe of some fifty dancers. There was very little activity by the stock company; the Walnut was now essentially operating as a rental house.

AN ACTORS' FEUD

Edwin Forrest returned to the Walnut again on November 20, 1848. The English actor William C. Macready was touring America, and William E. Burton booked him into the Arch Street Theatre. Forrest was still bitter about the reception he had received in England during his most recent tour there. He was convinced that Macready had encouraged his supporters in the press to pan his performances. He tailed Macready, playing the same parts at the Walnut that Macready was performing at the Arch.

Forrest had many supporters in his hometown, and a number of them attended Macready's performance of *Macbeth,* showering the stage with eggs and pennies and calling for cheers for Forrest. Macready addressed the crowd directly, protesting that he had no "feeling of unkindness" toward his American rival and denying that he had turned the London critics against him. Macready's remarks were published in the next day's paper. Forrest published a response, accusing Macready of having surreptitiously encouraged the British critics to pan his performances. This exchange of cards "intensified the excitement and improved the business of both theatres," wrote Charles Durang, and both houses had sold out crowds. "Curiosity to compare the two great actors in the same parts ran to fever heat."[15]

Macready cut short his Philadelphia engagement and returned to New York before setting off on his tour of the southern and western states. Forrest remained at the Walnut until December 9, then followed Macready to Baltimore, where he played the same roles at Marshall's Holliday Street Theatre that Macready was playing at the Front Street Theatre.

THE GENERAL AND THE COUNT

On Monday, December 11, 1848, Charles S. Stratton, better known as General Tom Thumb, appeared on the Walnut's stage. This protégé of P. T. Barnum stood less than twenty-nine inches tall. He was eleven years old when he appeared at the Walnut, but Barnum announced his age as eighteen. General Tom Thumb had been touring with Barnum since he was four years old and had just returned from a lengthy European tour, where he had performed before many of the crowned heads of Europe. Stratton appeared in *Hop o' My Thumb, or The Seven League Boots,* a farce written especially for him, and a burlesque version of *Bombastes Furioso.* "He displayed considerable dramatic ability, and played with a great deal of spirit, appearing to fully enter into and enjoy the humor of his parts," wrote Joseph Ireland.[16] He also sang, danced, and posed as classic statuary. T. D. Rice performed the following week in what seems to have been his last appearance at the Walnut. His style of blackface entertainment had been replaced by the minstrel troupes, which offered a full evening's entertainment.

On January 24, 1849, the Walnut and Arch presented competing productions of *The Count of Monte Cristo,* based on the 1845 Alexandre Dumas novel. William Wheatley played the character of Edmond Dantès, the former prisoner who assumed the identity of a fictional count so as to take revenge on those who had falsely imprisoned him. The romantic spectacle "took the town by surprise, and every lover of amusement was anxious to witness the novel spectacle," Durang recalled. "The [Walnut] was crowded on the first night and every other night for a month, hundreds being frequently turned away." The play so fired the imagination of Philadelphians that "fancy balls were given all over town, at which all the characters in Monte Cristo flourish[ed] . . . the hero could be seen hopping the polka everywhere."[17] Local seamstresses were kept busy reproducing the fashions of the play for elegant costume balls. *The Count of Monte Cristo* became one of the most popular melodramas of the nineteenth century, with many actors taking on the role of Dantès, most notably James O'Neill, the father of playwright Eugene O'Neill, who played it regularly in the 1880s and '90s.

THE ASTOR PLACE RIOT

During the winter and early spring, William Macready toured the South and West, where he continued to be harassed by Forrest's supporters, which was duly reported by the East Coast press. Macready concluded his American tour and was booked into New York's fashionable Astor Place Opera House. He was announced in *Macbeth* for the night of May 8, 1849. Edwin Forrest, appearing at E. A. Marshall's Broadway Theatre, would play *Macbeth* the same night. Not to be outdone, the managers of the third premiere house in New York, the Bowery, also featured a production of the play. Once again, Forrest supporters disrupted Macready's performance, hurling apples, pennies, and even chairs at the actor and finally driving him from the stage.

Macready announced that he was canceling the remainder of his run. A group of prominent New Yorkers persuaded him to reconsider, guaranteeing his safety, and two nights later he again appeared in *Macbeth*. That night, a crowd estimated at ten thousand people collected in the square outside the theatre. Some began hurling rocks through the windows, while others attempted to break down the doors. The militia was brought in to support the poorly armed police force protecting the opera house. When the mob continued to attack, troops fired into the crowd, killing twenty-three people and wounding many others. The event shocked the nation. It was the first time American troops had fired on American citizens.

Edwin Forrest was accused of fomenting the mob violence, a charge he vehemently denied. He returned to the Walnut on June 2, 1849, where he "was received with loud acclamations by the audience."[18] In a curtain speech, Forrest acknowledged the acclaim as "a signal and triumphant rebuke to those who have . . . aimed their malignant and cowardly shafts at me professionally and personally."[19] Despite the dramatic demonstration of support, the Astor Place Riot permanently damaged Forrest's reputation. Although he remained popular with working-class audiences, more respectable theatergoers turned their backs on him.

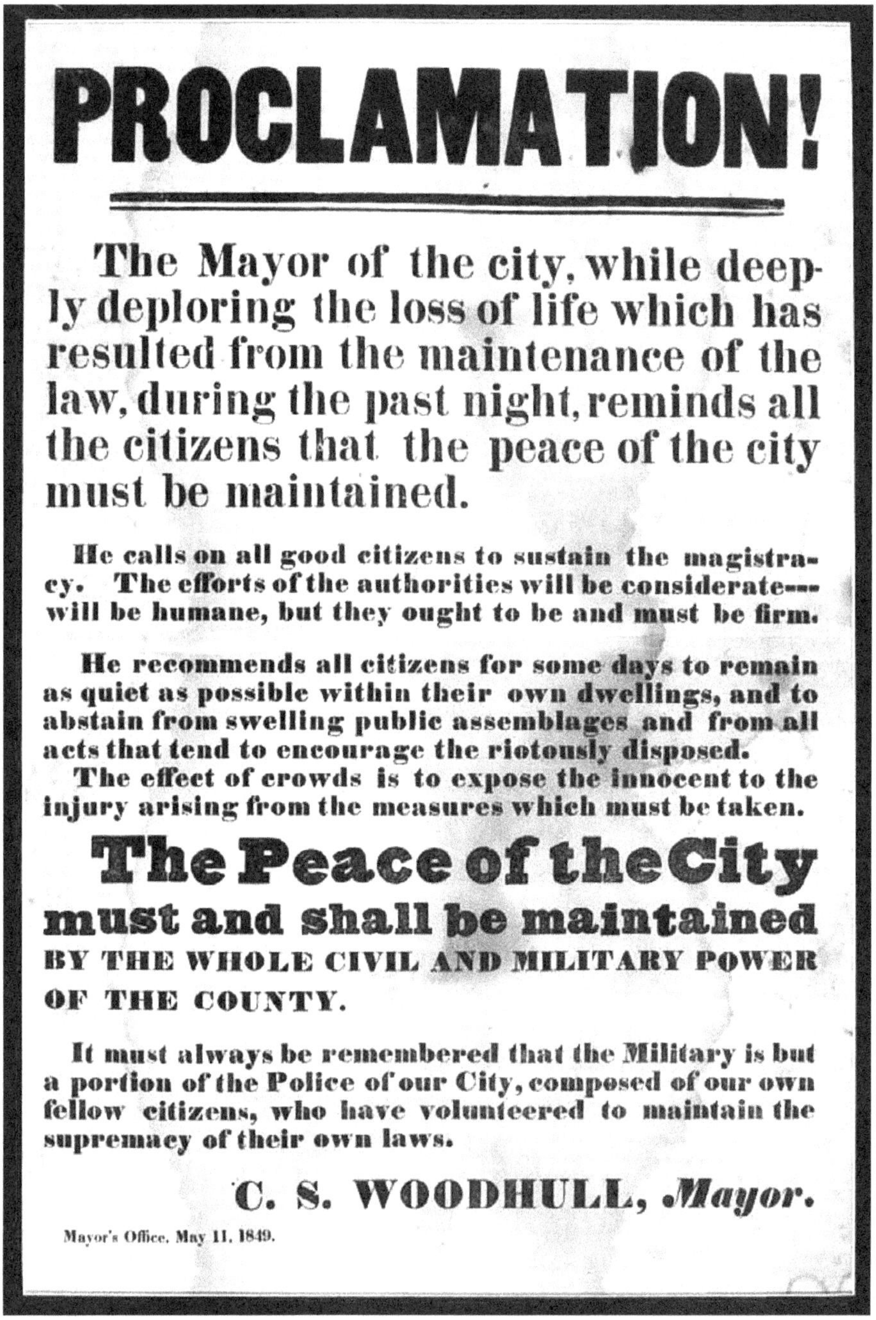

PROCLAMATION!

The Mayor of the city, while deeply deploring the loss of life which has resulted from the maintenance of the law, during the past night, reminds all the citizens that the peace of the city must be maintained.

He calls on all good citizens to sustain the magistracy. The efforts of the authorities will be considerate--- will be humane, but they ought to be and must be firm.

He recommends all citizens for some days to remain as quiet as possible within their own dwellings, and to abstain from swelling public assemblages and from all acts that tend to encourage the riotously disposed.
The effect of crowds is to expose the innocent to the injury arising from the measures which must be taken.

The Peace of the City must and shall be maintained
BY THE WHOLE CIVIL AND MILITARY POWER OF THE COUNTY.

It must always be remembered that the Military is but a portion of the Police of our City, composed of our own fellow citizens, who have volunteered to maintain the supremacy of their own laws.

C. S. WOODHULL, *Mayor.*

Mayor's Office, May 11, 1849.

fig. 8 The proclamation put forth by the mayor of New York City following the Astor Place Riot.

The Astor Place Riot marked a significant turning point in the history of American theatre. Raucous, even riotous, behavior that had been tolerated at the theatre acquired new, disturbing associations. The violence turned much of the public away from the obstreperous behavior that had characterized the typical audience of newsboys and others in the pit. The rowdy and disruptive behavior that had been considered a privilege of admission became less acceptable. Theatre owners cut back or eliminated liquor sales, an important source of their profits, in an effort to encourage more genteel behavior. They raised the price of admission to the pit so that poorer patrons were confined to the upper balcony, well away from the stage. Some theatres hired police to patrol the upper balconies to control patrons' behavior.

Beginning in 1849, E. A. Marshall focused his attention on his New York holdings. He now controlled four theatres in the Northeast. In addition to the Walnut and the Broadway, he operated the Holliday Theatre in Baltimore and the National Theatre in Washington, D.C. He also had arrangements to book shows in theatres in the Midwest and New Orleans. This gave him the biggest circuit in America, and on this basis he was able to attract leading European talent. With the demise of the old Park Theatre, Durang wrote, "Mr. Marshall was found to be in a position to carry out the great starring system most effectually; and he became, through these means . . . the successor of Price & Simpson."[20]

RESPECTABILITY, 1849–1860

Philadelphia was becoming industrialized, and new ethnic groups were establishing themselves. The 1840s had seen an upsurge in immigration, the largest numbers fleeing the potato famine in Ireland. Irish immigrants were filling unskilled jobs in factories, which brought them into conflict with native artisans who saw their livelihoods threatened by low-wage workers. The Industrial Revolution was creating a new middle class that was beginning to vie for power with the old elites for social and cultural leadership. Many of these newly affluent families were settling in the neighborhood of the Walnut. A gazetteer published in 1854 noted that the area "was thronged with stuccoed brick, giving abundant evidence of affluence, taste, and luxurious ease."[1]

These different groups sought out their own forms of entertainment. Opera appealed to the upper classes, for whom theatergoing was primarily a social occasion. Although Philadelphia did not have its own opera house, several concert halls catered to the wealthy with classical music. Saloons were siphoning off the working-class audience, turning their back rooms into entertainment centers known as "free and easies," where men could drink, engage in sing-alongs, and watch specialty acts. Philadelphia's first "free and easy" opened at the Mammoth Bowling Saloon in January 1849. Others soon followed. Modeled on English music halls, these were the earliest variety houses.

Middle-class Philadelphians were most likely to patronize one of the local museums, which offered dramatic and variety entertainment in their "lecture rooms," which they promoted as educational and moral. In this way they were able to attract patrons who viewed the theatre with disfavor. The most successful of these museum operators was the legendary P. T. Barnum, who had turned the American Museum in New York into the city's leading tourist attraction. In the fall of 1849 Barnum took over Philadelphia's Athenaeum Museum on Seventh and Chestnut streets, which he renamed Barnum's Museum. In his popularly priced lecture room he exhibited freaks, moving panoramas, and highly wrought moral melodramas like *The Drunkard.*

The established theatres were struggling. By this time Philadelphia had only three first-class theatres. The old National had been converted back into an equestrian arena and was presenting circus performances. William E. Burton controlled the Arch Street Theatre, but the 1849–50 season would be his last. He withdrew in January 1850 to concentrate his efforts on his New York venture. The Chestnut was not doing well either. The fashionable set that had supported the Chestnut for so many years had largely abandoned "Old Drury." It was now operated by a local hotel keeper named James Quinlan who ran theatrical bars around the city, through which he amassed a substantial fortune. Drama took second place in his mind to liquor sales, and the quality of the productions declined.

Only the Walnut remained profitable. But E. A. Marshall understood that he needed to attract a new audience if it was to remain so, and this meant going after middle-class audiences. They had the disposable income necessary to support the theatre, but they held the most negative attitudes toward it, often seeing it as immoral or frivolous. Upwardly mobile, they were especially concerned with demonstrating their newfound respectability, and they supported activities that showed off their moral character.

CHARLOTTE CUSHMAN AND THE FEMALE AUDIENCE

In the fall of 1849 Charlotte Cushman returned to America. She had been abroad for five years, where she had been enormously popular with English audiences. Under the influence of British companies, Cushman had acquired a technique and polish that, combined with her natural power onstage, gave her a majestic quality. London critics hailed her as the finest actress of the age, and she became accepted in fashionable literary circles. No other American actor—man or woman—had been as well received as "Our Charlotte," and American audiences embraced her with patriotic pride. E. A. Marshall booked her into the Broadway Theatre in New York, then into the Walnut, where she began a four-week run on October 29.

Cushman played most of her signature roles—Lady Macbeth, Rosalind in *As You Like It,* Julia in Sheridan Knowles's tragedy *The Hunchback,* and Queen Katherine in Shakespeare's *Henry VIII.* She did not attempt Romeo or any of her other "breeches" roles. Her most successful role was that of the gypsy fortuneteller Meg Merrilies in *Guy Mannering,* an adaptation of a novel by Sir Walter Scott. Cushman had taken a bit part and turned it into the most memorable figure in the play. Dressed in rags, her face aged by makeup, Cushman projected an eerie presence, "at once physically decrepit and charismatic, aging but timeless, demonic but maternal, elemental but unearthly," in the words of G. J. Williams.[2] So great was the demand that Peter Richings, the Walnut's stage manager, scheduled five performances of the play. Even so, hundreds had to be turned away.

Cushman's success was not lost on E. A. Marshall. According to one biographer, she brought in "the largest receipts ever taken in Philadelphia."[3] More important, however, Cushman was able to attract an audience that did not normally attend the theatre—women. Women were generally put off by the rowdy element in the pit and the prostitutes in the upper tier of boxes. When they did attend, it was only in the company of a male family member. Even so, the theatre had bad associations for middle-class women, and the violence at Astor Place reinforced those negative stereotypes. Cushman showed that women would support the theatre if their interests were taken into account. By presenting talented actresses in plays built around central female characters, theatre managers could bring women into the theatre. Marshall began to court the female audience. This created unprecedented opportunities for women in all aspects of the theatre. Although women had always been important in the theatre, they had largely been relegated to supporting roles. In the 1850s they began taking on leading roles as stars, playwrights, and even theatre managers. By the end of the decade, women would be running both the Walnut and the Arch.

THE FAMILY AUDIENCE

Marshall began to actively court the women's audience by appealing to their interest in domestic and family matters. In early January 1850 he booked the Bateman sisters into the Walnut. Kate and Ellen Bateman were another pair in the line of precocious child performers who performed adult roles. Six-year-old Kate played Richmond opposite four-year-old Ellen as Richard in the fifth act of *Richard III.* They also appeared in scenes from *Macbeth* and *Bombastes Furioso.* Like most child stars, the Bateman children came from a theatrical family. They were the granddaughters of Joe Cowell, who managed the Walnut in the 1820s. Their mother, Sidney Cowell Bateman, managed her children's career. The family had been touring the Ohio and Mississippi river valleys for several years, the parents playing supporting roles to their talented children. P. T. Barnum took notice of the precocious youngsters, signed them, and booked them into his American Museum, then sent them on a tour of Europe. Under Barnum's management they became the most renowned of the nineteenth-century child prodigies. The girls ended their careers as child actresses in 1856. Ellen Bateman retired from the stage, but Kate returned after several years and had a successful career as an adult.

The Ravels had always appealed to a family audience with their combination of dance, pantomime, and acrobatics. They returned in mid-January and remained for more than two months. On March 25 a new comedy titled *Extremes* depicted the growing tensions between the North and South. It had premiered at the Broadway Theatre in New York and "was produced with brilliant scenery, costly furniture and stage appointments, with also an unexampled combination of talent in the dramatis personae, embracing the names of a portion of the original cast, with the available strength of the regular company," wrote Durang.[4] The cast from the New York production was brought in to perform. The production ran for three weeks.

A former child prodigy, Jean M. Davenport, made her first appearance in mid-April. Davenport had toured in England and America for many years—too many—as a child star. Billed as the "infant phenomenon," she was said to be the model for Charles Dickens's satirical portrait of an overaged prodigy who still insists on playing child roles. Now twenty, Davenport was attempting to play the leading lady in Knowles's *Hunchback*, Bulwer-Lytton's *Lady of Lyons*, and other dramas with central female characters. She would remain in America for most of her career.

GEORGE HENRY BOKER

The concern for respectability renewed interest in literary drama, which created opportunities for a talented local dramatist, George Henry Boker. Boker came from a Philadelphia banking family; he had trained to be a lawyer but gave up the profession to pursue a literary career. He had written several plays since 1848 but had never had any of his works produced in America, only in England. Boker's *The Betrothal* received its world premiere at the Walnut Street Theatre on September 25, 1850, where it ran for ten nights. A romantic comedy set in Renaissance Italy, it concerned the efforts of an aristocratic family to marry a daughter off to a rich merchant in order to revive the family fortune. Based on the success of this production, Marshall brought out an earlier Boker work, *Calaynos*, a verse tragedy set in Spain that dealt with racial prejudice against those with Moorish blood. *Calaynos* had its American premiere on January 20, 1851, with James E. Murdoch in the title role. Another Boker play, a contemporary comedy titled *The World a Mask*, was produced at the Walnut the following April. Boker's reputation is based on two later works, *Leonor de Guzman*, which had its world premiere at the Walnut in 1853, and *Francesca da Rimini*, a verse tragedy based on an episode in Dante's *Inferno* that was produced in 1855.

Copyright laws worked against the development of American drama. While playwrights retained publication rights to their works, they had no control over performance rights. Once published, anyone could stage a play, and the author received nothing. For this reason few playwrights were willing to have their works published. Generally, playwrights received the proceeds from the third night's performance of a play, which might amount to several hundred dollars. It was by no means equal to what an author could make from a successful novel, and a number of leading playwrights had simply given up on the theatre. Boker campaigned to have the copyright laws changed but was unsuccessful, and he gave up writing plays for more profitable pursuits.

THE 1850–1851 SEASON

Charlotte Cushman returned for a four-week engagement at the Walnut beginning October 28, 1850. This time she attempted male roles. She opened her run with *The Lady of Lyons*, playing the male lead, Claude Menotte. On November 5 she brought out *Romeo and Juliet*. Several nights later she reprised the play, but, as Cushman's biographer Joseph Leach recounted, "by the end of the first act it was clear to players and audience alike that Fanny Wallack . . . the night's delicate Juliet, was gloriously drunk. By the end of act three, Fanny's hiccuping and giggling had made the play a shambles. A minute or so before the curtain, she stopped still, made one great sweep of her outstretched arms, then fell flat on her face, tangled and kicking in her draperies. The crowd burst into yells and laughter, and stagehands carried her off, her swollen red face shrieking. Watching it all, Charlotte stood dumb and helpless."[5]

Marshall continued to bring over European stars. Cushman was followed by Sir William Don, a British baronet who had taken to the stage. Also making their debuts were Mme. Ponisi, Mlle. Blangy and M. Durand, and Mlle. Celestine Franck, who headed up a French ballet troupe. Marshall brought in a pretty, blonde-haired English actress named Julia Bennett, who was making her first tour of the United States, to play in *All That Glitters Is Not Gold*. Her forte was comedy. Returning stars included Mme. Anna Bishop, John Collins, and Julia Dean, who appeared in *The Duke's Wager*, a play attributed to Fanny Kemble.

There were new opportunities for local talent as well. A twenty-year-old Philadelphia actress, Matilda Heron, made her stage debut on February 17, 1851, in *Fazio*, a verse tragedy by the English cleric Henry Milman. Heron grew up in the vicinity of the Walnut and regularly attended shows there. She studied elocution with Peter Richings, and he starred her in a benefit performance for the Walnut's prompter. Her stage debut must have been exceptional, for she was brought back two nights later to reprise the role and was booked for an entire week later in the season—an unusual opportunity for a beginner. Heron was known for her raw displays of emotion onstage, which both shocked and fascinated audiences. She made a name for herself with gold rush audiences in San Francisco and toured for many years, playing the Walnut frequently.

Opera was enjoying renewed popularity as a result of Jenny Lind's tour of America. P. T. Barnum lured the "Swedish Nightingale" to America with an unheard of offer of $1,000 a night. She played a total of eight nights in Philadelphia during the 1850–51 season, but never at the Walnut. Hoping to capitalize on the Lind phenomenon, Marshall and Richings engaged the Seguin Opera Company to play exclusively at the Walnut during the 1851–52 season. The troupe opened the fall season on August 18, performing a number of Italian operas in English, including *Sonnambula* and *Fra Diavolo.* The Walnut continued to bring in touring stars. On September 22 the Rousset family made their debut, performing a grand operatic ballet with the Seguin troupe. They produced "an unrivaled ballet spectacle," *La Bayadere.* New scenery and costumes were created for the production, and they were supported by the vocal and dancing talents of the company.

The Roussets remained until October 4, when Edwin Forrest opened a three-week run at the Walnut. It was Forrest's first appearance in Philadelphia in two years. Despite his association with the Astor Place Riot, he was still a guaranteed draw. He was engaged in a highly publicized divorce from his wife, Catherine Sinclair, whom he accused of infidelity. The tabloid press was already publicizing the upcoming divorce trial. On the eighth, Marshall staged a spectacular production of *Macbeth.* The operatic company was employed in the witches' scenes. Forrest remained for seventeen nights, drawing crowded houses during the entire run; hundreds had to be turned away.

An unprecedented number of women were brought in as stars during the season. Marshall continued to bring in new stars from England, which he debuted at the Broadway Theatre in New York and then sent on the road, beginning with the Walnut. Laura Addison, of Sadler's Wells, played for two weeks in November but did not make much of an impression. She was followed by Madame Céleste, who returned after an absence of seven years. The French-born actress began her career as a dancer, playing the Walnut in the 1820s, when she was a virtual unknown. She had developed into an extraordinary actress and was the most profitable star of her day. She appeared in *The French Spy,* which she alternated with *Harvest Home* and *The Wept of Wish-Ton-Wish.* Caroline Richings, the adopted daughter of the Walnut's stage manager, made her debut on February 9, starring in Donizetti's opera *The Daughter of the Regiment,* and following that up with several other popular operas, *L'Elisire d'Amore, La Sonnambula, Linda di Chamounix,* and *Norma* among them. She was to become one of the most famous singers in America and was a local favorite. Charlotte Cushman returned on April 19 for what was announced as her farewell engagement in Philadelphia. She planned to return to Europe and retire from the stage. Although she eventually resumed acting, it would be twenty years before she played the Walnut again. She reprised many of her roles during her two-week run and premiered a new work, *The Banker's Daughter,* by a Philadelphia playwright and critic, Mme. Julie de Marguerittes.

LOLA MONTEZ

E. A. Marshall's real coup came when he arranged to bring the notorious Lola Montez to America. Renowned as a dancer and a beauty, the eccentric and mercurial Lola had gained notoriety for her offstage exploits, including a celebrated affair with the king of Bavaria. She opened at the Walnut on January 19, 1852, playing two weeks in *Betley, the Tyrolean* and *Un Jour de Carnival da Seville,* two dance pieces specially prepared to highlight her dancing. Montez's signature piece was her "Spider Dance," a tarantella premised on her being bitten by a spider. Many called the dance obscene, as she writhed and tore at her clothing in order to get the spider out. Her dancing was unremarkable, but she was wildly applauded by the audience, which the *Public Ledger* noted "was composed, for the most part, of men, with a few of the other sex sprinkled here and there."[6]

Montez returned at the end of May, making her acting debut in *Lola Montez in Bavaria,* which purported to tell the story of her affair with Ludwig I. The play was full of court intrigue that eventually forced the king to abdicate his throne. The highlight of the piece came when Montez, confronted by an angry mob, drove them off with a whip. "Lola has succeeded in overcoming much of the prejudice which at first existed in the public mind against her," the *Public Ledger* noted, adding, "She is now as much talked of as some of the candidates for the Presidency."[7] Montez continued her tour of America, eventually settling in the California gold fields.

TRANSFORMING THE THEATRE

On February 10, 1852, the Walnut was sold at a public auction to satisfy a bill against the proprietors of the theatre. Although E. A. Marshall held the lease on the Walnut, the property was still owned by the Proprietors of the Walnut Street Theatre, the group of prominent Philadelphians who had purchased the property from Victor Pepin in 1818. The state legislature passed a special act authorizing the trustees to sell the building. The property was purchased by the president of the Walnut's board, Henry G. Freeman, for $43,000. Freeman spent an additional $10,000 on much-needed improvements to the auditorium. Box seats were cushioned and "constructed in the nature of stalls, as in the London theatres," according to Durang.[8] The orchestra seating, or what was known as the *parquet*, was enlarged by extending the seating underneath the first tier of boxes on either side of the auditorium. The proscenium was widened to provide greater visibility of the stage.

These alterations transformed the Walnut significantly. The new pricing meant that the seats closest to the stage were available for more affluent customers. A staircase was built connecting the parquet with the first-tier lobby, so that those with orchestra seats could mingle with those who paid for boxes. The pit, with its riotous behavior, became a thing of the past. Poorer people were now relegated to the upper balcony rather than the position closest to the stage.

FAMILY ENTERTAINMENT

Marshall retained the lease on the property and continued to offer a varied selection of entertainment designed to appeal to middle-class audiences. The 1852–53 season opened on August 30 with Mr. and Mrs. Barney Williams, who appeared in a series of Irish comedies. Irish-born Barney Williams had been one of the earliest blackface comedians, but he found his niche in playing lovable, hard-drinking Irish characters. His career took off after he married Maria Pray Mestayer in 1850, who played his Yankee wife in romantic Irish comedies. They were perennial favorites with Philadelphia audiences, returning regularly to the Walnut over the next twenty years.

The Ravel Family returned on September 6 after an absence of several years, offering their familiar blend of dance, acrobatics, and pantomime. The company included a young tightrope walker named Blondin. M. Blondin became famous some years later for walking a tightrope strung across Niagara Falls. During this run at the Walnut, he performed various stunts on the tightrope, including one in which he balanced with a large basket attached to his feet. More familiar names followed—the Bateman Children and John Collins, the Irish vocalist. Edwin Forrest made his first appearance that season on November 8, 1852.

December was devoted to opera, with Madame Anna Bishop and her company from England playing most of the month. There was more opera in February, when an Italian troupe led by Maria Alboni was engaged. They played through March 11, when a complimentary benefit was given for E. A. Marshall as a token of appreciation for his support of Italian opera in the city. The entire troupe volunteered their services for the evening.

The season closed May 21 but opened on the following Wednesday, May 25, for a farewell benefit for the stage manager, Peter Richings, who was resigning to help manage his daughter Caroline's career. "The entire company of comedians, with the orchestra and the artisans and attaches of the theatre, tendered their gratuitous services," Durang reported.[9] One hundred and twenty prominent Philadelphians were listed as patrons of the benefit.

CAMILLE AND *UNCLE TOM'S CABIN*

John Sefton, who had been a member of the Walnut's stock company under Francis Wemyss in the 1830s, took over as stage manager in the fall of 1853. Joshua Silsbee was brought in to open the season with his Yankee characterizations. Jean M. Davenport returned on September 12. On the twenty-third she brought out *Camille, or The Fate of a Coquette* for the first time in Philadelphia. The dramatization of the Alexandre Dumas novel was first performed in France in 1852 and became a favorite vehicle for melodramatic actresses like Matilda Heron, Fanny Davenport, and Sarah Bernhardt. The story of a courtesan, Marguerite Gautier, who falls in love with the dashing, aristocratic Armand Duval was considered too scandalous to be staged in America. Davenport transformed her into a flirt, but the play was not well attended and ran only two performances. When Davenport returned the following fall, it did much better.

The hit of the 1853–54 season was running at the Chestnut. *Uncle Tom's Cabin* opened there on September 26 and ran for six weeks. The play had had an extraordinary run in New York, and was to become the most popular play of the nineteenth century. Harriet Beecher Stowe, who disapproved of the theatre, did not assign the stage rights, but several stage adaptations were made, the most successful being George Aiken's 1852 version. Although the novel had sold well, it was the stage version that generated a mass audience. Troupes toured the country with the dramatizations of Stowe's novel of life on a slave plantation.

John Sefton did what he could to program against it. He premiered George H. Boker's drama *Leonor de Guzman* and brought in Edwin Forrest for a two-week engagement. Mr. and Mrs. Barney Williams followed, playing a comic repertoire that included *Uncle Pat's Cabin*, a send-up of *Uncle Tom's Cabin* set in Ireland. In December, Peter and Caroline Richings played their first star engagement at the Walnut. Twenty-six-year-old Caroline was featured in Donizetti's opera *The Daughter of the Regiment*. The Ravels arrived just after the first of the year and played through the end of April. Mr. and Mrs. Barney Williams closed out the 1853–54 season.

During the summer of 1854 the Walnut was renovated, the lobbies papered and decorated and the seats restuffed. Marshall continued to book stars into the Walnut who had first played at the Broadway in New York. Matilda Heron came in for a week early in the season. She was followed by Jean M. Davenport, who reprised *Camille*. Assured that the most objectionable features of the French version had been excised, audiences flocked to the play, which ran for twelve successive nights—a considerable run for the period. E. L. Davenport—no relation to Jean—followed in a new play, *St. Marc, or A Husband's Sacrifice* which he alternated with several Shakespeare plays. He had been touring in Europe with Anna Cora Mowatt and this was his first appearance in the United States in several years. Mrs. Mowatt had recently remarried and retired from the stage. Davenport had married an English actress, Fanny Vining, and they were touring together.

DION BOUCICAULT

Among those making their debuts at the Walnut were Agnes Robertson and her husband, Dion Boucicault, who arrived on November 27, 1854. Boucicault would become one of the most influential playwrights of the nineteenth century, writing or adapting more than 130 plays for the stage, including some of the greatest hits of the century—*The Octoroon, The Shaughraun, The Streets of New York*, and Joseph Jefferson's *Rip van Winkle*. Boucicault was already a well-known playwright and had a successful career in London following his early masterpiece, *London Assurance*. Boucicault discovered, however, that he could make more money adapting French plays for the English stage than creating original works. With no international copyright protection, English producers did not have to pay French playwrights, and the prolific Boucicault had several plays running in London's West End. By translating French works, he mastered the technique of the "well-made play," which had taken hold in France. He would turn the techniques of the French theatre to his own advantage, creating sensational melodramas.

Boucicault was forced to leave London when he became involved with the lovely nineteen-year-old Agnes Robertson, a minor actress at the Princess Theatre, where Boucicault was the resident playwright. Robertson happened to be the ward of the theatre's manager, Charles Kean. When their affair was discovered, Boucicault immediately resigned and married Robertson. Shortly thereafter the couple left for America, where Boucicault promoted his young wife's career. The couple had been in America for two years when they appeared at the Walnut. They had played the Chestnut the previous spring. They performed in a series of plays, most of them comedies Boucicault had adapted from the French, which showed off Robertson's charm, including *The Young Actress*, *Andy Blake*, and *The Devil's in It*. On November 27 they brought out *Apollo in New York*, a satire of local life in which the Greek god visits New York City. It was the world premiere of this minor work.

On January 8, 1855, Marshall and Sefton staged *A Midsummer Night's Dream*, with specially designed scenery, costumes, and machinery. They may have used the sets from a version that Marshall had staged at the Broadway Theatre the year before. The production featured "a new double panorama of a novel and beautiful construction, graphically illustrating through the progress of the piece the various passing incidents," Durang reported.[10] The play ran for more than a month. In February the Pyne and Harrison English Opera Company scored with a production of *Cinderella*. The remainder of the season was given over to star runs by Mr. and Mrs. E. L. Davenport, James E. Murdoch, Eliza Logan, and a Philadelphia actor named McKean Buchanan.

THE END OF OLD DRURY

The 1854–55 season was the last for the Chestnut Street Theatre. "Old Drury" had served the city of Philadelphia for sixty-two years. But it had fallen on bad times and had been abandoned by the fashionable set that had made it the premiere theatre in the city. The final performance was held on May 1, 1855, before a meager audience. Shortly afterward, the old building was demolished. Its spot on the corner of Chestnut and Sixth was filled with clothing bazaars, billiard saloons, and minstrel halls. That left only the Walnut and Arch as first-class houses.

The 1855–56 season was a particularly notable one for the old Walnut. Two of the productions stand out. The first was *Camille*, as played by the passionate Philadelphia actress Matilda Heron. After seeing the original version of *La Dame aux Camelias* in Paris, Heron was inspired to do a new translation of the play. Heron's version was written in a more realistic style than previous versions, and it allowed her to give full vent to her emotional style of acting. Her Marguerite Gautier was a suffering, passionate woman, and audiences responded. When Heron played it at Wallack's Theatre in New York in 1857, she created a furor, and the play ran for one hundred nights.

Heron was followed by E. L. Davenport, who starred in George H. Boker's new play, *Francesca da Rimini*, widely considered the finest romantic tragedy of the nineteenth century. Based on an episode in Dante's *Inferno*, the play recounts the tragic affair of a pair of thirteenth-century lovers caught up in the political intrigues of Italian city-states. Mrs. John Drew starred as Francesca, with A. H. Davenport as her lover, Paolo, and E. L. Davenport as the hunchback, Lanciotto. The play had a disappointing reception in part because of a lackluster performance by E. L. Davenport. Disappointed with the play's reception, Boker gave up writing for the theatre. It was only in 1882, when Lawrence Barrett revived the play, that it was embraced by critics and the public.

THE TRAGEDY OF RACHEL

On November 19, 1855, the renowned French actress Elisabeth Rachel Félix, better known simply as Rachel, made her one and only appearance at the Walnut Street Theatre in Corneille's tragedy *Horace*. Acclaimed as the greatest tragedienne in France, Rachel was often compared to Edmund Kean. Born to poor Jewish peddlers and reared in poverty, she had extraordinary power onstage. "Declaiming poetry in a golden voice, Rachel thrilled the audience by her magnificent diction, the expressiveness of her face and posture and gestures, and the way she moved about the stage 'with a panther's terrible and undulating grace,'" wrote historian Lloyd Morris.[11] At age thirty-five she was persuaded to make a tour of America; it had not proved successful.

Rachel was set to play a week's run at the Walnut, but freezing weather had set in, and her brother, who managed her tour, refused to pay the costs of heating the backstage area of the theatre. A member of her company, Léon Beauvallet, recalled, "No fire had been lit, and we were chilled to the bone. Everybody caught a cold. Mlle. Rachel, who had never completely recovered from her indisposition at the Metropolitan [Theatre in New York], and still had a bad cough, suffered so terribly that evening from the cold that on the following day she was seriously ill and had to take to her bed."

The company completed the week's engagement, joining forces with the Walnut's company. Rachel was unable to leave her hotel room, and without the star, houses were thin, and the company had to lower ticket prices. The low prices drew a less desirable audience than the company was used to attracting. "While the French people in the orchestra were applauding, the lads sitting in the 'gods' [the upper balcony] were dancing on the benches with young girls in low-cut dresses, whose demeanour was by no means staid, and who from time to time were gently reprimanded by the police," Beauvallet recalled. "During *Les Droits de l'Homme* these madcaps made so much noise in the gallery with their imitations of animal noises that it was quite impossible

fig. 9 The renowned French actress Rachel, who made her only appearance at the Walnut Street Theatre in November 1855 in Corneille's tragedy *Horace*.

for us to make ourselves heard. The French contingent downstairs swore at the Americans, who threw down nutshells and apple peelings on their heads. It was real pandemonium."[12]

The French company cut short its run and canceled scheduled performances in Baltimore, Washington, and Richmond. The company traveled to Charleston, South Carolina, to catch a ship back to France. There, Rachel played one engagement. It was to be her last appearance on any stage. The pneumonia she contracted at the Walnut inflamed an incipient case of tuberculosis. Within three years, the great tragedienne was dead.

As noted above, American playwrights had been severely hampered by the lack of legal protection. Although playwrights were allowed the rights to print and publish their works, until 1856 they had no control over how their plays were acted or staged. On August 18, 1856, Congress enacted the first copyright law, which finally gave playwrights the sole right to act, perform, and represent their plays. While this protection would benefit playwrights in the long run, in the short term it prompted many lawsuits, as the courts and theatre people tried to come to terms with the new law. Edwin Forrest understood the law to mean that he owned most of his signature roles, and he immediately applied for copyrights of *Jack Cade, Metamora,* and his other pieces, on the assumption that he had paid for them. It would be some years before the courts worked out an equitable system for rewarding dramatists.

Forrest returned to the Walnut on September 29 for what was announced as his final appearance. Forced by the courts to provide for his ex-wife, he did not want to add to his fortune. He was also suffering from periodic recurrences of gout, which hampered his ability to move onstage. His three-week run would be his last appearance on the Walnut's stage for more than a decade.

Two important actors made their Philadelphia debuts the following season. Laura Keene opened on October 20, 1856. Keene was the first woman in America to operate her own theatre. She had been forced out by William E. Burton, who took advantage of a flaw in her lease. A new theatre was being built for her in New York on Broadway near Houston Street, which would become her home for eight productive years. While the new facility was under construction, she took her entire company on the road. The company played the Walnut for two weeks with a repertoire of classic comedies and recent melodramas.

At the end of the season, Edwin Booth, the second son of Junius Brutus Booth, made his debut at the Walnut. Booth was twenty-three at the time. He had recently returned from California, where he had spent several years. He had joined a company that included Laura Keene, which had journeyed to Australia. He and Keene shared top billing in such productions as *The Lady of Lyons, The Merchant of Venice,* and other plays.

Booth made his debut at the Walnut on June 1, 1857, starring in a repertoire of Shakespeare tragedies identified with his father—*Othello, Richard III,* and *King Lear,* as well as playing the title character in *Brutus* and Sir Giles Overreach in *A New Way to Pay Old Debts.* He suffered by comparison with the elder Booth. Five foot six and slightly built, Booth lacked the commanding presence of his father. Many recognized an important talent, but he had yet to develop his own style of acting. Challenged by the inevitable comparisons with his father, Booth developed a quieter, subtler method of acting that would serve him well in such roles as Hamlet. In so doing, he would change the American acting style.

The big news that season was the opening of the American Academy of Music. The building still stands on the corner of Broad and Locust streets. Philadelphia had long needed a first-class opera house, and work began in 1855. E. A. Marshall was given the lease on the new facility. Marshall was expected to book the "highest class of dramatic representations from the works of standard authors." Peter Richings joined him as stage manager. The opening was celebrated with a formal ball on the evening of January 26, 1857. The first performance in the new opera house took place a month later, when *Il Trovatore* was performed. A season of Italian opera followed.

Although the need for a first-class opera house had long been acknowledged, the timing could not have been worse. That summer the country experienced another of its financial crises. What became known as the Panic of 1857 was brought about by overspeculation in railroad construction. The collapse of an investment house in New York in August led to the failure of the Bank of Pennsylvania a month later. Business declined in nearly every sector of the economy, workers were laid off, and the streets of Philadelphia filled with unemployed men demanding relief.[13]

E. A. Marshall was overextended and was unable to meet his payroll at the Academy of Music. On December 12, 1857, he gave up control of the Walnut Street Theatre in order to focus his efforts on the Academy of Music. Two days later, he withdrew from the Broadway Theatre in New York.

MRS. BOWERS'S NEW WALNUT STREET THEATRE

Periods of economic crisis gave new groups an opportunity to take the lead in the theatrical trade. This time it was a woman who took control of the Walnut. Inspired by the success of Laura Keene in New York, Mrs. D. P. Bowers took over the lease of the Walnut Street Theatre. Mrs. Bowers had been a prominent figure in Philadelphia theatre for more than a decade. Born in 1830, she made her Philadelphia debut at the Walnut at sixteen under her maiden name, Elizabeth Crocker. The following year she married a talented local comedian, David P. Bowers, and thereafter performed under her husband's name. The couple had been members of the Walnut's stock company, where Mrs. Bowers attracted considerable notice in tragic and melodramatic roles. Her husband died unexpectedly in the summer of 1857, leaving Mrs. Bowers with three small children to support.

The Walnut remained dark for a week while Mrs. Bowers had the theatre cleaned and new seats installed in the orchestra to accommodate ladies'

fig. 10 In December 1857, Mrs. D. P. Bowers, a former member of the Walnut's stock company, took over management of the theatre.

hooped skirts. She reopened the theatre on December 19, 1857, with a revival of Boucicault's *London Assurance*, playing the role of Lady Gay Spanker herself. In an opening address, she announced, "To-night the actress is not seen—she gives place to the new and more impressive character in which I now stand before you—the character of manager!" Bowers appealed to the public to support her efforts, assuring them that she would not neglect the older playwrights but would alternate them with new works. She made a special

plea to local playwrights "to give us original American Dramas and comedies, and not hybrid versions of French plays."[14]

Bowers was intent on reintroducing the stock system to the Walnut. She brought Peter Richings over from the Academy of Music to serve as her acting and stage manager and began building up the company. Mrs. Bowers's sister, Sarah, arrived on December 28 with her husband, Frederick Conway. John E. Owens played light comedy roles, and Cornelia Jefferson joined the company. Mrs. John Drew joined the company at the end of January, and her husband arrived the following month. It was by any measure a talented group of actors. The company performed classic comedies, in which Mrs. Drew specialized, and recent melodramas, in which Mrs. Bowers excelled. The company debuted several new plays during the spring of 1858, all by British playwrights: *White Lies* on February 25, *Sarah, the Creole* on March 8, *Esmeralda* the following week, and *Love Knot* in April.

During the summer of 1858 Mrs. Bowers traded theatres with Laura Keene. Keene opened her run at the Walnut on May 17, debuting two plays that had been successful in New York, a patriotic drama, *Blanche of Brandywine*, and a musical, *Elves, or The Statue Bride*. The principal comedian with the company was Joseph Jefferson, grandson of the Joseph Jefferson who had worked with Warren and Wood. Keene's run was cut short on June 9, William Dickey Coder reported, "due to the embarrassing fact that she found herself without the necessary funds with which to pay salaries."[15] Returning to New York that fall, Laura Keene brought out a new play that would revive her fortunes. *Our American Cousin*, a comedy by the English playwright Tom Taylor, made stars of its principal cast members—Keene, Jefferson, and E. A. Sothern.

Mrs. Bowers returned to the Walnut for a benefit performance on June 18, then closed the theatre again for renovations. The auditorium received a new paint job of white and gold. The first and second tiers of boxes were extended and lowered to provide a better view of the stage. Partitions between the boxes were removed to make the aisles "capacious enough for the accommodation of any wearable quantity of crinoline and extent of hoops," as a local newspaper reported. The boxes were supplied with cushioned armchairs and the fronts were painted in green and gold. One critic declared that "the whole effect of the decorations and alterations is apparently to enlarge the house—so light, graceful and harmonious is the house, in its new aspect."[16] The improvements were paid for by the theatre's owner, Henry G. Freeman, who raised the annual rent by $1,000.

Mrs. Bowers opened the fall season on August 21, 1858, with a production of *Romeo and Juliet* in which she starred as the female lead. She continued to operate the Walnut as a stock company, using in-house talent for all the productions and taking the lead roles herself. She had lost several important members of the company, most notably Mr. and Mrs. John Drew. Without their strengths in comedy, the productions were heavily weighted toward tragedy. She had some success with *Louise de Lignerolles, or A Wife's Devotion,* a romantic drama about marital infidelity, adapted from the French by Madame de Marguerittes, which ran for thirteen nights. Other productions were simply too grim. On September 25 the bill featured two tragedies, *Jane Shore* and *The Inconstant,* prompting one critic to comment that "not even the admirable cast . . . could tempt us to sit through these five acts of melodramatic horror and affliction."[17] Two nights later the company brought out *Cagot, or Heart for Heart,* a drama about the persecution of a people in the Pyrenees who suffered from a thyroid ailment that caused goiters. Audiences opted for the much more entertaining fare that William Wheatley and John Sleeper Clarke were offering at the Arch.

The Walnut's finances were also in disarray. Although the Panic of 1857 was not as devastating as that of 1837, the economy was still poor, but Mrs. Bowers failed to contain production costs. By November, financial problems were becoming apparent. Newspapers alluded to "a civil war" going on between Mrs. Bowers and her financial officers. She was pressured to bring in outside stars who could attract audiences. The first of these was John Drew, who brought in his popular Irish characters for two weeks in late November. Jean M. Davenport played for three weeks in December in old stalwarts *Camille* and *Medea.* The closing week of the year was given over to a series of benefit performances. The most talented members of the troupe were leaving, not content to play supporting roles to touring stars. On January 20, Mrs. Bowers relinquished control of the Walnut.

MRS. M. A. GARRETTSON

On January 22, 1859, Mrs. M. Augusta Garrettson took over the operations of the theatre. Not much is known about Mrs. Garrettson. She had no previous connection with the theatre. Her obituary indicates that she was born in New York City in 1823 and that her maiden name was Tucker.[18] She was apparently widowed in 1858. She was described as a "special partner" in the Walnut and it is likely that she or her late husband provided the financial backing for Mrs. Bowers.

Despite her lack of stage experience, Mrs. Garrettson had more success operating the Walnut than many of the veteran theatre people who preceded her. She accomplished this largely by putting her money into star salaries. A popular English actor, Barry Sullivan, played the first three weeks that Mrs.

Garrettson was in charge, appearing in the usual mix of Shakespearean tragedies. He was followed by James H. Hackett, James E. Murdoch, and Mr. and Mrs. Dion Boucicault, each of whom played a week. Mrs. Boucicault appeared in the title role in *Jessie Brown, or The Relief of Luchnow,* a new melodrama by her husband about the recent Sepoy Rebellion in India. Dion Boucicault played the part of the villainous Sepoy leader, Nana Sahib, when no other actor would take the part for fear of audience reaction.

The New Orleans English Opera Company presented a week of popular operas beginning in late March, and in May the Theatre Français de New York offered several nights of French-language productions. The season closed on June 4 following the usual end-of-the-season benefits for members of the company. During the summer the Walnut was made available to touring companies. The Theatre Français returned for several nights. The Ronzani Opera and Ballet Troupe was booked for a week in early July, and a company of children from the Academy of Music performed "their beautiful and innocent entertainments, consisting of floral beauties, garland exercises, petite ballets etc.," noted the announcement in the *Public Ledger.*

THE 1859 SEASON

The fall 1859 season offered more of the same. J. B. Roberts opened the season, playing a week of repertory while preparing a new production, *Faust and Marguerite.* Roberts played Mephistopheles in this retelling of the Faustus legend. The Walnut's music director, Dr. Cunnington, had prepared an original score for the production, and the cast included a full *corps de ballet.* It was a formula that would prove very successful several years later in *The Black Crook.* E. L. Davenport played the week of September 19. He was followed by Maggie Mitchell, a comedienne making the first of many appearances at the Walnut. Mitchell belonged to what theatre historian Garff B. Wilson termed "the personality school" of actresses, who challenged the overwrought style that predominated. She relied on her own charm and personality to put a play over, rather than creating a distinct character. Such actresses played a limited number of roles that were fashioned to their personalities. Mitchell appeared in *Katty O'Shiel, The Wept of Wish-Ton-Wish, Satan in Paris,* and *The French Spy.*

Emma Waller scored a triumph in a medieval epic titled *Geraldine, or Love's Victory,* playing a hunchback bride. The Walnut was said to be crowded from pit to dome for this production, a poetic tragedy by Sidney Cowell Bateman—mother of the Bateman sisters—that was proclaimed "the most perfect dramatic success of modern times."[19] The play was set in medieval times, and a local newspaper announced that the costumes had been carefully reproduced from period engravings. The production ran for three weeks, beginning in late October.

Mr. and Mrs. Barney Williams returned on November 28 for a four-week run of their Irish plays. Their performance for December 20 was canceled for a large testimonial benefit held for E. A. Marshall at the Academy of Music. The entire company of the Walnut performed. J. B. Roberts brought *Faust and Marguerite* back to the Walnut on December 26. Matilda Heron arrived on January 9, 1860, playing in *Camille*, *Medea*, and a new play called *Lesbia*. Other stars playing the Walnut that season were James E. Murdoch, Frank Chanfrau, Jean M. Davenport, and James W. Wallack Jr.

During the summer, the Walnut once again housed a circus, as Nixon's Royal Equestrian Troupe occupied the house for two weeks in June. The featured performer was Mlle. Ella Zoyara, a female impersonator considered one of the premiere equestrians of the day. James Robinson, billed as "the Star Rider of the Age," was also with the company, as were the six acrobatic Hanlon Brothers. Thomas Hanlon executed a leap from a swinging trapeze, flying some twenty or thirty feet before catching hold of a rope. It was an early version of the flying trapeze. Joe Pentland clowned, and there were stilt dancing by Herr Charlton and contortions by M. Duverna. It was a powerful group of circus performers.

A NEW DECADE

The Walnut was entering its sixth decade. In 1860 it was already the oldest theatre operating in the United States. Women had made extraordinary advances in the decade leading up to the Civil War. At the beginning of the 1850s there were only two touring female stars of any great renown—Charlotte Cushman and Anna Cora Mowatt. By the end of the decade, there were as many actresses starring at the Walnut as there were actors. Women like Sidney Cowell Bateman and Madame de Marguerittes were succeeding as playwrights. Most significantly, women were taking on the managerial and financial responsibilities of running the theatre. Though they met with resistance on the part of their male counterparts, women like Mrs. Bowers and Mrs. Garrettson proved that women were as capable as men of running a theatre.

Each of these women had limitations as a manager, however. Mrs. Bowers failed to pay close attention to the financial picture, and Mrs. Garrettson lacked the artistic vision to turn the Walnut into a prestigious theatre. They paved the way for another woman—Mrs. John Drew—who would be offered the management of the Arch Street Theatre in 1861 and would operate the theatre for the next thirty years.

Louisa Lane Drew combined the artistic vision of Mrs. Bowers and the business savvy of Mrs. Garrettson. To this she added other extraordinary talents of her own. She had a natural air of authority, and she was one of the best stage directors around. She filled her company with some of the best actors available, rather than choose supporting players who would make her shine. She had exacting standards, and she expected her company to meet them. She instituted regular acting classes, and a number of stars blossomed under her tutelage, including Ada Rehan, Fanny Davenport, and Clara Morris. Her own family benefited from her training and would become one of the most renowned acting families in America.

But even as Mrs. Drew was taking control of the Arch Street Theatre, America was entering the most wrenching period in its history. The Republicans nominated Abraham Lincoln for president, and the southern states threatened to secede if he was elected. On the eve of the America's Civil War, women were in charge of the two principal Philadelphia theatres.

THE CIVIL WAR YEARS, 1860–1867

In the fall of 1860, Philadelphia was preoccupied with the election that pitted Abraham Lincoln against Stephen A. Douglas and a southern candidate, John C. Breckenridge. Philadelphians were decidedly ambivalent on the issue of slavery. Nevertheless, they gave Lincoln 52 percent of the vote. On December 20, 1860, South Carolina seceded from the Union and was followed, in early January, by Mississippi, Alabama, Florida, and Georgia. Other southern states followed in February.

The Walnut opened for the fall season on August 27. The American Opera Troupe performed *The Daughter of the Regiment* and remained through September 8, performing *The Bohemian Girl*, *Fra Diavolo*, and other popular operas. The fall season featured such familiar stars as James W. Wallack Jr., Caroline and Peter Richings, and Mr. and Mrs. Barney Williams, with several new faces, including Annette Ince and Isabelle Freeman.

Military dramas had always been popular with audiences at the Walnut, but in the winter of 1860–61 they had special resonance. On January 7, 1861, a company of French Zouaves—brilliantly uniformed French infantrymen—occupied the Walnut. The all-male troupe had been organized during the Crimean War and specialized in farces, with the men playing both male and female roles. Their most popular feature was an afterpiece titled *Ambuscade in Inkerman*, which depicted an episode in which Russian forces attacked the city during one of their performances. The actors were forced to fight in their costumes—one member of the company was killed in female garb.

James E. Murdoch played in a *Grand Patriotic Combination*, featuring songs and recitations by the company, at the Walnut in February. Caroline Richings sang "Save the Union," and Murdoch recited an "Ode to the American Flag." During the war, Murdoch took a leave of absence from the stage in order to entertain Union troops at camps and hospitals with recitations of inspirational poetry.

Philadelphians were split on how to respond to the secession of the South. Some felt that the Declaration of Independence granted the southern states the right to secede. While most people were eager to hold the Union together, the public was not prepared to go to war. The prevailing attitude was that the North should acquiesce to southern demands. That attitude changed after April 12, when Confederate artillery in Charleston, South Carolina, fired on Fort Sumter. Philadelphia responded to President Lincoln's call for volunteers by enlisting forty thousand men in uniform in the first year of hostilities. Recruiting tents sprouted around the city and volunteers drilled in every public square, while local women sewed uniforms and set up refreshment saloons. At the Walnut, Anna Cowell sang a northern version of "Dixie" each night, with new lyrics for each performance, based on war news that came in by telegraph.[1] The 1860–61 season closed with an original military spectacle titled *The Patriot's Dream, or The Past, the Present, and the Future*. It depicted, in a series of tableaux, the firing on Fort Sumter, a march through Baltimore, and an imagined outcome to the hostilities with the punishment of the traitors.

Few people envisioned that the war would last more than a few weeks or months. Volunteers enlisted for only ninety days. Any illusion that the war would be quickly concluded came to an end when news came in late July that Union forces had been routed at the Battle of Bull Run. The Civil War was going to be more protracted and more costly than anyone had anticipated. Lincoln increased the enlistment period to three years and sent out a call for three hundred thousand new soldiers.

JOHN SLEEPER CLARKE

The Walnut remained closed for most of the summer, except for brief stands by a pair of local companies. Heading up one of these companies was a man who would have a long and profitable association with the Walnut, a twenty-eight-year-old actor named John Sleeper Clarke. Clarke was already a familiar figure to Philadelphia audiences when he made his first appearance at the Walnut. He had been a member of the Arch Street Theatre company since 1855, where he was the leading comedian. In 1858 he went into the management end of the theatre in partnership with William Wheatley. The two men had recently given up the Arch to Mrs. John Drew.

Clarke was married to Asia Booth, the daughter of Junius Brutus Booth. He had grown up near the Booth family in Baltimore and was a boyhood friend of Asia's brother, Edwin; the two made their stage debuts together. While Edwin Booth's forte was tragedy, Clarke found his niche in comedy. A small man, he was gifted with "a richly unctuous voice" and remarkably comic gestures. Unlike many comedians, he was not identified with a single comic character but played a wide variety of comic roles. Two of his most celebrated parts were that of Major Wellington de Boots in *Everybody's Friend* and the title role in *The Toodles*, a role originally created by William E. Burton. "His DeBoots is one of the most delightful characterizations of a good humored poltroon whose soldierly swagger is at odds with his bantam like person, feeble voice and satisfied pomp of manner," one critic wrote. "His Toodles is a masterly representation of a drunken countryman who tries to maintain his self respect under the most discouraging and ridiculous surroundings."[2] Clarke played both characters when he returned for a three-week run in November 1861, alternating them with Asa Trenchard in *Our American Cousin* and Salem Scudder in Boucicault's *The Octoroon*.

WAR STARS

The fall season was not a good one for the theatre. Although there was very little fighting during the fall and winter of 1861–62, the uncertainty of war depressed every area of entertainment. Few British stars were willing to cross the Atlantic given the obvious dangers. A number of leading American actors left the country. Dion Boucicault had returned to London in 1860 and would remain there for the next twelve years. Edwin Booth, newly married, had taken his wife to London the same year. Joseph Jefferson, mourning the death of his wife, departed for the West Coast, and in September 1861 set off for Australia. He would remain abroad until the end of the war. Mrs. Bowers was another of the actors who sought their fortune overseas.

The absence of leading stars created opportunities for lesser-known talent. A number of "war stars" emerged who were able to tour only as long as the hostilities continued. Typical of these stars was C. W. Couldock, a character actor who had appeared in supporting roles for both Charlotte Cushman and Mme. Céleste. Couldock opened the fall season, bringing in two of his signature pieces, *The Willow Copse* and *The Chimney Corner*, and presented another, *Jocrisse, the Juggler*, for the first time in America. Generally, Mrs. Garrettson relied on stars who had served her well before. She had the pick of the available talent, for her only serious competition was Louisa Lane Drew's company at the Arch Street Theatre, and Mrs. Drew was operating the Arch without stars, relying on her stock company. Caroline Richings returned to the Walnut in a new vehicle, *A Quiet Family*, then premiered two new plays, a comedy titled *Black Sheep* and a drama, *The Broken Sword*. Matilda Heron brought in a new production, *The Belle of the Season*, a play that mixed comedy, farce, and sensational melodrama. In December, J. B. Roberts brought back *Faust and Marguerite*. Mr. and Mrs. Barney Williams returned in early January with their repertoire of Irish comedies, playing for five weeks and presenting a new one, *The Lakes of Killarney*, that would remain in their repertoire for many years.

In March the Walnut was once again the site of circus exhibitions, when it was rented out to an equestrian company led by Dan Rice. Rice was now being billed as "the greatest living humorist." His troupe of equestrians included Madame Rournaire and her wonderful horse, Excelsior Jr., Ella Zoyara, and James Melville, "the greatest living bareback rider."

The shortage of major British and American stars opened up opportunities at all levels of the entertainment industry, and a number of local actors sought to improve their position. One of those making a successful transition from stock actor to touring star was Edwin Adams, who had been a member of the Walnut's stock company the previous year. He arrived at the end of the year in *The Dead Heart* and returned in February 1862 in repertory. During his final week he played Prince Hal opposite J. H. Hackett's Falstaff in *Henry IV.* Charlotte Thompson made her first appearance at the Walnut on April 7 and remained through the month. She had been playing juvenile roles at the Arch but was making the transition from stock actress to touring star, displaying her talent in emotional roles like Camille.

Even those who were not ready to take on starring roles took the opportunity to move to more prestigious companies. The Walnut's stock company suffered losses. William Dickey Coder reported that "towards the close of the season, the ranks of the stock company were badly depleted, to the detriment of capable production of plays: Mr. Shewell left for Niblo's Garden, together with Emma Taylor and Mary Wells, Edwin Adams left for New York; Alice Grey went to Canada; and Cornelia Jefferson had been kept away much of the season by illness."[3]

The war did not affect Philadelphia in any substantial way until the spring of 1862. Following the debacle at Bull Run, Lincoln placed the Union forces under the command of George B. McClellan, a popular and charismatic general. McClellan spent the fall and winter training and outfitting his troops, and did not engage the Confederates until the spring. Attempting to take the Confederate capitol at Richmond, the Union suffered a string of defeats at the hands of Robert E. Lee, culminating in a major defeat at the Second Bull Run on August 28–29, 1862. The greatest fear was that England would recognize the Confederacy and possibly come in on their side. British mills depended on southern cotton, and a blockade of southern ports was hurting the British economy. Lincoln felt that he needed a moral issue that would galvanize international support against the South, and he began thinking seriously about freeing the slaves.

The opportunity came in September 1862, as the theatrical season was getting under way. General Lee, following up on his earlier victories, took the war to northern soil, crossing the Potomac into Maryland. His advance would take him to Philadelphia, and there were public meetings to determine what could be done to defend the city should the Confederates prevail. But Union soldiers discovered Lee's battle plans and intercepted him at Antietam. It was the bloodiest single day in the war—the Union lost thirteen thousand men and the Confederates lost ten thousand—but McClellan forced Lee back across the Potomac.[4] The victory changed the tenor of the war. Philadelphia had its first real taste of the ugliness of battle as the first flood of wounded soldiers was brought to area hospitals.

THE 1862–1863 THEATRICAL SEASON

Despite the grim news from the battlefield, the 1862–63 theatrical season was a profitable one for Philadelphia theatres. While the war depressed attendance in much of the country, cities like New York and Philadelphia experienced an upsurge. Philadelphia served as a transfer point for troops being shipped off to battle, while wounded troops were treated in Philadelphia hospitals. Men in uniform filled the city and, incidentally, the theatres.

Although business was good, the quality of the productions at the Walnut declined. Mrs. Drew was bringing in touring stars to support her stock company at the Arch and drew most of the leading stars away from the Walnut, including Maggie Mitchell, Kate Bateman, Caroline and Peter Richings, Edwin Adams, and Mrs. D. P. Bowers. John Wilkes Booth played a starring engagement at the Arch Street Theatre as well. A former member of the Arch's company, he never appeared at the Walnut.

Mrs. Garrettson was able to get some stars that year—Mr. and Mrs. E. L. Davenport opened the season, and Laura Keene came at the end of the year. But most were relative unknowns who the previous year had been stock actors with various companies—Edward Eddy, Charlotte Thompson, Dan Setchell, Kate Denin, and others. The Walnut was in a rather sad state. The *Spirit of the Times* noted that the auditorium was not being properly cared for. Peanut shells were not being swept up between performances, there was tobacco juice on the floor, and the behavior of the audience in the upper galleries prompted comment. "We are sorry to see that no steps have been taken to make the nuisances of the Third Tier less disagreeable to the audience," the paper editorialized. "The matter is becoming so notorious that ladies cannot, with propriety attend, and we wonder that the fair Lessee can sit in her box, night after night, knowing that these shameless scenes are enacted in the theater, without some effort to remove them."[5]

Newspapers took note of the continuing decline of the Walnut's company. "The character of the Walnut continued on 'the down grade,'" wrote theatre historian William Dickey Coder. "There had been few serious attempts to replace the desertions which had taken place during the latter part of the previous season, and, in addition, throughout the present season, the company continued to dwindle both in size and quality. The rumblings of the critics concerning the 'Miserable character of the stock company,' 'the shabby manner in which new plays are produced,' and 'the meagre manner in which the house is lighted,' kept increasing in volume throughout the season."[6]

NEW ENTERTAINMENT VENUES

Competition was heating up. New entertainment venues were springing up around the city that catered to the audience of unattached young soldiers. The backroom "free and easies" had evolved into concert saloons, where a largely male clientele could drink and enjoy shows featuring Irish and blackface comics, singing and dancing specialties, and scantily clad chorines performing military drills onstage. The principal attractions of these establishments were the "pretty waiter girls" who served drinks and drank with the customers. Among the variety halls was Burton's old National Theatre, just down the block from the Walnut, now operating as the Continental Theatre and Music Hall.

The minstrel show was also popular. Though it was associated with southern culture, blackface minstrelsy was very much a northern phenomenon. Two Philadelphia companies were devoted to minstrelsy during the war years. Sam Sanford played at the Eleventh Street Opera House, which was later taken over by another minstrel troupe, Carncross and Dixey Minstrels. During the summer the Walnut was often rented out to traveling minstrel troupes. In 1861 Hooley and Campbell's Minstrels appeared; Campbell's Minstrels came in during the summer of 1863, and Sanford's Opera and Minstrel Company appeared in 1864.

Business was good enough for speculators to envision a third premier house in Philadelphia. The New Chestnut Street Theatre was hurriedly built on Chestnut Street between Twelfth and Thirteenth. William Wheatley returned to Philadelphia as the new lessee, and he booked Edwin Forrest for an opening engagement on January 26, 1863. Forrest remained at the theatre for an exceptionally long run, closing on April 17. This may have contributed to the failure of the new venture. Forrest was not the draw Wheatley had hoped for, and, as usual, Forrest kept half of the receipts for himself, and this eventually forced Wheatley out of business.

The spring season at the Walnut improved. Laura Keene brought her entire company to the Walnut on December 29, 1862. This was one of the first touring "combinations," in which the entire company traveled, rather than just the star. Other familiar stars followed. Mr. and Mrs. Barney Williams returned for two weeks in January. J. B. Roberts and Dan Setchell followed. Isabel Cubas made her Walnut debut on February 9. Señorita Cubas was primarily a dancer, but she was now touring in *The French Spy,* a play originally written for Madame Celeste. Edward Eddy returned for a four-week run. He debuted a new Boucicault play, *The Colleen Bawn,* the first in a series of romantic Irish plays that the popular playwright was churning out. John Sleeper Clarke followed, and Charlotte Thompson was back in April. Laura Keene returned with her company on May 11. She had closed her New York theatre two days before. She would now devote herself exclusively to touring. The season concluded on May 29 after a week of benefit performances for members of the company.

THE SUMMER OF 1863

As summer approached, Robert E. Lee determined to take the fighting north. In June 1863 Confederate troops crossed into Pennsylvania, and Philadelphians braced themselves for an attack on the city. The mayor issued a proclamation for the citizenry to prepare to defend the city. On July 1, Union forces under General George Meade met Lee's at Gettysburg, and during the three days that the battle raged, fear and speculation swirled through Philadelphia. On July 5, word came of Meade's decisive victory over Lee's army. Wounded troops poured into the city, quickly overwhelming local hospitals. On the seventh, reports arrived of General Grant's victory at Vicksburg. The victory gave the North control of the Mississippi River, effectively cutting the Confederacy in half. There was rejoicing in the streets. The entire city recognized this as a turning point in the war and once again anticipated a quick end to the bloodshed.

The Walnut was closed for most of the summer, undergoing a renovation designed to increase the seating capacity. Private boxes were eliminated, and the first and second tiers were brought forward about ten feet, adding some two hundred seats. The auditorium was repainted in white and gold and the seats covered in crimson damask. "The heavy, dull proscenium arch had been superseded by a light and graceful one. In the center was a carved figure of an

American eagle, and elaborately carved knobs jutted down from either end in a striking effect," wrote Coder.[7] The improvements were undoubtedly made with an eye toward selling the property, for on October 5, 1863, the Walnut was sold to Edwin Booth and John Sleeper Clarke. The purchase price was $100,000.

EDWIN BOOTH AND JOHN SLEEPER CLARKE

Edwin Booth was reaching the pinnacle of a career that is one of the most celebrated in the history of the American theatre. He had, by 1863, stepped out of the shadow of his famous father. He had developed an acting style that was naturalistic and refined; he disappeared into the characters. By managing his own theatres, he could now control all aspects of the production. It was John Sleeper Clarke who persuaded Booth to take the leap into theatrical management. Edwin Booth had lost his wife of two and a half years, Mary Devlin Booth, and was devastated by her passing. He spent much of the summer at the Clarkes' home in Philadelphia. Booth seriously considered giving up the theatre, but Clarke persuaded him that the responsibilities of management would help take his mind off his grief. They would use the Walnut as their base of operations. With both appearing there for lengthy runs, it could be quite profitable. Although Clarke is much less renowned a figure than Booth, he was certainly as big a draw in Philadelphia at the time.

Booth and Clarke made few changes at the Walnut. Mrs. Garrettson continued to operate the theatre, continuing the star policy of previous years. The venture would prove to be profitable both financially and creatively. They were able to pay back the entire mortgage in three years. It also pushed Edwin Booth into his most creative period. The following year the two men took over the lease of the Winter Garden Theatre in New York, one of the most fashionable theatres in the city. There, Booth would begin to stage impressive productions of classic plays.

POPULAR MELODRAMAS

The 1863 season introduced several new melodramas that became classics. A twenty-year-old actress, Lucille Western, made her first appearance at the Walnut in a new play, *East Lynne*, that became synonymous with melodrama. This play, adapted from a best-selling novel by Mrs. Henry Wood, was written especially for its star by Clifton Tayleure. Western played a well-born woman who deserts her family. Betrayed by the man she runs off with, and ill, she returns years later to take a job as governess of her own children. Her true identity is revealed and she begs forgiveness from her husband, but she is too ill to go on, and dies. Although *East Lynne* was dismissed by critics, it proved popular with touring companies; the play remained in Miss Western's repertoire for her entire career.

On October 19 Matilda Heron brought in a new play, *Aspasia,* which had to be withdrawn after local critics denounced it as indecent. Edward Eddy premiered another controversial play, *The Police Spy,* a thriller about government spying on its citizens that presented itself as "a truthful picture of our own government."[8] On November 9 a troupe of Arab acrobats arrived to support a minor star, Mary Provost. The troupe, which included Affid Ben Condour, the man of flexibility; Mahomet, emperor of vaulters; Ali Benside, Goliath of strength; and Bim Bomie, king of tumblers, was billed as the only genuine Arabs ever to appear in the United States.

John Sleeper Clarke, taking advantage of his new ownership position, was booked for a nine-week engagement, beginning November 23. He brought out a new play, *The Ticket-of-Leave Man,* a melodrama by Tom Taylor, the author of *Our American Cousin.* Clarke played a trusting prison parolee who is made a fall guy for a gang of counterfeiters. The play was having a lengthy run in New York, with W. J. Florence in the lead, and it became a favorite with nineteenth-century audiences. In early January 1864 both the Walnut and the Arch were presenting it.

The remainder of the season was mostly characterized by returning veterans. Lucille Western brought back *East Lynne* for a three-week run, beginning on January 25, and remained two more weeks, presenting a repertory that included *Lucretia Borgia, Oliver Twist, The French Spy,* and others. She was followed by Ettie Henderson, Edwin Adams, Laura Keene and her company, the Davenport-Wallack Combination, and W. J. Florence, who performed his version of *The Ticket-of-Leave Man.* Lucille Western returned one more time to finish out the season. There was a brief summer season, beginning on June 13, with Harry Pearson also performing *The Ticket-of-Leave Man,* J. B. Roberts returning in *Faust and Marguerite,* and a minstrel troupe, S. S. Sanford Minstrels, playing for two weeks in late July and early August.

THE DEEPENING WAR

In the spring of 1864 the war entered its bloodiest phase. In March, Ulysses S. Grant was put in command of all Union forces. Unlike Lincoln's previous commanders, Grant was not afraid to confront the South's greatest general. That spring, Grant launched an offensive to try to capture Richmond. Lee engaged him at the Battle of the Wilderness, at Spotsylvania, and at Cold Harbor. The battles were bloody and indecisive, but Grant forced Lee to dig his forces in, immobilizing his army. It was the kind of battle that the North, with its greater strength and supplies, could win. Simultaneously, William Tecumseh Sherman drove across Georgia from the west, laying siege to Atlanta.

Locally, the big event was the Great Central Fair, which opened on June 8, 1864. The fair was a fund-raiser for the Sanitary Commission, a volunteer group that provided services for wounded soldiers. Modeled on the Great Exhibition of London of 1851, it displayed local manufacturing and art and curiosities from around the world. Nearly thirty thousand people attended each day, among them the president and his wife, and raised more than $1 million.

Abraham Lincoln was nominated for a second term in June; in August the Democrats nominated his former commander, George B. McClellan. The election was essentially a referendum on the war—on whether the hostilities should be ended immediately or prosecuted to victory. Democrats claimed that the war was a failure, and this line resonated with many voters who were tired of the bloodshed. During the summer, both Grant and Sherman seemed to be mired in hopeless sieges in Richmond and Atlanta, respectively. In early September, however, Sherman captured Atlanta. The victory had enormous political significance to northerners, who saw the possibility of victory and reelected Lincoln by a large margin.

THE 1864–1865 SEASON

The Walnut opened the 1864–65 season on August 20 with a new production of *The Naiad Queen*, which ran for two weeks. Mrs. Garrettson continued as manager of the Walnut. There was turnover in the stock company. One of those brought in was nineteen-year-old James A. Herne, who would later gain renown as an actor and playwright. Edwin Booth arrived on September 5. It had been eight years since he had last appeared at the Walnut and he opened in *Hamlet*, his signature role. With his dark, brooding looks and slight build, he was destined to play the melancholy Dane. He had grown immeasurably as an actor. He still exhibited the great outbursts of emotion that had characterized his father's acting, but he had developed a more naturalistic style, acting as much with his body as with his voice. He was being hailed as the finest Hamlet America had ever produced. The critic William Winter wrote, "Surely the stage, at least in our time, has never offered a more impressive and effective combination than Mr. Booth's Hamlet of princely dignity, intellectual stateliness, glowing imagination, fine sensitiveness to all that is most sacred in human life, and all that is most thrilling and sublime."[9]

fig. 11 Sometimes called "the Hamlet of the nineteenth century," Edwin Booth went on to become one of America's greatest and most influential stage actors. He is shown here in his signature role as the prince of Denmark.

Booth remained at the Walnut for four weeks, alternating *Hamlet* with other tragic roles in *The Merchant of Venice, Richelieu, Richard III,* and *Don Caesar de Bazan.* On September 19 Booth revived *Ruy Blas,* Victor Hugo's romantic verse drama of a commoner who, disguised as a nobleman, gets involved in court intrigue. Booth's energies were now going into the Winter Garden Theatre, where he began to prepare lavish productions of classic plays. That winter, he would produce and star in a legendary production of *Hamlet* that ran for one hundred nights—by far the longest run of any Shakespeare play in the country to date.

Except for Booth's appearance, the fall season was unremarkable. Charlotte Thompson played for most of October. McKean Buchanan arrived on October 31 in a new play, *Waiting for the Verdict.* Lucille Western played a lengthy run, arriving in mid-November and staying through the first week of January. The Wallack-Davenport Combination arrived shortly after the first of the year. Appearing with James W. Wallack and E. L. Davenport was Rose Eytinge. Frank Drew arrived on January 30, 1865, and played for most of February. John Sleeper Clarke returned on February 27 with *Streets of Philadelphia,* an adaptation of Dion Boucicault's *Streets of New York.*

The war was rapidly coming to a conclusion. In mid-November Sherman set out on his legendary march to the sea. By early February he was moving north through the Carolinas, while Grant was making headway in his assault on Richmond. On April 3 word came that Union forces had captured the city. Flags were displayed all over Philadelphia, the statehouse bell was rung, and demonstrations were held at Independence Hall. On April 9 Lee's surrender at Appomattox was announced. Bonfires were kindled, cannons were shot off, and the festivities lasted into the following day. At the Walnut, Mlle. Felicita Vestvali was appearing in a new tragedy, *Gamea, the Hebrew Fortune Teller.* The next week, she brought out *Hearts Are Trumps.* Mlle. Vestvali's run was cut short after the news arrived, on the morning of April 15, that President Lincoln had been shot at Ford's Theatre in Washington. He had been sitting with his wife in one of the stage boxes, watching a benefit performance of *Our American Cousin* for its star, Laura Keene. The assassin leaped from the presidential box onto the stage and made his escape through the wings. As he did so, he brushed past Keene, who was waiting for her entrance. She was able to identify him as a member of the theatrical profession—John Wilkes Booth.

THE ASSASSINATION AND ITS AFTERMATH

The assassination provoked strong public reaction against the theatrical profession and the Booth family. Much of it was directed at John Sleeper Clarke and his wife, Asia. John Wilkes Booth was especially close to his sister and had been a frequent visitor to the Clarkes' home. There were rumors that Booth had made it a headquarters for his plotting. Asia Booth recalled later, "It was like the days of the Bastille in France. Arrests were made suddenly and in dead of night. No reason or warning given, only let anyone breathe a doubt of the most innocent person and arrest followed swift, and that incarceration meant to wait the law's leisure, innocent or guilty."[10]

The Walnut closed the day following the assassination and remained dark through the following week. Members of the theatrical profession gathered

fig. 12 This 1865 image is the earliest known photograph of the Walnut.

at the Continental Hotel on the afternoon of April 21 to "devise means to express in a suitable manner their deep and heartfelt sorrow."[11] They drafted resolutions expressing their regret that a member of their profession had been responsible and announced that they would gather as a body when the remains of the late president were brought to Philadelphia.

A crowd of some thirty thousand greeted the funeral train when it arrived on Saturday, April 22. The president's body was carried to Independence Hall, where it lay in state in the room where the Declaration of Independence had been signed. Lines stretched for blocks, and some eighty-five thousand people passed through the hall.[12] Early on Monday morning, the body was taken to the train depot to continue its journey to Springfield, Illinois.

The Clarkes' home in Philadelphia became the gathering place for members of the Booth clan. The elder Mrs. Booth arrived on Saturday, April 15. Junius Brutus Booth Jr. arrived the following Wednesday. Supposing that he might be needed to testify, Clarke took the younger Booth to the marshal's office, where he was arrested and jailed. Shortly thereafter, Clarke himself was taken into custody and quietly taken to Washington, where he was confined in the Old Capitol Prison, where the known conspirators were kept. Clarke

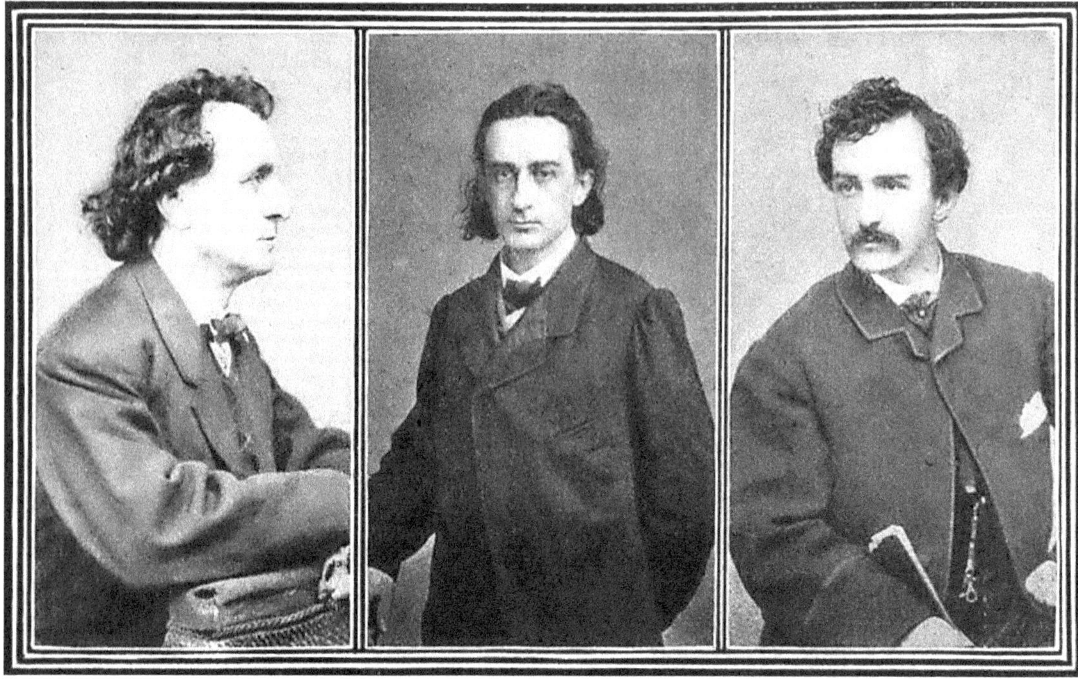

fig. 13 From left, the three sons of Junius Brutus Booth: Junius Brutus Jr., Edwin, and John Wilkes.

remained in jail until the end of May, when he was released for lack of any evidence connecting him to the conspiracy. John T. Ford, owner of Ford's Theatre, was in one of the nearby cells. Only Edwin Booth, supported by influential friends, remained free. He announced his retirement from the stage. Clarke was incensed that his brother-in-law was allowed to remain free while he himself was jailed. "The dishonor of the Booths in which he had become embroiled so infuriated him that he was ready to divorce himself from the entire family," reported historian Stanley Kimmel.[13]

CLARKE TAKES OVER THE WALNUT

John Sleeper Clarke had supported himself primarily by touring, letting Mrs. Garrettson handle the day-to-day running of the Walnut. The assassination severely undermined his ability to draw audiences, so in the fall Clarke took over the operations of the theatre, replacing Mrs. Garrettson. He brought in Thomas J. Hemphill as business manager and treasurer and W. S. Fredericks as the acting and stage manager. Clarke replaced the entire stock company, with the sole exception of James A. Herne. Among the new players was a handsome and dynamic young actor named John McCullough, a protégé of Edwin Forrest who carried on the tradition of robust acting.

Clarke himself opened the 1865–66 season with a two-week run. Mrs. D. P. Bowers followed, making her first appearance at the Walnut since she had lost control of the theatre in 1859. Since leaving the Walnut, Mrs. Bowers had built a successful career as a touring star. In all that time, however, she had never appeared at the Walnut. Now that Mrs. Garrettson was gone, Mrs. Bowers returned. She appeared in *Lady Audley's Secret*, a piece that was nearly as popular as *East Lynne* as a vehicle for romantic melodrama. Mrs. Bowers played a governess married to a nobleman who tries to hide her past, including a husband she never divorced. When her first husband unexpectedly appears, she murders him and sets fire to the house to cover up this crime. Confronted with her crimes, she feigns madness and poisons herself. It was a perfect vehicle for the highly emotional acting style popular at the time.

Other stars followed. John Brougham appeared for his first extended run at the Walnut, playing from November 12 through December 23. The Irish-born actor was known for his comic characters and was a prolific playwright as well. Brougham had made short appearances in Philadelphia, but this was his first extended run at the Walnut, and he played many of his most famous roles—*Po-Ca-Hon-Tas* and *Dombey and Son*. He played *O'Donnell's Mission* for the first time on any stage. Another comic great, Mrs. John Wood, made her debut after the first of the year. Mrs. Wood was operating the Olympic Theatre in New York and was considered the best burlesque actress of the day. Burlesque had not yet acquired the association it has today with erotic entertainment. John Sleeper Clarke played a second run in late January 1866 and remained until March 10. He was followed by Mr. and Mrs. Charles Kean, who were giving their farewell tour of America.

Edwin Booth arrived on April 23, 1866. It was his first appearance in Philadelphia since the assassination. Although he had announced his retirement from the stage, family finances and public pressure persuaded him to return. Booth mounted a spectacular production of *Hamlet*, which he debuted at the Winter Garden in New York shortly after the first of the year. Booth played for fifty-one consecutive nights, including twenty-one nights as Hamlet.

The Walnut remained open through the entire summer of 1866, with another spectacular revival of the *Naiad Queen* and a two-week run by Junius Brutus Booth Jr., Edwin's older brother, who appeared in *The Three Guardsmen*, based on Dumas's novel *The Three Musketeers*. The Buislay troupe—a family of aerialists, dancers, and pantomime artists in the mold of the Ravels—finished up the summer season.

THE 1866–1867 SEASON

John Sleeper Clarke continued to manage the Walnut and to improve the caliber of its stock company. Among those added to the company were J. B. Roberts, who came on as stage manager, and Mr. and Mrs. Charles M. Walcot, who headed up the acting company. These veterans would remain at the Walnut for many years, guiding the theatre through the next phase of its existence.

The 1866–67 season saw many returning stars. John Brougham opened on September 24 and remained for two weeks. He was followed by James H. Hackett, who was still touring at age sixty-six. Hackett played a week as Falstaff and Rip van Winkle. Edwin Booth arrived at the Walnut on October 15 for a six-week run, and John Sleeper Clarke returned for the month of December. During the Christmas season *The Naiad Queen* was once again revived. The piece was punctuated by operatic selections by Strauss, Donizetti, and others. It played for two weeks

John Sleeper Clarke and Edwin Booth had different ideas about theatre management. Booth was interested in putting together lavish productions of classic plays, and was not particularly concerned about making money. He could recoup whatever losses he sustained by touring. Clarke, always a more practical man, was concerned with the bottom line. That winter, he decided to withdraw from the New York venture and focus his efforts on the Walnut. Booth paid him $10,000 for his share of the Winter Garden; they remained partners in the Walnut. Clarke was fortunate, for in the spring of 1867 the Winter Garden was destroyed by fire, and with it Booth's wardrobe, scenery, costumes, and properties. The loss was estimated at $40,000. Booth was undaunted and announced that he would build his own theatre, which would "be devoted to plays and actors of the best kind."[14] It would take him two years to raise the money and build the theatre that bore his name.

TOURING COMBINATIONS

Clarke and Booth now went their separate ways. Booth went on tour to raise the funds for his new theatre. The assassination of Abraham Lincoln had done nothing to hurt his reputation. His response to the tragedy had been exemplary and ultimately enhanced his standing. Things were not so good for other members of the Booth family.

The association with John Wilkes Booth continued to haunt John Sleeper Clarke. In 1867 Clarke, possibly urged on by his wife, Asia, decided to relocate to England. England offered a more hospitable environment in which to raise their children—far away from the stigma of the assassination. That fall,

Clarke sailed for England. He was quickly accepted by London audiences, and in the spring, Asia and their five surviving children followed him. The Clarkes made their home in England after that. John Sleeper Clarke returned to America from time to time to look after his business interests. Asia never returned.

Clarke focused most of his managerial and acting activities in London, where he operated several theatres over the years. He had left a strong team behind at the Walnut that could guide the operations. He was able to function as an absentee manager because, once again, the theatre industry was changing. The era of the stock company that supported touring stars was coming to an end. Railroads made it possible to send an entire company on tour, along with the necessary scenery and props. Theatre managers in Philadelphia and other regional centers were increasingly functioning as landlords, renting the theatre out to a series of shows for one- or two-week runs. The old stock system would not disappear immediately, but the theatre industry was going through another transition.

THE LAST YEARS OF STOCK, 1867–1879

Augustus Pitou was nineteen when he joined the company at the Walnut in the fall of 1867. Pitou would later become a successful producer and playwright and was known as the "king of the one-night stands." In his memoir, *Masters of the Show,* Pitou provides a rare view of backstage life at the Walnut. Shortly before showtime, a call-boy went around to the dressing rooms announcing "half-hour," "quarter-hour," and "Overture! Everybody down to begin." The actors typically assembled in the green room, as they do today. "Its walls were usually adorned with old play-bills, portraits of actors and engravings of scenes from plays. In a prominent place was the call-board, on which casts for plays, calls for rehearsals, and communications from the manager were posted; and there was also a large mirror in which everybody took a last look before going on the stage," Pitou recalled.

According to Pitou's account, the Walnut's stage was raked. "The Walnut Street Theatre and a few others in the country had a considerable pitch in the stage from the back wall to the footlights, as had all theaters until about 1850."[1] Stages sloped down toward the audience, while the floor of the orchestra, or the pit, was level, and this enabled the audience in the back of the house to see the actors. Nowadays, the stage is normally level and the orchestra seating is inclined. The tradition of the raked stage survives in the stage directions of "upstage" and "downstage."

The company maintained the same "lines of business" that had prevailed since colonial times. Young actors like Pitou got their start as utility players, appearing in a variety of walk-on roles, delivering a few lines as a servant or messenger, or filling out the scene as supernumeraries. They advanced to "walking ladies" and "walking gentlemen," which offered larger, if somewhat less varied, roles. More talented actors would be advanced to a juvenile, or to the secondary rank of one of the other lines—a second low comedian or a second heavy. From there they progressed to one of the major supporting roles, the low comedian, the male or female heavy, the old lady or old man, or a leading actor.

Leading actors were expected to provide their own costumes, indicating that such roles incurred financial demands. "The leading members of the company of the Walnut Street Theatre had their own wardrobes; the others dressed their parts from the wardrobe of the theatre, consequently the old wardrobe woman and her daughter were constantly brushing and repairing the stock," Pitou pointed out. "The costuming of the plays was incongruous. Harmony of color was unknown and three or four characters might have been seen on the stage at one time, all dressed in the same colors. Frequently costumes of different epochs were used in the same play."[2]

The wardrobe mistress was identified as Mrs. Packer, while a Mr. Connellan was in charge of props.[3] "The property room was truly an 'old curiosity shop,'" Pitou remembered. "It contained every property that had been used in plays since the theater was built,—throne chairs, papier-maché gilded banquet set, Gothic furniture, and a thousand and one other things. All these properties were made by the property man, and were used season after season."[4]

A MIDSUMMER NIGHT'S DREAM

The acting company was headed up by J. B. Roberts, who held the title of stage manager but functioned as the Walnut's director and lead actor. Born in Delaware in 1818, Roberts made his acting debut in 1836 at the Walnut Street Theatre, playing Richmond to Junius Brutus Booth's Richard III. He had toured for some years as a star, finding his greatest success during the war years with *Faust and Marguerite*. When the Civil War ended and the major stars returned to touring, he decided to settle into a stock company.

The opening play of the 1867–68 season was an opportunity to introduce the new company and display the talents of the stage crew. The season opened with a particularly lavish production of *A Midsummer Night's Dream*. It featured scenery that Joseph Jefferson brought over from England, along with $35,000 worth of jewels and ornamental material that had been on exhibit at the recent Paris Exposition. The centerpiece of the production was a moving panorama by the English designer William Telbin, which depicted "hill and valley, woodland and meadow, rock and stream, rural road and classical temple," as it unrolled behind the lovers on their return from the forest. The Walnut's machinist and set designer were also inspired to do their best work.

At the close of act 3, Puck rose through the floor riding a glittering serpent that was twined around a globe of pearl. The production finished off with a triple transformation scene depicting the "Golden Vineyard of Aurora Fairy Land," which transformed into a valley of ferns and then into "the Temples of Arcadia, with groups of winged fairies upon rising pedestals."[5]

The Walnut had the services of one of the most celebrated scenic artists of the nineteenth century, Charles W. Witham. Witham made his reputation by creating the scenic effects for Edwin Booth at his theatre, and designed sets for Augustin Daly and Harrigan and Hart. Witham's work was known for its historical accuracy. His tasks at the Walnut were more mundane. Witham's "principal occupation was painting in and then painting out old scenery, of which there was a goodly stock in the scene-room," Augustus Pitou recalled.[6]

Old-timers like Edwin Forrest scoffed at these productions as "scene-painter's drama."[7] But improvements in set design were necessary owing to advances in stage lighting. The most important development was the adoption of the calcium light, or "limelight." Limelight was produced when a flame of oxygen and hydrogen heated a filament made of lime. The lime emitted an intense white light that could be used as a spotlight. Limelight had been invented in 1826 and was used experimentally in 1837, but it was only after the Civil War that it came into wide use. The calcium light made it possible to light an actor at any spot on the stage. Actors no longer had to play at the foot of the stage, where the footlights illuminated their faces. They could use the entire stage. They could engage in more subtle effects, letting "physicalization" communicate the inner life of a character rather than relying on broad posturing and rhetorical flourishes.

The man in charge of the lighting effects for the Walnut was John "Pop" Reed, an institution at the Walnut. He joined the Walnut in 1824 at the age of sixteen and remained with the theatre for the rest of his life. "He had gradually ascended the scale as lamplighter, gasman, captain of supernumeraries and general utility actor," theatre historian William Dickey Coder wrote. When they needed extras, "'Pop' Reed, who was a grandfather, furnished children of all ages from his own family when they were needed to take part in plays," wrote Pitou.[8] "During his long association with the Walnut he had become so attached to the theatre as to express a wish that, after his death, his skull should be placed in the property room to be used in *Hamlet*."[9]

REHEARSING THE SHOW

The company was busy during the early part of the fall. Monday was payday—the day when the "ghost walked," to use the parlance of the day. It was also the day when the actors rehearsed with the new star. Rehearsals were rather perfunctory affairs, as the members of the company were expected to know their lines and stage business. "One rehearsal usually sufficed to give a perfect performance as the actors had played the same parts with many stars," Pitou explained. "The dialogue had merely to be recovered, which was easily accomplished by the actors, as their capacity for memorizing was abnormally developed."[10]

This system functioned well only because the stock system relied on a heavy diet of revivals—in much the same way that opera is presented today. But there was a bigger emphasis on producing new works. Two important new works were debuted at the Walnut during the fall of 1867. J. B. Roberts took the starring role in *Caste*, an important new comedy by the English playwright T. W. (Tom) Robertson. The play depicted the marital difficulties of people of different social rank, and gave audiences an inside look at upper-crust British society. It was one of several unauthorized productions of the play, made possible by the lack of international copyright protection.

On October 28 the company brought out *The Grand Duchess of Gérolstein*, a comic opera by Jacques Offenbach that was having great success in Paris and New York. Mrs. William Gomersol played the title role of a duchess who falls in love with a common soldier and promotes him to general, hoping to win his affections. She and her husband had been hired a few years earlier to provide musical talent. Mr. Gomersol did the translation, probably the first English-language version. Critics complained that the translation was too literal and that "the introduction of American music was entirely out of place," but all gave high praise to Mrs. Gomersol's performance and proclaimed the production a success. Audiences were enchanted by the catchy melodies and energetic dance numbers, including the can-can, which was introduced in America with this show. Some considered the play, with its frivolity, satire, and bawdy sexuality, indecent, but sheet music from the operetta sold well, and waltzes and polkas were played everywhere.

SHAKESPEARE

Edwin Forrest returned on November 4, 1867, for a scheduled two-week run of his Shakespearean repertoire. Playbills announced that he would perform a different play each night, so the public could see all of his roles. It was Forrest's first appearance at the Walnut in more than a decade, and the theatre sold out every night. Forrest later boasted that his run was "the greatest ever known within the walls of the Walnut Street Theatre," and he was held over for a third week. But Forrest was in his sixties, and his physical decline was evident. He had a pronounced limp from a sciatic nerve that was partially paralyzed. Forrest had always depended on his muscular presence and vigorous acting style, and age severely undercut his presence. But his oratory was as majestic as it had ever been. He could fill the Walnut with his voice, even in the tenderest passages.

But Forrest's acting style had been developed for an earlier period. The broad movements, bold gestures, and strong facial expressions were necessary in the large, dimly lit theatres of the early nineteenth century. With improved theatre lighting, this style came to be seen as exaggerated. Like other stars of the antebellum period, Forrest was dismissed as old-fashioned.

If Forrest's acting style was considered passé, he still had a large following. A number of his admirers had commissioned the sculptor Thomas Ball to carve a full-scale marble statue of him. That fall, a statue of Forrest as Coriolanus was unveiled in Boston. Forrest was so impressed with the likeness that he purchased it from its subscribers and moved it into his home in Philadelphia. The statue remained in the house until 1984, when it was given to the Historical Society of the Walnut Street Theatre. The six-ton statue now stands in the lobby of the Walnut.[11]

Forrest was compared unfavorably with Edwin Booth, whose naturalistic style was more in keeping with current taste. On March 30, 1868, Booth opened a five-week run. He was trying to raise money for a new theatre in New York, which would bear his name. It was to be a state-of-the-art facility where he could mount productions that were historically accurate and technologically advanced. The cost of the theatre was mounting, and Booth went on tour to raise money for the project.

One of the great strengths of the stock system of training was that a young performer had the opportunity to play opposite the leading actors of the day. Just as Forrest had learned from Edmund Kean, young actors had a chance to study Forrest or Booth. Stars often ran their own rehearsals, so a young performer like Augustus Pitou received direction from some of the leading talents of the time. Supporting players had to adapt their style to a wide variety of acting styles. In addition to Forrest and Booth, Pitou played in support of John Brougham, in a sensational melodrama, *The Lottery of Life*, with Lucille Western in the domestic melodrama *East Lynne*, and with Mr. and Mrs. Barney Williams during a six-week run of their Irish plays.

Mr. and Mrs. Williams were among the most popular attractions at the Walnut. During their January run, they introduced a new play, *The Fairy Circle*, in which the character that Barney Williams played is supposed to have died. In one scene he is discovered in a wooded glen surrounded by fairies. The fairies explain that he is present in spirit and that only his body has been buried. Augustus Pitou played the body. Pitou sported a moustache at the

fig. 14 Mathew B. Brady, noted portrait and Civil War photographer, captured Edwin Forrest in some of his most notable roles in a photo shoot circa 1861. Clockwise from top left: King Lear, Brutus, Hamlet, and Richard III.

time, which he refused to shave off. "That night when the fairy queen waved her wand and summoned the dead body to appear I came up through the center trap stretched out on a green mossy bank," Pitou recalled. "The queen said: 'Behold your body!' Mr. Williams, loud enough for the entire audience to hear him, replied, 'Well, if that's my body, it has grown a very tidy moustache since they put it under the sod.'" By the next performance, the moustache was gone.

The spring brought James W. Wallack Jr. in repertory and Maggie Mitchell in *Fanchon the Cricket*. When no star was scheduled, the leading members of the company received benefits, which were typically held on Friday evenings and continued to be important sources of income. "In those days stars made very little money as compared with the stars of today," Pitou observed. "The minor stars often needed their benefit money in order to pay their hotel bills and go to the next city." Senior members of the company received one benefit per season, and this was important, for the income from the theatre was rarely enough to support a family. Many of the Walnut's actors had outside jobs, according to Pitou. "'Pop Bailey,' as he was called, who for many years played old men's parts at the Walnut Street Theatre, kept a thread and needle store on one of the side streets; the 'walking gentleman' of the company kept a drugstore in Baltimore, and J. B. Roberts, the stage manager, had a school of elocution."[12]

When the theatre closed for the summer, many of the actors had to continue to work. During the summer of 1868, Augustus Pitou went barnstorming. J. B. Roberts organized a troupe from the Walnut's stock company. In the smaller troupe, Pitou moved up to "walking gentleman's" roles. They played a week's engagement in Wilmington, Delaware, then worked their way through Pennsylvania, playing two or three nights in each town. Business was poor, and their salaries were cut. Their final destination was Reading, Pennsylvania, where they were to open a new theatre on July 4. When they got there, their baggage was impounded. Fortunately, advance ticket sales were enough to get their trunks released and pay for rent on the theatre, and the company had a successful run. They made enough money to take the company back to Philadelphia and give each cast member a few dollars.

LEG SHOWS

Touring was becoming a more important part of a typical actor's life. Railroads were expanding greatly in the postwar economic boom. The transcontinental railroad was under construction and would be completed in 1869. Most of the Northeast was already connected by rail. This made taking a show on the road considerably easier. Producers were able to transport an entire cast, along with necessary wardrobe and scenery, from one city to the next. This also created an incentive to invest more heavily in scenic effects, which could be used on the road. Local theatres could not compete with the level of spectacle offered by these "touring combinations," and the stock system began to decline.

The 1868–69 season commenced on August 3, 1868, with a touring production of *The Black Crook* put together by Philadelphia producer J. E. McDonough. Set in the Hartz Mountains of Germany, it featured a French ballet troupe who performed peasant dances, ballet, and an Amazonian march and drill. The original production of *The Black Crook*, which opened in New York in 1866, had created a rage for "leg shows," as audiences flocked to see the display of a hundred chorus girls in tights. McDonough's revival had all the spectacle of the original, including a dazzling transformation scene that revealed the "nymphs of the golden realm."

Burlesque followed, with M. W. Leffingwell doing parodies of *Cinderella* and the opera *Fra Diavolo*. Burlesque did not have the sexual connotations that it does today but was simply a form of parody. Burlesques of the time were written in rhymed couplets and relied heavily on punning humor, dancing, and musical parodies set to popular songs. Erotic content was about to become central, however, for Lydia Thompson and her British Blondes opened at Wood's Museum in New York in the fall of 1868. They presented *Ixion, or The Man at the Wheel*, a send-up of a Roman tragedy. The roles were all played by women, who were outfitted in togas. These, of course, revealed their legs, which brought in the crowds.

The success of the British Blondes prompted a host of imitators. One such burlesque company, the London Burlesque Combination, opened at the Walnut on March 29, 1869, with their version of *Ixion*. The production starred Jenny and Lizzy Willmore and featured Felix Rogers in the low comedy role. They extended their run with *Female Forty Thieves*—an "oriental extravaganza" by Henry J. Byron. The company remained to support J. H. Hackett as Falstaff in *Henry IV* and *Merry Wives of Windsor*. These three-act parodies had very little to do with the burlesque show as it eventually developed in America. But they helped to shift the meaning of burlesque from a comedy form to one featuring scantily clad women, an association that endures today.

THE COMPETITION

The Arch and the Walnut remained the two major theatres in Philadelphia. Mrs. Drew continued to operate the Arch Street Theatre with a repertoire of melodramas, novelties, and comedy classics. Her company had gained a considerable reputation for developing young talent. "What makes Louisa Lane Drew's management of the Arch Street Theatre notable is the evidence it provides of what we call directing," theatre historian Rosemary K. Bank observed. "Accounts indicated that Mrs. Drew was skilled at picturization and movement. . . . [She] attended to all aspects of production from cleanliness backstage to play selection and interpretation."[13]

The other major theatre, the New Chestnut, was having trouble. The theatre, which had been hastily built during the war, was poorly designed. The audience could not see the stage from certain parts of the house, and odors from a restaurant in its basement permeated the building. Several managers had tried their luck with the theatre, with little success. In the fall of 1869, Laura Keene took it over. She undertook major renovations, fixing most of the uncomfortable aspects of the auditorium, and introduced such innovations as children's matinees on Saturday. But her repertoire of sophisticated comedies failed to attract much interest. She took her company on tour after the first of the year and rented the theatre out to various touring combinations. She closed her season on March 26. It was the last time she would operate her own theatre. She continued to tour, but her health was failing, and she died of tuberculosis in 1873. E. L. Davenport took over the Chestnut for the 1870–71 season, where he presented "Shakespeare; eighteenth- and nineteenth-century British romantic and heroic pieces; and light, witty comedies."[14] Davenport relied on the stock company without the aid of visiting stars, often taking the leading roles himself, and ran the theatre for several years.

New theatres were going up to satisfy the demand for popular entertainments. The Arch Street Opera House, built on the corner of Tenth and Arch streets, became a center for blackface minstrelsy. The building, which still stands, became best known as the Trocadero, or the Old Troc. Restored in 1979, it is one of the only surviving variety houses of the late nineteenth century. Another famous minstrel house, Dumont's Theatre, opened that season at Ninth and Arch streets. It originally housed a museum and menagerie, and offered short plays and variety entertainment.

BOOTH AND CLARKE

Although Edwin Booth and John Sleeper Clarke continued to operate the Walnut, their attention was elsewhere. After many delays and cost overruns, Booth's Theatre finally opened in New York in 1869. As Booth had intended, it was a state-of-the-art facility, with a full basement beneath the stage. The hydraulics in the floor made it possible for the stage crew to raise and lower three-dimensional stage sets. Booth mounted exciting productions of classic plays.

Clarke had met with considerable success in London, where English audiences flocked to see him in classic comedy roles. He returned to America in the spring of 1870, ostensibly to purchase Booth's share of the Walnut Street Theatre. After a successful run in New York, he set out on an American tour, finishing up at the Walnut on October 17, 1870. He remained at the Walnut through the end of November, playing many of his familiar comic roles and a new farce, *Fox and Goose*. According to one account, "the houses were so crowded that the orchestra had to be removed to accommodate the public."[15] Clarke was followed immediately by Edwin Booth, who came in for three weeks in December. Clarke and Booth were undoubtedly negotiating Clarke's purchase of the Walnut, for in March 1871 Clarke bought out his brother-in-law. The Walnut would remain in the hands of the Clarke family for nearly half a century.

Clarke returned to America periodically after this but made his home in London, where he managed several theatres. During a visit to Philadelphia in January 1871, he and E. A. Sothern played the Walnut and Arch, respectively, and arranged to perform at each other's theatre. At the conclusion of their performances, each man left his theatre and drove to the other's and repeated the performance before a different audience. Both houses were sold out, as Philadelphians were eager to see the two renowned comedians appear in different theatres on the same evening.

THE WESTERN

If John Sleeper Clarke sought his future in England, most Americans were looking westward. The transcontinental railroad, completed in 1869, opened up the frontier, while the telegraph instantly transmitted news coming out of the West. The public was fascinated by stories of frontiersmen like "Buffalo Bill" Cody, whose exploits were detailed in newspaper accounts and dime novels.

A new entertainment form was evolving, which tied the fascination with melodramas to interest in the frontier—the western. One of the first westerns to be presented at the Walnut was *Kit, the Arkansas Traveler*, in March 1870, a frontier melodrama about a farmer whose wife and daughter are kidnapped by a former suitor. Most of the action is set aboard a Mississippi riverboat rather than the frontier, but the play contains many of the elements associated with the western, including a poker game and a thrilling knife fight at the end. It starred Frank Chanfrau, who had made his name as Mose the Bowery

B'hoy. Chanfrau was touring the play prior to bringing it to New York. While clearly a melodrama, *Kit* was a realistic depiction of life in the West, and it became Chanfrau's principal vehicle; he played it well into the 1890s. His company included an eight-year-old prodigy, Minnie Maddern, who would gain renown years later as Mrs. Fiske.

Over the next few years, the frontier drama evolved into the formula that we identify today with motion picture westerns—a tough, resourceful frontiersman fights and ultimately defeats one villain or another. On May 12, 1873, Frank Mayo introduced *Davy Crockett*, a role that would soon establish him as a star. The legendary frontiersman would become his most famous part, and Mayo would be identified with the character for the remainder of his career. The play has very little to do with Crockett's actual exploits. Gerald Bordman characterizes it as "more like a drawing-room melodrama set incongruously in the wilderness."[16] The climactic scene comes when the protagonist's cabin is attacked by a pack of ravenous wolves. Mayo, as Crockett, puts his arm in the door where an oak bar should have been, preventing the wolves from entering.

The play was not well received initially, and Mayo had to work out the kinks before bringing it to New York. A reviewer for the *Press* commented, "The language of the part, though presenting a good many glimpses of the dialect common in the Southwest, is not at all consistent in that particular, and Mr. Mayo does not improve it by the decided New England twang and drawl with which he renders it."[17] The play did have more to recommend it than most of the frontier dramas then circulating, however, and it established Mayo in the role of the legendary frontiersman.

Several literary figures tried their hand at writing plays. Bret Harte adapted his story *Two Men of Sandy Bar* for the stage. Stuart Robson commissioned the play for $3,000, as a vehicle for himself. However, it did not do well. Harte had more luck with *M'Liss, Child of the Sierras*, which was also adapted for the stage. It played the Walnut for the first time when McDonough and Lamb's Combination brought it there in December 1878. The play was most identified with Annie Pixley, who played it in early 1880. It became a popular touring show for much of the century, particularly in backwater areas.

EDWIN FORREST'S FAREWELL TOUR

Edwin Forrest opened on October 2, 1871, for what was to be his last run at the Walnut Street Theatre. He was sixty-six years old and had planned an ambitious tour—128 performances in fifty-two cities over four months, to commence at the Walnut. Wisely, Forrest concentrated on *King Lear* and *Richelieu*. The two characters were old men, so his own infirmities were less noticeable. It was clear, however, that time had passed him by. Booth's biographer, Eleanor Ruggles, reported that "after one neglected performance a reporter cried to him: 'Mr. Forrest, I never in my life saw you play Lear so well as you did tonight.' The old actor rose. 'Play Lear?' he retorted. 'What do you mean, sir? I do not *play* Lear. I *play* Hamlet, Richard, Shylock, Virginius, if you please, but by God, sir I *am* Lear!'"[18]

Forrest played for the last time at the Walnut on Friday, October 20, 1871, appropriately enough in the role of King Lear. The audience had a suspicion that this would be his last appearance onstage. "It would not surprise us if he never trod again the stage over which he has reigned the almost undisputed monarch," the *Press* reported.

Midway through Forrest's run, Chicago suffered a catastrophic fire, and the local papers were filled with the news. Flames swept through four square miles of densely populated neighborhoods. Half the population of Chicago, which numbered three hundred thousand, was left homeless. The business district was devastated, and all the theatres in the area burned to the ground. The night after Forrest closed, the Walnut produced Boucicault's labor drama, *The Long Strike*, as a benefit for members of the theatrical profession who had suffered by the recent fire.

On December 12, 1872, Edwin Forrest was found dead in his home. Members of the theatrical profession met at the Walnut on Saturday morning to plan a memorial. Attempts to organize a small funeral were quickly overwhelmed by the crowds that turned out to pay homage to America's first international star. Although Forrest had been a controversial figure, the outpouring of sentiment was immense. Newspapers across the country were filled with tributes. The funeral was held at the Forrest home on Monday, December 16. Crowds of people filled the streets outside, as a cortege of fifty carriages accompanied the casket through a cold rain to St. Paul's Episcopal Church, where Forrest was interred in a vault he had provided for his family. He is buried six blocks away from the site of his initial Walnut triumph.

Edwin was the last of the Forrest clan. With no living blood relations, he left the bulk of his estate to establish a home "for the support and maintenance of actors and actresses, decayed by age or disabled by infirmity."[19] The Edwin Forrest Home opened in 1876 in Forrest's country estate at Springbrook. In the 1920s it was moved into the city, to a house on Parkside Avenue overlooking Fairmount Park. Forrest's will also stipulated that stars should entertain at the retirement home on Shakespeare's birthday, should read the Declaration of Independence every July 4, and should assemble at Forrest's graveside for services on his birthday, March 9. This tradition is carried on today by the Walnut Street Theatre and the Actors Fund of America.

A GALAXY OF FEMALE STARS

The spring of 1873 saw a succession of talented actresses, several of them making their debuts at the Walnut. Adelaide Neilson, a beautiful English actress, appeared in *Romeo and Juliet* on January 13, 1873, and remained for three weeks in a repertoire that featured her in romantic Shakespearean roles. Blessed with a musical voice, dark eyes, and thick chestnut hair, she was unsurpassed in romantic parts. Neilson remained on tour for the next two years, and returned three more times in the 1870s.

Henrietta Chanfrau, the wife of Frank S. Chanfrau, was touring on her own in a production titled *The Elopement*. The Philadelphia native arrived in the first week of February and remained two more weeks playing in repertory. Nineteen-year-old Agnes Ethel followed, playing the title role in *Agnes*, a play reportedly written especially for her by Victorien Sardou, the French master of the "well-made play." Ethel was a protégé of Augustin Daly, who had starred her in a number of productions when she was only seventeen. Daly did not believe in the star system, and when actors enjoyed success, he assigned them to supporting roles. Ethel was the first of many Daly stars to strike out on her own.

On March 31, 1873, Charlotte Cushman opened a two-week engagement at the Walnut, her first appearance there in more than two decades. She had spent most of the intervening time in Europe, returning to America periodically. She played for two weeks with her standard repertoire, which included Meg Merrilies and Lady Macbeth. Though she no longer played Romeo, she continued to play breeches roles in Shakespeare's *Henry VIII*, appearing one night as Queen Katherine, the next night as Cardinal Wolsey. She also tried her hand at comedy in *Simpson & Co.*, a two-act comedy by English *farceur* John Poole.

Another *grande dame* of the theatre followed. Czech-born actress Fanny Janauschek made her Walnut debut on April 14 in *Chesney Wold*, an adaptation of Dickens's novel *Bleak House*. She remained for nearly a month in a repertoire of tragic dramas that included *The Winter's Tale*, *Medea*, *Mary Stuart*, and *Deborah, the Jewish Maiden*. A short, stocky woman, she was known for the intensity of her emotions and her powerful presence. Janauschek had been a favorite in Europe before coming to America in 1867. She met with limited success performing in German, but by 1873 she had learned English well enough to act in English-language productions. She toured America for many years, returning many times to the Walnut.

Among those making their debut at the Walnut was a tiny, red-headed entertainer who had made her reputation in the mining camps of California. Lotta Crabtree first appeared at the Walnut Street Theatre on August 25, 1873, in *The Little Detective.* The role allowed her to assume all sorts of disguises, which displayed her acting and musical talent. Lotta had grown up in the gold country of California, and it was said that she learned to sing and dance from Lola Montez, who was living in Grass Valley. She began her career as a child, performed in the mining camps and variety halls of California, singing and dancing and playing the banjo. Lotta was daring—she wore her skirts six or eight inches off the ground and she smoked onstage—but she had an impish quality that made her actions seem less shocking.

Lotta remained at the Walnut through the month of September, performing many of her standard roles in such plays as *Little Nell and the Marchioness, Old London,* and *Firefly,* light pieces designed to show off her charm and versatility. She also brought out *Zip, or Point Lynde Light,* in which she played the daughter of a lighthouse keeper who foils a plot to wreck a passing ship by blacking out the lighthouse. Her birth mother is aboard the ship, and Zip is taken to England to receive her inheritance, where she must outsmart another set of villains who are out to steal her fortune. Crabtree tended to play the same character in all of her plays—a gamine who stands up for what's right and is rewarded for her efforts.

The variety halls were producing a number of talented people like Crabtree who were moving into legitimate theatre. One of these was a German-dialect comedian named Joseph K. Emmet, who scored with *Fritz, Our Cousin German.* Emmet played a German immigrant who comes to America seeking his long-lost sister. There had been an upsurge in German immigration—particularly of German-Jewish immigrants—and their Old World ways, including their tendency to fracture the English language, were lampooned onstage. A former blackface entertainer with Bryant's Minstrels, Emmet had spent several years on the variety stage, where he developed his "Dutch" character, a German-dialect act in which he sang and spoke in broken English. *Fritz* was especially tailored to his talents and was a vehicle for the rest of his career.

THE PANIC OF 1873

The fall of 1873 produced another financial panic, when a Philadelphia banking firm failed. Once again, it was caused by overspeculation in railroads.

fig. 15 As demonstrated in this photograph, Lotta Crabtree was known for playing roles that allowed her to assume many disguises and show off her versatility.

The failure of the New York branch of Jay Cooke and Company burst the inflationary bubble and caused a nationwide depression that lasted most of the 1870s. The panic had devastating effects on the theatre industry. People were thrown out of work across the nation. Theatres in smaller cities and towns could no longer support stock companies and were forced to close. The depression that followed effectively put an end to the stock system, replacing it with a system that relied on touring combinations.

The impact was felt most in already marginal operations. The panic brought an end to E. L. Davenport's management of the Chestnut, which was briefly reopened as an equestrian theatre, then rented out to touring companies. "It did not remain under one management during this season but was rented for individual performances, the lessees of which are difficult to find," Coder explained. Another casualty was Edwin Booth, who was forced to declare bankruptcy on January 26, 1874. He had sunk more than $1 million into Booth's Theatre and had enormous debts. Though he was able to recoup his investments on tour, creditors were pressing. His father-in-law eventually consolidated the loans, but his debt ended Booth's career as a manager.

The financial panic did not immediately affect the Walnut, and the fall season was a good one. The company was improved by several additions to its stock company, with Charles Walcot taking over as acting manager. Coder stated that "the Walnut could now boast of possessing the finest company in the city," and noted that "the Walnut was still favored by the best of those who visited the city."[20]

THE CLASSIC TRADITION

The 1873–74 season was especially strong in drama. The older acting tradition was being carried on by John McCullough, who came in on November 24, 1873, in *Coriolanus*. The handsome and muscular McCullough was a protégé of Edwin Forrest and had toured with him for several years, playing second leads. McCullough spent several years in San Francisco managing a theatre, but after Forrest passed from the scene he returned east. He appeared in two of Forrest's signature roles, Jack Cade and Spartacus in *The Gladiator*. "To follow so quickly in the footsteps of the mighty artiste who was dear to the nation is a bold experiment, and Mr. McCullough deserves respect for the ability and energy which have made it a successful one," commented a reviewer for the *Philadelphia Press*.[21] McCullough became a favorite with Philadelphia audiences, returning regularly during Christmas week.

Charlotte Cushman came in for a two-week run in early March 1874. She was fifty-seven, and this was to be her last appearance at the Walnut. She had given farewell tours before, but it was generally known that Cushman was suffering from breast cancer. She played a week as Meg Merrilies in *Guy Mannering*. Eleanor Ruggles reported, "Actors playing with her these days whispered that as she gave her final death shriek in the part, she pounded her breast, which was known to be on fire with cancer, so as to make her famous cry one of real agony."[22] Given her failing health, acting was becoming too stressful, and Cushman chose to give dramatic readings instead of full productions. She played her last full performance at the Walnut on March 14, 1874, as Lady Macbeth, and made her final stage appearance on October 31. She continued to give readings until her death in February 1876.

An Italian star, Tommaso Salvini, was also making his mark with American audiences, despite the fact that he and his company performed in Italian. He opened a week of repertory on June 1, 1875, in *Samson*, but it was his Othello that really impressed the critics. A critic from the *Press* declared that Salvini's performance as Othello "was in all probability the greatest piece of acting that historic stage has ever seen or will ever see again." Salvini had a rugged, leonine quality onstage that served him well, and great emotional intensity and range that gained him applause for creating a controversial interpretation of Shakespeare's Moor. Some years later, Salvini toured with Edwin Booth, playing Othello to Booth's Iago.

COMEDY AND SPECTACLE IN THE 1870S

With the country in economic crisis, lighter fare proved most popular. Several first-rate comedians came through the Walnut in the mid-1870s. John T. Raymond played the grandiose Colonel Mulberry Sellers in *The Gilded Age*, a dramatization of Mark Twain and Charles Dudley Warner's novel. Colonel Sellers constantly comes up with grandiose schemes to make money, insisting each time that "there's millions in it." Raymond's Sellers captured the extravagance of the time, while the title of the novel gave the corrupt era, golden on the surface but rotten within, its name.

On May 10, 1875, Dion Boucicault brought out *The Shaughraun*, considered one of his best works. Boucicault played the part of Conn, a vagabond described as "the soul of every fair, the life of every funeral, the first fiddle at all weddings and parties." The play had a three-week run. It had grossed nearly a quarter-million dollars during its New York run, and Boucicault had drawn full houses in Boston. For the next few years, Boucicault toured the show around the country, earning half a million dollars.

A very different type of comedian appeared at the Walnut at the end of the summer. George L. Fox made a name for himself in pantomime and performed in whiteface. He appeared in *Humpty Dumpty in Every Clime*, a sequel to his extraordinarily successful pantomime *Humpty Dumpty*. Fox was the leading clown on the American stage and for a time its highest-paid performer. His behavior was becoming increasingly erratic, however, owing to the effects of untreated syphilis. During the New York run of *Humpty Dumpty in Every Clime*, he had to be institutionalized. He died of paresis in 1877.

fig. 16 The 1854–55 season included the debut of one of the most influential playwrights of the nineteenth century, Dion Boucicault, shown here in a much later photograph. Image courtesy of the Theatre Collection, Free Library of Philadelphia.

The excesses of the Gilded Age were reflected in W. J. Florence's depiction of an unethical congressman in *The Mighty Dollar,* which Florence brought to the Walnut on March 13, 1876. Florence's portrayal of the Honorable Bardwell Slote was "one of the richest, most memorable of American theatrical creations," according to Gerald Bordman. Florence and his wife toured this show for many years. "Whatever failings and vulgarities the play displayed," Bordman wrote, "the Florences' brilliant acting won the original production . . . kept it on the boards with some regularity for another decade."[23] *The Mighty Dollar* established the unethical blowhard congressman as an American icon.

On January 10, 1876, the Kiralfy Brothers opened in a spectacular production of Jules Verne's *Around the World in Eighty Days.* The Verne novel was an ideal vehicle in which to display the fantastic stage and mechanical effects of Hungarian-born Imre and Bolossy Kiralfy. The production featured eighteen scenes depicting Phileas Fogg's tour of the world. The Kiralfys brought a real helium balloon onstage for a flight over the Alps. A live elephant was used for a procession of Brahmins and worshippers leading up to a funeral pyre. Still another scene depicted the sinking of a steamship. The production established the Kiralfys as the premiere producers of spectacle in the country.

The Kiralfys built a theatre on the corner of Broad and Locust streets—opposite the Academy of Music—which they named Kiralfy's Alhambra Palace. Moorish in design, with spires and minarets, it featured a garden behind the theatre where the public could stroll in grottos of stone and courtyards with statuary. The Kiralfys planned to use their facility to develop their productions, then move them to New York. For their opening on May 17, they revived *Around the World in Eighty Days,* scheduled to coincide with the opening of the Centennial Exposition. The Kiralfys hoped to draw audiences away from the exposition, but the summer was extraordinarily hot, and the expected crowds failed to materialize. They did not exercise their option to purchase the property, and closed after a year. The new owners renamed it the Broad Street Theatre and operated it with more success. The Kiralfys retreated to New York, where they continued to churn out their spectacles.

THE CENTENNIAL EXPOSITION

Plans for Philadelphia's Centennial Exposition had been under way for nearly a decade. The city was the focus of the entire nation on the hundredth anniversary of the signing of the Declaration of Independence. The previous year, John Sleeper Clarke had arranged a series of benefit performances to help raise money for the exposition. For one benefit, Augustin Daly's company came down from New York for a matinee performance of their new hit, *The Big Bonanza,* starring John Drew Jr., the son of Mrs. Drew. The company returned to New York City in time for their evening performance.

More than two hundred buildings were built at Fairmount Park for the exposition. President and Mrs. Grant were on hand for the opening, and the president threw the switch on the immense Corliss engine, which powered eight hundred machines at the fair.[24] Among the exhibits were Alexander Graham Bell's telephone, the air brake, and the Pullman palace car. The torch for the proposed Statue of Liberty was another attraction. During the first two months of the exposition, there were parades, conventions, and other ceremonies. The highlight came in early July, with special ceremonies at Independence Hall and a torchlight parade on the night of July 3. Streets around the Walnut were densely packed with people. Independence Square was the site of the Independence Day events, with oratory, commemorative ceremonies, and a military parade. The two-day celebration was capped by a fireworks display.

The Walnut remained open through the summer to take advantage of the crowds drawn to the city for the centennial. Advertisements for the Walnut the weekend of July 4 announced that it was the oldest theatre in America—the first time this tag was used in its publicity. E. A. Sothern occupied the house during the month of June, appearing as Lord Dundreary in *Our American Cousin* and alternating it with other productions, such as Boucicault's *David Garrick*. Sothern took ill in July and had to be replaced. Salsbury's Troubadours filled in for a week, performing a "comic absurdity" titled *Patchwork*, about a comic group of scullery workers. The five-member comedy troupe was formed by Nate Salsbury, who would later run Buffalo Bill's Wild West Show. The piece was essentially a series of sketches. Though the show never made it to New York, *Patchwork* is considered one of the early works of the American musical theatre. Several other stars filled out the summer season. Emma Waller took on Charlotte Cushman's role of Meg Merrilies in *Guy Mannering*. John Brougham brought in a historical extravaganza titled *Columbus Reconstructed*. It advertised a *corps de ballet* of fifty young ladies. Tony Pastor arrived at the end of August to finish out the season with his vaudeville troupe.

EVANGELINE AND THE AMERICAN MUSICAL

Crowds began to pick up in the fall, when the weather cooled. The fall season at the Walnut officially opened on September 4 and mostly featured returning stars—Dion Boucicault, John T. Raymond, Lotta Crabtree, and Adelaide Neilseon. The hit of the fall season was *Evangeline, or The Belle of Arcadia*, a musical extravaganza loosely based on the Longfellow poem. It had had a brief run in New York two years earlier, but it was remounted with better production values for the 1876 tour. *Evangeline* is significant in that it was the first full-length American musical. It had an entirely original score, with music by Edward E. Rice and lyrics by J. Cheever Goodwin, who also wrote the book. The play was a parody of Longfellow's poem about French Acadians expelled by the British, and it followed the English burlesque tradition of having a woman play the male love interest and a man in drag as a comic elderly woman. Two lovers seek each other in various locales, including the Wild West and Africa. In the end, the lovers are reunited. The play also featured a dancing heifer, an amorous whale, and a lone fisherman, who wandered mournfully through scenes with his telescope, never uttering a word. The production starred Eliza Weathersby as the male lead, Gabriel, and Lizzie Harold as Evangeline. Among the minor cast members were Nat C. Goodwin and Henry E. Dixey, both of whom would have important careers in musical theatre.

PASSAGES

Lucille Western played her last dates at the Walnut beginning on January 1, 1877. She caught a cold on Friday night, January 5, playing the title role in *Leah, the Forsaken*, and died the following Thursday. She was only thirty-three. The following week, E. L. Davenport made his first appearance at the Walnut in a number of years, in a sentimental play by W. S. Gilbert titled *Dan'l Druce*. He returned late in the season, making his last appearance at the Walnut the week of May 14. Davenport died later that year, at the age of sixty-two. Despite his skill as an actor, he never enjoyed the following that came to many of his peers. Four of his children made careers in the theatre; his oldest daughter, Fanny, became one of the leading stars of the late nineteenth century.

Fanny Davenport made her first starring appearance at the Walnut in *Pique* in late September 1877. She had previously appeared as a member of Augustin Daly's Fifth Avenue Theatre company but, like many of Daly's talented players, had struck out on her own. Daly wrote *Pique* especially for Davenport, and it ran for 238 performances in New York. There was a parting of the ways, and Davenport took her show on the road, alternating *Pique* with other plays. The high point in her career would come in the late 1880s, when she obtained the American rights to Sardou's plays, which were identified with Sarah Bernhardt.

Also making her debut that season was Mary Anderson, who appeared in a repertory that included *Evadne*, *Ingomar*, and *Romeo and Juliet* during the week of October 8. Tall and willowy, Anderson was considered by many the most beautiful actress in America. Raised in Louisville, Kentucky, she was largely self-taught, but her beauty, her virginal appeal, and her rich, melodious voice charmed audiences and critics alike. Only eighteen years old, she was about to make her New York debut when she appeared at the Walnut.

THE END OF THE STOCK COMPANY

The era of stock was drawing to a close. More and more stars were touring with their own companies and did not need the support of local talent. If

Clarke and Goodwin wanted to get touring stars into the Walnut, they had to dismiss the resident company or send them on tour. In the fall of 1877 John Sleeper Clarke purchased Kiralfy's Alhambra and renamed it the Broad Street Theatre. He organized a small stock company and opened it on Christmas Day. When a company came into the Walnut with a full cast, as E. A. Sothern did on January 14, 1878, the Walnut's company shifted over to the Broad Street Theatre to augment the company there.

The Walnut continued to mount its own shows, most notably *The Exiles,* a play by Victorien Sardou, Eugene Nus, and Prince Lubormiski. This drama of "five scenes and nine tableaux" opened on February 25, 1878, for a five-week run. The play had been a hit in Paris, and there was a legal battle over the performance rights in America, which stimulated popular interest in the production. The play was set in Russia, which provided opportunities for spectacular sets and tableaux. It recounted the troubles of a countess who rebuffs the advances of the head of the secret police, who has her exiled to Siberia. Using elaborate interior sets and winter exteriors in the Siberian wilderness, the production featured a team of reindeer and a team of dogs.

The 1877–78 season proved to be the worst financially since the end of the Civil War, and it wreaked havoc with the amusement industry. "Time and again we read of stranded road companies everywhere in the United States," wrote Thomas F. Marshall. "Ticket prices were cut as a last resort. The standard price of admission at the principal theatres was $1.50 for a reserved orchestra seat, $1.00 for a reserved balcony seat, fifty cents for general admission in the lower parts of the house, and twenty-five cents for admission to the gallery."[25] Among the casualties of the economic downturn was Mrs. Drew. At the end of the season she dismissed her company and shifted to booking touring shows.

The 1878–79 season was the last year in which a stock company was employed at the Walnut. One of the members of the Walnut's company was nineteen-year-old Otis Skinner, who left an account of it in his autobiography, *Footlights and Spotlights.* Skinner would later join Augustin Daly's company and tour with both Helena Modjeska and Edwin Booth. Known for his energy and swagger, he was most successful in romantic roles.

The company that year featured Mr. and Mrs. Charles Walcot, who played most of the leading roles; Mrs. E. L. Davenport, who played old ladies; Lizzie Creese, the juvenile woman; and Atkins Lawrence, the male juvenile. George Howard and Sam Hemple were the theatre's comedians, and George K. Goodwin managed the company. Goodwin had gotten his start in the banking and brokerage trade, and as a young man he bought an interest in a moving panorama of Italy, which he toured. He became involved in circuses and menageries and for a time managed Josh Billings and other comic lecturers. In 1869 he established a "dollar store" at Chestnut above Seventh.

He briefly managed the Chestnut Street Theatre before joining the Walnut in 1875.

Otis Skinner reported that Goodwin knew very little about the artistic side of the theatre, which he left to Charles Walcot. Skinner recalled that Walcot "selected all the 'fat parts' for his own playing, sometimes to the disgust of the heavy man or the leading juvenile." During the year that Otis Skinner spent at the Walnut, he worked with such varied talents as Lotta Crabtree, Fanny Janauschek, John McCullough, Lawrence Barrett, and Fanny Davenport. "When a number of pieces were to be produced during the engagement, the star's stage director would precede him (or her) to conduct rehearsals in advance; the star and company coming together on Monday morning for the first time to run through the lines 'perfect,' and the bill presented that night," Skinner wrote. Often the star would run these rehearsals, so a young actor like Skinner received coaching from perhaps a dozen leading actors each season.

The process could be grueling, particularly when an actor played in repertory, which most serious actors did. "The procession of stars brought Lawrence Barrett and Fanny Davenport in adjoining engagements. Each had a huge repertory, and I played thirteen separate parts in two weeks," Skinner reported. Barrett appeared in *Richelieu*, *Hamlet*, *The Lady of Lyons*, and *Richard III* during the week of February 24. Fanny Davenport followed this up with *London Assurance*, *As You Like It*, *Divorce*, *The Hunchback*, and *Cymbeline*.

It became evident that 1878–79 would be the last season for the resident company. "With the ending of the dramatic year in Philadelphia, the old type of provincial, star-supporting company went out of existence in that city," Skinner recalled. "It was disappearing everywhere: the public was growing tired of seeing the same people in the same clothes season after season, and welcomed the change that brought each week a set of new faces, fresh costumes and complete scene settings. The local scene-dock was still kept stocked with the familiar Gothic Chamber, Rocky Pass, etc. but the dust of neglect and decay was settling on the things of yesteryear."[26] When the season ended, Skinner remained in Philadelphia for a few weeks, performing with Mrs. Drew's company, then moved on to New York, where he joined Augustin Daly's company.

The nature of the acting profession was undergoing a profound change. Stock companies were disappearing everywhere. Two years before, there had been five resident companies in Philadelphia. Now only one remained, the Chestnut, and it was one of only seven in the entire nation. Actors no longer were settled members of the community but made their lives on the road. The stock system relied on frequent changes of plays, and actors had to be prepared to perform a different show each night of the week. Once they began to tour, they played a limited repertoire, usually a single show, for months on end.

Skinner reflected on the strengths and weaknesses of the old stock system. "The fault of the old stock companies was that it allowed actors but little time for introspection. Efficiency it did give them—easy adaptability for whatever might be called for, but the true meaning of the character was very apt to escape them. Now and then, one would rise out of the ranks into greatness, but such a one would have succeeded, no matter what his obstacles. Yet the old stock company laid foundations not to be secured in these days of long runs and the specialization in 'types' of acting," Skinner concluded. "It put into the hands of the actor the tools of his trade, and it bred versatility and competence. He was always at work.[27]

A COMBINATION HOUSE, 1879–1895

The shift from stock to a combination system changed the theatre in a fundamental way. Under the stock system, the creative and commercial aspects were handled by the same person—the theatre manager. Under the combination system, these two functions became separated. Most plays were produced in New York or Chicago, while theatre managers outside these cities essentially functioned as landlords, booking touring shows into their houses. During the summer, managers from across the country traveled to New York to arrange the bookings for the following season. George K. Goodwin was among them. In 1879 he managed two Philadelphia theatres, the Walnut and the Arch Street Opera House, which he had recently taken over and renamed the Park.[1] The following year Goodwin took over the lease of the twenty-eight-hundred-seat Chestnut Street Opera House, and during the fall of that year he operated three Philadelphia theatres.

The new system created an incentive for managers to begin building circuits, since it was as simple to book a single production into several theatres as to arrange for one booking. This new system also led to the rise of booking agents. "In those days the transacting of the theatrical business was not methodized," Augustus Pitou recalled. "Managers of theaters came to New York from different parts of the country during the summer, and booked such attractions as they could secure direct with the managers of the attractions, and many of them returned to their homes with only a half, or a third, of their seasons filled. Few contracts were passed between the parties, and disputes were frequent as to what each was to furnish."[2]

Most companies were operated by actor-managers, who now toured with their entire productions. Several large-scale production companies emerged.

The Kiralfy Brothers were the foremost producers of spectacle. They had several shows on the road at any one time. E. E. Rice also kept several companies touring in various musical extravaganzas. They were joined by such entrepreneurs as J. H. Haverly, who had several minstrel troupes on tour, one featuring more than a hundred performers. Augustin Daly was emerging as a leading producer of dramatic vehicles. Such productions were a natural outgrowth of the combination system.

THE MULLIGAN GUARDS' BALL

While George Goodwin was in New York arranging bookings for the fall 1879 season, Edward Harrigan and Tony Hart brought their company to the Walnut for a two-week summer run. Harrigan and Hart had just finished an extraordinary season at the Theatre Comique in New York and were touring their newest hit, *The Mulligan Guards' Ball.* This play is cited as a seminal work in the development of American musical theatre. It featured original songs by Ned Harrigan and David Braham, the company's musical director, and depicted immigrant life on New York's Lower East Side. It was significant in moving the musical away from the far-off realms of European operetta to the gritty reality of urban American streets.

The Mulligan Guards' Ball was the second in a series of plays depicting the travails of Dan Mulligan and his paramilitary social group, the Mulligan Guards. Ned Harrigan played Mulligan, and Tony Hart played his son, Tommy, who is in love with the daughter of the local butcher, Gustave Lochmuller. Dan Mulligan disapproves of the mixing of Irish and German blood and does everything he can to derail the budding romance. As this is going on, the Mulligan Guards are planning an annual party at a local hall. Unfortunately, the room is rented out to an African American group, the Skidmore Guards, for the same night. The Skidmores are persuaded to take the ballroom directly overhead. They party so wildly that the floor collapses, and the entire party of Skidmores falls in on the Mulligans. In the confusion, the young lovers elope.

The production was a huge success, and Harrigan and Hart were acclaimed the funniest performers working on the American stage. The duo populated their plays with figures one would see in the Bowery and on the Lower East Side. They had developed their characters in a series of sketches and used the stock ethnic characters common on the variety stage. Harrigan, however, who wrote all the plays, infused them with individuality and careful observation that raised these works to a higher quality than the standard comedies of the time.

As America entered the 1880s, musical comedy was just beginning to take hold. Gilbert and Sullivan's *H.M.S. Pinafore* had been the smash hit of the 1878–79 season. Because there was still no international copyright protection, American companies were free to mount their own productions without paying royalties. During the spring of 1879, twelve Philadelphia companies, including an all-black company and an all-child company, presented the musical.[3] During the fall of 1879, musicals dominated the Walnut's stage. The Kiralfys mounted a spectacular revival of *The Black Crook*, which had a six-week run at the Walnut. It starred Maria Bonfanti, the premiere dancer of the original 1866 production, supported by a cast of two hundred, and reportedly cost $60,000 to produce. The Kiralfys returned in January with another fairy spectacle, *Enchantment*, which "tried to be an opera, a ballet, a play, a variety show, a gymnasium, a spectacle, and a pantomime, all rolled into one," in the words of Bolossy Kiralfy. "The great charm of the production lay in the transformation scenes, the familiar sight of women-laden pedestals and ballerinas flying in and out on wires, partially masked by shifting gauze curtains."[4]

This was just part of the rich and varied musical offerings at the Walnut that season. The Colville Opera Burlesque Company presented *The Magic Slipper*, a retelling of the Cinderella story set in the present day. E. E. Rice brought in his latest musical concoction, a farce titled *Revels*, and returned several weeks later with *Evangeline*. Emma Abbott's English Opera Company played two engagements that season. A genuinely populist diva, Abbott wore extravagant costumes and interpolated popular songs into her productions (an interpolation is any passage in a text—musical or otherwise—that was not written by the original author). Maurice Grau's French Opera Company played in April. In early May, Augustin Daly's company presented *The Royal Middy*, about a gypsy who disguises herself as a sailor to find her lover. Adapted from a German operetta, it was the first production to be billed as a musical comedy.

BUFFALO BILL CODY

The most notable star to appear during the 1879–80 season was Buffalo Bill Cody, who opened on February 2, 1880, in *The Knight of the Plains, or Buffalo Bill's Best Trail*. Cody had just published his autobiography, which sparked interest in the dashing frontiersman. *Knight of the Plains* owed more to the conventions of melodrama than to Cody's real-life exploits. But crowds flocked to see a genuine western hero, and the theatre took in about $5,000 a week.[5] Cody

fig. 17 Buffalo Bill Cody appeared at the Walnut in western melodramas before creating his highly successful Wild West Show.

played four different characters in the piece and entertained the audience with displays of marksmanship. "The scenes in the four acts were illustrative of frontier life and, with groups of Indians, scouts, interpreters and bordermen in each, presented a realistic effect," wrote the reviewer for the *Public Ledger*.[6] Cody toured that show and others in the intervening years, spending winters on the theatrical circuit and heading west during the summer to scout.

The following season, Cody returned in *The Prairie Waif*, and in December 1882 he presented *Twenty Days, or Buffalo Bill's Pledge*. When the 1882–83 season closed, Cody organized a Wild West show that could tour during the summer. The venture proved so successful that he gave up the stage to present the outdoor extravaganzas for which he is best remembered. The Wild West show was recognized as a major theatrical innovation, combining elements of the stage play with outdoor entertainments like the circus. Buffalo Bill toured the show for thirty years.

FARCE-COMEDY

Communities that could not support a permanent stock company were building "opera houses," and small-time producers mounted shows that could play these smaller venues. Traveling without scenery and with a small company, they could play one-night stands in smaller cities and towns in the Midwest and South. The Walnut hosted a number of these now forgotten troupes—Leacock's English Burlesque Company, Harrison's Musical Comedy Company, Duff Opera Company, Mitchell's Jolly Pleasure Company. These companies changed their names from year to year and, somewhat less often, their repertoire.

The early 1880s saw the emergence of "farce-comedy," a primitive form of musical comedy. Farce-comedies were essentially a series of vaudeville turns linked in a loose narrative framework. The appeal of these plays was that they were cheap to produce. "Farce-comedy could be mounted at extremely small cost, with an infinitesimal company and minimal settings, properties, and machinery," musical theatre historian Cecil Smith explained. "It required no specialized techniques of pantomime and burlesque, no chorus, no French ballets, no transformation scenes. . . . The form gave free opportunity to each performer to exploit whatever talent he might possess. As time went on, the freedom of farce-comedy from fixed traditions enabled a number of original and gifted comics to develop their individual styles of performance."[7]

Among the companies working the form were Harrison's Musical Comedy Company, which presented *Photos*, and Willie Edouin's Sparks Company, which staged *Dreams, or Fun in a Photograph Gallery*. Various characters enter the studio to have their picture taken and perform their specialty. Smith and

Mestayer presented *Tourists in a Pullman Car,* about adventurers on their way to California. It used songs from a variety of sources. Confusion erupts in this play as a result of a diamond robbery and complications arising from mistaken identity. The heyday of farce-comedy lasted only five years, although the companies toured for much longer.

MELODRAMA AND REALISM

Melodramas continued to be the favorite dramatic form, and they were produced with elaborate stage effects and thrilling sensational scenes. The 1881–82 season at the Walnut opened on August 11 with *The World,* a melodrama that had played New York the previous season. Its stage effects included the explosion of a ship onstage. After two weeks it moved over to the Chestnut and Lyceum theatres.

The most important production of the fall season was James A. Herne's *Hearts of Oak,* which he brought to the Walnut on October 24. Co-written by Herne and an up-and-coming director and playwright, David Belasco, it is regarded as one of the first examples of realism in theatre. The story was taken from an English melodrama, *The Mariner's Compass,* and told the story of an old sailor who raises a pair of orphans, a boy and a girl. He falls in love with the girl but loses out to the boy, who also loves her. *Hearts of Oak* was unusual, for it did away with the conventional hero and villain. The situations were less sensational and violent than those of most melodramas, and the play was populated with characters recognizable in real life. The dialogue was simple and colloquial, and although the plot seems contrived to modern audiences, an effort was made to make it realistic, even in the staging. When dinner was served in one scene, real food was used, and the audience could see the steam rising from the food and smell the aromas that drifted from the stage.[8] The scenery and effects were prepared especially for the production, and it featured a working mill and an onstage storm that drenched the characters. "There was plenty of 'realism' in the piece," the *Public Ledger* reported, "the first act closing with a storm, shipwreck, vivid forked lightning, and a shower of real water. A baby, not of the stuffed sort, but a bright little thing of flesh and blood, kicked and crowed its way into the affections of the audience."[9]

HALL AND FLEISHMAN

The balance of power in Philadelphia changed during the summer of 1882, when George K. Goodwin took ill and died. After much negotiating and many threats of lawsuits, Goodwin's widow turned over the lease of the Walnut to J. Fred Zimmerman and his partner, Samuel F. Nixon. Zimmerman and Nixon already held the lease on the Chestnut Street Theatre (then called Haverly's). A few weeks later Mrs. Goodwin sold them the lease on the Chestnut Street Opera House, giving them firm control over most of the major theatres in Philadelphia. Zimmerman and Nixon offered the Walnut's lease to Frank L. Gardner, who turned it over to Thomas A. Hall and Israel Fleishman.[10]

Hall and Fleishman already controlled the Broad Street Theatre. Hall had worked at the Walnut briefly in 1874 as "acting manager," another name for a business manager. Fleishman was primarily a businessman and undoubtedly provided the financial backing. He had been infatuated with the theatre from an early age and had toured for a season as an actor. He was forced to give up acting because of family pressure, and he became a salesman for a wholesale notions house. In 1868 he went into business for himself as a gentleman's clothier, opening a shop on Chestnut Street and eventually operating seven stores. Through his business ventures he amassed a substantial fortune.

Hall and Fleishman's first season, in 1882–83, was quite run-of-the-mill. Melodramas and musicals predominated. The season opened on August 14 with *Ranch 10*, a melodrama set in the West that its star, Harry Meredith, was bringing to New York. It featured several realistic effects, including an onstage blizzard and a fire. For the most part, the season consisted of returning stars. Mrs. G. C. Howard appeared in *Uncle Tom's Cabin*. She had originated the part of Topsy in 1852 and was still playing the role thirty years later. Alice Oates and her Comic Opera Company presented a week of *opéra bouffe* that included Offenbach's *Princess of Trebizonte*. They were followed by Rice's New Surprise Company, which presented *Pop*, a musical set aboard an ocean liner and another farce-comedy in which various people on the ship performed their specialties. Rice returned with *Iolanthe*, the latest Gilbert and Sullivan operetta, while the Kiralfy Brothers revived *The Black Crook* and *Around the World in Eighty Days*.

ETHNIC COMEDIANS

Ethnic comedians continued to make inroads into legitimate theatre. Many of them, like Harrigan and Hart, had gotten their start on the variety stage and now presented legitimate shows for the characters they had developed there. Ned Harrigan, breaking away from his Mulligan Guard plays, penned *Squatter Sovereignty*, which revolved around the conflict between the owners of land near the East River and the squatters who had settled there. It depicted an assortment of ethnic types and had a run of more than 150 nights in New York. M. W. Hanley's Company brought it to the Walnut on September 4, 1882.

New stage types were emerging, reflecting the new immigrants from eastern Europe. As with previous immigrant groups, their behavior and accent were spoofed onstage. J. K. Emmet appeared at the Walnut in January 1881 in *Fritz in Ireland*, the first of many sequels to *Fritz, Our Cousin German*. Another German-dialect, or "Dutch," comic was Gus Williams, who appeared in 1885 in *Oh! What a Night* and returned for a reprise the following year. Frank Bush presented *Ikey Solomons* on September 18. Bush, who was not Jewish and had gotten his start on the variety stage, was one of the first to present a stereotypical Jew onstage.[11]

Older stereotypes continued to be popular. The Yankee character had been taken up by Denman Thompson, who created a vehicle, *Joshua Whitcomb*, based on a character he had developed in vaudeville. He brought the play to the Walnut on January 29, 1883. Unlike other ethnic comedians, according to Bordman, "Thompson eschewed the broad characterization, verging on caricature, of so many earlier stage Yankees. His was a warm, totally believable New Englander, albeit one not without a few flaws, such as occasional irascibility and a penchant for spitting."[12]

The Irish comedians were going through the same evolution, reflecting the growing power and acceptance of Irish Americans in society. The hard-drinking, hard-fighting Irish comedian had given way to a romantic figure, often a singer. Joseph Murphy returned year after year in two plays—*The Kerry Gow* and *Shaun Rhue*. In *The Kerry Gow* he played a blacksmith who is framed for forgery by a rival, and he actually shoed a horse onstage. In *Shaun Rhue* he sang his celebrated song "A Handful of Earth" to open the show.

W. J. Scanlan was another important Irish singer and comedian. He first appeared at the Walnut in 1878 in *The O'Donovans*, as half of the comedy team of Scanlan and Cronin. Scanlan made his first solo appearance in *Friend and Foe* on October 29, 1883, a play in which he introduced the song "Moonlight in Killarney." He teamed up with Augustus Pitou, and the following spring they staged *The Irish Minstrel*, returning repeatedly after that to play half the week in each show. In 1885 Scanlan introduced *Shane-Na-Lawn*, in which he played the typical quick-witted, lovable Irish lad who falls in love with a girl whose family is feuding with his own.

COMEDY TEAMS

The premiere comedy team of the 1880s was Stuart Robson and William H. Crane. They teamed up in 1877 and toured for more than a decade. They were best remembered for their *Comedy of Errors,* in which they played the two Dromios, performing the play at the Walnut for the first time in 1882. Among their other pieces were *Forbidden Fruit, Our Boarding House,* and *Our Bachelors.* Robson and Crane did not appear at the Walnut after 1884, although they continued their partnership until 1889.

The comedy team of Barry and Fay kept alive the tradition of low comedy. Tall, thin Hugh Fay played opposite rotund, red-headed Billy Barry in *Irish Aristocracy at Muldoon's Picnic* on December 4, 1882. They made frequent returns to the Walnut in 1886. In 1889 they presented *McKenna's Flirtation,* an urban comedy with interpolated songs, reminiscent of the Harrigan and Hart vehicles. Their low, knockabout comedy offended Irish groups, who picketed their shows. By 1894 the team had broken up and each man appeared in his own shows.

Husbands and wives still toured as comedy partners. The most notable of these were Mr. and Mrs. W. J. Florence, who continued to tour through the mid-1880s. Mr. and Mrs. George S. Knight picked up the tradition, making their first appearance at the Walnut on March 15, 1886, in *Over the Garden Wall,* a farce-comedy that centers on a baby who is sent to live with various characters. This play displayed the talents of the Knights as well as those of supporting players Eddie Foy and Minnie Dupree. Dupree, who was only fourteen at the time, was quickly recognized as a talent and played supporting roles regularly. She gained her greatest fame after the turn of the century. Eddie Foy, then in his mid-thirties, was known for his acrobatic dancing. He had toured in vaudeville and minstrelsy and was now establishing himself in musical comedies. He is remembered today as the father of the untalented Seven Little Foys.

TRAGEDY

Tragic actors continued to pursue the tradition of acting in repertory, which demonstrated their versatility and talent, for acting ability was still identified strictly with tragedy. Several tragedians appeared at the Walnut over the years. Thomas W. Keene played for a week in January 1881. English-born Frederick Warde appeared for a week in early 1883, and W. E. Sheridan had a three-week engagement in November that year. Though they were lauded in their time, none of them made a lasting mark.

John McCullough appeared regularly at the Walnut and was a great favorite, returning each year for Christmas. He played his last date at the Walnut in the winter of 1881–82. McCullough was suffering from syphilis and was forced to retire from the stage. He returned in the fall of 1884 but suffered a collapse. In June 1885 he was committed to a sanitarium, and died on November 8, 1885, at his home in Philadelphia.

Tragedy was most strongly identified with Edwin Booth. Booth's business failures, and his association with the Lincoln assassination, greatly contributed to his tragic presence. He appeared for two weeks in January 1884, and the reception was tremendous. It had been eight years since Booth had last played the Walnut. Thomas F. Marshall wrote that "his second week was without precedent in the history of the theatre in Philadelphia. Standing room was the only thing that could be had any night after the doors had opened, and thousands were turned away at every performance. Top gallery seats were sold by speculators for five dollars, and special officers were required to restrain the crowd that surged around the box office every time the doors were opened."[13] Booth's two final appearances netted $4,600, and the total receipts were well over $25,000. On his closing night at the Walnut he played Richard III. This was to be Booth's final appearance at the Walnut, although he was only fifty years old. He continued to tour, however, including important tours with Lawrence Barrett and Tommaso Salvini, but he never again played the Walnut.

PHILADELPHIA'S ACTING FAMILIES

Acting remained something of a family business, and the Drew-Barrymore clan is Philadelphia's most illustrious example. Mrs. John Drew continued to manage the Arch Street Theatre, even though she had dismissed her company in 1878. Mrs. Drew turned her attentions to acting, touring while she continued to manage the theatre. By the 1880s, two of her children were established in the profession. John Drew Jr. was a member of Augustin Daly's company when it presented Arthur Wing Pinero's *The Squire* at the Walnut in April 1883. He played opposite Ada Rehan, the only time either of these longtime co-stars played together at the Walnut Street Theatre.

Louisa Lane Drew's daughter, Georgiana Drew Barrymore, appeared for a week in September 1883 in *A Possible Case*, a farce about a woman who finds herself married to several men at once. She had married a strikingly handsome British actor named Maurice Barrymore and was the mother of Lionel, Ethel, and John Barrymore—ages five, four, and one, respectively. Georgie Drew Barrymore had inherited her mother's skill at comedy, but this was to be her only appearance at the Walnut. She continued to tour until her early death, in 1893, at age thirty-seven. Maurice Barrymore made his first appearance at the Walnut in early 1887, supporting Lillie Langtry in *As in a Looking Glass.*

fig. 18 Ethel, Lionel and John Barrymore with their mother, Georgia Drew Barrymore.

Another Philadelphia acting family was beginning to make tentative steps onto the stage. John Sleeper Clarke returned on October 10, 1887, supported by his son, Creston. The next year they presented a dramatic repertory, evidently designed to showcase Creston Clarke, who was setting out on his own career. Roland Reed, the son of the Walnut's gasman, "Pop" Reed, had also taken up the acting profession. His first starring appearance was at the Walnut on March 29, 1886, in *Blackmail,* the story of an aristocrat condemned to death through the machinations of a cousin. Reed made numerous appearances at the Walnut over the course of his career.

SARDOU AND THE WELL-MADE PLAY

The most influential actress of the 1880s was the French star Sarah Bernhardt, who made several American tours, beginning in 1881. Bernhardt never appeared at the Walnut, but her passionate acting style and glamorous life influenced several actresses who did. Many of Bernhardt's most successful vehicles were written by Victorien Sardou, the French master of "the well-made play." Well-made plays were extremely formulaic, designed to maintain maximum suspense, typically by withholding a secret from the characters until the very end of the play, when the secret is revealed, tipping the balance in favor of the hero or heroine. In such works as *Fedora, Theodora,* and *La Tosca,* Sardou created melodramas full of passion and pageantry that overwhelmed audiences.

Madame Rhea opened the 1885–86 season in a new vehicle by Sardou called *A Dangerous Game.* A radiantly beautiful woman, Rhea projected elegance and sophistication through her extravagant costumes. She had first appeared at the Walnut in 1882 and had returned numerous times. She played many of the roles identified with Bernhardt, such as Camille and Adrienne, but gave them a fresh interpretation. She remained in the United States for the entirety of her career, rarely going into New York but touring successfully in cities and towns across the country.

Minnie Maddern returned on November 16, 1885, in Steele MacKaye's *In Spite of All,* which was a reworking of Sardou's *Andrea.* MacKaye turned "what Sardou, and all his translators had crafted as a standard contemporary social-melodrama into what later generations would call a black comedy," noted Gerald Bordman.[14] The play established the twenty-year-old actress as a star and attracted the notice of the influential editor of the *Dramatic Mirror,* Harrison Grey Fiske, whom she married in 1890. The play was superbly cast, with Richard Mansfield supporting Maddern as her cynical manager. Mrs. Fiske and Mansfield would become the most influential American actors of the 1890s.

The actress who most modeled herself after Bernhardt was Fanny Davenport, who began to secure the rights to Bernhardt's vehicles. She did this first in 1884 with Sardou's *Fedora,* which she performed at the Walnut on March 31, 1884. Davenport persuaded the author not to publish the play in France, thereby preventing other actresses from performing it. She later acquired several other tragic roles identified with Bernhardt, notably *La Tosca, Cleopatra,* and *Gismonda.*

The Walnut Street Theatre received one of its periodic remodelings for the 1885–86 season. Once again the interior was torn out and new flooring laid for the stage. A new ventilator was installed in the center of the dome. "Medallions of famous actors were to be seen in the entry amid the splendors of an interior decoration which one writer politely referred to as baroque," wrote Thomas Marshall. The front of the house was repainted and illuminated with electric lights. "In fact, the whole theatre has been so beautified as to be almost beyond recognition," the opening night program boasted. The Walnut sat 312 people in the orchestra, 342 in the dress circle, 360 in the balcony, and 400 in the upper gallery.

In his "History of the Philadelphia Theatre," Marshall noted that "a rather noticeable feature of 1886 was the reluctance of Manager Fleishman at the Walnut to introduce new plays. During the year, only eight first productions were recorded there." He added, however, "Although it produced few new plays during the year, it gave the public all their favorite actors, generally in favorite parts, and managed to secure the services of a large number of newer stars."[15]

One of these rising stars was nineteen-year-old Viola Allen, who was featured for the first time in *Talked About,* the opening show of the 1886–87 season. Allen would get greater notice in 1889 with her performance in *Shenandoah.* Richard Mansfield returned on September 13 in *Prince Karl,* his first starring role. He played an impoverished prince who served as a tour guide for American visitors. Critics were divided on the merits of the play but praised Mansfield for his performance. He played the role with a light, polished German accent rather than the exaggerated stage dialect common at the time. Robert B. Mantell had his first starring role in *Tangled Lives,* which opened at the Walnut on September 27. Mantell's acting style was described as "flamboyant" and "full of feverish emotions," and the play was written to show off these attributes.[16] The handsome Scottish-born actor had come to America in 1878 to support Helena Modjeska, and later toured with Fanny Davenport. He continued to play romantic leads through the 1880s and '90s, later turning to Shakespearean roles. Rose Coghlan followed in a week of repertory after the first of the year. The Irish-born beauty had a commanding presence onstage, and her performance as Rosalind in *As You Like It* was a special favorite.

Outshining them all was the legendary beauty Lillie Langtry, who made her Walnut debut on January 17, 1887, in *A Wife's Peril.* She remained a second week, during which she presented *The Lady of Lyons.* The tall, statuesque blonde was the reigning beauty in London society. She had come to America in 1882. This was the second of several tours she made to the United States, and she traveled in a private railroad car lavishly decorated to her specifica-

fig. 19 Actress Lillie Langtry was known not only for her stage career but for her legendary beauty, social status, and many notable lovers.

tions. She returned the following year in *As in a Looking Glass,* about a woman who falls in love with the man she married for money, then commits suicide to save him from disgrace. Maurice Barrymore played her husband.

THEATRE CONSTRUCTION

In the fall of 1889 Israel Fleishman opened the sixteen-hundred-seat Park Theatre on the northeast corner of Broad and Fairmount streets. Fleishman's dream was to construct the perfect theatre, and the Park was fully illuminated by electricity. The Walnut also received some upgrading. The exterior of the theatre was marbleized and the interior brightened. However, the repairs could not hide the fact that "evidence of its age was too apparent for the comfort of cast and audience."[17]

The economy was good, and a number of theatres opened in Philadelphia at this time. The Grand Opera House at Broad and Montgomery gave Philadelphia a second venue for opera. The Bijou at Eighth and Race streets became Philadelphia's most important variety house. There were nineteen theatres operating in Philadelphia by the end of the 1880s, up from thirteen a decade earlier. Most of these were popularly priced houses that offered some combination of melodramas, farces, variety and minstrel shows, and dialect plays. Samuel Nixon and Frederick Zimmerman controlled the three most important theatres in Philadelphia—the Broad Street Theatre, the Chestnut Street Opera House, and the Chestnut Street Theatre. The Broad Street Opera House was generally considered the leading theatre in the city. The Chestnut Street Opera House was the more fashionable theatre and catered to a younger clientele. Edgar Leroy Potts observed that the three theatres controlled by Nixon and Zimmerman "were high-priced houses, offering the best traveling productions and the star players, both native and foreign. Of the three, it would be difficult to say which came first in distinction."[18]

COMEDY IN THE 1890S

In this increasingly competitive market, the Walnut found its niche as a family house. Fleishman relied heavily on comedy to attract this audience. As a result, the fall of 1890 was a good one for comediennes. Annie Pixley opened the season on September 13 in *Kate*, a play about a woman who follows her beloved into battle during the Civil War. Lotta Crabtree arrived on October 27, after an absence of exactly a decade. She presented *Musette* and introduced two new pieces, *A Faint Heart* and *Ina*. It was also her last run at the Walnut, for she suffered a bad fall during a performance the following year and retired shortly thereafter. Russell's Comedians arrived on November 10 in *The City Directory*, a musical starring William Collier and featuring May Irwin in a supporting role. The plump, blonde soubrette with an infectious sense of fun became one of the most popular entertainers of her day. The following month, Fay Templeton made her Walnut debut in *Miss McGinty of the Comédie Française*. The twenty-five-year-old actress had begun her career as a child, touring with her parents. She became a great favorite with Weber and Fields's company, and introduced "Mary's a Grand Old Name" in George M.

Cohan's *Forty-Five Minutes from Broadway.* Kate Castleton played the following March in *Faust Up-to-Date.*

Several comedy teams toured. Despite protests from Irish antidefamation groups, Billy Barry and Hugh Fay continued to perform their knockabout Irish comedy roles in *McKenna's Flirtation,* which they brought out in April 1890. Other comedians were developing more individualized "eccentric" characterizations—among them the comedy team of Donnelly and Girard, who appeared in *Natural Gas* on February 24, 1890. The play was written by Philadelphia-based minstrel Frank Dumont. The pair returned to the Walnut five times between 1890 and 1893, a sure sign of their popularity. The diminutive Frank Daniels played a man who must take his son's place in school in *Little Puck,* in which he appeared for the first time on April 15, 1889, returning several times in the ensuing seasons. Dialect comedian Gus Heege appeared as *Yon Yonson,* a Swede from North Dakota. Richard Golden revived the homespun Yankee character in *Old Jed Prouty* in March 1892.

The leading comedians of the time found steady work in musicals. Henry E. Dixey was already an established musical comedy star when he first appeared at the Walnut in *The Seven Ages* during the spring of 1890. He depicted the seven ages of man referenced in Shakespeare. The show featured Dixey's clowning, along with music and dance and pretty chorus girls. Dixey had made his reputation in *Adonis,* playing a statue that is brought to life. He performed it at the Walnut for the first time in 1893. James T. Powers was a "small, red-headed, rubber-faced comedian" who made his first appearance in September 1891 in *A Straight Trip* and made return appearances in 1892 in *A Mad Bargain* and the following year in *Walker, London,* as a barber who has one last fling before his marriage to a domineering woman. Nat C. Goodwin made his first starring appearance at the Walnut in *The Nominee* in January 1891. He returned in *Art and Nature* in February 1892. Goodwin scored a triumph in *A Gilded Fool* the following season, in which he played a young man who must prove to his fiancée that he can make a fortune on his own. Peter F. Dailey made his mark in *A Country Sport* in the fall of 1893, as a man demonstrating that he is a "thorough-bred sport" in order to win an inheritance. Dailey gained his greatest renown with Weber and Fields's company, where he was known for his quick-witted ad-libs.

CHANGES IN MANAGEMENT

On July 28, 1891, the Walnut's longtime gasman, John "Pop" Reed, passed away at the age of eighty-three. He had been connected with the Walnut Street Theatre for sixty-six years. He had long expressed interest in donating his skull to the Walnut, so that future Hamlets "might, in a side speech, exclaim, smiting it playfully over the plate, 'So this is all that is left of poor old John Reed.'"[19] In his will he requested that "my head . . . be separated from my body immediately after death, the latter to be buried in a grave; the former duly macerated and prepared to be brought to the theatre where I served all my life, and to be employed to represent the skull of Yorick."[20]

Less than a month later, the Walnut suffered a second loss, when Israel Fleishman passed away. He had been ill for some time with Bright's disease and his death was not unexpected. Both the Walnut and the Park were taken over by Rich and Harris, a Boston firm, and Frank Howe Jr. was installed as manager of both theatres. The productions were not particularly noteworthy, a mix of comedies and musicals. *The Country Circus* was performed for two weeks in mid-October. Publicity announced that more than $50,000 had been spent on the production and that five hundred people were employed in putting on the play. In addition to the actors, the production called for forty horses, sixteen trained dogs, four goats, several monkeys, a donkey, and more. Seven train cars were needed to transport everything.

James A. Herne directed the show. "It was a potboiler that Herne despised," his biographer, John Perry, asserted. "It forced him to compromise his artistic integrity for a menagerie of dogs, cats, baboons, and monkeys." Perry indicates that Herne's staging was highly imaginative. "*The Country Circus*' big scene unfolded beneath a tent rigged on stage with ring and sawdust. Its top held brightly colored posters and flags with the producers' names: Klaw, Erlanger and Jefferson."[21] The play moved to Broadway in late December and ran for a hundred nights.

Popular tastes favored swashbuckling characters, and the term "matinee idol" came into common usage around this time. Young ladies often attended matinees on their own, and preferred dashing, good-looking actors in romantic roles. The leading matinee idol of the time was Robert B. Mantell, a handsome Scottish actor. He appeared in such plays as *The Corsican Brothers, The Marble Heart,* and *Monbars* at the Walnut in December 1891. Alessandro Salvini, the son of Tommaso Salvini, rejected tragedy for romantic roles. He made his first appearance at the Walnut in February 1892 in romantic melodramas like *Don Caesar de Bazan* and *The Three Guardsmen.*

THE CENTRAL THEATRE FIRE

Theatre building continued into the new decade, with several smaller, popularly priced theatres opening up—the New Standard, the Kensington, and the People's Theatre in 1890, the Empire and the Girard in 1891, and the Gaiety and the Star in 1893.

On the evening of April 27, 1892, Philadelphia lost one of its premiere houses when the Central Theatre, a thirty-four-hundred-seat theatre located one block east of the Walnut, went up in flames. The Central was primarily used for extravaganzas. The curtain was about to go up on a production of *The Devil's Auction* when a piece of the canvas scenery touched one of the gas jets and caught fire. The flames quickly spread along the borders to the curtain. Panic ensued, as the crowd in the upper galleries struggled down the inadequate stairways to safety. Dozens were trampled, and some leaped from the upper windows onto the street below. The cast featured a large company of ballet dancers, acrobats, and chorus girls, and the large number of players created confusion backstage, too.

News of the fire reached the Walnut Street Theatre, where an audience was assembled for a new comedy titled *Imagination*. The curtain had not yet gone up. Concerned that news of the nearby fire would cause panic, the Walnut's manager announced that one of the principal cast members was sick and that the performance would have to be canceled. The audience filed out of the theatre and only discovered the truth when they reached the street.

The scene on the street was chaotic. "Actors searched wildly for friends or relatives. Half clad women wept in fear, as they sought for missing husbands. At a nearby theatrical hotel, the broken company reassembled in an effort to learn who had still to be accounted for. Ambulances worked late into the night, carrying away the injured and the burned," wrote Edgar Leroy Potts.[22] It was several days before the true extent of the tragedy could be determined. In the smoking ruins of the Central Theatre, rescue workers found the bodies of four actresses and two actors. Seven spectators also lost their lives.

The tragedy naturally raised concerns about fire safety at the Walnut, and during the summer recess, new firewalls were built above the cornices and a fire escape was added to the Ninth Street wall to allow a quick exit from the gallery. Gas fixtures were replaced by electrical ones. The ornamentation and hangings were "in shades of yellow ranging from cream to salmon. The effect is rich and pleasing, and the subdued character of the decorations in the front of the house enhances the brilliancy of the stage picture," the *Public Ledger* reported.[23]

TRANSITIONS

The 1891–92 season was the last for Mrs. Drew at the Arch Street Theatre. She had been managing the house for more than thirty years. Philadelphia's theatrical community gathered together for a tribute to Mrs. Drew at the Academy of Music on June 6, 1892. The Arch Street Theatre was then leased to Charles B. Jefferson, the son of Joseph Jefferson. After 1892, however, "the Arch Street Theatre was no longer of any importance in the theatrical life of Philadelphia. It declined at an ever increasing rate; the rest of its history is simply that of a fine old theatre fallen upon evil days," according to Potts.[24]

Joseph Jefferson returned to the Walnut for the first time since 1878, appearing in *Rip van Winkle.* He had been touring with Mrs. Drew for some years in an all-star production of *The Rivals.* With Mrs. Drew in retirement, the sixty-three-year-old comedian returned to his most famous role. "His comedy has a subtle charm; his pathos a winning interest, and his personality a magnetism that seems to lend an air of enchantment," the program stated. Jefferson would return for two more runs at the Walnut, appearing there for the last time in 1894.

The only play of any significance to be staged at the Walnut that fall was a musical comedy titled *Miss Helyet,* produced by David Belasco and starring Mrs. Leslie Carter. A temperamental society lady, Carter turned to the stage following a sensational divorce. She persuaded David Belasco to train her and star her in his productions. *Miss Helyet* was billed as a play with "musical attachment" and featured Mrs. Carter as a Quaker girl who goes on a spree in Paris. She did not do well, and Belasco withdrew her for more training; she returned to the stage with more success several years later in the Civil War melodrama *The Heart of Maryland.* Mrs. Carter had subsequent success with *Zaza,* a French drama about a music-hall singer, and *Du Barry,* the story of a courtesan, but she never returned to the Walnut.

Also making his first appearance on the Walnut's stage was a romantic tenor specializing in Irish roles named Chauncey Olcott. He made his debut on January 23, 1893, in Augustus Pitou's Irish drama *Mavourneen,* taking over the part created by W. J. Scanlan. During the New York run of the show, Scanlan became increasingly erratic owing to paresis, and Pitou needed another romantic Irish tenor to fill the role. Olcott not only replaced Scanlan, he surpassed him, appearing regularly at the Walnut for the next twenty years. Beginning in 1895, Olcott took over the profitable Christmas week run.

Although Olcott is little known today, he wrote or introduced some of our most familiar Irish melodies, among them "My Wild Irish Rose," which he introduced in the 1899 *Romance of Althone,* and "Mother Machree," which was featured in the 1910 production *Barry from Ballymore.* Another song Olcott popularized was "When Irish Eyes Are Smiling," from *The Isle of Dreams,* a 1913 production. All of these plays were sentimental portrayals of Irish life. "Chauncey's delight and forte were in the scenes that smacked of fairyland, glimpses of that fanciful world where all is beauty and love is master," wrote one observer.[25]

THE PANIC OF 1893

In the spring of 1893, the nation suffered yet another of its economic meltdowns. The Panic of 1893 was caused by a drop in gold reserves, which sent stocks tumbling. A month later, banks called in their loans, businesses failed, and the country entered a depression that would last four years. Banks failed nationwide, nearly fifteen thousand companies shut down, and workers struck. The summer of 1893 also marked the loss of Edwin Booth, who died in his apartment atop the Players Club in New York City early on June 7, 1893. The fifty-nine-year-old actor had been ailing for some time. Newspapers across the country ran front-page obituaries. The funeral was held at the Church of the Transfiguration, the actors' church known as "The Little Church Around the Corner." His body was carried to Boston for burial.

Despite the looming economic crisis, the 1893–94 season was a good one, particularly for musicals. Lottie Collins arrived on September 25 in a piece titled *A Naughty Substitute*. She was supported by the Howard Athenaeum Company of Boston, one of the best-known vaudeville companies in the country. Collins played a chorus girl who is asked to substitute for a mind reader at a charity event. The role showcased her specialties, which included "Ta-ra-ra-boom-de-ay," Collins's saucy, show-stopping musical number. "Like our own Lotta [Crabtree], she can commit, what might be in another most outré acts, but in Miss Collins, are simply graceful picturings of the dancer's art," the program noted. Peter F. Dailey returned in *A Country Sport*, a farce-comedy with interpolated songs that had been the hit of the 1891–92 season. He played a small-town man who must visit the Bowery in order to inherit a fortune. May Irwin had a supporting role in the show. On November 6, Henry Dixey debuted in *Adonis*, a burlesque extravaganza, playing a statue that is brought to life. He had been touring in the play for nearly a decade. During its New York run it won the distinction of being the longest-running show on Broadway up to that time.

Several musicals by Charles H. Hoyt had their Walnut premieres that season. Hoyt's 1888 satire on superstition, *The Brass Monkey*, played the week of October 16, 1893. *A Texas Steer* played for two weeks the following month. Described as a farce with interpolated songs, it depicted the troubles of a rich Texan elected to Congress who gets fleeced by the sharpies around Washington. The play had originally been produced in 1890. Hoyt's most successful musical, *A Trip to Chinatown*, debuted in mid-February. Bessie Clayton starred in this revival of the 1891 musical, which introduced such songs as "The Bowery," "Reuben, Reuben," and "After the Ball."

Among the dramatic actors who appeared at the Walnut that season were Thomas Keene and Robert Mantell. Each came in with a week of repertory.

Rose Coghlan appeared in Oscar Wilde's *A Woman of No Importance,* and Julia Marlowe made her Walnut debut in *Romeo and Juliet* and other plays.

FRANK HOWE JR.

During the summer of 1894, Frank Howe Jr. took over the lease of the Walnut. He had been running the theatre on behalf of Rich and Harris, but now he was making the decisions. The fall season saw much the same offerings as in previous years. Eddie Foy had his first starring role in *Off the Earth,* a comic trip to the moon. Lottie Collins returned, heading up her own company, Lottie Collins's Troubadours. Robert Mantell also returned, and Joseph Jefferson played his last run at the Walnut the week of November 12.

On November 19, 1894, Canary and Lederer presented *The Passing Show* at the Walnut. It was described as a "topical extravaganza," but it is recognized as the first musical revue. *The Passing Show* satirized events of the previous year, with parodies of *Cleopatra* and other recent stage hits. Reviewers, unacquainted with the revue form, called it "a variety show . . . based on the operas and plays of the day." The show was successful both in New York and on the road, and others soon followed. Over the next several seasons, the Casino produced annual revues, among them *In Gay New York* and *The Whirl of the Town,* which also came to the Walnut.

By December 1894 there was a distinct shift in the offerings, with a strong emphasis on drama and a greater investment in star power. Howe engaged Lillie Langtry for Christmas week. She appeared in *A Wife's Peril,* co-starring Maurice Barrymore.

The New Woman, which opened on February 4, 1895, took as its theme the controversy over women's rights. Annie Russell played a woman who marries above her station to find that her husband, E. M. Holland, is being pursued by a freethinking woman. Russell had recently returned to the stage after a three-year absence due to illness. Appearing in a supporting role was Mrs. D. P. Bowers as the aristocratic Lady Wargrove. She had not been seen at the Walnut for twenty years. Mrs. Bowers had toured as a star until 1885, after which she acted in support of other stars, most notably the Booth-Salvini combination. This was to be her last run at the Walnut. She passed away the following September at the age of sixty-five.

Julia Marlowe opened on March 3 with her repertoire of Shakespeare plays. The slender beauty with dark, wistful eyes had chosen to operate her own company and play starring roles outside New York rather than take on supporting roles at the Empire Theatre. She was touring with her husband,

Robert Taber, and Rose Eytinge, who at age sixty was also taking on supporting roles. The company had a successful four-week run.

The following season saw more dramatic actresses. Mme. Helena Modjeska played two weeks of repertory in late November, featuring *Mary Stuart, Camille,* and other emotional vehicles. The Polish actress had come to America in 1877, but this was her first appearance at the Walnut. A reviewer noted that in her portrayal of Mary Queen of Scots, "Modjeska plays with surpassing power, exhibiting every emotion and thrilling her hearers with her final denunciation of Elizabeth. As of yore, Modjeska carried her audience with her, and was recalled many times after the fall of the curtain."[26] The tall beauty was known for the grace and poetry of her acting. Supporting her was William S. Hart, who became famous as a cowboy star in movies.

Minnie Maddern Fiske followed for a week in a minor play, *The Queen of Liars,* a melodrama translated from the French by her husband, Harrison Grey Fiske. A reviewer for the *Public Ledger* captured her unique appeal. "There is about her none of the greatness that doth hedge in some members of her craft, nor is she the less welcome on this score; rather let it be said that she is so intensely human, so like the rest of us poor mortals, that she almost seems to belong in the audience."[27] During that week Mrs. Fiske played a single performance of Ibsen's *A Doll's House.* She was a leading proponent of Ibsen's work, although many critics and audience members rejected the pessimism of his plays. The reviewer had mixed feelings about the production, calling it "disagreeable," but noted that the play contained "much matter for the thoughtful to ponder over." Mrs. Fiske's portrayal of Nora was singled out. "The development of her character from that of a light frivolous lark without moral sense of the ordinary pattern, to a self-resourceful woman, determined to learn the lessons of life by herself was wonderfully well pictured."[28]

Fanny Janauschek had a supporting role in a melodrama called *The Great Diamond Robbery,* staged on December 9, 1895. No longer able to attract audiences, Janauschek was reduced to appearing in cheap melodramas. "Denied star billing, she still received a huge, show-stopping welcome on her first appearance," Gerald Bordman reported. "As a criminal mastermind, she brought remarkable shadings to her interpretation, suggesting the cruel injustices of her early years as much as any naturally evil bent had determined her chilling course."[29] Chauncey Olcott closed out the year, bringing back Augustus Pitou's *Mavourneen,* inaugurating a tradition of appearing during the Christmas season that would last more than twenty years.

THE SYNDICATE YEARS, 1896–1920

By the mid-1890s, Samuel F. Nixon and J. Fred Zimmerman had emerged as the most powerful theatre managers in Philadelphia. They controlled the four leading theatres in Philadelphia—the Broad, the Park, the Chestnut, and the Chestnut Street Opera House. In 1896 they joined forces with New York booking agents Marc Klaw and Abe Erlanger, producer Charles Frohman, and theatre owner Al Hayman to form what became known as the Theatrical Syndicate. In a secret agreement, the partners agreed to share the profits from the thirty-three theatres they directly owned or leased, and from several hundred smaller theatres they booked. They were now poised to take control of the entire theatre industry.

In doing this, they were operating like the other trusts of the day. The 1890s was the era of the robber barons, and the Syndicate sought to control theatrical bookings as John D. Rockefeller was doing with oil, and other industrialists were attempting in railroads, banking, and steel. This move was not simply based on greed: some kind of consolidation was necessary. The number of theatres and touring companies had grown enormously, and the informal method of booking shows no longer worked. Actors and theatre owners complained about wasteful competition, double bookings, and empty houses. By organizing a circuit, the members of the Syndicate would be able to reduce competition and systematize theatrical bookings. They would also be able to dictate their terms.

Because they controlled access to so many theatres, the members of the Syndicate were able to exert a great deal of control over any producer who wanted to book a national tour. A producer who played a Syndicate house in one city was forced to play a Syndicate house wherever he went. The men

fig. 20 Walnut Street Theatre, circa 1900.

of the Syndicate began to demand a third of the theatre's profits in the larger cities, and 5 or 10 percent in small towns.[1] They also took a fee from producers—as much as 50 percent to guarantee good bookings. During the fall of 1896, the members of the Syndicate began buying up theatres. By February 1897 they owned or leased fifty-five theatres in the United States and Canada. The following month, Klaw and Erlanger took over the lease on the Walnut Street Theatre, bringing it into the Syndicate.[2]

MUSICALS

All Syndicate shows were booked through Klaw and Erlanger's agency in New York. This meant that the Walnut got the leading shows of the era. Musical comedy featured prominently in the 1897–98 season. Thomas Seabrooke opened the fall season in *Papa Gou Gou,* an adaptation of a French play that he was touring prior to its New York opening. *The Whirl of the Town* followed. It was an early musical revue, which had had a successful summer run at the Casino Theatre in New York. *The Widow Jones* provided May Irwin with her first starring role, as a woman who pretends to be married to escape the attention of suitors. "There is never a dull moment while she is on the stage," a reviewer noted. "Her unaffected way of seeming to enjoy the fun as much as any of the audience adds a charm of its own to her most happy passages."[3] Irwin introduced her famous "Bully Song," a classic "coon song," done in a pseudo–African American dialect. The kissing scene from the play was filmed by the Edison Company and released as *The Kiss;* it became one of the most famous film clips of the silent era. Camille D'Arville, "the Queen of Comic Opera," appeared in an early Victor Herbert operetta, *Peg Woffington.* Marie Dressler followed in *Courted into Court,* a farce-comedy.

The most notable production of the season was *The Belle of New York,* which debuted in early December. This precursor to *Guys and Dolls* centered on a Salvation Army girl who reforms a man-about-town. The musical had only a modest New York run but was very successful on the road. It was brought back for two more weeks near the close of the season. Chauncey Olcott returned for his year-end run of *Sweet Inniscarra,* a romantic drama by Augustus Pitou, who had long since given up acting for a career as a playwright and producer. The new year saw Eddie Foy in a musical revue titled *In Gay New York,* May Irwin in *The Swell Miss Fitzwell,* and Louis Mann and Clara Lipman in *The Telephone Girl.*

Among the dramatic productions that season was *A Ward of France,* a historical romance featuring Maurice Barrymore as the pirate Jean Lafitte. It was to be Barrymore's last appearance at the Walnut. He died a few years later—yet another victim of paresis. Fanny Davenport made her final appearance in early 1898. A heart condition forced her to retire in March, and she passed away in September, at the age of forty-eight. Lionel Barrymore made his Walnut debut on February 28 in *Cumberland '61,* a Civil War drama about a family of mountaineers divided by the conflict. His younger sister Ethel and brother John would soon follow him into the profession.

WAR WITH SPAIN

On February 15, 1898, the battleship *Maine* exploded in Havana's harbor, killing 260 crewmen. The tabloid press seized upon the incident to lobby for war against Spain, accusing Spanish officials of setting off the blast. Throughout March there were patriotic displays in the theatres, with speeches and singing of anthems. On March 11, Frank Howe Jr. and the Walnut's company joined other Philadelphia companies in a benefit at the Academy of Music to aid the survivors of the *Maine.* In early April, President McKinley asked Congress for a formal declaration of war, which was quickly passed. Caught up in the jingoistic fervor, Americans took to the war. The conflict lasted only 113 days and was over before the fall theatre season was under way. Spain signed an armistice on August 12, 1898, and America acquired Cuba, Puerto Rico, and the

Philippines. Philadelphia celebrated "Peace Jubilee Week" during the week of October 24. That week, *Way Down East* debuted at the Walnut. Florenz Ziegfeld co-produced this melodrama with William A. Brady. Standard melodramatic fare, it was set on a New England farm, where a woman with a past has sought refuge as a servant. The star of the show, Phoebe Davis, played the role more than four thousand times, although the play is best remembered in the silent film version that starred Lillian Gish. On November 14 the Syndicate brought in the Hugh Morton and Gustave Kerker revue *Yankee Doodle Dandy*, which played on anti-Spanish sentiments, as a couple sets out on a tour of New York in search of two Spanish spies. Each location they visit provides the theme of a song-and-dance number. The chase takes them to Washington for a cakewalk production titled "Coon Chowder Party." The show played for three weeks.

Rose Coghlan came in for three weeks in *The White Heather*, a melodrama set in Scotland. It featured an underwater scene in which two deep-sea divers battle it out at the bottom of the ocean, as they try to retrieve crucial evidence from a sunken ship. Chauncey Olcott finished out the year in *A Romance of Althone*, a new musical by Augustus Pitou. Olcott introduced his own composition, "My Wild Irish Rose," which quickly became a standard. Roland Reed, the son of the Walnut's gasman, "Pop" Reed, returned in *The Woman Hater*, a comedy about the troubles besetting a man who proposes to three different women. Madame Modjeska appeared in repertory that included *Mary Stuart* and *Antony and Cleopatra* the week of January 16, 1899, for what would be her last run at the Walnut.

THE SYNDICATE AND *CYRANO*

As the Syndicate solidified its position in the entertainment business, it became clear that it was largely serving the interests of its partners. Attractions owned or managed by a member of the Syndicate were given the best routes and theatres. Those who resisted were booked into second-rate houses or forced to make long jumps between venues. Few actors and producers had the clout to resist. Several leading stars—notably Francis Wilson, Nat C. Goodwin, Minnie Maddern Fiske, Fanny Davenport, James A. Herne, and Richard Mansfield—agreed not to book through Klaw and Erlanger's agency but deal exclusively with individual theatre managers instead.

The Syndicate responded by offering them extremely generous terms. The first to succumb was Richard Mansfield, who was widely regarded as the best actor of his day. In the summer of 1898 he began appearing in Syndicate-controlled houses. On March 27, 1899, Mansfield opened at the Walnut in

Cyrano de Bergerac, Edmond Rostand's classic story about a man who courts the woman he loves on behalf of a much handsomer man. The play had debuted in Paris the year before and was the kind of colorful heroic role in which Mansfield excelled. His production featured more than a hundred actors in period costumes.

Seats for the three-week run were sold out well in advance, and ticket scalpers had a field day. Mansfield's biographer related that on the closing night of his Philadelphia run, three men presented themselves at the Walnut's box office, only to find that no tickets were available. A scalper had one seat left, which they purchased. "The problem of how three men were to see the play on one ticket was met in this way," Paul Wilstach explained. "One man went in for the first act. He handed his pass off to the second man for the next act. The last man watched the third act. They flipped a coin for the remaining two acts."[4]

Shortly after the fall 1899 season opened, news arrived that John Sleeper Clarke had passed away at his home in London at the age of sixty-six. He had last been seen in Philadelphia in 1888, but he had held on to both the Walnut and the Broad Street Theatre. The Walnut passed to his sons, Creston and Wilfred Clarke, who both had thriving acting careers of their own.

The Syndicate continued to operate the Walnut and booked in most of the leading stars and productions of the day. Even those who originally spoke out against the Syndicate eventually caved in. Among them was James O'Neill, best remembered as the father of playwright Eugene O'Neill, who depicted him in *Ah, Wilderness!* and *Long Day's Journey into Night*. James O'Neill came into the Walnut on September 18 with two Alexandre Dumas plays. The first week he played D'Artagnan in *The Musketeers*, and the second week Edmund Dantès in *The Count of Monte Cristo*, the role for which he was most famous. Although O'Neill had been touring *Monte Cristo* since 1883, this seems to have been his first appearance at the Walnut.

Among the other leading stars to appear that season was Viola Allen, who opened a six-week run on November 13 in *The Christian*, about a music hall singer who falls in love with a young clergyman and gives up her career to help him minister to the poor. Allen produced the play herself. She had been a member of Charles Frohman's stock company at the Empire Theatre, but when Frohman dismissed the play as trash and refused to produce it, she went out on her own. It was a shrewd move, for it established Allen as an independent star, and she toured successfully for many years. A Christian theme was also at the heart of *Quo Vadis*, a costume drama set in Roman times, which had a three-week run beginning March 19, 1900. Based on a best-selling novel, it told the story of a Christian girl who is pursued by a Roman tribune. The play concluded with a spectacular burning of Rome.

Josephine Hall played in *Mam'sell 'Awkins* on April 23, about an impoverished nobleman who tries to fend off the advances of the daughter of a nouveau riche soap manufacturer. Her husband, Alfred E. Aarons, wrote and produced the play. *Mam'sell 'Awkins* played for seven weeks, before transferring to Atlantic City for the summer. It inaugurated a tradition of long season-ending runs by the actress. She returned in 1902 in *My Antoinette,* in 1903 in *The Knickerbocker Girl,* and in 1904 in *A China Doll.*

VAUDEVILLIANS AT THE WALNUT

In the summer of 1900, Paul Furman, the manager of the Walnut, experimented with vaudeville, putting together a bill that featured Maggie Cline and Pauline Hall. Cline sang Irish songs, and her rendition of "Throw Him Down, McCloskey" delighted the gallery. Hall sang selections from various operas. "Variety had been popular at the Bijou during the summer months, and Furman felt that, with good bills, he could make a success of it," theatre historian Joseph Meconnahey explained. "In a special effort to attract the public, he had a liquid air plant installed in the theatre, the first in the city. The expenditure was unnecessary, however, for the public was not interested in summer entertainment, and, after three unprofitable weeks, the house closed until fall."[5]

This was the only time that vaudeville was attempted at the Walnut, although a number of leading vaudevillians appeared at the Walnut in legit productions. The Four Cohans opened on April 29, 1901, in *The Governor's Son,* a musical based on their vaudeville act. The production was only moderately successful, but it allowed twenty-two-year-old George M. Cohan to make the leap from vaudeville into legitimate theatre. Eddie Foy opened the 1902 season in *The Wild Rose,* a musical based on *The Bohemian Girl,* about a pair of infants switched at birth. The cast included a pretty young showgirl, Evelyn Nesbit, playing a gypsy girl. Nesbit would be involved in the era's greatest scandal when her husband, Harry Thaw, murdered celebrity architect Stanford White at a rooftop theatre. Eddie Foy later went on to a career in vaudeville, doing impersonations of important public figures, and after 1910 he toured with his seven children as Eddie Foy and the Seven Little Foys. Evelyn Nesbit capitalized on her notoriety by touring in vaudeville, pulling in $1,750 a week in 1913.[6]

On November 10, 1902, two future vaudevillians, Trixie Friganza and Eva Tanguay, appeared in *The Chaperones.* Friganza was a large woman, and she made her weight the subject of her self-deprecating humor. She worked in musical comedy for some years, appearing at the Walnut in *His Honor the*

Mayor, *The Girl from Yama*, and *The Sweetest Girl in Paris*. From 1912 on she worked primarily in vaudeville. Tanguay went into vaudeville in 1904 and by 1910 was its highest-paid performer. "Eva Tanguay *was* American vaudeville," wrote Anthony Slide, "and for its entire existence, she was the medium's greatest female star."[7] Plump and not particularly attractive, she was deliberately outrageous. She had boundless energy onstage and sang suggestive songs, most famously "I Don't Care."

Two important figures made unheralded appearances at the Walnut that season. Will Rogers appeared between the acts of *The Girl Rangers*, doing his rope-spinning act. It was a brief venture into legitimate theatre. He returned to vaudeville shortly after the three-week run closed on October 26, 1907. On January 6, 1908, the blackface team of McIntyre and Heath put on *The Ham Tree*, a musical adventure about two African Americans who are stranded in a small town and pretend to be a rajah and his minister in order to get a room. W. C. Fields played a supporting role as a tramp juggler. Sophie Tucker had success playing a supporting role in *Louisiana Lou*, which played at the Walnut in 1912. She reportedly brought down the house each night with "The Puritan Prance," a spoof of underworld dancing.

A NEW CENTURY

By 1900 the Theatrical Syndicate dominated professional theatre in America. Only Mrs. Fiske refused to submit, and she was forced to play second-rate houses. The Syndicate controlled all the first-class theatres in Philadelphia. Only Gilmore's Auditorium, a block east of the Walnut, and the Academy of Music were available for non-Syndicate shows. Tensions were growing within the Syndicate, however. Abe Erlanger had emerged as the most powerful figure within the Syndicate. Nixon and Zimmerman were particularly unhappy with the bookings they were getting for their theatres, protesting that the best shows were going to the Walnut.[8] They threatened to withdraw and form a rival organization. On April 23, 1900, however, they signed a new agreement that extended the Syndicate for another five years, although their portion of the profits was cut from one-third to one-quarter.

The Walnut continued to get the best of the touring shows. A new touring company brought in *The Belle of New York* to open the fall season. It was produced by the Shubert brothers, who would establish themselves as the main competition to the Syndicate. Sam, Lee, and J. J. Shubert, then in their twenties, had gotten their start in upstate New York, where they put together a small chain of theatres. They purchased the touring rights to *The Belle of New York*, and the profits allowed them to move to New York, where they leased the Herald Square Theatre and began to produce their own shows. The Shuberts booked their shows through Klaw and Erlanger, gradually building a chain of theatres that would eventually compete with the Syndicate.

During the fall 1900 season the Walnut hosted a number of musicals. Dan Daly starred in *The Cadet Girl*, Peter F. Dailey in *Hodge, Podge and Co.*, Louis Mann and Clara Lipman in *All on Account of Eliza*, and Sam Bernard and Trixie Friganza in *The Belle of Bohemia*. All were leading musical comedy stars. Cecil B. DeMille had a supporting role in *Hearts Are Trumps*, an English melodrama that ran for four weeks in November.

Richard Mansfield returned on December 12 in a magnificent four-and-a-half-hour production of *Henry V*, presented with great pageantry. "One long scene was a color-strewn pantomime representing the return of Henry's troops from Agincourt," Gerald Bordman noted. "In a large plaza at the end of London Bridge, townspeople and officials gathered to welcome the soldiers. Venders hawked their wares, watched from windows and housetops by citizens unable to crowd the street below. Flags and banners waved in the breeze as trumpets heralded the arrival of the army. Company after company of battle-worn fighters paraded by. Wives and sweethearts broke through the mob to kiss loved ones."[9] The Walnut was the first stop on a successful tour; Mansfield returned in March, alternating *Henry V* with his other important plays.

CAPTAIN JINKS OF THE HORSE MARINES

The new year saw even more important productions. On January 7, 1901, Ethel Barrymore made her Walnut debut in *Captain Jinks of the Horse Marines*. It was the first starring role for the lovely twenty-one-year-old actress. Barrymore played a European opera star who is romanced by a cavalry officer who has bet his friends that he can win her affections. What begins as a cynical wager turns into real affection in the course of the play. Written by the popular playwright Clyde Fitch, the play was not well received at the Walnut. Barrymore's nervousness was evident to the opening night crowd, and one voice called out from the gallery, "Speak up, Ethel! All the Drews are good actors!" She rallied, but the critics lambasted her, and the show played to half-empty houses. *Captain Jinks* was scheduled to open on Broadway on February 4. Ethel Barrymore tried to persuade the producers to close the show, but Fitch had two other plays running on Broadway and was eager to have a third. This time Barrymore overcame her shyness, and both audience and critics responded. She became the toast of Broadway during the show's six-month run.

The same night that Ethel Barrymore had her New York debut, James A. Herne brought *Sag Harbor* to the Walnut. The play was essentially a rewrite

fig. 21 This publicity photo of the lovely Ethel Barrymore was taken twenty-one years after her Walnut Street Theatre debut, in the midst of her highly successful stage and screen career.

of *Hearts of Oak,* set in a New England fishing village. Two brothers vie for the affections of a girl, played by Herne's daughter Julie. Herne played her father, Captain Dan Marble, an homage to an earlier specialist in Yankee roles. It was to be his last run at the theatre where he had once worked as a stock actor. At sixty-one, Herne was ailing. When *Sag Harbor* played Chicago, he had to take himself out of the show. He died at his home a few weeks later.

Local color was the major appeal of Augustus Thomas's *Arizona,* which opened at the Walnut on February 18, 1901, for a three-week run. *Arizona* depicted the lives of soldiers in the desert Southwest. Filled with melodramatic elements, the dialogue was poetic and the production well mounted. The Shubert brothers produced the play, and the profits it made were key in establishing them as a viable alternative to the Syndicate.[10]

REVIVALS AND SEQUELS

The fall 1901 season failed to live up to the quality of the spring, relying mostly on revivals. *The Christian* opened the fall season, with Elsie Leslie replacing Viola Allen in the lead role; *Arizona* was revived as a vehicle for Dustin Farnum, who was establishing himself as a leading cowboy star. The Four Cohans brought back *The Governor's Son,* and James O'Neill appeared in *The Count of Monte Cristo.* Augustus Thomas tried to follow up the success of *Arizona* with *Colorado,* a conventional shoot-'em-up that failed to live up to the original. Lottie Blair Parker wrote *Under Southern Skies,* a successor to her highly successful *Way Down East.* It too had a disappointing run.

Otis Skinner appeared on December 2 in a highly regarded revival of *Francesca da Rimini,* George H. Boker's 1855 poetic drama. Skinner had built a successful career since his early years at the Walnut, acting opposite Edwin Booth and joining Lawrence Barrett's company, when he revived *Francesca da Rimini* in 1882, and acting with Augustin Daly's company for five years. Skinner had starred in the play in Chicago, and he brought it to the Walnut for two weeks prior to opening in New York. Despite the stilted language, the compassionate view of the characters and the well-acted and excellent production values made it one of the important revivals of a classic American tragedy.

ETHNIC MASQUERADE

Ethnic characters, which had fallen out of vogue in the 1890s, were making a comeback. Most would be viewed as stereotypical and racist today, but at the time they were considered realistic character types that could be found in the streets of America's major cities. Yankee, Irish, and blackface characters appeared regularly on the Walnut's stage during the 1902–3 season. Denman Thompson returned as the Yankee in his old warhorse, *The Old Homestead.* Ezra Kendall mined the same vein, playing a Yankee peddler from Buscomb's Corners in *The Vinegar Trader.* Chauncey Olcott was the leading Irish comedian of the era, brought into the Walnut each year for the profitable Christmas week. He premiered a new play, *The Old Limerick Town,* based on an old premise—an Irish émigré returns to the old sod and falls in love with a local girl. Andrew Mack also specialized in Irish roles, appearing in *The Bold Soger*

Boy. James O'Neill put aside his Monte Cristo character to attempt a Scottish dialect role in *The Manxman*, which played the first week of 1903. *San Toy* took advantage of the contemporary vogue for all things Oriental, with James T. Powers made up for an Asian role. The big minstrel company of the era was Primrose and Dockstaeder's Minstrels, who appeared at the Walnut for a week in March doing traditional blackface.

Eastern European Jews were represented onstage by Hebrew comics. The most capable comic specializing in Hebrew roles was David Warfield, who was Jewish. He first appeared at the Walnut in 1897 in the role of Solomon McCarthy in the musical revue *In Gay New York*. Warfield went on to work with Weber and Fields, where he specialized in playing a comic stereotype of an orthodox eastern European Jew—bearded, dressed in black, with a derby pulled low over his ears.

Warfield teamed up with producer David Belasco to produce *The Auctioneer*, the story of a Jewish used-furniture dealer on New York's Lower East Side. Critics hailed Warfield's portrayal as "the best stage characterization of a local type since the heyday of Edward Harrigan's Mulligans."[11] The play was co-written by David Belasco, Lee Arthur, and Charles Klein. Because Warfield was not well known outside New York, Klaw and Erlanger demanded 50 percent of the play's profits. Belasco agreed to these ruinous terms in order to get the play into first-class houses. It was a good gamble. *The Auctioneer* was a great success for both Warfield and Belasco. It established Belasco as a serious producer and allowed Warfield to be taken seriously as an actor.

RESTORATION WORK

During the week of May 17, 1903, the *Philadelphia Public Ledger* carried an article announcing that the Walnut would be remodeled. The Walnut Street Theatre Company had been formed, with Frank Howe Jr. as president. The company hired architect Willis G. Hale and spent $100,000 on altering the theatre, inside and out. The exterior was returned to the original 1829 design, and interior improvements included a women's lounge, a smoking room for men, and a promenade where theatergoers could stroll before the play started. The company also announced that it would begin to present operas as well as plays at the Walnut, but this never happened.

The Syndicate continued to tighten its hold on the theatre industry. That summer, it took control of three more theatres in Philadelphia, bringing the total to thirteen of the twenty-five theatres operating in the city.[12] But opposition to the Syndicate was mounting. The Shubert brothers were buying up and building theatres around the country. In the fall of 1903, the competition between the Shuberts and the Syndicate heated up, as Sam Shubert "aggressively sought out stars, producers and theatre owners who would join him in his challenge to the theatrical leviathan."[13] The Shuberts' goal was to acquire enough theatres in major cities to assure producers of a full year's bookings.

More improvements had to be made to the Walnut in the aftermath of the Iroquois Theatre fire in Chicago. A total of 387 people—mostly women and children—were trampled to death when flames swept through the Iroquois during a matinee performance on December 30, 1903. The tragedy sparked concern over safety at Philadelphia theatres, and the mayor appointed a special commission to investigate conditions in all places of amusement in the city. Two theatres were closed because of defective wiring. The Walnut had to reduce seating in its balcony from 850 to 50 until adequate exits were provided. Nearly every theatre in Philadelphia required better exits.

Tyrone Power appeared on January 11, 1904, in *Ulysses*, a verse drama based on Homer's *Odyssey*. Power was the grandson of the Irish comedian of the same name and the father of the movie star. Mabel Taliaferro followed in *Mrs. Wiggs of the Cabbage Patch*, an adaptation of the popular novel about a woman and her three daughters who live in a ramshackle house by the railroad tracks in Louisville. The play had had a successful premiere in New York in the fall. The night of February 29, Thomas W. Ross presented *Checkers*, about a young man who promises his fiancée he will give up gambling if she marries him. Her father insists that he earn $5,000 before he will give his consent to the marriage. This piece of fluff must have been well produced, for Ross brought it back the next two seasons. Josephine Hall finished out the year with *A China Doll*, a minor musical by Harry B. Smith, which played for seven weeks during April and May. Critics took note of the excellent sets, including a Chinese palace.

TWO LANDMARK PRODUCTIONS

The plays of the early 1900s were generally forgettable, as commercial considerations beat out artistic ones. The 1904–5 season saw two productions of lasting significance. Dustin Farnum starred in *The Virginian*, which opened on October 3, 1904. Farnum played an incorruptible ranch foreman who must pursue his best friend, who is in league with a gang of cattle rustlers. The play was based on a best-selling novel by Fanny Kemble's son-in-law, Owen Wister, who adapted it for the stage. The play established Farnum as a cowboy star and introduced the timeless line "When you call me that, smile." Farnum went on to a successful film career, reprising the role of the Virginian in the silent film version.

fig. 22 This photograph of George M. Cohan, in his characteristic song-and-dance-man pose, was taken around 1905.

Two weeks later, on October 19, George M. Cohan brought out his new musical, *Little Johnny Jones,* which he was touring before taking it to Broadway. Cohan played a jockey who goes to England to ride in the derby. He is offered a bribe to throw a race but refuses. He loses anyway, and the villain spreads the rumor that he lost intentionally, and Johnny Jones returns to America in disgrace. In the end, a detective unearths evidence that clears his name, but the villain kidnaps his sweetheart, and Johnny must rescue her. The musical was a breakthrough role for the show's twenty-six-year-old creator and star. The musical introduced two timeless musical numbers—"Give My Regards to Broadway" and "I'm a Yankee Doodle Dandy."

The rest of the season was undistinguished. *Resurrection*, a dramatization of a Tolstoy novel, played for two weeks in November. *The Earl of Pawtucket*, a new comedy by Augustus Thomas, followed. Lawrence d'Orsay played a British lord who tries to pass himself off as an American to win the woman he loves. Comedy had replaced melodrama as the most popular genre, and it was represented that season by *The Heir to the Hoorah* and *Weather Beaten Benson*. Musicals included *The Isle of Spice*, a formulaic piece about American sailors on a South Sea island, and *The Maid and the Mummy*, about a man who tries to pass himself off as an Egyptian mummy. Chauncey Olcott and Andrew Mack provided romantic Irish comedies. Several shows returned to the Walnut, including *Mrs. Wiggs of the Cabbage Patch*, *Checkers*, and *The Pit*.

THE SYNDICATE WARS

Shortly after the season closed, news arrived that Sam Shubert, the driving force behind the Shuberts, had died. He was traveling to Pittsburgh on May 12, 1905, when his train sideswiped an army transport train loaded with blasting powder. The explosion killed twenty-two passengers, including Shubert. He was only twenty-nine. Sam's death devastated the surviving brothers and raised Klaw and Erlanger's hopes that this threat to the Syndicate would collapse. Instead, Lee and J. J. Shubert redoubled their efforts. In July they severed relations with Klaw and Erlanger. With the help of backers, they acquired funds for the construction of eighteen new theatres, and that fall they opened a new theatre, the Lyric, located at Broad and Cherry streets, specifically designed to house non-Syndicate attractions.[14]

In the winter of 1905–6, the Shuberts booked Sarah Bernhardt for what was announced as her farewell tour of the United States. The Syndicate refused to allow the French tragedienne to perform in any Syndicate-controlled house, so she toured part of the country in a circus tent. The tour generated immense publicity against the Syndicate, and its six members were indicted in New York for conspiracy to restrain trade. The indictment was finally dismissed, but the Syndicate's reputation was badly damaged. Opponents of the Syndicate rallied around the Shuberts. David Belasco, the Fiskes, and the Shuberts organized the Society of Independent Managers and promoted an open-door policy, allowing companies that had played Syndicate theatres to play Shubert houses as well. They mounted a publicity campaign portraying themselves as champions of freedom and art against the mercenary commercial interests of the Syndicate.

As it became known that the Shuberts were determined in their opposition to the Syndicate, many stars who were dissatisfied with their bookings left the Syndicate and turned their booking rights over to the Shuberts. Seeing that such figures as E. H. Sothern, Julia Marlowe, and Mrs. Patrick Campbell were allied with the Shuberts, a number of theatre owners also came over to the opposition.

THE RISE OF MOTION PICTURES

While the Shuberts and the Syndicate were battling it out for control of the theatre industry, a far more important threat was emerging. In 1905 the first nickelodeon opened in Philadelphia in a converted storefront on the corner of Eighth and Market. The theatre held seventy-five seats; admission was a nickel. Theatre owners paid little attention, for the movies were still primitive, but the low ticket prices appealed to low-income patrons. Within two years, between four and five thousand nickelodeons dotted the country, and two million people attended each day.[15] The effect on the theatre industry was dramatic. Road companies soon discovered that they were losing one-night stands in smaller towns, while larger theatres reported fewer and fewer people in the galleries.

During this period a number of actors appeared at the Walnut who would make their reputation in films. Douglas Fairbanks made his Walnut debut in *The Pit* in 1903, in a supporting role. He returned in 1906 in George Broadhurst's *The Man of the Hour,* which played for a week prior to a highly successful run in New York. Fairbanks would return again in 1910, supporting Thomas Wise in *A Gentleman from Mississippi,* before abandoning the stage for films. William S. Hart made several appearances at the Walnut before leaving the stage for a film career as a cowboy star. Hart had begun as a Shakespearean actor supporting Madame Modjeska in 1895. He returned the following year, starring as an Arctic explorer in *Under the Polar Star,* and in 1903 in *Hearts Courageous,* a costume drama set in colonial times. Hart found his niche playing western characters, however, taking over for Dustin Farnum in *The Virginian* in 1907.

THE *CLANSMAN* CONTROVERSY

Many of the plays from this period acquired fame as silent movies. The most notorious was *The Clansman,* which became the basis of D. W. Griffith's silent film epic, *The Birth of a Nation. The Clansman* was a best-selling novel by an openly racist ex-minister named Thomas Dixon, who depicted the sufferings of a white South Carolina family during Reconstruction. Seeking a broader audience, he adapted the novel into a stage play, which, according to the program, told "how the South threw off the yoke of negro and carpet bagger bondage two years after the Civil War and reasserted the rights of white manhood and the honor of white womanhood." The play was a propaganda piece for Dixon's radical racist views. Dixon toured the play through the South and Midwest, making curtain speeches about "the awful suffering of the white man during the dreadful reconstruction period."[16] It had a brief run in New York earlier in the year and opened at the Walnut on April 23, 1906, to capacity crowds. Despite the controversial nature of the play, it played for four weeks.

When Dixon brought the play back to Philadelphia in the fall, it met with organized opposition from Philadelphia's black community. Local clergymen sent out flyers saying that the play encouraged lynching. When city officials failed to take action against the play, an African American newspaper asked for "10,000 colored men to make a demonstration." Some twenty-five hundred people assembled outside the Walnut on the night of October 22. "Despite the vigorous efforts of seventy five police, there was some disorder," Joseph Meconnahey wrote. "When the curtain was raised, a man in the audience stood up, vehemently denounced the play, and hurled an egg on the stage. He was removed, and the performance continued without interruption."

The following day, a delegation of African American community leaders met with the mayor, who issued a statement prohibiting further performances on the grounds that the play had a "tendency to intensify racial hatred and incite riot."[17] The Walnut's managers tried to get an injunction against the mayor's order, but a judge refused, and the theatre remained dark for the rest of the week. Despite organized opposition, *The Clansman* continued to tour for the next five years.[18]

POPULAR GENRES

Melodrama still remained popular, but playwrights increasingly applied the formula to contemporary social problems. George Broadhurst's *Man of the Hour* depicted a politician who defies the local political machine. It played for a week in October 1906 before moving on to New York, where it became the season's biggest hit. *The Jungle* was a dramatization of Upton Sinclair's muckraking novel about the meatpacking industry, adapted for the stage by Margaret Mayo. It came in for two weeks in December 1906. *The Spoilers*, which played for two weeks in February 1907, was another dramatization of a muckraking novel about the coming of law to the Klondike gold fields. Eugene Walter had been a newspaperman before turning to playwrighting. *Paid in Full* depicted a husband who is caught embezzling and turns to his wife, asking her to visit his employer and beg for his freedom. Julia Dean starred when the play came to the Walnut in late 1908.

The musicals of the period were derivative, heavily influenced by the European operetta. Many followed a formula of introducing Americans in a far-off locale, as in *The Isle of Spice*, which was so successful that two separate road companies were sent out. Even works with a nominally American theme used this formula, as with *His Honor the Mayor*, a musical by Alfred E. Aarons that played for fourteen weeks in the spring of 1907. Harry Kelly played a politician who is forced to leave town when it is revealed that he bought the election. Most of the action took place in Paris and a Hungarian spa. Among the better offerings was *The Time, the Place and the Girl*, which had a record-breaking run in Chicago and played for seven weeks at the Walnut in the spring of 1908 before moving on to New York. In this instance the protagonists were two drinking buddies who take refuge in a sanitarium, where they find romance with the women inmates.

Comedy continued to be popular, and even serious playwrights tried their hand at it. Augustus Thomas wrote *The Education of Mr. Pipp*, based on cartoons by Charles Dana Gibson, whose "Gibson Girls" defined the spirit of the period. Digby Bell played the henpecked husband of a social-climbing wife. May Robson had success in January 1909 in *The Rejuvenation of Aunt Mary*, playing a small-town spinster who goes to the city to rescue her nephew, only to succumb to all the temptations of urban life. Robson reprised the role for the 1927 film version. *Brewster's Millions*, which premiered at the Walnut on January 25, 1909, depicted the difficulties of a man who must spend $1 million within a year in order to win a $7 million inheritance. The production was in its second week when the Walnut reached its centennial. There was no acknowledgment of the milestone.

THE DECLINE OF THE ROAD

Beginning in 1910, the number of road shows began to decline markedly. The number of touring companies fell from 236 in 1910 to 97 in 1915.[19] This created turmoil in the theatre, for most productions made the bulk of their profits on the road. Producers could afford to lose money on a Broadway run in the expectation that they would recoup their investment on the road. But the number of theatres available for road shows was also declining, as less profitable theatres converted to film. The Shuberts and the Syndicate continued to engage in mutually destructive business practices. Both sides exploited the public with misleading advertising, claiming that the original Broadway cast was performing in a play when it was not. Many of the shows that came through the Walnut during this period never made it to New York—they were productions specifically designed for the road.

Edgar Selwyn's *The Country Boy* was the big success of the 1910–11 season, playing from January 9 through May 14, 1911. It told the story of a small-town boy who heads to New York to prove his worth. There he meets some people, and they return to start a newspaper in his hometown. Despite the holes in the story, it was "a real play, with real characterizations and a real plot," according to Gerald Bordman.[20] During its opening week, every visitor received a souvenir program that contained a history of the Walnut, along with portraits of actors and actresses who had appeared there. It was announced that the history was to be published in book form by J. B. Lippincott, but this never came to pass.

During the week of January 23, the modern dance pioneer Ruth St. Denis appeared in a series of four matinee performances entitled *Dances of Ancient Egypt*. The production included dances that St. Denis had introduced in vaudeville, along with selections from a dance theatre piece, *Egypta*, which she had introduced in New York the previous month.

Edgar Selwyn starred in his own play, *The Arab*, which opened the 1911–12 season. He played a Middle Eastern tour guide who falls in love with an American tourist and foils a plot by radical Islamists to massacre Christians. The production, which was on its way to New York, featured real Arabs, a bazaar, palm trees, and a live camel. Frank McIntyre starred in *Snobs*, about a milkman who suddenly inherits $70 million. Frank Reicher followed in *The Scarecrow*, a fantasy by Percy MacKaye based on a Nathaniel Hawthorne story about a seventeenth-century witch who brings a scarecrow to life. MacKaye was a leading proponent of the little theatre movement, which encouraged amateurs to take to the stage as an alternative to the overcommercialization of the professional stage.

On April 15, 1912, news arrived that the *Titanic* had sunk during its maiden voyage. Fifteen hundred people lost their lives, including Henry B. Harris of the theatrical firm of Rich and Harris, which held the lease on the Walnut Street Theatre. His wife, who survived the voyage, sued the White Star Line for $1 million, for the loss of his creative talent. John Kellerd finished out the season with a weeklong Shakespeare festival beginning April 22. The English actor had recently performed *Hamlet* for 102 nights, breaking Edwin Booth's record. The Walnut remained dark for a week, then was leased out for six weeks to millionaire-adventurer Paul J. Rainey, who presented his African hunt films, in which a lecturer provided live narration of films made during a big game hunt. This was the first time the Walnut was used as a movie house, but hardly the last.

MORE NEW THEATRES

Despite the decline of road shows, the years leading up to World War I were an affluent time, and speculators invested in building new theatres. Two new theatres opened in Philadelphia in 1909—the William Penn Theatre opened as a two-a-day vaudeville house, while the Victoria Theatre offered a combination of movies and vaudeville. Two more vaudeville houses, the Liberty and the Nixon, opened the following year. In 1911 the Keystone and the Princess were built to show silent movies, and the following year two large vaudeville houses, the Allegheny and Keith's Orpheum, opened for business. "In 1913," Irvin Glazer noted in *Philadelphia Theatres, A–Z,* "seventy vaudeville and motion picture theatres were under construction in Philadelphia. Virtually all of them were open by the fall, making an approximate total of 350 theatres including nickelodeons in the city."[21]

Vaudeville and motion pictures continued to chip away at the audience for legitimate theatre. By 1913 the Syndicate and the Shuberts were ready to call a truce. "So many new theatres had been built in cities and towns throughout the country, that there were not enough worthy attractions to fill these theatres," Monroe Lippman explained. "Cities which were able to satisfactorily support only one first-class theatre, had two or more: one controlled by the Syndicate and another controlled by the Shuberts or by an independent manager affiliated with the Shuberts." In order to keep their theatres filled and theatre managers satisfied, both factions had been forced to send out second-rate companies, often billing them as the original New York casts. The public quickly caught on, and theatre attendance plummeted.

The Shuberts and the Syndicate signed an agreement in February 1913 aimed at reducing competition in Philadelphia and three other major cities.[22] In the future, first-class productions in Philadelphia were to be confined to the (Old) Forrest, Garrick, Broad Street, Adelphi, and Lyric theatres.[23] The two factions agreed to stop their predatory business practices, hold on to their best theatres, and turn the rest into movie and vaudeville palaces.

LOUIS B. MAYER TAKES OVER

On March 2, 1913, the *Philadelphia Public Ledger* announced that the Walnut's lease was to be put up for sale, a development clearly tied to the agreement between the Syndicate and the Shuberts. The sale was ordered by Edgar J. Pershing, a trustee of the court appointed to sort out the legal difficulties that followed Henry Harris's death aboard the *Titanic.* The lease was taken over by two young entrepreneurs, Ben Stern and Louis B. Mayer. Mayer would later

fig. 23 A portrait of young mogul Louis B. Mayer, who began his career as a producer in theatre and managed the Walnut before making it big in Hollywood.

become the driving force behind Metro-Goldwyn-Mayer, but at twenty-eight he was still in the exhibition business. He and Stern had formed a company "to conduct a general amusement business in New York City, the U.S. and Canada." The Walnut was to be a showplace for touring shows they would produce.

The new managers did not realize it, but the Walnut needed extensive repairs. Local fire laws had recently been stiffened, and the theatre lacked the proper equipment for fire safety. Mayer and Stern were uncertain whether they could bring the Walnut up to code, and newspapers announced that the building might have to be razed. They eventually spent $6,000 refitting the theatre, and the fall season opened on schedule on August 30, 1913, with a production of *The Firefly,* a new operetta by Rudolf Friml and Otto Harbach.

The 1913–14 season inaugurated a distinct change in booking patterns. Long runs disappeared, and one- and two-week runs became the norm. The Walnut was a starting point for Mayer and Stern's touring shows. After a week's engagement, the plays toured up and down the eastern seaboard. For the most part these were low-budget productions of plays that had debuted on Broadway several years before—*A Fool There Was, Madame X, The Round Up, Way Down East,* and *Rebecca of Sunnybrook Farm.*

The policy was evidently successful, for the Walnut's owners increased the rent for the following year. The increase was more than the traffic would bear, however, and Mayer and Stern went to court to retrieve the $6,000 they had sunk into the theatre. It was also the end of their partnership. Mayer went on to distribute films like *The Birth of a Nation,* and in 1916 he moved to Hollywood, where he started his own production company. After a series of mergers, it became Metro-Goldwyn-Mayer, where Mayer was production chief from 1924 to 1951.

LEON LEOPOLD AND THE MOVIE INDUSTRY

Mayer's assistant, Leon Leopold, took over management of the Walnut for the 1914–15 season. Leopold was a Philadelphia native and the brother of comedian Ed Wynn. He continued to operate the Walnut as a road house, bringing in shows that had played the previous season. The stars were touring actors whose names are all but forgotten today—Shep Camp, Eugenie Blair, Rose Melville, and others.

A marked change from this regular fare was *Damaged Goods,* which opened on November 15, 1914. The play dealt with syphilis and its effects on marriage and was promoted by a medical journal. "Everyone should see the play, which has no scene of scandal or disgust or obscene words unless we must believe that ignorance and folly are necessary conditions of female virtue," the promotional materials read. Audiences flocked to the play during its one-week run, despite the fact that protesters picketed outside the theatre, and the play was brought back for two more runs.

The spring of 1915 saw the premiere of D. W. Griffith's *Birth of a Nation.* The film played to packed houses in New York City and opened at the Forrest Theatre in Philadelphia the following September. From this point on, films would compete more directly with the stage—to the detriment of live performance. One performer who did attract audiences to the Walnut was John Bunny, a former stage actor who had quit the stage in 1910 to pursue a film career. In the five years since, Bunny had made 150 comedy shorts for Vitagraph Pictures, establishing himself as the first comedy star in films. He arrived at the Walnut in March 1915 in *Bunny in Funnyland*, which combined a minstrel "first part" with song-and-dance specialties by blackface musicians, a burlesque scene set in a movie studio, and a concluding vaudeville show. Critics panned the show, but crowds filled the theatre, eager to see a leading film actor in the flesh. Sadly, the stress of the tour ruined Bunny's health. He was already suffering from kidney disease, and he passed away at his home the following month.

Bunny was followed by the magician Thurston, making the first of several appearances at the Walnut. He produced a girl and a donkey from an apparently empty cabinet. A reviewer described Thurston as "essentially a good-humored entertainer" and noted that "his familiarity with the audience and his rapid-fire style of talk create an atmosphere of fun which does away with the air of mystery with which former masters of the 'black art' clothed their doings."[24]

THE RETURN OF STOCK

In the fall of 1915 the Walnut returned to a policy of stock, when William H. Leahy established a company calling itself the Walnut Street Players. Stock had not entirely died out, and in most major cities one or two stock companies still operated. The stock company could survive on lower admission prices. With fewer road companies coming through and a continued decline in the quality of touring companies, operating a stock company regained some appeal. The Walnut Street Players produced *Fine Feathers*, *The Governor's Lady*, and *The Sign of the Cross* to start off the 1915–16 season. The cheapest seat at the Walnut cost ten cents, the highest, seventy-five.

Leahy failed to make a go of it, however, and in October the Walnut was taken over by Grant Laferty, who had previously operated a stock company at the Chestnut, with a company calling itself the Penn Players. They played for several weeks, with *The Man from Home*, *Within the Law*, and *Ready Money*, all modern dramas that had had their Broadway debuts a few years before. The company's leading man was Edward Everett Horton, best known for his supporting roles in several Fred Astaire and Ginger Rogers films. He later became the voice of "fractured fairy tales" on the *Rocky and Bullwinkle* cartoon series.

The experiment in stock proved to be a financial failure, and Laferty was unable to meet payroll. On November 8 the stagehands refused to work, demanding the two weeks' salary due them. The manager lacked funds, so a scheduled production of *The House of Bondage* was canceled. Left almost penniless by the strike, the cast and stagehands did not have the money to return home or pay their hotel bills. This sort of predicament was growing increasingly common and had led to the founding of Actors' Equity three years earlier. This labor union made little headway in improving working conditions for actors until an actors' strike in 1919.

The Walnut remained dark until Christmas Day, when Andrew Mack opened a two-week run of *The Irish Dragoon*. The rest of the season was given over to the usual selection of touring productions of shows that had premiered in New York several years before. None remained longer than a week, until *Twin Beds* opened in early May. Margaret Mayo's farce about a married couple tormented by an intoxicated Italian tenor was one of the most popular comedies of the era.

The season concluded with an all-black production of *Othello*, which had originally been produced at the Lafayette Theatre in Harlem on April 23 to mark the three-hundredth anniversary of Shakespeare's death. The *Public Ledger* claimed that it was the first performance of Shakespeare in Philadelphia by African Americans. The players were an amateur company organized by Edward Sterling Wright, a dramatic lecturer for the New York City Board of Education. Wright played Othello; the supporting cast members were college-educated students of Shakespeare.[25] On the opening night in Philadelphia, Mrs. Patrick Campbell and Sir Herbert Beerbohm Tree were in the audience.

WORLD WAR I

Although America was not yet involved in the fighting, World War I affected the theatre industry. The war was brought home to Americans in the spring of 1915, when the *Lusitania* was torpedoed by a German submarine. One of the passengers who lost their lives was the producer Charles Frohman. His death dealt a further blow to the Syndicate. When the agreement officially came up for renewal on August 31, 1916, it was allowed to lapse. Marc Klaw and Abe Erlanger continued to book shows, but their hold over the theatrical industry was at an end. The Shuberts, who had invested heavily in New York theatres, would take over as the most important producers and theatre owners in America.

The 1916–17 season relied on tabloid melodramas, most of them specifically designed for the road. *The Natural Law* depicted an out-of-wedlock pregnancy. *While the City Sleeps* and *Broadway After Dark* gave the public a view of underworld life. Several plays were adapted from popular cartoon strips—*Bringing Up Father in Politics, Mutt and Jeff's Wedding,* and *Hans and Fritz, the Katzenjammer Kids.* A touring version of the popular 1912 comedy *Peg o' My Heart* played for three weeks in April, with Virginia Carewe-Carvel in the part created by Laurette Taylor. *Her Unborn Child* dealt with the issue of birth control. Crowds were so large during its weeklong run in March that it was brought back for an additional four weeks in May. The season finished up with a company of Negro entertainments called *The Smartest Set.* The thirty-member troupe who performed it was headed by the comedy team of Salem Tutt Whitney and J. Homer Tutt, who wrote the material. The production, *How Newtown Prepared,* provided a thin story line for fifteen specially written musical numbers.

Woodrow Wilson narrowly won re-election in the fall of 1916, campaigning on the slogan "He kept us out of war." But that promise was soon to be broken. In January 1917 Germany announced that its U-boats would attack all ships, including America's. During the first two weeks of March, four American merchant vessels were torpedoed, prompting Wilson to ask Congress for a declaration of war. On April 6, Congress obliged. In June, a national draft was instituted, and by fall a million men were in uniform. The loss of men to the military devastated the theatre industry. "Box office receipts dropped with a sickening thud," Abel Green and Joe Laurie Jr. reported. "Ticket money went into buying Liberty Bonds. Parents stayed home to scan newspapers for reports of their sons' regiments. Close to a million men abandoned theatre attendance for close-order drill."[26]

The 1917–18 season opened on September 24 with *The White Feather.* Chauncey Olcott appeared during Christmas week in *Once Upon a Time.* The most successful production was a touring production of *Fair and Warmer,* Avery Hopwood's 1915 comedy, which played for four weeks in March. Several of the productions had titles clearly meant to titillate—*The Marriage Question, His Bridal Night, The White Slave,* and *The Little Girl in a Big City.* The season closed with a tabloid melodrama, *The Unmarried Mother,* which played for three weeks in May.

THE FLU EPIDEMIC

The 1918–19 season opened on September 18 with *Lady Bountiful's Minstrels,* which featured sixty "classy looking singing dancing girls," according to an announcement in the *Public Ledger.* The Walnut was open only a week when it had to close because of the flu epidemic. Philadelphia was hit particularly hard. Nearly sixteen thousand Philadelphians lost their lives, some eleven thousand in October alone.[27] The Walnut reopened on November 4, presenting *Hearts of the World,* a D. W. Griffith film starring Lillian Gish, set in a French village during the German occupation. The film featured footage shot on actual battlefields. A week later, the armistice was signed, and the city erupted in celebration. *Hearts of the World* continued to play through early December and was followed by another World War I picture, *The Woman the Germans Shot*, the story of Edith Cavell, a British nurse executed by the Germans for helping Allied soldiers escape.

On December 23 the Walnut resumed its theatrical offerings, presenting *The Garden of Allah*, the story of a monk who leaves his monastery for an affair with a beautiful girl but is persuaded to return to religious life. It had originally played on Broadway in 1911 but had recently been revived as an elaborate touring production that featured real donkeys and camels and a violent sandstorm. Chauncey Olcott gave up his usual Christmastime slot but opened on St. Patrick's Day for a two-week run of *The Voice of McConnell*, a play George M. Cohan wrote especially for him. It was more of Olcott's usual fare: he played a famous ballad singer who wins the heart of a lovely Irish girl after helping her brother. It was to be Olcott's last appearance at the Walnut, although he remained active in the theatre for another decade.

The remainder of the season was given over to drawing room comedies that had played on Broadway the year before—*Twin Beds, The Brat, The Naughty Wife, Eyes of Youth, The Boomerang*. The season finished off with a production by the Twenty-eighth Division of the U.S. Army Theatrical Troupe, performing *Who Are You?*—a comedy set in the European battlefield at the time the armistice was signed. It featured interpolated songs and soldiers in drag. The governor of Pennsylvania, the mayor of Philadelphia, and top military personnel were all on hand for the opening. A marching band paraded from City Hall down Chestnut Street to Independence Hall for a special ceremony, followed by a march to the Walnut for the show.

THE ACTORS' STRIKE

A strike by Actors' Equity in August delayed the opening of the 1919–20 season. The union had been formed in 1913 to protect the interests of actors, who were forced to rehearse for weeks without pay, were often stranded on the road, and had to endure other indignities. The strike originated in New York in August but quickly spread to eight other cities, including Philadelphia, delaying the opening of the fall season until September 29. The productions were as undistinguished as they had been for the previous few years. The Walnut booked shows that had been on the road for several years, with stars who are forgotten today. The only production of any note was *Business Before Pleasure*, which featured the characters of Abe Potash and Mawruss Perlmutter, two Yiddish men in the garment trade who decide they will get rich by going into films. It was the third in a series of farces featuring the two characters, played by Barney Bernard and Alexander Carr, and ran for a week. The Walnut limped through the season with such forgettable pieces as *My Honolulu Girl*, *The Little Shepherd of Kingdom Come*, and other plays designed specifically for the road.

On January 14, 1920, the heirs of John Sleeper Clarke signed the Walnut Street Theatre over to James P. Beury, a millionaire coal dealer. Beury kept the theatre going with popular plays like *Pollyanna*, Margaret Mayo's comedy *Twin Beds*, and *Seven Days' Leave*, a war drama. Two plays—*The Gumps* and *The Katzenjammer Kids*—were based on popular comic strips. Fiske O'Hara closed out the season in *Down Limerick Way*, taking over the Irish roles that Chauncey Olcott had popularized. The season ended in late April, and the theatre did not reopen in the fall.

The twenty-five years of Syndicate domination had seen tremendous changes in the entertainment industry. Movies were well on their way to replacing live theatre as Americans' primary form of entertainment. The Walnut "had become wearied, worn, aged and frail and seemed to be singing 'neath the mortal burden of years during the last decade," the *Public Ledger* declared.[28] As America entered the Jazz Age, the Old Walnut was once again slated for demolition.

BOOM AND BUST, 1920–1940

James Beury, the Walnut's new owner, hoped to build a new modern theatre on the lot. A city ordinance required that any new building had to be set another ten feet back from the street. This would have meant a much smaller theatre, so Beury decided to rebuild within the confines of the original walls. He hired Charles H. Lee, a noted theatre architect, to oversee the renovation, while a wrecking crew began removing the old interior.

The workmen unearthed an interesting architectural feature. When Pepin and Breschard enlarged the theatre in 1812 to accommodate a stage, they had evidently acquired a house standing on the property behind the theatre. "They left the old house standing," the *Public Ledger* reported, "building the walls of the (at that time) new house around it, turning it into dressing rooms, where it lay concealed from view all these years." The back portion of the stage, including three dressing rooms, is part of this original house.

Workmen also came upon a number of interesting relics. "Two full hampers of costumes used by Edwin Booth and also by John Sleeper Clarke in Shakespearean repertoire, most of them in good state of preservation, were found under the eaves," the *Public Ledger* noted. "Several hand-carved chairs of the early period, an antique mirror, the solid wood block letters that for over a century occupied a place on the Walnut Street front of the theatre, a windlass, used to haul up the curtain, and which consists of the solid trunk of a tree, two antique desks and other relics."[1] There was a diary belonging to Junius Brutus Booth that dated back to 1820, and in an unused property room, workmen discovered a skull that had been carefully packed away. It was assumed to be that of "Pop" Reed.

fig. 24 This image of the Walnut Street Theatre shows the 1920 interior design by architect William Lee. The production onstage is unknown.

While the wrecking crew gutted the building, Charles Lee drew up plans for the new building. The exterior remained much the same, although a cigar store that occupied the corner spot was removed to make room for the new box office. There were entrances on both Walnut and Ninth Street that led into a foyer extending across the length of the theatre. The biggest changes were made in the auditorium, which was completely renovated. A single balcony replaced the two tiers of the old balcony, supported by a heavy girder that spanned the house. A large chandelier, taken from the ballroom of the Bingham House, was set in a recess in the ceiling. A new ventilating system was installed to ensure plenty of heat during the winter months, with an independent cooling system that blew millions of cubic feet of fresh air into the auditorium during the summer.

THE NEWEST OLDEST THEATRE IN AMERICA

The renovation delayed the opening of the fall 1920 season until after Christmas. Opening night playbills proclaimed that the Walnut was the "newest-oldest theatre in America." A distinguished assemblage attended the gala opening on Monday evening, December 27. James Beury's brother, Dr. Charles E. Beury—banker, lawyer, and the future president of Temple University—acted as master of ceremonies. Philadelphia's mayor, J. Hampton Moore, spoke about the Walnut's importance to the city's cultural life and its role in the American theatre. James Beury had several canes made from the walnut beams that had once supported the roof of the theatre, and these were presented to several of the dignitaries.

The audience "was quite taken aback by the genuine beauty of the theatre's interior," the *Public Ledger* observed. The Victorian details were gone. "There are no 'gingerbread' effects in decoration. It is all in severe white, though with the element of color warmth added in the rich red of upholstering and a few hangings behind the four well-placed boxes."[2] The *Inquirer* also noted the change. "Gone are the fusty draperies, the ancient boxes. Gone, too, is the sense of smallness and confinement. In their places stands now a flawless and splendid temple of acting which is, very likely, the best example of its school in the United States." One important architectural feature remained. "The golden shield, surmounted by the trusty eagle," was "perched above the proscenium arch, a single telling spot of color against the immaculate white paneling of the spacious rectangle."[3]

THE GREEN GODDESS

The production that night was *The Green Goddess*, a new work by an influential English drama critic, William Archer, that was having its world premiere. Winthrop Ames, one of the leaders of the art theatre movement, produced and directed. George Arliss headed up the largely British cast, which included Ronald Colman in a minor role as a priest. Arliss played a western-educated rajah who imprisons three British travelers after their private plane crash-lands in his Himalayan kingdom. Although he treats them graciously, they discover that he plans to kill them if the British government executes his three half-brothers, who have been sentenced to death for political subversion. Most of the play involves the travelers' attempts to escape. In the end, they manage to get a message out by shortwave radio and are rescued in the nick of time by British troops.

Critic Arthur Hornblow dismissed the play as "commercial melodrama of the most conventional kind." But the dialogue was literate and the play was a triumph for Arliss, who dominated the stage "with a countenance at once gentle and diabolic."[4] *The Green Goddess* became one of the era's most successful plays. Arliss went on to perform his role more than one thousand times, reprising it for the 1929 film, for which he received an Oscar nomination. The play even inspired a salad dressing, when, at the height of its popularity, a chef at the Palace Hotel in San Francisco created a new recipe, which he named green goddess dressing.

BEURY AND WANAMAKER

The involvement of prestigious people like Winthrop Ames and George Arliss indicated to the theatergoing public that "the Walnut is making a promise to present only the best of attractions in various fields of entertainment."[5] Like many of his contemporaries, James Beury was influenced by the art theatre, or "little theatre," movement that had arisen in the 1910s to combat the shallow commercialism of the theatre. Largely an amateur movement, it was beginning to influence the commercial theatre, as playwrights, directors, and designers moved from smaller off-Broadway houses to professional Broadway theatres.

Beury and his manager, Charles C. Wanamaker, tried to balance commercial considerations while raising the standards of the theatre by freely mixing popular fare with more prestigious productions and relying heavily on European imports. After *The Green Goddess* closed, comedian Ernest Truex arrived in *Pitter-Patter*, a musical about a bashful young man who saves a mine owner and his daughter from financial ruin. A young dancer named Jimmy Cagney appeared in the show. Walter Hampden followed with two weeks of Shakespeare repertory. Brooklyn-born Hampden was the leading proponent of the classic repertoire, vying with John Barrymore as the country's foremost Hamlet. He opened in *The Merchant of Venice* and followed it up with *Hamlet*, *The Taming of the Shrew*, and *The Servant in the House*, a 1908 drama that had first established Hampden as a star.

Beury and Wanamaker revived the tradition of benefits at the Walnut. On March 11, 1921, they held an all-star benefit to aid the Charlotte Cushman Club, which had been organized in 1907 to provide safe and inexpensive housing for actresses appearing in Philadelphia. The organization had recently moved from its original building on Twelfth and Locust streets to a larger facility at 1010 Spruce Street. Cast members from all the shows playing in Philadelphia were on hand, including John Drew, William Collier, Francis Wilson, Victor Herbert, and Hal Skelly. De Wolf Hopper served as master of ceremonies.

Among the other productions finishing out the season were *The Masquerader*, which featured English actor Guy Bates Post in dual roles, and *Opportunity*, a Wall Street melodrama by Owen Davis, a Harvard-educated author of touring shows. Victor Herbert was on hand to conduct the orchestra when his musical *The Girl in the Spotlight* debuted on April 18, 1921. It was a clichéd story about a chorus girl who takes over the lead when the prima donna cannot go on. Nance O'Neil finished out the season in *The Passion Flower*, a drama by the Spanish playwright Jacinto Benavente, who would receive the Nobel Prize for Literature the following year.

The fall season followed the same formula, relying on a mix of comedies, operettas, and spectacles. A backstage operetta titled *Love Dreams* opened the fall season with a monthlong pre-Broadway tryout. European imports dominated the 1921 fall season. *Happy-Go-Lucky* was a Cinderella story about a girl from a working-class British family who is about to marry into an aristocratic family. O. P. Heggie stole the show as a drunken bailiff pressed into service as the family's butler. *A Dangerous Man* was the first-time offering of the son of the Peruvian ambassador. *In the Night Watch* was adapted from a French play about a ship that is sunk in the hours after war breaks out.

THE EMPEROR JONES

The first production of real significance arrived during Thanksgiving week 1921, when the Provincetown Players presented *The Emperor Jones*, Eugene O'Neill's landmark drama about an ex-Pullman porter who becomes the ruler of a Caribbean island. Founded in 1915 as an amateur group, the Provincetown Players became the most influential theatre group of the era, functioning as a sort of laboratory for developing important actors, designers, and playwrights. When *The Emperor Jones* opened at the Provincetown Playhouse on November 1, 1920, word quickly spread that it was something special. The demand for tickets overwhelmed the tiny Greenwich Village theatre, and the play was moved to Broadway, where it ran for more than two hundred performances before going on the road.

The story follows the emperor's downfall as he hurries through the jungle to a gunship waiting to take him to safety. The play is essentially a monologue, as the deposed emperor confronts the demons of his past. Charles S. Gilpin, a veteran of black theatre companies and the former director of the Lafayette Theatre in Harlem, played the title role. It was the first time an African American played the lead in a play produced by a white company. The role would normally have gone to a white actor performing in blackface, but Eugene O'Neill insisted on having a black actor in the role. Opportunities for African American actors were limited, and Gilpin was working as an elevator operator at Macy's department store when he was tapped for the role. His performance was electrifying. Moss Hart recalled that Gilpin "had an inner violence and a maniacal power that engulfed the audience."[6] The reviewer for the *Public Ledger* lauded Gilpin's acting as "a unique exhibition of histrionic artistry."[7] *The Emperor Jones* lasted only a little longer than an hour and was preceded by a one-act comedy, *Suppressed Desires*, a satire of psychoanalysis written by George Cram Cook and Susan Glaspell, the husband-and-wife team who were the driving force behind the Provincetown Players.

EUGENE O'NEILL

At thirty-four, Eugene O'Neill was emerging as the finest playwright that America had ever produced. While *The Emperor Jones* was playing at the Walnut, his next play, *Anna Christie*, opened on Broadway and would win the Pulitzer Prize for Drama that year. *Anna Christie* is the story of a woman who is sent as a child to live with relatives by her seafaring father, to keep her away from the influence of "the old devil sea." Rather than being "saved," she becomes a prostitute. Believing that the sea air will benefit her, her father takes her on a voyage to Boston. En route, they rescue some shipwrecked sailors, and one of them, an Irish stoker, falls in love with Anna. Her father is determined that she will never marry a sailor, and the two men come to blows. A touring production of the play came to the Walnut on December 4, 1922. The Walnut production, directed by Arthur Hopkins, featured the original cast—Pauline Lord as Anna, George Marion as her father, and Frank Shannon as the rough sailor who falls in love with her.

An earlier version of the play, *Chris*, had had a Philadelphia tryout two years earlier but never had a New York run. O'Neill withdrew the play and reworked the story, shifting its focus from the father to the daughter. Critics called Pauline Lord's Anna "a perfect portrayal." "She has the beauty admired in her sort: there is that curious raucousness of voice, the vocal betrayal of whisky-drinking dwellers in a submerged world: she has that evanescent artificial smile, the mark of the official and forced entertainer," C. H. Bonte wrote in the *Ledger*, adding, "Miss Lord's Anna Christie is a veritable triumph of naturalness in acting."[8]

POPULAR DRAMA

While O'Neill exemplified the best in American playwrighting, most plays by American authors were more pedestrian and formulaic. Melodramas retained their hold on the theatergoing public, although they had changed form, reflecting the concerns of the time. Crime dramas grew in popularity as Prohibition

fig. 25 Eugene O'Neill is considered one of the most renowned American playwrights of all time. In the early 1920s, at the young age of thirty-four, he had two landmark dramas—*The Emperor Jones* and *Anna Christie*—play at the Walnut.

began to wear more and more on the public. The Eighteenth Amendment had little support in eastern cities like Philadelphia, and speakeasies operated openly in parts of the city. The 1923–24 season opened with *Thumbs Down*, a melodrama about a district attorney's campaign against bootleggers and corrupt policemen produced by the Walnut's manager, C. C. Wanamaker. Mary Ryan played the title role in *Red Light Annie*, which opened later that season. It depicted a small-town couple who move to the city and fall under the influence of underworld figures. Liquor featured heavily in *The Old Soak*, a play by humorist Don Marquis, which starred Raymond Hitchcock as a drunk who discovers that the town's self-righteous banker is funding the local bootleggers.

There was a brief interest in war dramas, as playwrights began addressing the effects of World War I. James Beury produced *A Man's Job*, which played at the Walnut for a week in the summer of 1924. George M. Cohan and Augustus Thomas both attended opening night, and Thomas declared it "two-thirds of a hit," but the play never made it to New York. *Simon Called Peter* was a dramatization of a best-selling novel, set in World War I, about a priest who falls in love with a nurse and leaves the priesthood to marry her. H. P. Trevelyan's *The Dark Angel* had its world premiere at the Walnut prior to opening in New York. It depicted a man who returns from the war to discover that his fiancée is about to wed someone else.

Mystery plays enjoyed a vogue. Generally, they were set in a haunted house and relied on lighting and stage effects to deliver chills to the audience. A second-rate production called *The Haunted* closed out the 1921–22 season at the Walnut. The fall season opened with *The Charlatan*, a somewhat better representative of the genre. Frederick Tilden starred as a man who assumes the role of a magician and helps a millionaire clear his father's name and expose the real culprit. New Year's Day 1923 saw the debut of *The Monster*, in which a group of people take refuge in the home of a mad scientist where eerie mechanical and electrical effects take place—fire that emits poisonous fumes, clocks that strike thirteen, doors that open by themselves.

Tropical melodramas also became something of a rage after the extraordinary success of *Rain*, a 1922 staging of a short story by Somerset Maugham. *Aloma of the South Seas* played the Walnut for three months in the fall of 1925. It was a drama about a man who is saved by a beautiful native girl from drinking himself to death. The production advertised authentic native music on the ukulele. Another tropical drama, *White Cargo*, arrived immediately on its heels, playing six weeks beginning on January 18, 1926. It depicted the lives of four British men on a rubber plantation off the coast of Africa. A newly arrived Englishman succumbs to the weather and to a sultry native girl of mixed race named Tondelayo. The play was uneven, but critics found it superior to the "silly twaddle" of *Aloma*.

COMEDY

Some of the best American playwrighting of the 1920s mined the comedy vein. Comedies of manners enjoyed a revival, reflecting the growing prosperity of the country and burgeoning interest in the goings-on of the rich and powerful. Several major comic playwrights—George S. Kaufman, S. N. Behrman, George Kelly, and Philip Barry—were all starting out in the early 1920s. Barry made a splash with *You and I*, which appeared at the Walnut for a two-week run in February 1924. A young man is about to give up a promising artistic career to marry his sweetheart, but his father, who gave up similar dreams and regretted it, dissuades him. The twenty-seven-year-old playwright had written the play as a student in George P. Baker's class at Harvard and received the Harvard Prize for his work. Barry went on to become one of the principal social critics of the era and is best remembered for the 1939 play *The Philadelphia Story.*

The 1920s saw many opportunities for women playwrights, many of them also writing comedies. Anita Loos had her first success at the Walnut with *The Whole Town's Talking*, a comedy about a man who invents an affair with a film star, only to have her arrive in his hometown. Loos is best known for her novel *Gentlemen Prefer Blondes*, which she adapted for the stage in 1926. It was later made into a film starring Marilyn Monroe and Jane Russell.

Rachel Crothers was the leading female playwright of the time, often producing and directing her own shows. *Expressing Willie* came to the Walnut after an eight-month Broadway run to close out the 1924 calendar year. This was a sharp, witty comedy about a toothpaste magnate who has surrounded himself with pseudo-intellectual friends. Determined to prove to her son that his sophisticated friends are freeloading off him, his mother invites his old sweetheart to spend the weekend. Critics called it "ultra-smart theatrical fare," with clever repartee and bon mots.[9]

Cornelia Otis Skinner had a local success with *Captain Fury*, a comic melodrama about an innkeeper whose daughter persuades him to take command of a pirate crew so that she can take revenge on a faithless lover. Her father, Otis Skinner, starred in this play, which ran for three weeks in March 1926—it would be his last appearance at the Walnut. The *Ledger* called the play "a rousing yarn, colorful, flamboyant, gaily improbable, and full of exciting action."[10] *Captain Fury* never made it to Broadway, but it encouraged Cornelia Otis Skinner to continue writing for the stage. She developed a series of one-woman shows that she toured for some years.

VAUDEVILLIANS ON THE LEGITIMATE STAGE

Vaudeville, which had been the most popular form of entertainment during the first two decades of the twentieth century, was beginning its decline. In 1920 ticket sales at the nation's vaudeville houses began to sag, and many converted to films or a combination of film and variety acts. The decline continued through the 1920s. By 1926 there were only six big-time vaudeville theatres in the East, and another six scattered throughout the country.[11]

Scottish balladeer Harry Lauder organized his own company of variety artists, which toured legitimate theatres. Lauder had made his first appearance at the Walnut on October 24, 1921, with a company that included acrobats, comedy cyclists, and musicians. Members of Philadelphia's Caledonian Club marched to the theatre en masse to attend the opening night performance and, after the show, initiated Lauder into the organization. Lauder returned to the Walnut in 1922, 1924, and 1926.

A number of vaudeville acts were expanded into full-length shows. The father-and-son team of J. C. and Elliott Nugent had a huge success with *Kempy* in 1923, a comedy about a plumber who is nearly enticed into a bad marriage. The play was developed out of the Nugent family's vaudeville act.

THE MARX BROTHERS

Among those making the leap from vaudeville to the legitimate stage were the Marx Brothers, who debuted their first stage show, *I'll Say She Is,* at the Walnut in the summer of 1923. Harpo, Chico, Groucho, and Zeppo Marx were already established vaudeville stars, but they had never been in a legitimate show. They had alienated E. F. Albee, the powerful head of the Keith-Albee vaudeville circuit, who blacklisted them, and were eager to hook up with a Broadway producer who would put them in a show. They found him in Joseph M. Gaites, a low-end producer known as "Minimum" Gaites. Gaites had a script titled *Love for Sale,* written by Will and Tom Johnstone, about a millionairess looking for adventure.

James P. Beury, meanwhile, was looking for a summer revue that could go into the Walnut. Summer revues had grown quite popular in New York, and Beury saw this as a means of keeping his theatre open during the summer. The Marx Brothers and the Johnstones cobbled together a show from *Love for Sale* and pieces from the Marx Brothers' vaudeville act—notably an opening scene in a theatrical agency, where the four brothers enter one by one to try out. The production had a two-day tryout in Allentown, Pennsylvania, and opened at the Walnut Street Theatre on June 4, 1923.

The audience was meager. "June Philadelphia weather featured suffocating heat encountered elsewhere only on the upper reaches of the Amazon," the Marx Brothers' biographer, Kyle Crichton, wrote. "Only Quakers and sailors from the Philadelphia Navy Yard could be imagined going to a theatre in such weather."[12] But the critics did attend, and praised the production as "ideal hot weather entertainment." The reviews identified the Marx Brothers by their given names. "Arthur [Harpo] Marx did remarkable things on a harp and Leonard [Chico] Marx performed on a piano with unbelievable dexterity there

fig. 26 A publicity photo from the Marx Brothers' Walnut debut, *I'll Say She Is.*

was little to complain of," the *Public Ledger* declared, "and Julius [Groucho] Marx, impersonating Napoleon, had moments of gutsy humor."[13]

I'll Say She Is proved to be a hit, playing for thirteen weeks that summer, then went on a national tour. The Marx Brothers returned to the Walnut for a three-week run prior to their New York opening on May 19, 1924. When it finally opened in New York, *I'll Say She Is* established the Marx Brothers as stars.

PRODUCING ORGANIZATIONS

By now, the Walnut was the only independently owned theatre in Philadelphia. The other first-class houses were controlled either by the Shubert Organization, which leased or owned the Forrest, Adelphi, Lyric, and Shubert, or by Abe Erlanger (the only member of the Syndicate still active in the theatre), who operated the Broad and Garrick theatres. The other theatres had either converted to film or were offering vaudeville, burlesque, or, in the case of the Arch Street Theatre, Yiddish drama. The Walnut was the only venue in Philadelphia available for independent producing organizations.

The Theatre Guild, based in New York City, was the most prominent of these. Growing out of the little theatre movement of the 1910s, the Guild was founded in 1919 to present artistically important works by modern playwrights on Broadway, and during the 1920s and '30s it became the most important producing organization in America, premiering many significant works by European and American playwrights. In January 1924 the Theatre Guild produced three weeks of repertory at the Walnut. The English actor Basil Sydney starred in Bernard Shaw's *The Devil's Disciple,* Henrik Ibsen's *Peer Gynt,* and Leonid Andreyev's *He Who Gets Slapped.* It was the first time the Theatre Guild had been seen in Philadelphia, and the first important revival of *Devil's Disciple* since it premiered in 1897. *Peer Gynt* received its first staging since 1906, and Grieg's music was used as incidental music.

During the winter of 1924–25 an organization called the 7 Arts Club put together a series of seven Sunday night events. The first of these took place on November 16, when Paul Robeson appeared in *The Emperor Jones.* Drama critic Heywood Broun opened with a talk titled "Confessions of a Dramatic Critic." On January 18 the Elkins-Payne Negro Ensemble performed a concert of spirituals. Playwright Zoë Akins gave an address titled "Within Three Walls."

During Christmas week of 1924, the Hedgerow Theatre Company offered a production of Lady Gregory's *The Dragon,* a children's theatre piece about a fierce dragon that becomes a lovable house pet when a prince tears out its heart and replaces it with a squirrel's heart. Ann Harding, a founding member of the Hedgerow Theatre, starred. She returned again in Bernard's Shaw's *Misalliance*, which the company presented on January 11, 1925. The Hedgerow Theatre Company was formed in 1923 by Jasper Deeter and was housed in a mill in Moylan-Rose Valley, which was converted into a 170-seat theatre. The company performed in repertory style, giving different plays nightly during a season that ran from early spring to late fall, touring in the winter months. The repertory consisted of more than two hundred plays, with classics by European dramatists predominating.

MUSICAL COMEDIES

The Walnut was not Philadelphia's premiere house for musical comedies, which usually played at the Broad Street Theatre. But from time to time musicals came to the Walnut. *Marjorie*, the first production of 1925, told the story of a woman who passes off her brother's play as her own. The 1924–25 season closed in mid-May with *Broke*, a comedy with music, and then *When You Smile* came in for an extended summer run. This was a musical adaptation of a 1923 play, *Extra*, about a newspaper publisher who is determined to ruin his newspaper so that he can buy out its outstanding stock at a bargain rate. He puts his son in charge, but the son manages to turn the paper into a goldmine. *When You Smile* played the entire summer but quickly flopped when it reached New York that fall. Imogene Coca had a supporting role in the show.

Blossom Time depicted the life of Franz Schubert and his love for a student who inspires him to write his *Unfinished Symphony*. The operetta using Schubert's melodies had been one of the hits of the 1921 season. "Song of Love," an important song in the show, was taken from his *Unfinished Symphony*. Gerald Bordman writes that "the operetta was revived and toured constantly over the next quarter of a century, in increasingly cheap productions, until 'a road company of *Blossom Time*' became synonymous with the shabbiest theatrical commercialism."[14] One of these touring productions played the Walnut for three weeks in April 1926.

In May of that year, *Kosher Kitty Kelly* had a five-week run. The musical borrowed the premise of the era's longest-running show, *Abie's Irish Rose*. This was a musical about two families, one Irish, one Jewish, living next door to each other, whose children develop romantic attachments to each other. The critics noted that Irish brogues and Jewish mothers were hoary stage conventions that bore little relationship to actual life on the Lower East Side.

THE SESQUICENTENNIAL

The year 1926 marked the 150th anniversary of the signing of the Declaration of Independence, and once again Philadelphia marked the occasion with a major exposition. "Tremendous efforts were called for to complete the Forum of the Founders, the state buildings, foreign pavilions, a 'Gladway,' a 'High Street' in a colonial village, numerous small structures for restaurants, a bank, a radio broadcasting station, and a gigantic Liberty Bell, eighty feet tall, placed at the entrance to the Exposition," Philadelphia historian Arthur Dudden wrote.[15] The fair opened on May 31 with much fanfare, but few of the exhibitions were complete and the streets were still unpaved. Early reports that the fair was not worth seeing kept crowds away.

The Walnut remained open through the summer, in the hope of attracting visitors from the exposition. Tennis champion William "Big Bill" Tilden opened the summer season on June 14 in a romantic comedy titled *They All Want Something.* Tilden, who was born into a Philadelphia banking family, dominated men's tennis during the 1920s. He lost much of his fortune backing unsuccessful Broadway shows. He played a well-to-do young man who disguises himself as a hobo to woo the neighbor girl he has worshipped from afar. Tilden garnered good reviews, and the play went on to have a moderate run in New York. Two minor plays finished out the disappointing summer: *Arlene Adair,* starring Grace George, with support from Robert Montgomery, and the minor musical *Cynthia,* featuring another Philadelphia favorite, Jack Whiting.

The fall 1926 season relied heavily on family comedies, precursors to television sitcoms. "Every year a half-dozen or more of those naïve trifles come to town, all of them serving to pass an entertaining evening, and none of them boasting any outstanding features of originality, ingenuity, novelty or glamour," the *Ledger* noted.[16] Larry Oliver and Marion Wells co-starred in *Laff That Off,* a comedy about a young actress who moves in with three bachelors. The Nash sisters, Florence and Mary, opened in Rachel Crothers's *A Lady's Virtue,* a comedy about the marital troubles of a small-town couple, when the husband falls in love with an opera singer. In *One of the Family,* Grant Mitchell starred as a well-to-do young man rescued from his oppressively pedigreed family. Robert Montgomery and Beulah Bondi had supporting roles. Claiborne Foster garnered good reviews for her performance as a put-upon younger sister in *The Patsy.*

RODGERS AND HART

Peggy-Ann introduced the songwriting team of Rodgers and Hart. Richard Rodgers was twenty-four and his partner, lyricist Lorenz Hart, was thirty-one when *Peggy-Ann* came to the Walnut on December 13, 1926, for a two-week pre-Broadway tryout. The book, by Herbert Fields, was a reworking of Marie Dressler's 1910 comedy *Tillie's Nightmare*. Helen Ford played the title role as a boardinghouse maid who dreams of a glamorous life. The musical incorporated Freudian thinking on dreams, and although it produced no classic songs, it ran nearly a year on Broadway.

Rodgers and Hart had another success at the Walnut in the fall of 1927 with *A Connecticut Yankee*, a musical version of Mark Twain's novel. William Gaxton starred as an affluent New Yorker who is knocked unconscious and finds himself transported back to the court of King Arthur. The musical successfully juxtaposed a Jazz Age sensibility with the mannered style of a medieval court. The show produced two Rodgers and Hart standards—"Thou Swell" and "My Heart Stood Still"—and proved to be one of their most successful musicals, running 418 performances on Broadway. The dance director on this production was a youngster with no formal choreographic training named Busby Berkeley.

Helen Hayes made her first appearance on the Walnut's stage on January 10, 1927, in a revival of James M. Barrie's *What Every Woman Knows*. The twenty-six-year-old actress was already a show business veteran when she took on the role of Maggie Wylie, a part originated by Maude Adams. Hayes had a sweet, impish quality that made her successful in romantic comedies. *What Every Woman Knows* was a stretch for her. "When I was cast as Maggie in the 1926 revival, many thought I was stepping out of my class," Hayes recalled. "They still remembered Maude Adams' performance vividly, and I took pride in eventually being recognized as a worthy successor."[17]

Hayes played a mousy, unassertive Scottish woman who bends everyone to her iron will. "What every woman knows," she wrote years later, "is that she must never allow her man to realize that she is helping him, but must allow him to think that it is his own intelligence and ingenuity that are getting him on. In the play, Maggie plays an important part in the successful rise of her husband in Parliament. But she also must see him through an affair she knows he is having with Lady Sybil Lazenby. Maggie is shrewd enough to know that by giving Lady Sybil enough rope she will win back her man, which she does. And she charts a shrewd course that guarantees his re-election to Parliament."[18]

THE IMPACT OF TALKING PICTURES

The year 1927 was to be the high point of theatrical production in the United States. A total of 264 productions opened on Broadway that year, a record that has never come close to being matched, for the summer of 1927 saw the

fig. 27 Helen Hayes, who first appeared at the Walnut in 1927, became known as the First Lady of American theatre.

release of the first talking picture, *The Jazz Singer.* Although many theatre people insisted that talking pictures were a passing fad, the impact would soon be felt, as films took over as America's principal form of public entertainment. "There seems to have been a gradual change in the habits of theatergoers," Jack Poggi pointed out. "As they had more opportunity for satisfactory entertainment from movies at a low price, they began to go to the theater less frequently, and naturally they chose the plays with the most outstanding reputations."[19] The production of plays became a riskier business as they began to fall into the categories of "hits" and "flops." Fewer plays were produced each year, beginning a decline that has continued to the present day.

The new medium required actors who could speak, which created opportunities for stage actors. A number of actors who played at the Walnut were about to make their names in talking pictures. Basil Rathbone received glowing reviews for his portrayal of a military attaché carrying on an affair with the wife of one of his superiors in *The Command to Love,* which opened the Walnut's 1927–28 season. Melvyn Douglas had a supporting role in a touring production of Sidney Howard's drama *The Silver Cord.* George Arliss returned to the Walnut in *The Merchant of Venice.* It was his last stage show. When the tour ended, he left for the West Coast, where he became one of the most recognizable character actors in Hollywood. Leslie Howard played a gentleman serving a sentence for manslaughter in John Galsworthy's *Escape.*

The 1928–29 season saw more future film stars on the Walnut stage. The season opened with a domestic drama titled *The Lady Lies,* which starred William Boyd, who would become famous in the movies as Hopalong Cassidy. James Cagney was one of the featured dancers in *The Grand Street Follies,* the fourth edition of this popular revue. Joan Bennett co-starred with her father Richard in *Jarnegan,* a story about exploitation in Hollywood.

CRIME DRAMAS

The spring 1928 season turned out to be a banner one for crime dramas. Interest in underworld figures was piqued by the violence of mobsters engaged in turf wars, much reported by the press. February 7, 1928, saw the Walnut debut of *Chicago,* a dramatic version of the story that became the basis of the 1975 Kander and Ebb musical. Francine Larrimore starred as Roxie Hart, "a coarse, selfish" wife who kills her husband, then builds a vaudeville career on her notoriety. The reviewers commented on "the boisterous and often harsh humor" of the story. The *Ledger* noted that "the audience was moved by this altogether coarse and brutal story which is so electrified by the broad spirit of satire that it becomes a rollicking, entertaining one."[20]

Felix Krembs played the leader of a gang of bandits in *Kidnapper,* said to be based on a highly publicized kidnapping. It was unsuccessful because it was too close to the actual events—the play lacked the surprise twists that audiences had come to expect from crime dramas. *The Racket* followed. It was a cut above the other thrillers. The action took place in a Chicago police station, where mobster Nick Scarsi, played by Edward G. Robinson, threatens to squeal on politicians in his pay and is enticed into trying to escape, whereupon he is shot dead. This was Robinson's first role as a gangster, and the only time he played one on the stage. The physical resemblance between Robinson and Chicago mobster Al Capone was obvious and, as a result, Chicago authorities canceled the play's run there.

The opening of the 1929 season was delayed by a musicians' strike that kept Philadelphia theatres dark until the end of September. A touring company from Detroit opened the fall season on September 28, reviving Dion Boucicault's 1868 melodrama *After Dark*. The following day, the stock market experienced its worst one-day loss in history. The Depression that followed was to be the most prolonged and devastating in American history. The effects were not immediately felt in the theatre industry, as most of the season had already been booked.

Maggie the Magnificent, a new play by Pulitzer Prize–winning playwright George Kelly, followed. He was a member of Philadelphia's illustrious Kelly clan, which included Walter C. Kelly, a popular monologist known as "the Virginia judge." A younger brother, John, was an Olympic rowing champion and the father of Grace Kelly, the princess of Monaco. George Kelly got his start in vaudeville, writing comedy sketches for himself. He had his first success in 1922 with *The Torch-Bearers*, a satire of the little theatre movement. A 1924 comedy, *The Show-Off*, is generally considered his best play and just missed winning the Pulitzer Prize, which was awarded to Kelly the following year for *Craig's Wife*. *Maggie the Magnificent* was one of his lesser efforts, and starred Shirley Warde as a refined girl who rebels against her vulgar family. James Cagney, as Maggie's jaunty, lowbrow brother, and Joan Blondell, as his wisecracking new bride, stole the show.

The remainder of the season featured run-of-the-mill fare—mostly comedies and melodramas that had brief Broadway runs. *Courage* was a down-east drama about paying off the mortgage of the old homestead. *The Sap from Syracuse* revolved around a man who is mistaken for an important politician while on a trip to Europe. *Rope's End* depicted the notorious Leopold and Loeb thrill killing. *Everything's Jake* was a comedy based on Don Marquis's newspaper characters.

LYSISTRATA

The high point of the 1929–30 theatre season came at the end, when the newly organized Philadelphia Theatre Association mounted *Lysistrata*, Aristophanes' two-thousand-year-old antiwar satire. Fay Bainter played Lysistrata, the leader of the Greek women determined to force a halt to war by denying sex to their husbands. The supporting cast included film star Miriam Hopkins as Kalonika, Ernest Truex as the comic servant Kinesias, and Sydney Greenstreet as the president of the Senate. Doris Humphrey and Charles Weidman choreographed the dances, and José Limón was among the dancers. *Lysistrata* had previously been presented in Philadelphia by the Moscow Art Theatre, but this was the first production in English. The author and critic Gilbert Seldes translated the play into colloquial English and freely interpolated new scenes, "as Aristophanes might have done if he were alive today."

A play dealing openly with sexuality might have been censored by local authorities, but the Philadelphia Theatre Association had a socially prominent board. It was organized by Horace Howard Furness Jr., a distinguished Shakespeare scholar, to present historically important dramas from earliest times to the present day. An equally prestigious team was involved in mounting the production. Norman Bel Geddes directed a cast of seventy. Bel Geddes was principally a set designer, known for his innovative use of theatrical space. For *Lysistrata,* he transformed the Walnut's interior into a Greek temple. Front row seats were removed and the stage was extended into the auditorium. Huge platforms were built, and a cyclorama enclosed the stage, "showing not only a greater perspective but a higher extension of vision to the very limit of the structural proscenium arch," according to the *Public Ledger.*[21]

A fashionable audience of Philadelphia's cultural and social leaders, joined by a delegation from New York, attended the opening night on April 28, 1930. The play proved very successful, and its three-week run was extended to five weeks. In the final week, Violet Kemble Cooper took over the title role from Fay Bainter, who had a film commitment. Most of the cast moved on to New York. Plans to open other productions never materialized owing to the death of H. H. Furness. His extensive library of Tudor and Stuart drama was donated to the University of Pennsylvania and became the basis for the H. H. Furness Memorial Library.

THE PROFESSIONAL PLAYERS

A group calling themselves the Professional Players took over the Walnut in the fall of 1930, inaugurating the first subscription series. Organizations like the Theatre Guild had discovered the value of subscription series for attracting audiences to quality productions. The Professional Players had been formed the year before to bring prestigious plays to Philadelphia and had been producing at the much smaller Adelphi Theatre. They had already started their season at the Adelphi when the Walnut became available. James Beury was preoccupied with a family tragedy. On October 11, Beury's fourteen-year-old son, Harry, was bitten by a rabid dog outside their home in Ventnor,

New Jersey. Although the bites were treated immediately, the boy succumbed to the disease on November 6.

Grace George directed and starred in the first production by the Professional Players, *The First Mrs. Fraser,* which opened on November 3, 1930. She played a divorcée who helps her ex-husband get rid of his second wife. It was followed in early December by a new play by Luigi Pirandello, *As You Desire Me,* which was on its way to Broadway. Judith Anderson played dual roles as a cabaret singer and a madwoman, both claiming to be a man's long-lost wife. The reviewer for the *Ledger* was not pleased with the translation, which he described as "uneven and stumbling," but he praised Anderson for a performance "that will send tingle after tingle up and down your spine even in the dull and profitless moments of the second act."[22]

During the week of December 18, Ruth Draper offered her one-woman show for two matinee performances. She performed on a bare stage, with only a table, a chair, and a shawl as props. She played an Englishwoman opening a bazaar, and followed this up with *A Scottish Immigrant at Ellis Island.* In addition to her finely wrought characterizations, she was praised for her ability to evoke throngs of unseen characters onstage. In *Three Women and Mr. Clifford* she played three different women whose lives revolve around a businessman who is never seen. Among the other plays produced by the Professional Players as part of their subscription series were *Topaze,* a drama by Marcel Pagnol; *Michael and Mary,* a comedy by A. A. Milne, already best known for his Christopher Robin books; and *Silent Witness,* an English thriller starring Lionel Atwill.

TOURING PRODUCTIONS

Evidently, the Professional Players were unable to attract audiences consistently, for by the fall of 1931 they had departed from the Walnut, and the theatre was rented out to touring productions. Harry Green opened the fall season on September 7 in *Twisting the Law.* Leslie Banks and Vera Allen brought in an English drama, *Lean Harvest,* for its American premiere. Grace George returned in *A Golden Cinderella,* playing a Victorian heiress who goes out for a night on the town.

A production of *Hamlet* finished the brief season. It was directed by Norman Bel Geddes and starred Raymond Massey, making his American debut. The Canadian-born actor was "a tremendously sincere and moving Hamlet," according to the *Public Ledger,* but it was Bel Geddes's set design and lighting effects that most impressed the reviewers. He used irregularly shaped platforms and cubes set around the vast stage. Scenes were played on different platforms, while fluctuating lights established the shifting moods of the drama. "Few, indeed could deny that, pictorially it was the finest Shakespearean presentation ever seen in this city," wrote the reviewer for the *Ledger*.[23]

Not everyone was pleased, however. One reviewer noted that "conventions were overturned, formulae were forgotten and traditions sometimes scorned." Bel Geddes cut the play severely, eliminating several famous soliloquies. When *Hamlet* closed on October 31, 1931, the Walnut went dark for the longest period in its history—nearly a year and a half.

THE DEPRESSION YEARS

Business continued to decline in all sectors of the economy. Some fifty Philadelphia banks went out of business, wiping out people's life savings. By 1933, when the Depression reached its nadir, 11.5 percent of Philadelphia's whites, 16.2 percent of blacks, and 19.1 percent of foreign-born workers were unemployed. Even so, Philadelphia suffered less than single-industry cities like Pittsburgh and Detroit. The national average for unemployment was 25 percent.[24] With 175 theatres operating in Philadelphia in 1931, the city was vastly oversupplied. As the economic situation continued to worsen in 1931 and 1932, theatre owners experimented with different policies in an effort to keep their theatres open.

During the winter of 1932–33, a New York company took over the Walnut, rewired it for sound, and turned it into a movie theatre, offering continuous shows from 11:00 A.M. to 11:00 P.M., with five acts of vaudeville accompanying the feature film. Admission was 15 cents before 1:00 P.M., 15 and 20 cents until 6:00 P.M., and 20 to 25 cents for evening performances. Unemployed men used the theatre as a flophouse, buying tickets early in the day and remaining until the theatre closed.

The pictures were second-rate. Lila Lee starred in the opening production, *Exposure*, which played during the week of February 6, 1933. It was followed by such films as *Blame the Woman*, starring Adolph Menjou; *Mazie*, with Dorothy Lee; *Pride of the Legion*, with Victor Jory; and *Divorce Racket*. The feature changed twice a week. The vaudeville acts are forgotten now. Buddy Walker served as emcee. Doyle and Donnelly did a song-and-dance act. Bob, Bob, and Bobbie were jesting jugglers, Everett Sanderson performed *A Musical Hodge-Podge*, and Smith, Rogers, and Eddy announced themselves as "Wits of Pantomime."[25] The shows failed to find an audience and closed before the end of February.

After its stint as a vaudeville and film house, the Walnut was taken over by a newly formed Philadelphia group calling themselves Theatregoers and

Producers, which operated it as a pre-Broadway tryout house beginning in August 1933. The fall season opened with *The Pursuit of Happiness,* a drama set in New England during the American Revolution. Film star Jean Arthur starred in a backstage drama, *The Curtain Rises.* Blanche Yurka appeared in *Spring in Autumn,* a Spanish comedy notable for the fact that Yurka sang a Puccini aria while standing on her head. Florence Reed—the granddaughter of "Pop" Reed—returned to the Walnut after an absence of ten years in a drama about horse racing called *Thoroughbred.*

Henry Fonda and Jane Wyatt played the juvenile leads in S. N. Behrman's drama *Love Story,* which played for half a week in December. The play was a disappointment after Behrman's hugely successful *Biography* the previous year. Though the actors garnered good reviews, *Love Story* was much too serious for audience tastes, and it folded before getting to Broadway. Theatregoers and Producers folded as well.

BURLESQUE

The Walnut was next taken over by burlesque impresario Isadore Hirst, who already operated two burlesque theatres in Philadelphia, the Bijou and the Trocadero. The Walnut reopened on February 22, 1934, offering movies and a live stage show titled *Parisian Fantasies,* described as "a mixture of standardized vaudeville, modern revue and musical comedy." "There is a large cast of comedians, comely leading ladies. Billy Arlington was the principal comic and the cast included Leo Lee and Argo, Mullen and Vincent, the Pezzetti Sisters and Frank Smith, a stuttering master of ceremonies," the *Public Ledger* reported, assuring readers that "the show is of the 'clean' variety, generally free from that dirt sometimes considered a substitute for wit."[26]

The theatre was open from 11:15 in the morning till 11:15 at night, and admission was only twenty-five cents. As before, the films were standard B movie fare. Randolph Scott starred in *Broken Dreams* during the opening week, and a crime drama, *Sin of Nora Moran,* opened the following Friday. The policy lasted until the end of March, with such forgettable films as *Son of Kong, Murder on the Campus,* and *Social Register.* For the week of March 23, Lou Costello, who had yet to team up with Bud Abbott, appeared on the bill. The stage show was too clean to appeal to the burlesque crowd, and Hirst abandoned the project.

The Walnut was open intermittently the following season, as various touring shows were brought in. *She Loves Me Not,* a farce by Howard Lindsay that had had a successful run on Broadway the previous season, opened the 1934–35 season. Joshua Logan directed this "gorgeously haywire farce," about a nightclub dancer who seeks shelter in a dormitory of an elite men's college. It was Logan's first professional directorial assignment. He would go on to direct such important Broadway shows as *Knickerbocker Holiday*, *Annie Get Your Gun*, *Mister Roberts*, and *South Pacific*.

Slightly Delirious had its world premiere at the Walnut, appearing for a week in February before moving on to Broadway. It featured Hall Shelton as a stodgy professor who becomes a sexual athlete after spending time in a nudist colony. A British company brought in a vampire thriller, *Death Comes at Sunset*, which played for five weeks beginning in late December. *Cross Ruff* depicted a couple living together out of wedlock who decide to marry when they suspect that their children plan to follow in their footsteps. Then, once again, the Walnut went dark.

THE WALNUT GOES YIDDISH

In the mid-1930s the Walnut became a Yiddish theatre. Two Jewish actors, Irving Jacobson and Max Rosenblatt, organized a stock company to support traveling companies. In the spring of 1936 they booked Herman Yablokoff to star in a musical based on his 1932 hit song *Papirossen*, a sentimental ballad about a young boy who sells cigarettes (or *papirossen*) to eke out a meager living. Yablokoff brought in his leading lady, Bella Mysell, and a youngster named Chaim'l Parness to play the leads. Jacobson and Rosenblatt provided everything else: singers and dancers, sets, and décor.

The following Passover season, Maurice Schwartz, the leading producer of Yiddish drama, appeared in *The Water Carrier*. The Russian-born actor had come to America as a child and had acted in various Yiddish theatre companies before taking over the Irving Place Theatre in 1919, which he turned into the Yiddish Art Theatre. Schwartz operated the Yiddish Art Theatre for the next thirty years, presenting a mixture of classics and popular material and touring part of the year to other cities with large Jewish populations. During the Depression the company toured under the auspices of the Federal Theatre Project, established in 1935 to provide employment for theatre professionals put out of work by the economic crisis.

Often called the Yiddish Barrymore, Maurice Schwartz starred in most of his productions. In *The Water Carrier* he played a simpleminded Polish Jew whose wife tricks him into believing he is a great rabbi. The company returned the following spring with *The Brothers Ashkenazi*, an epic drama about twin brothers living in the Polish city of Lodz. Schwartz played the weaker but more clever brother, while Samuel Goldenberg played his powerfully built but naïve twin, Jacob. "As performed by the Yiddish Art Theatre,

The Brothers Ashkenazi becomes an historical pageant. It is a century of Lodz, through the center of which runs the thread of the history of the Ashkenazi family," wrote Sidney B. Whipple of the New York production.[27]

More Yiddish productions followed. Molly Picon appeared in an operetta titled *Mein Makele* (My Little Molly), playing a Polish girl pressured by her family to marry a man she does not love. Instead she marries an American who promises to take her to the United States. The diminutive impish actress was raised in Philadelphia and had made her stage debut in a vaudeville act at a local nickelodeon. She spent most of her early career in the Yiddish Theatre and was a leading comic star, turning to the Broadway stage during her later years. Julius Nathanson starred in an opera called *Bei Mir Bist Du Schoen* (To Me You Are Beautiful), and in *Semele's Bar Mitzvah,* a romantic musical about a simple man in love with a wealthy girl.

THE FEDERAL THEATRE PROJECT

In the fall of 1938 the Walnut was taken over by the Federal Theatre Project. The season opened on October 17 with *One Third of a Nation*, a product of the Federal Theatre Project's controversial Living Newspaper series. This documentary play dealt with slum conditions, employing slides and live action, which we now call multimedia. "Through spotlights, through black-outs, through the dance, through an explanatory voice, through films, through by-play between actors and audience . . . the story of slums, of the disease and crime they produce is graphically told," the *Inquirer* reported.[28] Originally presented in New York, *One Third of a Nation* was adapted to Philadelphia and told the history of tenement housing from the days of William Penn to the recent collapse of a tenement, depicting the plight of families living in the midst of poverty, crime, and disease.

Not all Federal Theatre Project productions were so controversial. In December a touring company brought in *Prologue to Glory*, a reverential depiction of Abraham Lincoln's years as a small-town lawyer in Illinois, which the *Inquirer* dismissed as "a modest footlight fabric fashioned of homespun and hokum dramatic materials."[29] The Federal Theatre Project's Gilbert and Sullivan Opera Company arrived in early January, presenting *The Mikado, The Pirates of Penzance, H.M.S. Pinafore, Trial by Jury,* and *The Gondoliers* to generally good reviews. On January 28, 1939, they presented *The Playboy of the Western World*, John Millington Synge's comedy of Irish peasant life.

Meanwhile, the Philadelphia Company was rehearsing a documentary piece tracing the history of syphilis and the efforts to find a cure for the disease. *Spirochete* was produced in late February and ran for five weeks. It was generally less successful than *One Third of a Nation,* for the subject matter did not lend itself to effective drama, although certain scenes "packed plenty of punch."[30] Such works alienated more conservative members of Congress, who accused the organization of leftist bias and refused to fund the Federal Theatre Project beyond June 30, 1939.

Shortly before the Federal Theatre Project's funding was eliminated, the Philadelphia Negro Unit came out with an original production, *Prelude to Swing.* This dance piece traced the development of African American music from its roots in African drumming and chants through slave dances to the jitterbug. The cast included Norman Johnson, Edward G. Robinson, and Mattie Washington, and a gospel choir accompanied the dancers. Hallie Flanagan called *Prelude to Swing* "Philadelphia's contribution to original theatre composition, a history of the development of Negro music by the dance unit, the Negro choral group, and the swing orchestra. To the music of the swing band and chorus the dancers, boldly accented by costume and light, achieved, on the steps and levels of a simple functional setting, luminosity and a striking emphasis on three-dimensional form and movement. African jungle rhythms, slave songs, work songs, play songs, spirituals, jazz and swing, were given visual definition. Plantation songs in unconcertized arrangement were fresh and vigorous."[31] The production continued through the end of June, when the curtain came down on the Federal Theatre Project.

Without the support of federal dollars, the Walnut remained dark. The Yiddish Art Theatre returned for a week in March 1940 in *Salvation,* a drama by Sholem Asch about Jewish life in Poland under Russian rule. Another Yiddish comedy, *Three Daughters,* played for several nights beginning December 31, 1940. The theatre then remained shuttered until March 3, 1941, when producer Oscar Serlin brought in a touring production of *Life with Father.*

Life with Father was setting box office records in Boston, Chicago, and New York, where it was on its way to becoming the longest-running nonmusical play in Broadway history. Howard Lindsay and Russel Crouse adapted the play, about growing up in a well-to-do family, from *New Yorker* sketches by Clarence Day Jr. The play depicted family life on Park Avenue in the 1880s and captured the public's yearning for a safer, simpler time. The Broadway version, which starred Howard Lindsay as the irascible head of the Day household and Dorothy Stickney as his slyly manipulative wife, Vinnie, opened on Broadway on November 8, 1939.

In the audience on opening night were silent film stars Lillian and Dorothy Gish. "We thought it was a wonderful play," Lillian Gish told biographer Stuart Oderman, "the kind of play our audience, who remembered us from our Griffith films, would like to see us do."[32] The Gish sisters approached Howard Lindsay that very night about doing the play. Lillian Gish headed up the Chicago company and was kept busy for eighteen months, while Dorothy Gish opened in Boston, then moved on to Philadelphia, playing opposite her longtime lover, Louis Calhern. The play held the Walnut's stage for nearly three months during the last days of the Depression.

Despite frequent closures, the Walnut Street Theatre had pulled through the most devastating economic crisis in American history. Many others did not survive. The Casino Theatre, two doors down from the Walnut, was torn down in 1935. It had been a burlesque theatre for some years. The historic Arch Street Theatre, at the time the second-oldest theatre in America, was razed the following year, after 112 years of operation. The Garrick, built in 1901, staged its last show in 1936 and was torn down to make way for a Woolworth's. The Broad Street Theatre, built in 1876 by the Kiralfy brothers, was demolished on August 20, 1937. The following month, the Adelphi and Lyric theatres, located side by side on Broad near Cherry, were victims of the wrecking ball. The Chestnut Street Opera House was demolished in 1940, after eighty years in operation. The Philadelphia houses that survived had mostly converted to film. The Bijou, at Eighth and Race, had become a burlesque theatre and was eventually converted into a second-run movie house. The Erlanger, built in 1927 as a legitimate theatre, was rewired for sound and became a film house two years later. Forepaugh's on North Eighth Street had shifted to a film policy in 1913. The only surviving legitimate theatres, apart from the Walnut, were owned by the Shubert Brothers, and served primarily as tryout houses for shows that were about to open on Broadway. In the 1940s the Walnut, too, would become a Shubert house.

A TRYOUT HOUSE, 1941–1954

In booking *Life with Father* into the Walnut in the spring of 1941, producer Oscar Serlin bypassed the Shubert Organization, thereby avoiding the percentage that the Shubert-controlled United Booking Office demanded. "They asked $52,000 to be paid weekly on a percentage basis, and exclusive of the usual house arrangements," Serlin told *Variety* shortly before he brought the play to the Walnut. Serlin did more than complain to *Variety*, however. According to the Shuberts' biographer, Foster Hirsch, he also told Eleanor Roosevelt that the Shubert Organization was a dangerous monopoly. Mrs. Roosevelt set in motion a federal investigation into the Shuberts and their business practices, an investigation that would result in antitrust charges against the Shubert Organization.[1]

The Shuberts had emerged from the Depression stronger than ever. Abe Erlanger, the last of the Syndicate partners, had died in 1930, and Lee and J. J. Shubert acquired most of the Syndicate's properties. The Shubert Organization had gone into receivership in 1932, but Lee Shubert bought their properties at a bankruptcy auction in 1933 for $400,000. He was the only bidder. As the economy began to improve by the end of the 1930s, the Shuberts bought up theatres in New York and the major tryout cities. By 1941, "more than 75 percent of Broadway's attractions were in one form or another Shubert 'investments,' partially, 50 percent, or otherwise," Shubert biographer Jerry Stagg reported. "Of those that had no part of the Shuberts' dollars, 90 percent were compelled to play Shubert theaters. It was a monopoly, in the truest sense."[2]

Central to the Shuberts' dominance was their control of the principal tryout cities of Philadelphia, New Haven, and Boston. All were convenient to New York City, so that productions could be transported without much cost and Broadway theatre owners could attend the shows. Ninety percent of all Broadway shows opened out of town. New York theatre owners attended the tryouts to decide which shows they wanted to book. The tryout productions allowed producers and directors to gauge the reactions of an audience and make any changes in the script, cast, or staging before putting the show in front of the New York critics.

In the fall of 1941 the Shuberts took over the Walnut, leasing it from James P. Beury. They already owned three Philadelphia theatres—the Shubert, the Forrest, and the Locust—and their takeover of the Walnut meant that they now controlled all the first-class theatres in the city. "Translated into practicality, this meant that if a show wanted to play Boston or Philadelphia, it would have to sign a life contract with UBO [the United Booking Office]," Jerry Stagg explained, noting that "shows had to play one or both cities."[3]

THE WALNUT UNDER THE SHUBERTS

The man in charge of the Shuberts' Philadelphia operations was Lawrence Shubert Lawrence. Lawrence was the son of Lee and J. J.'s sister, Fanny. Both he and his brother Milton joined their uncles' company as teenagers. "At sixteen, Lawrence began as a telephone boy in the Winter Garden box office. In four years, he worked his way up to treasurer and house manager; but he left in 1915 for Philadelphia, where he remained head of Shubert operations until his death on April 17, 1965," Foster Hirsch wrote in *The Boys from Syracuse*. Lawrence had little use for the political battles of the family-run organization, "and cared more about alcohol and about collecting books than he cared about the theatre."[4]

Under Lawrence's auspices, the Walnut became an important tryout house for shows headed to Broadway, and it entered a golden age. The opening production in the fall of 1941 was *Separate Rooms*, a farce by Joseph Carole and Alan Dinehart, which came in after a successful run in New York, despite a thin plot and mediocre reviews. The theatre was dark for two weeks, and then Grace George returned for a week in a comedy, *Spring Again*, that had its world premiere at the Walnut prior to a profitable Broadway run. The theatre went dark for another week, after which Fredric March appeared in a Theatre Guild production of *Hope for a Harvest*.

The Walnut was used intermittently during its first season as a Shubert house. Thus, nothing was playing on December 7, 1941, when news of the Japanese attack on Pearl Harbor reached Philadelphia. The theatre did not reopen until Christmas week, when Owen Davis Jr. brought in a road company production of *Mr. and Mrs. North*, a comic murder mystery written by his father about a young married couple living in Greenwich Village. Striptease star Ann Corio followed in early January in a revival of the tropical potboiler *White Cargo*. Principally known as a burlesque stripper, Corio was moving into legitimate drama in roles that took advantage of her sultry good looks. Mary Anderson starred in *Guest in the House,* which had its world premiere at the Walnut on February 10, 1942, but failed on Broadway.

NATIVE SON

The show that followed, on February 23, was one of the most powerful dramas of the era, a stage adaptation of Richard Wright's best-selling novel *Native Son*. The play brought together a strong original story, a visionary producer, a talented director, and an actor of uncommon ability. *Native Son* is a tragedy about an embittered black youth, Bigger Thomas, who accidentally kills the daughter of his white employer, then burns her body in the family's furnace to avoid being caught. Wright adapted it for the stage with playwright Paul Green, who tried to soften the bleakness of the novel. Producer John Houseman refused to tone down the tragedy and had it rewritten, then turned it over to his longtime collaborator Orson Welles to direct. Welles was then at the height of his fame. He had recently completed *Citizen Kane* and was struggling to get the film distributed when he began work on *Native Son* in the spring of 1941.

Welles cast Canada Lee, a former prizefighter, jockey, and nightclub owner, as Bigger Thomas. Lee had remarkable range, and the part displayed his virtuosity. Lee—who had gotten his start with the Negro unit of the Federal Theatre Project—was able to capture the extremes of the character: his bitterness over the injustices of race, his panic at being caught in the bedroom of a white girl, and the sense of power and achievement the murder gives him, even as he is hunted down, captured, and convicted. The *Philadelphia Inquirer* noted that Lee "plays the part of Bigger with unflinching honesty and great forcefulness. He makes startlingly vivid the mental and emotional processes of the character, from the braggart and bully, to the primitive creature overwhelmed by abject panic."[5]

Welles made innovative use of realism and expressionism, creating an oppressive world closing in on the protagonist. The play ran without an intermission, and programs were not distributed until after the show, to prevent any distraction from the rustling of pages. Yellow brick was used in the sets to give a bleak, institutional feel to the environment, and Welles made effective use of sound and other effects. The sounds of the burning furnace followed Bigger through his descent into the legal system, which culminated in a trial scene in which the defense attorney gave a powerful indictment of the racist system that had created Bigger Thomas. The scene brought bravos from the audience.

The play reaffirmed Welles's place as the most talented director on the American stage. Sidney Whipple wrote that "Orson Welles, whether you like to admit it or not, is no boy wonder but actually the greatest theatrical director of the modern stage. He is bold, ruthless and unashamed in his assault upon your emotions. He tricks your senses and pounds upon your feelings. And he brings this play through constantly rising tension and continuously mounting passion to a climax that makes the brain reel with the impact."[6]

KATHARINE HEPBURN

Katharine Hepburn made her only appearance at the Walnut in a new play by Philip Barry, *Without Love,* which opened on March 23, 1942. She had previously collaborated with Barry on *The Philadelphia Story,* a triumph for Hepburn on both stage and screen. The role in *Without Love* was well suited to the star, although the plot was contrived. Hepburn played a New England widow who operates a boardinghouse in Washington, where an American diplomat takes up residence as he tries to persuade the Irish government to assist in the war effort. The two embark on a marriage of convenience, only to discover that they have fallen in love.

Hepburn had recently completed her first film with Spencer Tracy, *Woman of the Year,* and wanted Tracy to play opposite her, but the producers refused, concerned about Tracy's well-publicized drinking problem. They cast Elliott Nugent instead. It was a mistake—Nugent had drinking problems of his own, and he lacked Tracy's charisma. The pairing failed to click. "As a result of Kate's feeling about Nugent not 'working' with her, she overplayed extremely, trying to make up for his deficiency, his inadequacy, and her whole performance failed to soar," Lawrence Langner wrote.[7]

Hepburn was then at the height of her popularity, and despite mediocre reviews tickets were sold out well in advance in tryouts in New Haven, Boston, and Washington. Langner recalled, "we traveled through the country like a circus, all the comings and goings of Kate being accompanied by the wildest demonstrations on the part of tumultuous admirers."[8] But the script had problems, and the producers decided not to open in New York, bringing the show to the Walnut instead.

The play generated negative comparisons with *The Philadelphia Story.* "While there are flashes of Mr. Barry's sparkling and sophisticated wit, there is little sense of plausibility or persuasiveness in the plot," wrote the reviewer for the *Inquirer.* The play was withdrawn for rewrites, and Hepburn returned to Hollywood that summer. *Without Love* eventually opened on Broadway the following fall but played only a few weeks. Hepburn eventually did play opposite Tracy when the play was made into a movie in 1945.

fig. 28 Katharine Hepburn poses for a publicity photo for Philip Barry's successful play *The Philadelphia Story.* Hepburn's only appearance at the Walnut was in another Barry production, *Without Love.*

THE WAR YEARS

World War II was generally good for the theatre industry. After more than a decade of steady decline, the number of new productions increased in the 1941–42 season. "A portion of the stupendous amount of money put into circulation during the war inevitably found its way into box-offices," observed theatre historian Glenn Hughes, "and the mass migration of workers to war-industry cities created larger audiences for road shows than had existed for a long time."[9] Philadelphia played an important role in manufacturing goods for the war effort. The shipbuilding yards in Camden and Philadelphia produced warships, and locomotive works were refitted to turn out tanks. High-wage jobs in the war plants had workers flocking to Philadelphia. Flush with money, many workers attended the theatre for the first time in their lives.

Russel Crouse and Howard Lindsay, who had such a success with *Life with Father,* had another hit on their hands with *Arsenic and Old Lace,* a dark comedy about two sweet old ladies who lure lonely old men into their home and murder them. The play, written by Joseph Kesselring, had originally been conceived as a serious thriller, but Crouse and Lindsay, who produced the play, turned it into a comedy. It was an inspired choice, for the play broke box office records when it debuted on Broadway in January 1941, and it has been revived regularly ever since. A touring company brought the play to the Walnut for three weeks beginning on April 29, 1942. It returned the following January with the original Broadway cast, which included Josephine Hull and Jean Adair as the two murderous women and Boris Karloff as their eccentric nephew.

Several producers hurried out war-related plays in time for the fall season. Gladys Cooper and Gregory Peck opened the 1942–43 season in *The Morning Star,* a war story set in London during the blitz. The play failed to capture an audience in New York, and Peck was back in November trying out a new play, *The Willow and I.* Dean Jagger and John Forsythe had supporting roles in *Yankee Point,* a melodrama about Nazi spying. Maxwell Anderson's *The Eve of St. Mark* dealt with the emotional impact a soldier's death has on the woman he leaves behind. Anderson dedicated the play to his nephew, who had been killed in action in the early months of the war.

Several major playwrights were represented that season. Gloria Swanson appeared in *Three Curtains,* actually a trio of one-act plays by Shaw, Barrie, and Pinero, respectively. It was headed to Broadway until Swanson's co-star began acting strangely during the Boston run. Rather than recast and re-rehearse the play, the production was shut down. William Saroyan penned *Hello Out There,* which played on a bill with a revival of G. K. Chesterton's *Magic*—Eddie Dowling starred in both. *Life with Father* was revived, with Percy Waram and Margalo Gillmore in the roles played by Louis Calhern and Dorothy Gish. John Barton appeared in a touring production of *Tobacco Road,* Erskine Caldwell's record-setting comedy about southern sharecroppers.

As usual during wartime, the public sought escape, and comedies proved to be popular. Edward Everett Horton returned to the Walnut after a twenty-five-year absence in *Springtime for Henry.* Fans of the character actor jammed the theatre for a special matinee opening on Washington's birthday in 1943. Horton had already racked up more than eight hundred performances of the play. Among the other comedies that spring were *Those Endearing Young Charms*, with Mabel Taliaferro; *Dark Eyes*, with Minnie Dupree; and *The Doughgirls*, a comedy about gold diggers set in wartime Washington, directed by George S. Kaufman.

Fred Stone starred in a revival of Kaufmann and Hart's 1937 Pulitzer Prize–winning comedy, *You Can't Take It with You*, which opened the fall 1943 season. *Life with Father* also returned, with June Walker and Harry Bannister in the roles of Vinnie and Clarence Day. The brightest spot in the season was a production of Noël Coward's *Blithe Spirit*, which opened at the Walnut on October 10, 1943, after an eighteen-month run on Broadway. It was a high-spirited tale of a writer who is tormented by the ghost of his first wife, after she is summoned during a séance. Most of the Broadway cast—including Clifton Webb, Peggy Wood, and Mildred Natwick—played in the touring version, which the critics pronounced "irresistible, uproarious amusement."[10]

TRYOUTS AND REVIVALS

Several plays had pre-Broadway tryouts in 1943–44. Stella Adler directed Eddie Dowling in *Manhattan Nocturne*, about a writer who helps a prostitute suffering from amnesia. *What's Up?* brought together lyricist Alan Jay Lerner and composer Frederick Loewe for their first Broadway show. Jimmy Savo starred as a Middle Eastern potentate whose plane makes a forced landing near a girls' boarding school, where the passengers are quarantined for measles. It was not an auspicious beginning for the songwriting team that would create *Brigadoon*, *My Fair Lady*, and *Camelot*.

Hollywood stars tried their luck on the stage. Margaret Sullavan played the lead in *The Voice of the Turtle*, a romantic comedy about a struggling actress and a soldier on leave. It proved to be popular with the home front audience, and Sullavan toured it for two years. Zasu Pitts managed to keep *Ramshackle Inn* alive with her vague character and fluttery mannerisms, despite negative reviews from the critics. Ruth Chatterton was not so lucky in *A Lady Comes Home*. The critics concluded that "it would have been better for actors and audience if this lady hadn't come home," and the show never made it to Broadway.[11] Billie Burke had the lead role in Zoë Akins's *Mrs. January and Mr. X*, which came in on February 28 for a two-week run prior to its Broadway opening.

Walter Hampden played Thomas Jefferson in Sidney Kingsley's *The Patriots*, a historical play that had received the New York Drama Critics' Circle Award the previous spring as the best American play of the year. Louis Calhern returned to the Walnut in *Jacobowsky and the Colonel*, a "comedy about a tragedy" written by Franz Werfel and S. N. Behrman, based on Werfel's experience fleeing the Nazis. Calhern played an aristocratic Polish army officer fleeing occupied France with a resourceful Jewish refugee, played by Oscar Karlweis. Elia Kazan directed this Theatre Guild production. Maurice Schwartz brought in the Yiddish drama *The Family Carnovsky* for a week in March, and Herman Yablokoff appeared in *Mazel-Tov Mama* in May.

THE FALL 1944 SEASON

The fall season got off to a slow start. It was an election year, and although Roosevelt was a shoe-in for a fourth term, producers were not eager to promote their new offerings during a political campaign, so touring shows were brought in. Film star Una Merkel opened the fall season in a touring version of *Three Is a Family*, a domestic comedy about living in a tiny apartment. Will Geer, Jack Albertson, and Eddie Nugent followed in *Champagne for Everybody*, a disappointing comedy about an eccentric Brooklyn family. Sonya Stokowski, the daughter of the Philadelphia Orchestra's conductor, Leopold Stokowski, headed up a road company of *Wallflower*, a romantic comedy that had had a successful Broadway run the previous season. Yet another production of *Life with Father* came through, with Carl Benton Reid and Betty Linley in the leading roles.

On October 16, 1944, the Theatre Guild presented *Embezzled Heaven*, which brought Ethel Barrymore back to the Walnut for the first time since *Captain Jinks of the Horse Marines* established her as a star back in 1900. Sanford Meisner co-starred in this stage adaptation of a Franz Werfel novel. The effort was disappointing. Barrymore played a pious cook who sends all her savings to a nephew studying to be a priest in order to guarantee her place in heaven, only to discover that he has swindled her. It was to be Ethel Barrymore's last Broadway show.

More substantive productions were timed to come to Broadway after Election Day, so late autumn was a busy time at the Walnut. On October 30, Richard Widmark opened in *Trio*, playing a college student in love with a girl engaged in a lesbian affair with an older woman. Despite the dignified treatment of the theme, the producers had trouble finding a New York venue. Concerned about New York's "padlock law," which allowed the city to close any theatre putting on an obscene play, the Shuberts refused to let the play appear at any of their theatres. Eventually, *Trio* went into a non-Shubert house, opening after Christmas. But city officials found the subject matter obscene, and it was forced to close.

Playwright Arthur Miller had his debut with *The Man Who Had All the Luck*, which had a Broadway tryout at the Walnut beginning November 13, 1944. The play explored the subject of fate, and how a man can be destroyed by the illusion of his powerlessness. It was not well received. The critics concluded that "despite some good and stimulating lines, the pace is pedestrian, and the character-drawing is conventional."[12] Miller would get a much better reception for his next play, *Death of a Salesman.*

THE CHERRY ORCHARD

Eva Le Gallienne appeared at the Walnut for the first time in a production of *The Cherry Orchard*, which she also directed. The play is considered Chekhov's masterpiece, completed just months before he died in 1904. Le Gallienne played Madame Ranevskaya, the head of an aristocratic Russian family forced to sell off their ancestral estate to a former servant. "The play discloses qualities of comedy not hitherto suspected," wrote Linton Martin.[13] Le Gallienne's frequent co-star, Joseph Schildkraut, played her vacillating brother.

Born in England and educated at the Royal Academy of Dramatic Art, Eva Le Gallienne had come to the United States in 1920, and was featured in the Theatre Guild's production of *Liliom*, where she first acted opposite Joseph Schildkraut. In 1926 she established the Civic Repertory Theatre, where she offered low-priced productions of classic drama. Over the next six years she directed and starred in many of its productions. Schildkraut got his start in German-language productions and later worked in Germany with the celebrated director Max Reinhardt. He joined Le Gallienne's Civic Repertory Theatre in 1932 and performed with her company for several years. He divided his time between New York and Hollywood, where he won the Academy Award for his portrayal of Dreyfus in *The Life of Emile Zola.*

THE WAR WINDS DOWN

By the winter of 1944–45, the end of the war was in sight. Roosevelt had won the 1944 presidential election, despite rumors of failing health. By mid-December, Allied troops were poised to enter Germany. Hitler massed his troops for one last desperate offensive in the Ardennes forest, the Battle of the Bulge, but was turned back after ten days of bitter fighting.

Comedies proved popular with a population tired of the war and the separations it entailed. Ruth Gordon had a success in a vehicle she wrote for herself, *Over Twenty-One*, which opened on Christmas Day. George S. Kaufman directed this madcap comedy about a celebrated Hollywood writer who follows her husband to Florida, where he is attending officer candidate school. It proved very popular with audiences on the home front. Gordon was unable to perform on opening night owing to influenza, and an understudy replaced her. Gordon continued to be ill, and Dorothy Gish took over the role later in the run and went on to tour army bases for two years with the play.

Romantic comedies particularly appealed to audiences anticipating the return of the fighting men. Gene Lockhart played a justice of the peace who is exposed as a fraud in *Happily Ever After*. *Kiss and Tell* played a two-week engagement; six road companies were touring the country with this romantic comedy at the time. *I'll Be Waiting*, a comedy about war wives, followed; then *Too Hot for Maneuvers* had its world premiere at the Walnut. It featured film star Richard Arlen as an air force veteran who takes over his family's military academy.

On April 12, news reached Philadelphia that Franklin Delano Roosevelt had died. Philadelphians lined the train tracks to greet the funeral train bearing the president's body back to Hyde Park, New York. Less than a month later, Germany surrendered. Celebrations were restrained, since the public anticipated a difficult and bloody invasion of the Japanese homeland. Maurice Schwartz brought in Sholem Aleichem's *It's Hard to Be a Jew* on May 14 to close out the season. The play was about a Christian student who exchanges identities with a Jewish student to prove that not all Christians are intolerant, only to fall in love with a Jewish girl, whom the Jewish student also loves. But the title had special significance, as reports and photographs from liberated concentration camps circulated, and the true horror of the Nazi regime sank in.

The United States dropped the atomic bomb on Hiroshima and Nagasaki in August, and on August 14 Japan surrendered. The city went wild. Downtown Philadelphia was filled with celebrants from late afternoon until early morning the next day, and the governor declared a two-day holiday. The fall season opened on September 8 with French actress Simone Simon playing an invalid in *Emily*, a psychological drama set in a Philadelphia mansion. But it was a new play by Howard Lindsay and Russel Crouse, *State of the Union*, having its world premiere at the Walnut, that was the first important production of the season. Ralph Bellamy starred as a millionaire businessman who is selected as the Republican presidential candidate, despite the fact that he is estranged from his wife, played by Ruth Hussey, and is carrying on an affair with an important newspaper publisher. The play had a two-year run in New York and garnered a Pulitzer Prize for Lindsay and Crouse.

Hollywood stars continued to be featured on the Walnut's stage during the 1945–46 season. Leo G. Carroll reprised his Broadway success in George S. Kaufman and John P. Marquand's *The Late George Apley*, as a stuffy Bostonian whose children frustrate and infuriate him by making unsuitable marriages. Louis Calhern and Dorothy Gish were reunited in *The Magnificent Yankee,* a historical drama about Justice Oliver Wendell Holmes and his wife, Fanny. Walter Huston returned to the stage in *Apple of His Eye,* which also featured Mary Wickes and Tom Ewell. Arlene Dahl had a supporting role in *Questionable Ladies,* which featured an all-woman cast and failed to make it to Broadway. *Flamingo Road,* with Will Geer, based on the best-selling novel, debuted that season. *Twilight Bar* featured Luther Adler and Mercedes McCambridge. *Woman Bites Dog* starred E. G. Marshall and Kirk Douglas. Miriam Hopkins was featured in *Laura,* a mystery drama. *The Dancer* finished out the 1945–46 season, providing dancer Leon Fokine with his first dramatic role.

POSTWAR THEATRE

The end of World War II soon brought an end to the revival of Broadway. Although the country was entering a new era of prosperity, these were not good years for legitimate theatre. There was new competition from television, which began to replace radio and movies as the country's principal entertainment medium. Productions dwindled to prewar levels and continued to decline through the 1940s and 1950s. This meant that fewer productions tried out in Philadelphia. But if the financial times were not good for the theatre, artistically they were excellent. While lighthearted fare had predominated during the war, playwrights now began to tackle more substantive themes.

One such work was *Deep Are the Roots,* a play about racial prejudice. The play followed a black soldier returning from the war who confronts bigotry in his hometown. When he refuses to display the deference expected by southern whites, he is framed for a theft and run out of town. A touring version of the play came to the Walnut on March 4, 1946, with Henry Scott as the black veteran and Frances Waller as a white woman who falls in love with him. The play was directed by Elia Kazan, who was emerging as the most important theatre director of the postwar period. The characters are two-dimensional, designed to put across the themes, but the play contained elements found in Kazan's best work.

Kazan had begun his career with the Group Theatre in the 1930s, where he was influenced by the politically challenging work of the Depression playwrights and the method acting style of Constantin Stanislavsky. Kazan had directed one play at the Walnut—S. N. Behrman's comedy *Dunnigan's Daughter,* a Theatre Guild production about the downfall of a ruthless industrialist living in Mexico, which opened on November 5, 1945. Kazan went on to found the Actors Studio and directed such plays as *A Streetcar Named Desire*, *Death of a Salesman*, and *Cat on a Hot Tin Roof*, as well as such films as *On the Waterfront*.

Perhaps the most important group to bring productions to the Walnut after the war was the Theatre Guild. Based in New York City, the Theatre Guild presented three road shows each year, which were presented along with three plays by other producers. The plays were sent out on the road through the American Theatre Society as part of a subscription series. The Shubert Organization was a partner in these ventures. It had merged its subscription series with the Theatre Guild's subscription series during the Depression to help reduce costs. At the time, the road was virtually dead, but this "single deal changed the so-called 'road' from a liability and a headache for everyone in the theatre, into an asset," the Theatre Guild's executive director, Lawrence Langner, noted. Langner observed that by 1951, when he was writing, "the Theatre Guild–American Theatre Society subscription system reaches from coast to coast and now includes twenty-one cities with a total of well over one hundred thousand subscribers."[14]

ANTITRUST INVESTIGATION

On August 5, 1946, the Ninth and Walnut Corporation, representing the Shubert Organization, purchased the Walnut from James P. Beury. The sale was ordered by the sheriff in an action against Beury, evidently for debts. The same month, the Justice Department began to take a look into the Shuberts' domination of the legitimate theatre. "In the early part of August 1946, [Lee Shubert] was visited by some gentlemen from the Anti-Trust Division of the Department of Justice," wrote the Shuberts' biographer, Jerry Stagg. "They wanted to talk with him about Shubert Theater Enterprises and the United Booking Office." While producers could bring their shows into New York in a non-Shubert theatre, if they wanted to use any UBO-controlled houses on the road, they had to remain with the Shuberts for the entire life of the play. The Shuberts were playing the same game the Syndicate had played so effectively at the turn of the century. Producers who refused to go along with these terms were effectively shut out of Philadelphia, since the Shuberts controlled all the legitimate theatres in the city.

The Justice Department was putting together an antitrust case against the movie studios, and the "Anti-Trust Division callers promised to come back, and the press covered the story," Stagg reported. "The articles pointed out that the Shuberts owned seventeen theaters in New York, controlled the booking of an eighteenth and that in Philadelphia they owned all the theaters, and all of them were UBO, and in Boston they controlled all theaters but one and *they* were all UBO. Translated into practicality, this meant that if a show wanted to play Boston or Philadelphia, it would have to sign a life contract with UBO (and shows had to play one or both cities). It was not necessary to add that if the play didn't sign with UBO, it might have trouble getting a New York theater. It was a very cozy setup."[15]

The Walnut was central to this arrangement and continued to be used regularly as a tryout house for new productions. Several minor plays appeared there in the fall of 1946 prior to their Broadway openings. *Mr. Peebles and Mr. Hooker* was a parable of good and evil set in the Tennessee Hills. Ina Claire starred in a new comedy, *The Fatal Weakness*. Philadelphia playwright George Kelly directed this Theatre Guild production. Among the other plays that opened at the Walnut was *The Temporary Mrs. Smith*, co-written by Jacqueline Susann, who would go on to write best-selling novels like *The Valley of the Dolls*. The play opened on Broadway some weeks later under the title *Lovely Me*. Claire Trevor starred in a cold war drama, *The Big Two*, about an investigator who enters Russian-occupied Germany to arrest an American collaborator, then falls in love with her Russian counterpart.

ANATOMY OF A FLOP

The principal reason for a Philadelphia tryout was to allow the producers to observe the reactions of an audience and make whatever changes were needed. The author, the director, and the designers were generally all on hand for out-of-town openings. Sometimes it was necessary to fire an actor, and occasionally the director had to be replaced. Usually rewrites were needed, and the playwright often worked late into the night making changes in the script. From time to time the problems were so substantial that the show folded out of town. Such was the case with *Heartsong*, an early work by playwright Arthur Laurents. *Heartsong* was a domestic comedy exploring the marital difficulties of a young couple. Laurents had one Broadway play under his belt, a critically acclaimed study of anti-Semitism during World War II titled *Home of the Brave*. The producer was Irene Mayer Selznick, the daughter of MGM studio chief Louis B. Mayer and the ex-wife of film producer David O. Selznick.

From the very beginning there were problems, Laurents recalled in his autobiography. The original leading lady quit after three days of rehearsal. In New Haven, the original leading man was replaced by Lloyd Bridges. In Boston, the original director was fired, replaced by Mel Ferrer. Meanwhile, the play was undergoing extensive rewrites. Before the Philadelphia opening, Bridges quit. Frantic calls to Hollywood rounded up Barry Nelson and Phyllis Thaxter, two players under contract at MGM. "I was surprised to find they were delighted, even ecstatic," Laurents remembered. "Hollywood scripts, they enthused, didn't have dialogue this wonderful! That, in a way, was the mainspring of the problem: the dialogue, like a good wig, deceived too well. It made the play seem better than it was."

Only one cast member—Shirley Booth—remained throughout the play. She was "a godsend," Laurents recalled. "Playing an alcoholic, her dry delivery, her vulnerability and her timing from God made her big scene the one surefire scene in the play."[16] *Heartsong* opened in Philadelphia on March 17, 1947, to bland reviews. "The very unpretentiousness of this play is its most engaging asset," Linton Martin wrote for the *Inquirer*. "It may be a somewhat negative asset, and there is no denying that the pace is pedestrian and much of the talk is trite. But at least the characters are more than the cardboard cutouts that too often clutter comedies, and the playwright has provided a couple of secondary individuals who are intermittently amusing."[17]

"My play wasn't good enough and I couldn't fix it," Laurents admitted. "I told [Irene Selznick] it would not do her or me or even Shirley Booth any good to bring it into New York. I asked her to close in Philadelphia, to let it die." Selznick complied. "This was my learning experience with the foremost reason for failure in the theatre," Laurents explained. "The signposts say STOP but the show continues anyway. Why? Because it started. It may get better, sick productions often do, but better doesn't make it good."[18] Despite the failure of the production, most of those connected with the show had successful careers. Laurents provided the libretto for such shows as *Gypsy* and *West Side Story*. Shirley Booth received a Tony for her performance in *Come Back, Little Sheba*. And Irene Selznick would go on to produce *A Streetcar Named Desire*.

THE ICEMAN COMETH

Touring shows continued to be booked into the Walnut. Magician Harry Blackstone arrived on November 11, 1946, making the first of four annual appearances at the Walnut. Known for his full-stage illusions, Blackstone had started in vaudeville. During World War II he toured military bases under the sponsorship of the USO, and he had briefly starred in his own radio show. For his current production, he traveled with a cast of thirty. He "produced a rabbit out of a bottle, a garden of paper flowers from his tailcoat, and a spouting fountain from an afghan." He did a variation on sawing a woman in half by using an electrical buzz saw, "which surprisingly gave off sawdust," and distributed rabbits that he pulled out of his hat to children in the audience. "His show has lavish color and costuming, and it has a sustained flow of comedy. But not the least of its qualities is Blackstone's talent as an actor. Alternately he is roguish, suave, villainous and fatherly—as the skit demands," the *Inquirer* noted.[19]

A touring production of *Dream Girl,* a comedy by Elmer Rice (who also directed) came in during Christmas week. It starred June Havoc and Richard Widmark. Later that year Widmark had his first screen success, playing a psychopathic hoodlum in *Kiss of Death.* But the most anticipated production of the 1946–47 season was Eugene O'Neill's *The Iceman Cometh,* which arrived at the Walnut on April 7, 1947.

It had been a dozen years since Philadelphia had seen a new O'Neill play. O'Neill had completed *Iceman* in 1939 but delayed production until after the war, judging that the public would not support such a bleak tragedy during wartime. The play opened "cold" in New York—without an out-of-town tryout—at the Martin Beck Theatre on October 9, 1946. James Barton starred as Hickey, a hardware salesman who arrives at a seedy New York saloon, circa 1912, where an assortment of has-beens and ne'er-do-wells live on pipe dreams and drink to kill their pain. Hickey tries to goad his friends out of their alcoholic stupor and force them to face the truth of their existence. When Hickey admits to killing his wife and is taken away by the police, the men return to their whiskey and their pipe dreams.

Most of the original cast reprised their roles when the play came to the Walnut, although E. G. Marshall took over the role of Hickey from Barton, a move that was labeled "a distinct improvement." The play ran nearly four hours, and the curtain had to be moved up to 7:30 P.M. Reviews were mixed. Jerry Gaghan, writing for the *Daily News,* found it "overlong, windy and static in stretches," but noted that "even when he is overwriting, [O'Neill] can make most of his competitors seem as uninspired as business college students."[20] The play failed to garner either the New York Drama Critics' Circle Award or the Pulitzer Prize. It was not until a 1956 revival, directed by José Quintero and starring Jason Robards, that it was fully realized to be a masterpiece.

POSTWAR PLAYWRIGHTS

Lillian Hellman's *Another Part of the Forest* arrived at the Walnut on September 24, 1947. It was a prequel to her 1939 hit *The Little Foxes,* set twenty years before the action of the other play. Patricia Neal starred as the matriarch of a moneyed and vicious clan, and the *Inquirer* praised the production as "a gripping evening in the theatre."[21]

Musicals almost never played the Walnut while the Shuberts were in charge, but a pair of musical plays by Gian Carlo Menotti, *The Telephone* and *The Medium,* arrived on November 3, 1947, following an eight-month run on Broadway. *Medium* was a two-act tragedy about spiritualism; *The Telephone* was a one-act curtain-raiser. The Italian-born composer had studied at Philadelphia's Curtis Institute of Music and was best known for operas such as *Amahl and the Night Visitors,* which was commissioned by NBC and presented on Christmas Eve 1951.

British playwrights were also featured. *The Winslow Boy,* Terrence Rattigan's drama, had won the New York Drama Critics' Circle Award as the best foreign play of the previous season. It dealt with the trial of a naval cadet falsely accused of stealing a money order. J. B. Priestley did not have much luck with *The Linden Tree,* despite the presence of Boris Karloff in the cast and direction by Maurice Evans. It lasted a week on Broadway after its stint at the Walnut.

A STREETCAR NAMED DESIRE

On November 17, 1947, Tennessee Williams's *A Streetcar Named Desire* opened for previews at the Walnut prior to its Broadway opening. Irene Mayer Selznick produced and Elia Kazan directed. The play arrived at the Walnut after tryouts in New Haven and Boston. Jessica Tandy starred as Blanche DuBois. The action was set in New Orleans's French Quarter, where Blanche has come to stay with her sister, Stella, played by Kim Hunter, and her low-life husband, Stanley Kowalski, played by a relative newcomer, Marlon Brando.

Brando was not the first choice for Stanley Kowalski. Selznick and Kazan originally wanted John Garfield, but Garfield felt that the role was secondary to Blanche DuBois. Marlon Brando had only one Broadway role under his belt and was virtually unknown outside New York. But he impressed director Elia Kazan and playwright Tennessee Williams with his animal magnetism.

The Philadelphia critics immediately recognized the play as a landmark. Linton Martin wrote that "the new Tennessee Williams play is certain to be the sensation of this season in New York."[22] Reviewers focused mostly on Tandy, who would receive the Tony Award for Best Actress in the role of Blanche DuBois. The *Inquirer* noted that "Jessica Tandy last night gave an arresting and infinitely skillful though at times uneven performance. Marlon Brando was superb as Stanley."[23]

It was Brando, however, who came to dominate the play, creating an iconic image in blue jeans and a white T-shirt. Costume designer Lucinda Ballard created that image by tailoring a T-shirt so that it was form-fitting and removing the pockets of the jeans. Of Brando, the *Evening Bulletin* observed, "his transitions from animal brutality to a sort of crude affection are flowing, convincing, never jerked."[24]

MISTER ROBERTS

Streetcar lost the Tony Award for Best Play to *Mister Roberts,* a wartime comedy about a soft-spoken navy lieutenant serving on a supply ship in the Pacific, which starred Henry Fonda. Fonda had recently been discharged from the navy, where he had served in the Pacific during World War II, and he used his own uniform in the play. *Mister Roberts* opened for a pre-Broadway tryout at the Walnut on January 27, 1948. Joshua Logan directed and co-wrote the play with Thomas Heggen, based on Heggen's novel.

"In lieutenant (j.g.) Roberts," *Billboard* reported, "Fonda has found a role which fits him like a glove, and he plays it with beautiful restraint and skill."[25] The supporting cast included David Wayne playing the eccentric Ensign Pulver; William Harrigan, Logan's brother-in-law and son of Ned Harrigan, as the surly captain; and Marlon Brando's sister, Jocelyn Brando, in the sole female part, as an army nurse.

Although it is a comedy, the play has serious themes. On one level it satirizes a tyrannical commanding officer who operates his ship like the totalitarian regimes America had just fought against. In a departure from the comedy formula, the protagonist dies at the end of the play. The crew learns that Mr. Roberts has been killed in a kamikaze attack after he is transferred to another ship.

Reviewing it for the *Philadelphia Inquirer,* Linton Martin proclaimed *Mister Roberts* "easily the roughest, rowdiest, and most uproariously amusing of war comedies. And Philadelphia is fortunate in seeing it before Broadway, for *Mister Roberts* is a smash hit of the season, and no mistake about it."[26] It was—running for 1,157 performances. In addition to the Tony Award for Best Play of the year, Tonys also went to Henry Fonda, producer Leland Hayward, and authors Thomas Heggen and Joshua Logan.

THE IMPACT OF TELEVISION

By 1948 the impact of television was beginning to be felt. Ticket sales on Broadway slumped by 50 percent during the 1947–48 season, and the film industry experienced a similar decline.[27] During the summer of 1948, both the Democratic and Republican conventions were held in Philadelphia, and were

fig. 29 Newcomer Marlon Brando starred as the rugged, sensual Stanley Kowalski in *A Streetcar Named Desire.*

televised for the first time. The new medium was changing the leisure-time habits of the nation, as movies and radio had done before. By 1949 two million television sets were in operation in the United States, and within ten years 85 percent of the population had access to TV.[28]

Television captured the nighttime audience, leaving radio to dominate during the day. The number of radios in use remained static through the decade. Radio responded by giving rise to the disc jockey, who provided patter between playing records, plugging the songs he liked. This created a change in music listenership. Pop music, mostly by Broadway composers, declined as DJs began playing a wider variety of songs. Folk, hillbilly, and blues-based music grew in popularity, while the Broadway songwriters, who had dominated the popular music charts with their sophisticated, urbane lyrics, no longer monopolized the *Billboard* chart.

The Justice Department was going after the movie studios, which controlled not only the production of films but their distribution as well. In 1948 the Supreme Court handed down a decision forcing the major movie studios to divest themselves of their theatres within five years.[29] The Justice Department began to turn its attention to the legitimate theatre and to prepare a case against the Shubert Organization.

ELECTION YEAR

In 1948 the nation was preoccupied with the presidential campaign between Harry Truman and the Republican nominee, Thomas E. Dewey. The fall season opened on September 20, with Basil Rathbone starring in *The Heiress*, an adaptation of Henry James's novel *Washington Square*. Rathbone received a Tony Award for his performance. Howard Lindsay and Russel Crouse wrote *Life with Mother*, a sequel to *Life with Father*, which had recently concluded its Broadway run after eight years. Lindsay and his wife, Dorothy Stickney, reprised their roles as Clarence and Vinnie Day, and the response was good. Reviewing for the *Inquirer*, Edwin Schloss gushed that the authors "have not merely written a supplement to *Life with Father*. They have given us a play that in its own dower right is a triumph of hilarity and charm."[30] Expectations were high, so its six-month run on Broadway was disappointing.

A pair of English productions followed. Maurice Evans directed and starred in George Bernard Shaw's *Man and Superman*, and Cyril Ritchard was featured in a Theatre Guild production of *Make Way for Lucia*. Garson Kanin directed his wife, Ruth Gordon, in *The Smile of the World*. Ossie Davis and Ruby Dee had supporting roles, and during rehearsals for the play they slipped off to New Jersey to get married. The Theatre Guild brought in another production by French film star Jean Pierre Aumont, *Figure of a Girl*. Aumont also starred in the play opposite Austrian beauty Lilli Palmer. The title was changed to *My Name Is Aquilon* when it moved to Broadway the following month. "The play was a failure," Norman Nadel wrote. "Reviewers were fairly scornful of a playwright who writes himself a role as a devil with women, especially when he had failed to make it entertaining."[31]

The big production that season was *Harvey*, which featured Joe E. Brown in the role of Elwood P. Dowd, a small-town eccentric whose closest companion is a mythical white rabbit that nobody else can see. It was a touring version of the show, which had premiered on Broadway in 1944. Joe E. Brown had taken over the role originated by Frank Fay and had played the role more than a thousand times. Antoinette Perry, for whom the Tony Award is named, directed.

YIDDISH THEATRE IN DECLINE

The Walnut continued to be used for Yiddish-language productions, and Maurice Schwartz brought in a production of *Hershel, the Jester* on February 21, 1949. His Yiddish Art Theatre was celebrating its thirtieth anniversary. One reviewer noted he was "an eloquent pantomimist, which is a great help to non–Yiddish speaking members of the audience."[32] A Yiddish-language version of *Anna Lucasta,* about a woman who becomes a prostitute after being thrown out of her Pennsylvania home, closed out the 1949 season. The play had previously had a successful Broadway run with an all-black cast.

Schwartz returned in January 1950 in *Yosele, the Nightingale,* a folk drama that told the story of a choir singer who forsakes his childhood sweetheart for a heartless siren, nearly ruining his career. Schwartz starred as the choirmaster, who involves himself in the romance to get the young man back in the choir. The production contained a good deal of music, dance, and festivity. It was the last production by Maurice Schwartz's Yiddish Art Theatre; after thirty-one years, the company was forced to disband.

Schwartz continued to tour, even after the demise of his Lower East Side theatre. In Christmas week of 1950, Schwartz presented *Riverside Drive,* a modern drama about a Jewish couple who have survived the Holocaust and come to live at their son's plush New York apartment. The younger generation resents their elders' Yiddish speech and Old World manners. "The combination of Yiddish-English dialogue was appreciated by the younger generation not too well versed in Yiddish," the *Inquirer* noted.[33]

PRODUCTIONS DECLINE

The Yiddish Theatre was not alone in having problems surviving in a new era. The number of productions coming into the Walnut declined from an average of twelve or more a year to approximately nine. And, for a time, touring productions outnumbered tryouts. The fall 1949–50 season did not open until early November, when Monty Woolley appeared in Kaufman and Hart's

1939 comedy *The Man Who Came to Dinner*, a role he originated. George S. Kaufman directed the next offering of the season—*Metropole*—a thinly disguised satire of *New Yorker* editor Harold Ross. Magician Harry Blackstone was back in early December with his *Show of 1001 Wonders.*

The spring season was filled primarily with revivals and touring shows. The Shuberts presented a British comedy, *Yes M'Lord*, on January 23, 1950. *The Barretts of Wimpole Street*, a 1931 drama about Robert Browning and Elizabeth Barrett Browning, was revived, with Susan Peters in the lead role. In early March the Theatre Guild brought in *The Silver Whistle*, another revival. Lloyd Nolan starred, replacing José Ferrer as the raffish imposter who revives the residents at an old age home.

THE MEMBER OF THE WEDDING

The hit of the 1949–50 season opened just before Christmas week, when Carson McCullers's *The Member of the Wedding* played a week-and-a-half tryout. Although reviewers found the play static, they cited the remarkable acting by Ethel Waters, Julie Harris, and seven-year-old Brandon De Wilde. Harris, then twenty-four, played Frankie Addams, a lonely twelve-year-old tomboy who yearns to escape her small southern town. Her only real friend is the family's black cook, played by Ethel Waters. When Frankie's older brother returns home from the army with his fiancée and asks Frankie to be a member of the wedding, Frankie expects to accompany them on their honeymoon, and is shattered to learn she will be left behind.

McCullers adapted the play from her novel, working on the play at Tennessee Williams's cottage on Nantucket while he labored over *Summer and Smoke.* Harold Clurman directed. Despite mixed reviews in Philadelphia, the play became a hit on Broadway and won the New York Drama Critics' Circle Award in 1950. It went on to become one of the classics of modern American drama. Clurman directed several other important shows at the Walnut, notably Arthur Laurents's *Time of the Cuckoo* in 1952 and William Inge's *Bus Stop* in 1955.

ANTITRUST SUIT

On February 21, 1950, the U.S. attorney general launched a massive antitrust suit against the Shubert Organization and its subsidiaries. The complaint alleged that Lee and J. J. Shubert forced producers to book through their agency, the United Booking Office, discriminated in favor of their own productions when booking and presenting shows, and sought to stifle free trade through their combined power in booking and presenting shows. The Justice Department had won a similar lawsuit against the movie studios in 1947, forcing them to divest themselves of their theatres. That decision fundamentally changed moviemaking and led to the demise of the old studio system.

The Shuberts, never ones to shy away from a legal dispute, fought the government's case, arguing that "the business of producing or booking theatrical attractions is not 'trade' or 'commerce' within the meaning of the Sherman Anti-Trust Act of 1890." The case would drag through the courts for the next six years. Indeed, the Shuberts controlled 60 percent of the theatres in New York and 90 percent throughout the country.[34]

THE THEATRE GUILD

Despite the ongoing legal troubles, productions continued at the Walnut Street Theatre. The 1950–51 season was an important one for the Theatre Guild. The fall season opened with its revival of *The Relapse, or Virtue in Danger,* a seventeenth-century comedy of manners the Theatre Guild brought over from London. Cyril Ritchard directed the show, about a sex-starved widow who lures a notorious rake out of retirement and back into London society. Ritchard stole the show as the bewigged Lord Foppington, a role that foreshadowed his most famous role as Captain Hook in the 1954 production of *Peter Pan.*

In January 1951 Sidney Blackmer and Shirley Booth appeared in William Inge's *Come Back, Little Sheba,* playing an alcoholic chiropractor and his slovenly wife, which was touring following a successful Broadway run. Booth and Blackmer received Tony Awards in 1950 for their performances, and the play established Inge as an important dramatist. The following month, the Guild presented Alfred Lunt and Lynn Fontanne in S. N. Behrman's *I Know My Love,* a romantic comedy that followed a couple over the course of fifty years. Lunt and Fontanne were celebrating twenty-five years as an acting team and saw the play as a parable of their own marriage. They had insisted on extensive script changes when the play was produced on Broadway the previous year. It was their first appearance at the Walnut, and the only time this influential acting couple played there. The play was plagued with problems, however, and Lynn Fontanne spent much of the tour with her left arm in a sling.

GIGI

Audrey Hepburn was an unknown when she graced the Walnut's stage for the world premiere of *Gigi.* The twenty-two-year-old beauty played an innocent sixteen-year-old whose aunt has been training her for a career as a courtesan. When Gigi falls in love with a rich playboy, she threatens to upset the family plans. The play was written by Anita Loos, based on a novel by Colette. Colette reportedly selected Hepburn for the role after seeing her on a movie set in a Paris hotel. Hepburn gave "a highly animated and wholly captivating performance," according to reviewers, who also praised the sets and costumes. "Grandma's parlor is a masterpiece of late Victorian knick-knacks, hanging and other bizarre furnishings. . . . Moreover, the frocks of the womenfolk are right out of Godey's Ladies Book (circa 1900), even to the feat of donning them, including lacing up the corset by sheer strength."[35]

The newspapers were as fascinated by Hepburn's biography as by her delicate beauty. Born in Brussels of a Dutch mother and Scottish father, she grew up in Holland under German occupation. She trained to be a ballerina but, as the *Sunday Bulletin* reported, "Food became more and more scarce during the next five years and finally she was so weak from the near-starvation diet that she was forced to give up dancing."[36] In 1948 Hepburn left for England to study ballet, but she realized that she was too far behind her peers and joined the chorus of the London company of *High Button Shoes*. She came to America alone and was tapped for the role of *Gigi*. Film producers had already taken note of the continental beauty and cast her in her first film, *Roman Holiday*, which was to begin shooting the following spring.

HOLLYWOOD ACTORS

José Ferrer played a suicidal theatre director in *The Shrike* at the Walnut for one week in early January 1952 before opening on Broadway. He played a man who wakes up in the psychiatric ward of a hospital and learns that he can be released only if he subdues all his emotions and places himself under the control of his wife. The play won the Pulitzer Prize for Drama that year, and Ferrer, who directed the play as well as starred, received Tony Awards for both. Although Ferrer is remembered primarily as an actor, particularly for his performance as Cyrano de Bergerac onstage and in the movies, it was principally as a director that he made his mark at the Walnut.

Later that season Ferrer directed *Stalag 17*, a World War II comedy about POWs trying to uncover a traitor in their midst. The cast was populated with Hollywood character actors and included Jason Robards and Robert Lansing. It later became a movie starring William Holden and was the inspiration for the television series *Hogan's Heroes*. In 1959 Ferrer directed an all-star cast led by George C. Scott in *The Andersonville Trial*.

A number of actors whose reputations were made in Hollywood appeared at the Walnut in the early 1950s. Melvyn Douglas played a washed-up screenwriter in S. N. Behrman's comedy-drama *Let Me Hear the Melody!* Supporting him were Cloris Leachman, Morris Carnovsky, and Anthony Quinn. David Niven played opposite Gloria Swanson in *Nina*, a French farce. "Swanson, who had loudly protested during the play's tryout that she wanted to be released from a patent dud, was seen as miscast," writes Gerald Bordman.[37] Later that season Basil Rathbone returned in *Jane*, while Edmund O'Brien starred in *I've Got a Sixpence* in 1952. Veronica Lake tried to revive her stalled career in "a frail bit of whimsy" titled *Masquerade*.

Lillian Gish played an old woman searching for her hometown in Horton Foote's *The Trip to Bountiful*. This Theatre Guild production originated as a television play. Jo Van Fleet and Eva Marie Saint had supporting roles, and Van Fleet received a Tony for Best Supporting Actress. Burgess Meredith co-starred with Una Merkel in *The Remarkable Mr. Pennypacker*, playing an 1890s businessman who keeps one family in Wilmington and a second in Philadelphia. Maurice Evans reprised his Broadway role in *Dial "M" for Murder*, about a man who has married for money, then arranges to have his wife killed. Jackie Cooper tried his hand at the stage in *The King of Hearts*. Donald Cook and Cloris Leachman had supporting roles in this comedy about an egocentric cartoonist.

COMMEMORATION

The season had concluded when, on April 22, 1952, Katherine Cornell presented a plaque to the Walnut from the Council of the Living Theatre, commemorating the two-hundredth anniversary of the American Theatre. The inscription read, "The Walnut Street Theatre is the oldest theatre in the English-speaking world still devoted exclusively to legitimate stage productions." Participants in the ceremony included Lee Shubert and Lawrence Langner, co-founder of the Theatre Guild and secretary of the Council of Living Theatre, respectively.

The fall season was a series of tryouts. Shirley Booth opened the season in Arthur Laurents's *Time of the Cuckoo*, playing a spinster who travels to Venice to find romance, only to discover that her Latin lover has a wife and family. She received her third Tony Award for Best Actress. Laurents recalled that "Shirley Booth looked like a bargain-shopper, not an actress; not even onstage where she never appeared to be acting. She was heartbreaking because she was walking vulnerability; her laughs were surefire because she had an intuitive comic talent and was immensely skilled."[38]

It was to be Lee Shubert's last visit to Philadelphia. Shortly before Christmas 1953, he collapsed. He lingered for several days and passed away on Christmas Day. Three days after Shubert's death, Eva Le Gallienne, Mary Astor, and Christopher Plummer opened for previews at the Walnut in *The Starcross Story*. Le Gallienne played the widow of a polar explorer who discovers the sordid truth about her dead husband when she assists on a biographical film about him. The production itself was star-crossed—it closed after one night on Broadway. It was the last production to bear the Shubert name. In the future the company would be involved only in managing its theatres and booking plays. Lee Shubert had run the company virtually singlehandedly, and there was no one ready or qualified to take up the reins.

THE SHUBERTS IN DECLINE, 1954–1969

Five days after Lee Shubert's death, a federal district court announced that because "theatrical bookings, like organized baseball, are not subject to antitrust laws," the government's case against the Shuberts could not proceed. The Justice Department quickly appealed the case to the Supreme Court, arguing that the legitimate theatre was more like the movie industry than like baseball. While the threat from the Justice Department was evident, the real crisis was taking place within the Shubert Organization and among the Shubert heirs.

In his will, Lee Shubert named his nephew Milton Shubert to succeed him as head of the Shubert Organization. This was a slap in the face to his brother, J. J., who had worked for many years in Lee's shadow. Volatile and stubborn, seventy-five-year-old J. J. Shubert moved quickly to take over the organization, ousting his nephew from the executive offices and contesting the will. He used his new authority to settle old grievances, firing Milton Weir, the attorney who had successfully fought the government's antitrust suit, and insisting on making every decision himself. Incapable of delegating authority, "he bombarded everyone with memos, notes, orders, picayune and pettifogging inconsequentials," Jerry Stagg wrote. "A sour and twisted man who had never been able to be articulate, to communicate, he insisted on communicating with everyone about everything."[1]

THE 1953–1954 SEASON

The difficulties were not immediately apparent at the Walnut Street Theatre. Lawrence Shubert Lawrence continued to oversee the family's interests in

Philadelphia, assisted by his son, Lawrence Shubert Lawrence Jr. The 1953–54 season closed early. Jack Warden and Mary Boland appeared in *Lullaby*, a comedy about an older woman married to a much younger man, which arrived at the Walnut on January 18, 1954, for a two-week tryout. The theatre remained dark until March 1, when Maurice Evans appeared in *Dial "M" for Murder*, which had already had a successful run on Broadway. Jackie Cooper, Donald Cook, and Cloris Leachman starred in Jean Kerr and Eleanor Brooks's comedy *The King of Hearts*, which finished out the 1953–54 season. It went on to have a successful Broadway run despite a late-season opening.

The fall 1954 season opened in late September with *Reclining Figure*. It starred Mike Wallace, who would go on to greater renown as a television newsman and host of CBS's *60 Minutes*. It was followed by *The Rainmaker*, a play by Philadelphia-born playwright N. Richard Nash, which was having a pre-Broadway tryout. Darren McGavin played a handsome con man who romances a small-town spinster, played by Geraldine Page. It had only a moderate run on Broadway but became an American classic.

The World of Sholom Aleichem followed in early November. It featured three different one-act plays by the master Jewish storyteller—*Mendele the Book Seller*, *Bontche Schweig*, and *The High School*. Three important figures of the Yiddish theatre starred—Morris Carnovsky, Jacob Ben-Ami, and Herschel Bernardi. The play drew the ire of anticommunists. Some of the actors had belonged to radical organizations in the 1930s and, as Brooks Atkinson explained, the play "became the focal point of McCarthyites all over the nation. They stigmatized the actors as traitors; they excoriated the critics who had praised the production."[2]

Playwright Sidney Kingsley tried his hand at comedy with *Lunatics and Lovers*, about the raffish characters in a seedy New York hotel. Buddy Hackett, who was primarily known as a nightclub comedian, inaugurated his acting career in this comedy, which went on to a yearlong run on Broadway. It was followed by *Anastasia*, a drama about a demented girl who claims to be the only surviving daughter of the czar of Russia. Several con men take her under their wings and train her to act the part of the czarina. The great moment in the play is a melodramatic recognition scene, when she is presented to the dowager empress. It was played for every scrap of emotion by Viveca Lindfors as Anastasia and Eugenie Leontovich as the empress.

A SUPREME COURT RULING

The Justice Department's antitrust appeal against the Shuberts had been wending its way through the courts. In January 1955 the Supreme Court overturned the lower court, ruling that the Shuberts were indeed subject to antitrust laws. Chief Justice Earl Warren noted that the justices had not decided whether the Shuberts had actually violated the Sherman Act. The decision simply allowed the Justice Department to proceed with a case. The Shuberts' case depended mainly on the claim that the theatre was not an industry and could not be treated as such. With the Justice Department free to pursue an antitrust case, the Shubert lawyers "urged J. J. to submit to a consent decree and thereby avoid a Supreme Court decision that [they] predicted might be unfavorable to the Shuberts."[3] The Shubert lawyers were not eager to let the case proceed, given J. J. Shubert's erratic nature, and began negotiating with the Justice Department.

That month, Eva Le Gallienne returned to the Walnut in *The Southwest Corner*, playing a widowed schoolteacher who hires a caretaker, then finds herself dominated by her. Many people thought it one of Le Gallienne's finest roles, but the play had only a short run on Broadway. A touring company brought Max Shulman's comedy *The Tender Trap* to the Walnut in mid-January, following a moderate Broadway run. It had greater success as a film.

Harold Clurman directed Kim Stanley in William Inge's *Bus Stop*, about a nightclub singer and a cowboy who are stranded by a storm. Jerome Courtland, who played Stanley's love interest, was replaced by Albert Salmi before the play opened on Broadway. The reviews were tepid. "It seldom flares into stirring action," Henry T. Murdock complained in the *Inquirer*. But the play had a lengthy run on Broadway and is regarded as one of the finest plays of the postwar period. It is best remembered today in the film version, which starred Marilyn Monroe.

The spring was given over to comedies. Jessica Tandy returned to the Walnut with her husband and frequent co-star, Hume Cronyn, in Roald Dahl's *The Honeys*. Tandy and Dorothy Stickney played two ladies married to nasty twin brothers, both played by Hume Cronyn, who decide to bump their husbands off. Oscar Karlweis closed out the season in *Once upon a Tailor*, playing a tailor who tries to get some money as a marriage broker to raise a dowry for his eldest daughter. The comedy moved too slowly and cumbersomely for the critics.

THE DIARY OF ANNE FRANK

"There are times when the theater reaches a higher plane of entertainment that lifts the spectator's eyes, not just in appreciation, but in something close to awe," the *Inquirer* raved about *The Diary of Anne Frank*, which had its world premiere at the Walnut on September 15, 1955. The public was already familiar with *Diary of a Young Girl,* by the thirteen-year-old Holocaust victim, which had been a best-seller in 1952. The problem of adapting the work to the stage was turned over to the husband-and-wife team of Frances Goodrich and Albert Hackett, who had scripted such films as *It's a Wonderful Life*, *The Thin Man*, *Father of the Bride*, and *Easter Parade*. They "turned a monologue into a dramatic pattern filled with intense characterization, taut excitement and, in spite of the sense of doom, a touch of humanity in its humorous guise," the *Inquirer*'s reviewer noted, adding that "they have managed to look at the other people in the story with older wiser eyes. . . . to give these people fuller dimensions and the right to their own displays of 'nerves' caused by cramped quarters, lack of privacy, scarcity of food and an outlook shadowed by terror."[4]

Seventeen-year-old Susan Strasberg—the daughter of Actors Studio head Lee Strasberg—was cast as Anne Frank. Joseph Schildkraut played her father, Otto, giving "one of the best performances of his distinguished career." The cast also included Lou Jacobi as Mr. Van Daan and Jack Gilford as the fussy Mr. Dussel. Eva Rubinstein, the daughter of pianist Arthur Rubenstein, played Anne Frank's sister, Margot. Garson Kanin directed the production and supervised the writing of the script.

"Actress Ruth Gordon, who was married to Gar[son Kanin], was present most of the time, advising and lending moral support," Susan Strasberg remembered. "During rehearsals, whenever I was having difficulty interpreting a reflective passage or timing a laugh line, she'd come to my room and talk to me about her struggles when she was a young actress. She never directly or specifically told me what to do, but afterward, when I'd had time to digest what she had said, I'd realize her stories always pertained to the problem I was having."[5]

For Joseph Schildkraut, *The Diary of Anne Frank* was the highlight of his career in the theatre. "I have appeared in plays of greater literary value and in parts that were not less important. And I had won acclaim and praise before. Yet never before have I felt such an intimate relationship with a play, never such an identification with a part," he wrote. "For *The Diary of Anne Frank* is not only an epitaph to an era, but also the promise of a new world. Not merely an end, but also a beginning. In her child's wisdom, Anne has left us not only the legacy of her doom but her hope and faith in the future: 'In spite of everything I still believe that people are really good at heart.' I see in these few words the essence of Anne's work and the real meaning of her death."[6]

The Diary of Anne Frank played for two and a half weeks at the Walnut, and opened on Broadway on October 5, 1956, where it ran for two years. It swept the awards for Best Play that year, garnering the New York Drama Critics' Circle Award, the Pulitzer Prize for Drama, and the Tony Award for Best Play. "In presenting *The Diary of Anne Frank* the theater, once more, fulfilled its noble mission of a 'moral institution,'" Joseph Schildkraut concluded.

THE REST OF THE SEASON

The Walnut was dark for much of the fall of 1955. *The Chalk Garden*, a British comedy by Enid Bagnold, played a two-week tryout prior to Broadway. Irish actress Siobhán McKenna made her American debut as a convicted murderess who is hired to look after the troubled granddaughter of an imperious aristocrat, played by Gladys Cooper.

The theatre remained dark from late September until the first week of January 1956, except for Thanksgiving week, when Marcel Marceau offered a week of pantomime. The Philadelphia critics were enchanted. "This artist of silence demands a theater rarity, a totally rapt public. Marceau is a man who has observed life fully and has applied most all that he has seen and experienced to his art," Barbara Wilson wrote in the *Inquirer*. "With the effortless grace of the most accomplished ballet dancers, this French mime is in complete control of every studied attitude and movement. His mouth turns down in a mournful moment, or curves upward in joy. His eyelids flutter and his lips twitch, and his adaptive hands are in constant movement."[7]

Leo G. Carroll appeared in mid-January in a mystery titled *Someone Waiting*. Dennis King and Betsy Palmer arrived in late February in a Theatre Guild costume drama, *Affair of Honor*. *Mister Johnson*, adapted from a novel by the Irish-born Nigerian writer Joyce Cary, that finished out the season.

THE CONSENT DECREE

On February 17, 1956, the Shubert Organization signed a consent decree with the Justice Department. "Under the terms of the decree, the Shuberts agreed to divest themselves of part of their empire," their biographer wrote. "In effect that meant giving up twelve theatres in six cities, including four in New York, and closing the UBO and LAB Amusement Corporation."[8] The government's main concern was to break the Shuberts' monopoly on the key tryout cities. Under the terms of the decree, the Shuberts had two years to sell off twelve theatres in six cities. J. J. Shubert announced that, in Philadelphia, the Forrest and Shubert theatres would be retained but the Walnut would be demolished. Mrs. Lawrence Shubert Lawrence favored the historic playhouse and pleaded with her husband to save the Walnut. He yielded, convinced that the Walnut should be rescued, and persuaded his uncle to spare the building.

In the wake of the Supreme Court decision, the Shubert Organization ceased to be as dominant a force in theatrical production. J. J. Shubert was nearing eighty and clearly on the decline. His son, John, took over the day-to-day management of the Shubert Organization, while Lawrence Shubert Lawrence

Jr. looked after the family's interests in Philadelphia. The younger generation of Shuberts lacked the drive and confidence of their elders. They no longer produced plays on their own and rarely invested money in Broadway shows. They largely operated as landlords, booking shows into their remaining theatres.

The Walnut continued to operate as a tryout house for Broadway-bound shows, although most of the productions that came in during the 1956–57 season were failures. The season opened on September 17 with *The Loud Red Patrick,* a period piece set in Cleveland, described as an Irish American *Life with Father,* which ran only six weeks on Broadway. The others did even worse. *The Best House in Naples* flopped in New York after three performances. Terence Rattigan's romantic comedy *The Sleeping Prince* closed after six weeks despite excellent performances by Michael Redgrave and Barbara Bel Geddes. Geraldine Page co-starred with Elliott Nugent, who portrayed an idealistic young physician in *Build with One Hand,* a disappointing drama by Joseph Kramm that never made it to Broadway. *Protective Custody* was also destined to close until its star, Faye Emerson, persuaded friends to bankroll a Broadway opening. When their money ran out after three days, so did the show.

Many of the plays were vehicles for film and television stars, who took a hiatus to return to the stage. Shelley Winters starred in *The Girls of Summer,* by Philadelphia's N. Richard Nash. George Peppard had a supporting role. Kim Stanley and Robert Culp appeared in Arthur Laurents's *A Clearing in the Woods,* while Robert Preston starred in *The Hidden River,* a drama about resistance fighters. Tom Ewell and Darren McGavin co-starred in a Peter DeVries comedy, *The Tunnel of Love.* Joyce van Patten, Paul Douglas, and Butterfly McQueen were featured in *A Hole in the Head.*

THREE IMPORTANT DRAMAS

Three important dramatic plays tried out at the Walnut in 1957. In March, Tennessee Williams's *Orpheus Descending* had a two-week run. The play was a reworking of an earlier Williams work, *Battle of Angels,* which had closed during tryouts in 1940. The critics agreed that *Orpheus Descending* was far from Williams's best, but one wrote that "it does have impact, technical assurance and is the vehicle for stirring performances." Maureen Stapleton played a Sicilian woman married to the owner of a dry goods store who carries on an affair with a guitar-toting stranger, played by Robert Loggia. He was replaced during the second week of the run by Cliff Robertson.

George Roy Hill directed a distinguished cast in *Look Homeward, Angel,* a stage adaptation of Thomas Wolfe's novel that opened for tryouts at the Walnut on November 9, 1957, and went on to win both the Pulitzer Prize and

Drama Critics' Circle Award as best play of the year. Jo Van Fleet played a manipulative operator of a boardinghouse who lords it over her family and guests. Hugh Griffith played the "roistering, alcoholic, alternately aggressive and self-pitying father of the clan," and Arthur Hill and Anthony Perkins played the two sons. When the older son dies of consumption, he leaves money to his younger brother, who stalks out of the house never to return. Van Fleet received applause at the end of all her major scenes.

Elia Kazan directed William Inge's *The Dark at the Top of the Stairs*, which followed on November 25, 1957. Like *Orpheus Descending*, this was a rewrite of an earlier play. Set in a small Oklahoma town in the 1920s, it depicts the desperation of a family that has failed to adapt to the modern age. Pat Hingle played a harness salesman whose company is going out of business. Teresa Wright played the wife, who pampers their son.

Among the other notable productions of the 1957–58 season was a performance of *The Day the Money Stopped*, a new play by Maxwell Anderson, which starred Richard Basehart, Kevin McCarthy, and Mildred Natwick. It inaugurated Sunday performances at the Walnut. The play did poorly on Broadway, closing after only five performances. The Theatre Guild brought in *Look Back in Anger*, the much heralded play by British dramatist John Osborne, which had won the New York Drama Critics' Circle Award for Best Foreign Play the previous season. Kenneth Haigh starred as Jimmy Porter, an embittered working-class shop owner who rails against everyone and everything from his attic apartment in London. Haigh, who originated the role in London and New York, gave a virtuoso performance. Budd Schulberg adapted his best-selling novel *The Disenchanted*, based loosely on the life of F. Scott Fitzgerald. Jason Robards went on to win a Tony Award for his portrayal of a writer slowly falling to pieces.

YIDDISH PRODUCTIONS

Periodically, Yiddish-language productions still played at the Walnut. Molly Picon starred in *Farblonjet Honeymoon* (Snafued Honeymoon), which arrived on October 28, 1957. Picon played the servant to an eligible widower who returns from Atlantic City with a statuesque blonde he plans to marry. The play had run for two years in New York before coming to the Walnut. *Borscht Capades* was described as an English-Yiddish musical revue, although the Yiddish occurred mainly in punch lines and songs. It played a one-week engagement at the Walnut beginning January 19, 1959. Mickey Katz headed the cast, which also included ventriloquist Rickie Layne and his dummy, Velvel, comedians Larry Alpert, Marty Drake, and Larry Best, and singer Jo-Ann Florio.

Maurice Schwartz remained active, returning to the Walnut one last time in April 1959 in Sholem Aleichem's comedy *It's Hard to Be a Jew,* performed in an English translation, which he alternated with *Tevye and His Daughters,* played in Yiddish. The latter became the basis for the musical *Fiddler on the Roof* in 1964. It was Schwartz's last appearance at the Walnut. He died of a heart attack in Israel the following year, while preparing a production of Sholem Asch's *Kiddush Hashem.*

These were the last years of the Yiddish theatre in America. Increasingly, Jewish playwrights were addressing Jewish themes and subjects in plays that were getting produced on Broadway. Paddy Chayefsky drew on Jewish folktales about the *dybbuk* in *The Tenth Man.* Lou Jacobi, Jack Gilford, and Gene Saks played members of a conservative synagogue who try to rid a young girl of a *dybbuk,* a malicious spirit that possesses her. Tyrone Guthrie directed this play, which played for three weeks at the Walnut in October 1959.

A RAISIN IN THE SUN

On January 26, 1959, an unheralded play by an unknown author opened at the Walnut. "When the curtain went down on that first performance, it was time to start putting together notes for a significant page in the history of the arts and an additional chapter in the story of Negro achievement in America," wrote Frank Brookhouser, the reviewer for the *Evening Bulletin.*[9] *A Raisin in the Sun* was the work of a soft-spoken twenty-eight-year old playwright named Lorraine Hansberry.

Claudia McNeil starred as Lena Younger, the matriarch of an African American family who hopes to use her late husband's life insurance policy to move the family out of the ghetto. Her son, Walter, played by Sidney Poitier, persuades her to give it to him to invest in a liquor store, only to discover that his partner has run off with the money. Ruby Dee played his wife, Ruth. Also featured in the play were Diana Sands, Ivan Dixon, and Louis Gossett.

Novelist James Baldwin was one of those who saw the play at the Walnut. He wrote later, "I had never before in my life seen so many black people in the theater. And the reason was that never before, in the entire history of the American theater, had so much of the truth of black people's lives been seen on the stage."[10] Amiri Baraka observed that "Hansberry had created a family on the cutting edge of the same class and ideological struggles as existed in the movement itself and among the people."[11]

There was no theatre available on Broadway, so the play went to Chicago for several weeks before opening in New York on March 11, 1959. It was the

fig. 30 *A Raisin in the Sun,* featuring Ruby Dee, Sidney Poitier, and Lonne Elder III, opened at the Walnut on January 26, 1959.

first time a play by an African American woman was produced on Broadway, and it received the Drama Critics' Circle Award for Best Play.

STAR TURNS

Hollywood stars continued to make appearances at the Walnut in 1959 and 1960. In November, Rex Harrison played a retired general in Jean Anouilh's

The Fighting Cock, a satire of French general Charles de Gaulle. Peter Brook directed a cast that included Roddy McDowall and Arthur Treacher. For the opening performance, Harrison was made up to look like de Gaulle, with a putty nose, bushy eyebrows, and a wig. De Gaulle, who had yet to ascend to the presidency of France, was not familiar to American audiences, and the makeup did not go over well. "The audience was horrified. They had come to see the star of *My Fair Lady* and were angry that they could barely recognize him under the disguise."[12] The offending prosthetics were quickly discarded.

Lauren Bacall was the principal attraction in *Goodbye, Charlie*, as a woman who insists that she is the reincarnation of Sydney Chaplin's late friend, Charlie. It turns out that God has forced him to return to earth as a woman, to see what it is like to be treated by men like him. George C. Scott played the prosecutor in *The Andersonville Trial*, a historical drama about the trial of the Confederate officer who was held responsible for a POW camp where thirty thousand Union soldiers died.

Jane Fonda showed "extreme depth and perception" in *There Was a Little Girl*, her first important stage role. She portrayed a rape victim whose friends and family refuse to believe the rape was not her fault. Joshua Logan directed. "I was suspicious of her career at first," Logan admitted, "as one always suspects newcomers who have successful parents. But as she matured she became so beautiful, I didn't care." The Philadelphia premiere on February 9, 1960, took place twelve years after her father's premiere in *Mister Roberts*, which Logan had also directed.

Jack Lemmon did not do so well in his first dramatic role, in *Face of a Hero*, which opened the 1960–61 season. He played an idealistic young prosecutor in a corrupt southern town. The supporting cast included Ed Asner, Sandy Dennis, and George Grizzard. "He secures neither the sympathy which the playwright seems to try to throw toward him nor the scorn a cold analysis of his actions demand[s]," Henry T. Murdock wrote in the *Inquirer*.[13] Claudette Colbert appeared later that season in *Julia, Jake, and Uncle Joe*, a comedy by Oriana Atkinson, the wife of the *New York Times* drama critic Brooks Atkinson, based on their experience living in Moscow in the mid-1940s. John Shubert produced the play, which closed after one night on Broadway.

Sunday in New York brought Robert Redford to Philadelphia for the first time in 1961. Garson Kanin directed the comedy by Norman Krasna. Redford played the music critic for the *Philadelphia Inquirer*, who gets involved in romantic entanglements with a music critic from Albany during a visit to New York. Local reviewers were lukewarm about the "one-joke play," but it had a moderately successful run on Broadway.

Jessica Tandy fronted a mostly British cast in *Five Finger Exercise,* a drama by Peter Shaffer about a well-to-do English family at war with itself. The play, directed by John Gielgud, had recently received the New York Drama Critics' Circle Award as the Best Foreign Play of the year. A comedy by Tennessee Williams, *Period of Adjustment,* followed. James Daly starred and received generally good reviews. The play went on to have a moderate run on Broadway.

Advise and Consent was a dramatization of the Pulitzer Prize–winning novel by Allen Drury. Set in the future, when the Russians are about to land on the moon, it concerns the Senate confirmation of a new secretary of state. When it is discovered during the Senate hearings that he has had a homosexual affair, the nominee kills himself. Otto Kruger played the role of the president but withdrew when revisions diminished his role. Judson Laire took over the role on Broadway. In *Send Me No Flowers,* David Wayne played a hypochondriac who misunderstands a remark by his doctor and assumes he is dying. On opening night, the Allied Florists of Philadelphia distributed carnations to the audience to protest the play's title.

During Christmas week, Bil and Cora Baird brought their marionette troupe for daily matinee performances at noon and 3:00 P.M. Stringed puppets performed a musical melodrama titled *Davy Jones' Locker,* about a little boy who runs away from home, gets shipwrecked, and joins a pirate crew. When he brags about his swimming ability, the pirates toss him overboard to retrieve a treasure chest from the bottom of the sea. The score was composed by Mary Rodgers, the daughter of Richard Rodgers. The second half of the program was a variety show that presented the history of puppetry around the world. The play enchanted children and critics, who announced that "not since the famed 'Teatro di Piccoli' of Italy appeared here 25 years ago has the art of puppeteering been so well demonstrated."[14]

NEIL SIMON'S DEBUT

The 1960–61 season concluded with *Come Blow Your Horn,* which introduced Neil Simon. Simon had been a scriptwriter on the TV program *Your Show of Shows* and had written sketches for camp revues, but this was his first full-length play. The play had had a summer tryout at the Bucks County Playhouse the previous summer. Hal March, best known as the host of the TV game show *The $64,000 Question,* played the older son of a plastic fruit manufacturer, played by Lou Jacobi. Warren Berlinger, Milton Berle's nephew, played his timid younger

fig. 31 Playwright Neil Simon's first full-length play, *Come Blow Your Horn*, closed the Walnut's 1960–61 season and launched his career.

brother, who comes to live with him. "The play fairly bristles with comedy lines, each topping its predecessor," wrote the *Inquirer*'s reviewer.[15]

While there was comedy onstage, Neil Simon recalled, there was tragedy in the audience. "Twenty minutes into the play, we heard a woman scream from upstairs, 'Harry!! Harry!! Oh, my God, help me someone!!' Then came the hustle and bustle of feet running up stairs and down stairs, ushers scattering everywhere. Most people, not knowing the seriousness of the screams, looked up at the balcony annoyed, thinking it was a family squabble or the misbehavior of an out-of-control drunk. Poor Harry died of a heart attack in the upstairs lounge, despite the efforts of the paramedics, who soon whisked Harry and his bereaved wife into a waiting ambulance. Somehow the play carried on, missing only a few beats before laughter soon replaced tragedy."[16]

"In the three and a half weeks we played Philadelphia, we were a virtual sellout," Simon wrote. "We had a hit. A huge hit. In Philadelphia, that is." The New York reviewers were less kind. Walter Kerr noted, "it is imperative that I report a blockbuster response on the part of the customers, no matter whether the jokes were satisfying, so-so, or seedy."[17] Nevertheless, the play ran for nearly two years and launched Neil Simon's playwrighting career. Critics never warmed to Simon's work, but plays like *Barefoot in the Park*, *The Odd Couple*, and *Plaza Suite* made Simon the most important comic playwright of the 1960s.

The 1961–62 season at the Walnut proved to be an important one, after a rough beginning. On October 2, *A Shot in the Dark* opened for tryouts. Julie Harris starred as a maid in the home of a French banker, played by Walter Matthau, who is accused of murdering her boyfriend, the family's chauffeur. William Shatner played the young magistrate investigating the case. He discovers that the aristocrat's wife, played by Louise Troy, did the shooting, thinking that she was murdering her husband.

The play was a turning point in the career of Walter Matthau, who received a Tony Award as Best Supporting Actor for his deliciously pompous performance. Though he had been cast in several Broadway shows that had tryouts at the Walnut—including *One Bright Day* and *The Grey-Eyed People*, both in 1952, and *Ladies in the Corridor* the following year—all of them failed on Broadway. Matthau was a late addition to *A Shot in the Dark*, brought in after Donald Cook died during tryouts. "Cook suffered the fatal heart attack in New Haven on a Saturday, and died Sunday. On Monday Matthau saw the play when it opened in Philadelphia, played by Ben Severs. Matthau signed the next day, rehearsed for two days and replaced Severs on Friday."[18]

ENGLISH IMPORTS

Robert Bolt's historical drama *A Man for All Seasons* had a two-week tryout at the Walnut before moving on to Broadway. British actor Paul Scofield made his American debut as Sir Thomas More, who accepts martyrdom rather than acknowledge Henry VIII as the spiritual head of the church. When he refuses to sign the requisite oath, he seals his fate, and the king and his henchman, Thomas Cromwell, convict him of treason with perjured testimony. Scofield's performance, "at once both lean and eloquent," won him a Tony. The play also received Tony Awards for Best Play, for its producers, for author Robert Bolt, and for director Noel Willman. Scofield went on to star in the 1966 film version, which won the Academy Award for Best Picture and a Best Actor award for its star.

London's Old Vic company came to the Walnut for one week beginning March 19, 1962, with *Romeo and Juliet* and *Macbeth*. The company had completed a successful six-week run at New York's City Center. The plays were directed by Franco Zeffirelli, previously known as a grand opera designer. *Macbeth* was conventionally presented, with John Clements in the title role, but *Romeo and Juliet* was entirely reconceived. Zeffirelli departed from tradition by creating a Verona of "dusty streets, often somnolent under the Italian sky but quick to erupt with hate and bloodshed as the bravos of the Montagues and Capulets whip out their rapiers," in the words of the *Inquirer* reviewer. The swordplay scenes were thrillingly staged. "There is authenticity in the desperate passages between Mercutio and Tybalt, followed by the sword and dagger clash of Romeo and Tybalt to form a hair-raising sequence."

Zeffirelli "has pulled the characters out of their classic frame and made them kin to our age," the *Inquirer*'s reviewer wrote. Romeo, played by John Stride, had "all the ardor and uncertainty one can find in a 16-year old boy of today," while Joanna Dunham's Juliet "approximated the 14 years which Shakespeare gave his heroine" in her reaction to sudden love.[19] Zeffirelli received a special Tony Award for his direction and design of the production, and went on to direct the highly acclaimed film version, starring Olivia Hussey and Leonard Whiting.

Eva Le Gallienne "gave one of the best performances of her career," as Elizabeth I in a pair of dramas about the English monarch—Frederich Schiller's *Mary Stuart* and Maxwell Anderson's 1930 blank-verse drama, *Elizabeth the Queen*. *Inquirer* critic Henry T. Murdock wrote of her performance in the latter that the sixty-two-year-old actress "gave the full-flashing, dominating star values to her intense performance of the lovelorn Queen. . . . With an almost mask-like makeup, a nose built to heroic proportions and a red-orange wig topping her royal head, there is a willful handicap of grotesquerie to overcome. Elizabeth overcomes it in sweeping terms."[20]

Le Gallienne's biographer wrote of the production, "She shaved her hairline back a quarter of an inch, blocked out her eyebrows and painted on thin, black arches, and created defined eye sockets and heavy lids. The makeup required several hours to apply, and the transformation was helped further by a copper-colored wig and stunning period gowns." The gowns each weighed more than sixty pounds. For the role in *Mary Stuart*, which took place twelve years later, "Le Gallienne used a darker wig in a more violent red. Feeling that Elizabeth had probably lost additional teeth in those years, she added a few more shadows to her cheeks."[21]

The remainder of the season was filled with productions based on the works of notable writers. Imogene Coca and Arthur Treacher headed a touring company in *A Thurber Carnival*, which opened on December 11, 1962.

Burgess Meredith directed the revue, based on works of humorist James Thurber. Cyril Ritchard appeared in Gore Vidal's comedy *Romulus*, an adaptation of Swiss playwright Friedrich Dürrenmatt's comedy about a onetime history professor who becomes Rome's last emperor by marrying the emperor's daughter.

A British cast headed by Maurice Evans and Wendy Hiller presented *The Aspern Papers*, based on a Henry James novella. Michael Redgrave wrote and directed the play. Garson Kanin directed Henry Fonda and Olivia de Havilland in *A Gift of Time*, which he adapted from the autobiography of a man dying of cancer.

A CRISIS OF SUCCESSION

The Shubert Organization suffered a major setback in November 1962 with the sudden death of J. J. Shubert's son, John Shubert, from a heart attack. He was only fifty-three. J. J. was still alive, but he was confined to a nursing home and was never informed of his son's death. "With John dead and J. J. grown senile, the company faced the gravest leadership crisis in its history," wrote Foster Hirsch.[22] Lawrence Shubert Lawrence Jr. took charge of the Shubert empire.

Like other members of the Shubert family, Lawrence Shubert Lawrence Jr. had been brought into the family business. After graduating from the University of Pennsylvania, he had become manager of the Locust Street Theatre. Moving to New York, he became the company manager of Olson and Johnson's *Hellzapopin* before settling in as the manager of the 44th Street Theatre. At the time of John Shubert's death, he was manager of the Majestic Theatre in New York, an important Shubert house.

Lawrence was not suited to running a major theatrical organization. "As an overseer of what was still the world's largest theatrical empire," according to Hirsch, "Lawrence Shubert Lawrence, Jr. lacked the relish for power and for making money that even John had revealed once he was in charge."[23] One result was that the number of productions was cut back. Tom Ewell and Joanna Pettet played until the end of the year in a touring production of *Take Her, She's Mine*, which had just closed on Broadway. After that, the Walnut essentially shut down for the season.

It was reopened briefly in late February to accommodate Helen Hayes and Maurice Evans, who came in for a week with their selection of Shakespeare scenes in *A Program for Two Players*. They were nearing the end of a grueling nineteen-week tour, during which time they played in sixty-nine cities. "Catching our breath at the Walnut Street Theatre in William Penn's City of Brotherly Love, there was light at the end of our touring tunnel," Evans remembered.[24] They performed on a simple stage, Evans appearing in a dinner jacket and Hayes in a series of gowns. "Great scenes there are, big speeches there are, but there is also a sense of continuity, not in time but in content, as comedy and drama and a dash of the sonnets crisscross in rhythmic patterns," Henry T. Murdock wrote in the *Inquirer*.[25]

THE 1963–1964 SEASON

Beginning with the 1963–64 season, the number of productions was cut in half, from an average of twelve per season to an average of six. Van Heflin had a minor success in *A Case of Libel*, the first offering of the season. It was based on Louis Nizer's best-selling autobiography, *My Life in Court*, and dealt with journalist Quentin Reynolds's suit against right-wing columnist Westbrook Pegler. The play ran for seven months on Broadway. The other productions flopped. *A Rainy Day in Newark* lasted four days on Broadway. The only thing notable about the play was that Gene Hackman had a supporting role. *Love and Kisses* lasted ten days, while *Conversations in the Dark* never made it that far. After the first of the year, the Walnut was dark except for the two weeks in February, when a touring production of *A Man for All Seasons* appeared, with Laurence Luckinbill starring as Thomas More.

It was a lackluster year in the theatre generally. Neither the Critics' Circle nor the Pulitzer committee saw fit to award a prize for best drama that year. The Walnut received recognition, however, when the U.S. Department of the Interior listed the theatre as a National Landmark. This ensured that the building was finally protected, for no landmark so designated may be razed by its owners, and no important part of the original fabric may be destroyed. The plaque stated that the Walnut "possesses exceptional value in commemorating and illustrating the history of the United States."

AMERICAN COMEDIES, BRITISH DRAMAS

Comedies dominated the Walnut's stage during the mid-1960s, although few did very well. Arlene Francis and Laurence Luckinbill lasted less than a month on Broadway in *Beekman Place* in the fall of 1963. Jean Simmons did not make it that long. After the Philadelphia critics derided *Rich Little Rich Girl* as a "poor little comedy," the producers closed the show after the Philadelphia tryout. Joshua Logan's luck was not much better. He returned to the theatre after several years in Hollywood to direct Julie Harris in *Ready when*

fig. 32 In 1964 the U.S. Department of the Interior designated the Walnut Street Theatre a National Landmark. Shown standing with the commemorative plaque, from left, are Lawrence Shubert Lawrence Jr., Dorothy Haas, and Philip Klein.

You Are, C.B., but the downbeat ending limited its appeal. Chicago's Second City troupe put in an appearance at the Walnut in March 1965. Reaction to the company's send-up of Republicans, folk singers, faith healers, and the University of Chicago football team was decidedly mixed. Other comedies that had tryouts during the 1965–66 season did even worse. *The Family Way* played three days on Broadway, *The Wayward Stork* and *UTBU* each closed after four, and *The Best Laid Plans* folded after two.

Only the British were having much success. The highlight of the season was John Osborne's *Inadmissible Evidence,* which proved to be a tour de force for British actor Nicol Williamson, who played a lawyer who has alienated his family, friends, and clients. "There is such macabre magic in the swift and pungent words of Osborne and in the almost incredible sustained portrayal of Nicol Williamson that one is moved close to tears at the protagonist's plight," Henry T. Murdock wrote in the *Inquirer.*[26] The play ran for more than seven months on Broadway.

Despite its title, *Philadelphia, Here I Come!* was actually an Irish play about a young man eager to emigrate to America who has a dialogue with his own inner voice. Producer David Merrick brought over the Dublin cast, and the play had its American premiere at the Walnut before moving on to Broadway.

WOODY ALLEN AND NEIL SIMON

Woody Allen had his first stage success with *Don't Drink the Water*, which arrived for a three-week tryout at the Walnut to open the 1966–67 season. Lou Jacobi and Vivian Vance played a New Jersey caterer and his wife who take refuge in the American embassy in an Iron Curtain country after being pursued by secret police for taking unauthorized pictures. Critics complained that the show lacked any real plot or character development, but Allen's one-liners were greeted with great laughter.

"There was no question in my mind that audiences were going to respond to it, though it was a true nightmare," Woody Allen recalled. "I remember David Merrick saying to me in Philadelphia, 'Well you're up to your ass in show business.'" There were thirteen cast changes during tryouts in New Haven, Philadelphia, and Boston. "The direction was the worst in the world," Allen told biographer Eric Lax. "No one knew what to do. People were standing around. It was a non-directed play."[27] Bob Sinclair, the original director, was fired, and Allen took over briefly. The play moved on to Boston, where Kay Medford replaced Vivian Vance, and the play began to come together. It eventually racked up 598 performances on Broadway.

Neil Simon dominated the 1960s with his comedies, although no other plays of his had tryouts at the Walnut. The theatre had to be content with touring productions. Dana Andrews and Robert Q. Lewis co-starred as Oscar Madison and Felix Unger in *The Odd Couple*, which opened the fall 1967–68 season. Another Neil Simon comedy, *Barefoot in the Park*, played later in the season. Margaret O'Brien, the former child star, played opposite Jack Mullaney in this touring production.

ARTHUR MILLER AND TENNESSEE WILLIAMS

America had not produced serious dramatists to match Arthur Miller and Tennessee Williams, each of whom had new productions at the Walnut in 1968. Miller had one of his successes with *The Price*, a drama about two estranged brothers who meet in the attic of the brownstone they grew up in to dispose of the family furniture. Pat Hingle played a self-sacrificing sibling who becomes a policeman to help pay for his brother's medical school education, played by Arthur Kennedy. In the process of going through the family belongings, the two men uncover unwelcome truths about their past. The director, Ulu Grosbard, had conflicts with the cast, and Miller had to take over directing duties when tensions between the actors and the director came to a head. Despite the problems, *The Price* became one of Miller's longest-running shows.

The Walnut remained dark for nearly two months before Tennessee Williams's *Seven Descents of Myrtle* came in on March 11. Williams was drinking heavily and taking amphetamines, which had caused his writing to become weird, sordid, and fascinating. Williams was rarely at rehearsals, and when he was present, his manner was disruptive. The three-character play featured Brian Bedford, Estelle Parsons, and Harry Guardino. José Quintero directed, but he was also drinking so heavily that Parsons received virtually no direction. "Estelle Parsons was quite brilliant in *The Seven Descents of Myrtle*," Williams recalled. "But the poor thing had no help. José Quintero didn't direct her properly so everything that happened onstage was her own invention."[28]

"We thought that in its climax it presented a denouement long forecast in the first two acts, that its ideas and some of its talk tended to become repetitious," wrote the *Inquirer*'s critic, Henry T. Murdock. "Estelle Parsons becomes an actress to be reckoned with," he wrote, adding, "She is funny and pathetic and obviously not too bright, but even in her final switch of allegiance she retains integrity and a sometimes claim on dignity."[29] Some saw the play, which was later published under the title *Kingdom of Earth*, as a work of great power. Most considered it an artistic failure, and it closed on Broadway after twenty-nine performances. It was to be Williams's last Broadway show.

OTHER PERFORMING ARTS

Flanders and Swann made their Philadelphia debut in *At the Drop of Another Hat* in early November 1966. The English songwriting team satirized topical issues such as Britain's financial worries, air travel, and scientific doubletalk. "They sing solo or in duet and while they must operate with hair-trigger timing, they give an impromptu effect," the *Inquirer* reviewer wrote. "Nothing is forced, everything indeed seems to come 'at the drop of a hat.'"[30] A dance company from the Republic of Guinea, *Les Ballets Africaines*, offered "a riotous extravaganza in sound and rhythm." Musicians played on native musical instruments, and the dances were derived from fertility rites, hunting adventures, village romances, and pleas for a good harvest.

The Teatro Stabile de Genova arrived on May 13, 1968, to finish out the season with an Italian-language production of Carlo Goldoni's farce *The Venetian Twins*. Performed in the style of the *commedia dell'arte*, the play follows the confusions of mistaken identity when twin brothers separated at birth arrive in the same town. Alberto Lionello played dual roles, which crescendo in the final act when both brothers emerge from different sides of an outhouse. The play was offered by the Theatre Guild as part of its subscription series. The language barrier seemed to be a problem, and a large portion of the audience left during intermission.

THE SHUBERTS' LAST SEASON

The 1968–69 season opened on October 13 with a revival of George Kelly's 1924 comedy *The Show-Off.* Helen Hayes played the matriarch of a lower middle-class Philadelphia family whose daughter marries a brash young man who believes he can succeed by bragging about his money and accomplishments. In the end, he is proved right. It was during the run of this play that a plaque was presented to the Walnut by the Interior Department designating it a National Historic Landmark. Helen Hayes accepted the award on behalf of the theatre.

Your Own Thing opened on November 6 for a lengthy run. It was a musical adaptation of Shakespeare's *Twelfth Night* and had received the New York Critics' Circle Award for the Best Musical of 1968—the first time the award had been given to an off-Broadway production. In this version, Viola and her brother Sebastian are both rock singers who are separated in a shipwreck. They arrive in New York City, where Viola disguises herself as a boy to get a job with a rock band, while Sebastian attracts the eye of the owner of a discotheque. The musical played for twenty weeks at the Walnut, closing in mid-March.

During this time, the Shubert Organization was approached by a consortium of local civic leaders about turning the Walnut into a performing arts center. Advertising executive Philip Klein spearheaded the project. Money for the project was provided by the Haas Community Fund. The idea of restoring the Walnut had originated several years earlier when the Theater of the Living Arts explored the possibility of turning the Walnut into a theatre museum.

An environmental theatre piece, *Big Time Buck White*, finished out the Shuberts' last season. The auditorium of the Walnut was transformed into the meeting hall of an imagined radical black organization, B.A.D.—Beautiful Allelujah Days. Tall, commanding Kirk Kirksey played Buck White and directed the production. The second half of the program featured a question-and-answer session, mostly from actors planted in the audience. The production was the product of Budd Schulberg's Watts Writers Workshop, designed to provide opportunities for black playwrights. The production played through the first week in May.

At its annual meeting on May 26, 1969, the Haas Community Fund endorsed the idea of a new theatrical venture to be located at the Walnut and provided a grant of $2 million for the purchase and renovation of the theatre. It further authorized the establishment of the Walnut Street Theatre Corporation, a nonprofit cultural and educational organization to preserve and operate the theatre. Philip Klein was named president.

In June the new corporation purchased the Walnut from the Shubert-controlled Select Theatres Corporation for $300,000. The signing ceremony took place on Monday, June 9, 1969. Lawrence Shubert Lawrence Jr. represented the Shubert Organization. The signing was to take place on the stage, but the stagehands' union viewed it as a performance, which required the presence of paid union personnel, so the ceremony was moved to the lobby. With that, the Walnut entered a new era as a community-oriented performing arts center.

PERFORMING ARTS CENTER, 1969–1982

At the end of the 1960s, the theatre industry was undergoing major changes. Broadway was losing its dominance. The cost of producing on Broadway was rising, and fewer productions were being mounted each year. New productions were likely to originate in an off-Broadway theatre or in one of the country's new regional theatres. As a result, Philadelphia had declined as a tryout city for Broadway-bound shows. Because it had been such an important tryout city, Philadelphia had little in the way of homegrown theatre. By the late 1960s there were only two professional theatre companies in the city. The Theater for the Living Arts, founded in 1965, occupied a converted movie theatre on South Street, and had acquired a good, if controversial, reputation under its director, André Gregory. The Freedom Theatre, established in 1966 by John Allen Jr., served the African American community.

A group of civic leaders saw a need for a medium-sized performing arts center suitable for a wide range of theatrical presentations and musical events. Similar arts centers had been built in New York, Los Angeles, and other cities. The Walnut was an attractive site because of its tradition, location, availability, and excellent acoustics. The effort was spearheaded by Philip Klein, a retired advertising executive, educator, and real estate investor. He envisioned the theatre as playing an important role in the city's cultural life, with a variety of attractions—drama, music, lectures, book reviews, travelogues, art exhibits, a theatre museum, and a repertory theatre—a true center for the performing arts.

Financial support for the new venture was provided by the Haas Community Fund (which changed its name to the William Penn Foundation in 1973), a private foundation set up by the Haas family, which owned Rohm and Haas, a local chemical and plastics firm. The fund provided a grant for the purchase and renovation of the theatre. A nonprofit organization, the Walnut Street Theatre Corporation, was established to preserve and operate the theatre. Philip Klein became the president of the new organization and Mrs. F. Otto Haas became vice president. The board also included William Kohler, who served as treasurer, and Frank C. P. McGlinn, a banker and theatre historian, who was the corporation's secretary. The board also included Mrs. John C. Haas, Richard K. Bennett of the Haas Community Fund, and Edwin P. Rome, a senior partner of Blank, Rome, Comiskey & McCauley, one of the city's largest law firms. They would guide the Walnut through the next phase of its history.

RESTORATION

Their goal was to restore the Walnut to its nineteenth-century grandeur so it could serve as an example of theatre of the early American period, and to recognize Philadelphia's place in the history of the American stage. The Haas Community Fund allocated $2 million for the restoration. The architectural firm of Dickey, Weissman, Chandler and Holt, which specialized in architectural renovations, was hired to oversee the project. John M. Dickey, a partner in the firm and a longtime advocate of historic preservation, oversaw the exterior renovations, while F. Bryan Loving, a specialist in theatre design, took charge of the interior.

On February 2, 1970, the Walnut Street Theatre Corporation purchased the six-story building next to the theatre. The twenty-five-foot-wide building at 825 Walnut would house the box office and business offices on the ground floor, with additional office and rehearsal space on the upper floors. The new entrance to the theatre would be at 825 Walnut.

Philip Klein supervised the project. In improvised offices in the 825 building, he worked directly with the architects, foremen, and workers. Thanks to his input and availability, decisions could be made promptly and implemented without recourse to meetings, avoiding expensive delays. He was assisted by twenty-four-year-old Randy Swartz, who was hired on as publicist.

The exterior required relatively minor changes to restore the façade to John Haviland's 1828 design. Marble columns, which had been embedded into the wall of the theatre, were freed, and steel supports were inserted into the masonry. The arched windows on the second floor were enlarged. The marble facing on the Walnut Street side of the theatre was replaced. Because the marble at the original quarry had been depleted, gray marble had to be imported from Italy. The old doors at the front of the theatre, which were designed to fold, were replaced by modern glass double doors. New alcoves for the gas lamps were put in, and new lamps were built to resemble those in early prints of the theatre. The steps leading up to the theatre were restored, and the floor of the lobby was raised to accommodate them.

Given the impossibility of restoring the interior to its nineteenth-century design, the architects decided to make the Walnut an up-to-date arts center. Randy Swartz visited performing arts centers around the country and came back with ideas that could be incorporated into the new design. His research resulted in such innovative ideas as a closed-circuit television system that would allow latecomers to see what was happening onstage, a double set of doors to prevent light from seeping into the auditorium, and pedestal seats that afforded extra legroom. The auditorium was finished off in a modernist style that the architects felt preserved the spirit of the Greek revival architecture of Haviland's original design. The walls, ceiling, and balcony of the auditorium were of sand-finished plaster, with smoothly sweeping lines joining the balcony to the walls. The house was fully air-conditioned, and a state-of-the-art lighting system was installed, featuring a computerized lighting board that allowed lighting changes for up to seven scenes to be set in advance.

The wooden stage itself was completely rebuilt. It was given a vinyl finish and equipped with twenty-three traps. Three floors of dressing rooms were installed, including one star suite and two chorus rooms, which could accommodate up to twenty performers. The dressing rooms were fully air-conditioned and equipped with shower and toilet facilities.

One feature from the nineteenth century that did remain was the old wooden grid. In a theatre, the grid is a structure made up of boards and beams that is suspended from the roof of the building over the stage. This grid serves as the support structure from which curtains, pieces of scenery, lighting equipment, and sound equipment can be hung. "Huge wooden wheels, axles and drums for the moving of heavy sets and a large superbly fitted and joined wooden drop-roller provide handsome indications of the craftsmanship and technology of this early period in the design of stage machinery," wrote Bryan Loving.[1]

The renovation costs far exceeded projections. The Haas Community Fund eventually provided more than $4 million, reflecting its commitment to creating a modern, all-purpose facility that would cater to all the arts.

THE GRAND REOPENING

Construction delays and labor disputes delayed the opening from February 1971 until the fall. Lillian Gish, the silent film star, was invited to give a lecture and demonstration on D. W. Griffith on October 17, 1971. The night before Gish was to appear, the public got its first look at the new theatre as the

Walnut opened its doors for a walk-through for one thousand invited guests. Dorothy Haas spoke on behalf of the Haas Fund about the restoration and the promising future of the Walnut as a center for the performing arts. A documentary film showing the theatre's restoration was screened. In the middle of the film, the sound failed, and the remainder was shown with organ accompaniment, as with a silent film. Lillian Gish made a surprise appearance. As she walked onstage, she exclaimed, "All the ghosts of the past—perhaps they are here tonight to bless this theatre."

The following morning the theatre opened its doors to the general public for a screening of the 1966 film *Born Free*, the first in a series of family movies held on Saturday mornings. The Empire Sinfonietta, a New York–based chamber orchestra, performed in the afternoon. In the evening, Lillian Gish spoke about her career, recalling her transformation from a "skinny, awkward girl, frightened to death by the camera," to one of the stars of the silent screen. She spoke about working with director D. W. Griffith, explaining how he staged battle sequences for *Birth of a Nation* with only a handful of men, and how she floated down a real river on an ice floe in *Way Down East*.

A COMMUNITY ARTS CENTER

Under the direction of Philip Klein and Randy Swartz, now promoted to artistic director, the Walnut embarked on an ambitious program of cultural offerings. The Walnut was to be much more than a theatre, providing a wide range of cultural attractions—films, live drama, ballet, classical music, rock, jazz, and pop music concerts, lectures, recitals, art exhibits, and children's theatre. This commitment to the arts included the visual as well as the performing arts, and the new performing arts center incorporated an art gallery off the east lobby.

Philadelphia impresario Moe Septee agreed to present a program of dance, classical and popular music concerts, off-Broadway theatre productions, and a children's series. His first production, *Don't Bother Me, I Can't Cope*, opened an eleven-day tryout on October 20, 1971, prior to a successful Broadway run. Produced in association with the Urban Arts Corps, an off-Broadway theatre company specializing in works by African Americans, *Don't Bother Me* was a musical revue depicting black men's response to living in a white-dominated society. At a time when most African American shows emphasized black rage, the revue stressed black pride. It proved to be popular with both black and white audiences and ran for 1,065 performances when it opened on Broadway the following spring. *Don't Bother Me* became the model for many other successful black musical revues of the 1970s. Other productions that

Septee brought in included the Black Light Theatre of Prague performing in fluorescent colors under ultraviolet lights. *You're a Good Man, Charlie Brown* was presented during the Christmas season. In late March, Yiddish theatre returned briefly to the Walnut with a production of *Only Fools Are Sad*.

A number of classical music groups planned to perform regularly at the Walnut. Sunday afternoons were given over to classical and pop concerts. There were appearances by the Pennsylvania Orchestra, which had been organized the previous spring by conductor Maurice Kaplow. Aaron Copland conducted the Empire Sinfonietta when it performed his Clarinet Concerto in December 1971. Several choral groups also gave concerts that first season, including the Singing City, the Philadelphia Chorale, and the Mendelssohn Club.

Dance also featured prominently in the Walnut's offerings. The Pennsylvania Ballet was invited to become the resident dance company. It performed two dance pieces that season—a Beethoven-inspired piece titled *Bagatelles*, and *Reconnaissance*, which featured electronic sounds and lights. The American Dance Festival brought six of America's most important dance companies to Philadelphia, including the Dance Theatre of Harlem, the José Limón Dance Company, Merce Cunningham, Alvin Ailey, Paul Taylor, and Erick Hawkins. The series was supported by the National Endowment for the Arts, and subscribers paid only $2.35 per concert, which included lecture-demonstrations by the performers.

THE PHILADELPHIA DRAMA GUILD

The new Walnut was to be a presenting house, not a producing house, and a well-regarded community theatre group was invited to become the resident theatre company. The Philadelphia Drama Guild had been founded in 1956 by a local dentist, Dr. Sidney Bloom, and over the years it had developed a considerable reputation for productions of Brecht, O'Casey, Shaw, and others, in plays designed for school groups staged at the 324-seat Plays and Players Theatre on Delancey Street. In order to present at the Walnut, the Drama Guild transformed itself from an amateur to a professional group, becoming an Actors' Equity signatory.

In making the jump from an amateur to a professional organization, Dr. Bloom was helped considerably by a neighbor, actor John Randolph, in bringing in guest stars. "John worked miracles," Bloom told the *Inquirer*, and he was able to attract some leading talent already interested in keeping regional theatre alive. Stars worked for considerably less than the usual minimum, receiving $1,000 a week for three weeks of rehearsal and three weeks of performance. E. G. Marshall played the title role in Moliere's *The Imaginary Invalid*, which ran the first two weeks of December 1971. The cast also included John Randolph, Ruby Dee, and Tammy Grimes. Hume Cronyn and Jessica Tandy starred in Richard Brinsley Sheridan's comedy *The Rivals.* Julie Harris arrived on March 1 for a two-week run in Bernard Shaw's *Pygmalion,* while Diana Sands and Chita Rivera finished out the Drama Guild's season in *Born Yesterday.*

THE SUMMER SEASON

With the restoration of the Walnut accomplished and a successful season produced, Philip Klein stepped down as president of the Walnut's board, although he remained an active board member. William Kohler took his place. The Walnut was booked solidly through the summer of 1972, although ticket sales for the summer shows were not good. A production of *Life with Father* ran for twenty-four performances in late June and early July. It was followed by *No Place to Be Somebody,* the Pulitzer Prize–winning play about a black bar owner who tries to make it big in the underworld. New York's La Mama Troupe arrived in August with *Tom Paine,* an avant-garde production depicting the life of the Revolutionary War pamphleteer. The play did so badly that it closed after one week and *No Place to Be Somebody* was brought back. The Walnut lost roughly $80,000 that summer—roughly equal to the cost of remaining dark.[2]

The fall season officially opened on August 22, 1972, with a touring production of *One Flew over the Cuckoo's Nest.* Jerry Orbach and Jane Alexander followed in Bob Randall's comedy *6 Rms Riv Vu,* which began a two-week Broadway tryout on September 25. Orbach and Alexander played a couple who have a brief affair after they find themselves locked in the last available rent-controlled apartment in New York.

On Sunday, October 15, the Walnut celebrated its first anniversary as a performing arts center. Three hundred invited guests turned out to hear Cornelia Otis Skinner talk about the history of the Walnut and her own family's involvement with the theatre. She was presented with a special plaque by the Friends of the Walnut. Two days later, a national touring company brought the controversial nude revue *Oh! Calcutta!* in for a three-week run.

RICHARD DUPREY

Oh! Calcutta! may have been too much for the Walnut's board, for Randy Swartz left in November 1972. A month later it was announced that Richard

Duprey would take over as artistic director and general manager. Dr. Duprey had been on the Theater Department faculty at Villanova for fourteen years and had been brought in as a consultant the previous summer to start an actors' workshop at the Walnut. Duprey was eager to develop local talent. He planned a short season of experimental opera and American dance, and sought to attract the black community with productions aimed at their concerns. "I see the Walnut as a place that will act as a catalyst in arousing community interest in the arts," he told the *Bulletin*. "It should also be a place for music, dance and off-Broadway productions that lend themselves to a theater the size of the Walnut."[3]

Dr. Duprey spearheaded the renovation of the upper floors of the 825 Walnut building, which would include a screening room, rehearsal space, a lab theatre, and corporate offices. The cost of the renovation was budgeted at $400,000, and the project was underwritten by the Haas Community Fund.

The American Dance Festival continued to bring in the leading names in modern dance. The Alvin Ailey American Dance Theater appeared in October and Martha Graham in November. The dance series had a difficult time. Each dance company supplied its own taped music, but the musicians' union forbade taped music and required five musicians for each performance, at a prohibitive cost. After negotiations with the Walnut's management, the union dropped the requirement to three musicians. The spring saw Alwin Nokolais (who performed multimedia dance) splitting the week of March 20–25, 1973, with Murray Louis. Paul Sanasardo and Louis Falco split the week of May 1–6.

TURNOVERS AT THE DRAMA GUILD

For the 1972–73 season, the Drama Guild sold nearly eighteen thousand subscriptions to its season of four plays. That season, the Guild offered Richard Kiley and Bernadette Peters in Moliere's *Tartuffe*, Eli Wallach and Anne Jackson in *The Waltz of the Toreadors*, and Tom Ewell in Sean O'Casey's *Juno and the Paycock*. Rosalind Cash and Douglas Turner Ward re-created their roles from the original production of Lonne Elder III's *Ceremonies in Dark Old Men*.

The 1973–74 season opened with Maureen Stapleton and Jerry Orbach in Tennessee Williams's *The Rose Tattoo*. Tammy Grimes returned to the Walnut playing Kate in *The Taming of the Shrew*, opposite Ron O'Neal, best known for his role in *Superfly*, as Petruchio. Malcolm Black directed. On February 26 the Drama Guild staged a twenty-fifth anniversary presentation of Arthur Miller's *Death of a Salesman*, with Martin Balsam as Willy Loman and Teresa Wright as his wife. George C. Scott directed, but he withdrew, reportedly because of conflicts with the playwright, who took over directorial responsibilities. On April 9, Geraldine Page and Rip Torn appeared in a revival of Lillian Hellman's *The Little Foxes*.

Despite some memorable productions, the quality was uneven, and subscriptions were down five thousand from the previous season. It was evident that the Guild needed a more experienced artistic director. The *Inquirer*'s theatre critic, William B. Collins, complained, "from the outset, the Guild has not had what could properly be called an artistic policy. It has had a business policy dedicated to the production of safe plays in a safe manner by reputable talent," nothing that "in most Guild productions, you encounter a bewildering variety of acting styles."[4]

In the summer of 1974 the Drama Guild hired Douglas Seale as artistic director. The sixty-two-year-old British-born director had extensive experience producing repertory theatre in England and Canada. Rather than rely on the star system that had been in place, Seale recruited four experienced regional theatre actors—Leah Chandler, Philip Kerr, Robert Pastene, and James Valentine—with the idea of establishing a permanent repertory company that would offer an expanded season of more adventurous productions.

Seale announced a new season of classic plays for the 1974–75 season, which opened with Bernard Shaw's *Misalliance*, directed by Paxton Whitehead. Other productions included Jean Anouilh's *Ardele*, Eugene O'Neill's *Long Day's Journey into Night*, and Oscar Wilde's *The Importance of Being Earnest*. The critics were pleased with the results, given the mishandling of the productions the previous year. It set the precedent for the Drama Guild's offerings for the next several years—high-quality productions of European classics.

REGIONAL REPERTORY COMPANIES

During the summer hiatus, the Walnut invited regional theatres to present. In the summer of 1973 the Baltimore Center Stage revived Robert E. Sherwood's 1935 drama *The Petrified Forest*, following it with a musical adaptation of *The Contrast*, the earliest known play by an American author, written in 1787. The Trinity Square Repertory Company, a Rhode Island–based company, offered Moliere's *The School for Wives* in a new translation by Richard Wilbur. It was followed by an original musical about Oscar Wilde titled simply *Oscar*. The third production was a musical version of *Lady Audley's Secret*, the nineteenth-century melodrama, which had once been a vehicle for Mrs. D. P. Bowers. The Goodspeed Opera Company of East Haddam, Connecticut, had a major success with its revival of John Philip Sousa's 1896 operetta *El Capitan*.

Raisin, a musical version of Lorraine Hansberry's *A Raisin in the Sun*, opened the fall 1973 season. Virginia Capers, Joe Morton, and Ernestine

Jackson starred. The cast included choreographer Debbie Allen in the role of Beneatha Younger. Originally produced at Washington's Arena Theatre, it was about to open on Broadway, where it was honored with a Tony for the Best Musical of 1974.

Jerzy Grotowski, the founder of the Polish Laboratory Theatre, whose experimental work exerted a great influence on avant-garde theatre in America, made his first appearance in this country under the auspices of the Walnut and the University of Pittsburgh's Speech and Theatre Department. Grotowski envisioned a poor theatre, stripped of essentials, which relied on the entirety of the brain and body of the actor. Grotowski's company was scheduled to perform *Apocalypsis Cum Figuris* at the Walnut, but the theatre was much too impressive for Grotowski's purpose, so the play was put on at the Saint Alphonsus Church at Fourth and Reed streets. Audience members sat cross-legged on the floor to view the production, which was spoken entirely in Polish. After the show, André Gregory, the noted theatre director, led a discussion that continued late into the night.

Several touring companies came through the Walnut during the 1973–74 season. Spanky McFarland, star of the Little Rascals comedies, brought *The Spanky Show* in for two shows on Friday, November 16. The Oxford and Cambridge Shakespeare Company presented *Romeo and Juliet* over the Christmas holidays. The company was made up of undergraduates from the two premier English universities. Despite professional direction, critics noted that the students were not up to the demands of the play. Pigmeat Markham was the featured comedian in *Kaleidoscope of Vaudeville*, which depicted the panorama of dance arising from the black experience, tracing the development of African American jazz from its roots in tap dancing, time steps, and jazz steps. Markham's career had revived after his appearances on the hit television series *Rowan and Martin's Laugh-In*. The entire country was repeating Markham's catchphrase, "Here come de judge."

The Trinity Square Repertory Company returned during the summer of 1974 to present a season that included Israel Horovitz's *Alfred the Great*, Robert Bolt's *A Man for All Seasons*, and Robert Penn Warren's verse drama *Brother to Dragons*, which he adapted from his poem about two nephews of Thomas Jefferson who cruelly murder one of their slaves.

CLASSICAL MUSIC AND DANCE

For the 1974–75 season, the music schedule was beefed up. The Curtis Institute of Music celebrated its fiftieth anniversary with five classical music concerts. The Curtis Opera offered three fully staged operas sung in English, including Offenbach's *Tales of Hoffman* and Handel's *Xerxes*. Music from Marlboro presented several chamber music concerts. Philadelphia's All-Star Forum presented piano virtuosos Claudio Arrau, Rudolf Firkusny, Ted Joselson, and Gina Bachauer. The Performing Arts Society presented three Sunday afternoon recitals during the spring—Jean-Pierre Rampal on flute, with Robert Veyron-Lacroix on keyboard. Soprano Jessye Norman performed in April, and the Tokyo String Quartet appeared in May. A twentieth-century music series featured works by Stravinsky, Ravel, Takemitsu, and Messiaen.

The Concerto Soloists began what would be a twenty-five-year affiliation with the Walnut with a concert of Italian music on November 11, 1974. The chamber ensemble had been founded ten years earlier by Marc Mostovoy; its repertoire consisted mainly of baroque and classical works. The Mostovoy Soloists gave three additional Monday concerts that season.

Dr. Duprey instituted a music program called Musicamerica, which would feature popular music on weekdays. Tuesdays were programmed with country and folk music, Wednesdays with gospel and blues, and Thursdays with jazz. Among those performing were Mike Seeger, Sweet Honey in the Rock, Sonny Terry and Brownie McGhee, and Earl "Fatha" Hines.

Paul Taylor premiered his first full-length dance piece, *Genesis*, to open the series in the fall of 1974. The dance drama traced the origins of American culture, drawing parallels with the biblical creation story. The forty-three-year-old choreographer was also the principal dancer with the company. Others companies presented that season included the Inner City Repertory Dance Company, which played a split week with the Martha Graham Dance Company. The Alvin Ailey American Dance Theater returned to the Walnut to present *Blues Suite*, which featured Philadelphia-born Judith Jamison. The Lotte Goslar Pantomime Circus appeared in late April, and Bella Lewitzky appeared in May.

The José Limón Dance Company was booked in October 1974, Dan Wagoner and Dancers in November, the Pilobolus Dance Theatre in February 1975, and the Dance Theatre of Harlem in March. Each company was booked for a Friday evening, Saturday matinee, and other evening performances, as well as a Sunday master class held at the Philadelphia Dance Academy.

Helen Hayes dedicated the theatre museum in November 1974. It was located on the mezzanine level of the Walnut. A mural designed by Shirley Tattersfield depicted the major stars who had appeared at the Walnut over the years, including Charlotte Cushman, Junius Brutus Booth and his son, Edwin Booth, Fanny Kemble, Edwin Forrest, the Marx Brothers, W. C. Fields, Will Rogers, the Drews and the Barrymores, the Lunts, Rachel, Otis Skinner, George Arliss, and Sarah Bernhardt (by mistake).

Al Stites took over as managing director of the Walnut Street Theatre in February 1975. The fifty-three-year-old business consultant was hired to make sweeping, efficiency-minded changes to the center's staff and organizational structure. Stites had previously helped the Bucks County Playhouse stave off bankruptcy, then worked at a Washington-area performing arts center. "The board wanted [Stites] to get more local dance, music and theater groups to use the center as a showcase and base of operations, and to help them develop audiences," the *Inquirer* reported. They were "looking for more community involvement in the center, more city performers and audiences utilizing its facilities."[5] Stites moved to replace the publicity director and created a new department of audience development. To help smaller arts groups with their publicity, he established a federation of twelve small drama groups to deal collectively with their common financial, staffing, and promotional needs.

The musical *Bubbling Brown Sugar* had its pre-Broadway tryout at the Walnut from June 12 through July 6, 1975. The revue celebrated the music of Harlem in the 1920s and '30s and featured the music of such celebrated black composers as Earl "Fatha" Hines, Eubie Blake, Duke Ellington, Cab Calloway, and Billie Holiday. It featured more than thirty musical numbers, including "It Don't Mean a Thing," "Take the A Train," "Sophisticated Lady," and other classic jazz numbers. Thelma Carpenter, Avon Long, and Vivian Reed starred. It was loaded with nostalgic hits of the '20s and '30s and energetic dance numbers staged by Philadelphia choreographer Billy Wilson. The run was extended through August 2, as the bugs were worked out.

In the summer of 1975 the Walnut became the first theatre in the country to install an "audio loop," permitting the hard-of-hearing to enjoy the performance clearly. The loop was a wire strung around the perimeter of the theatre and energized with amplified sound from the stage. The sound was picked up by an amplifier and fed into the loop, where it could be picked up by the telecoil in a hearing aid. The loop was completely inaudible to the unaided ear but eliminated distracting noises from the audience that prevented people wearing hearing aids from hearing the dialogue from the stage.

Renovations were completed that added a new film-screening room, a small theatre space, a dance studio, and a lecture room on the top four floors of the annex. That fall, Al Stites initiated an ambitious schedule of dance, film, theatre, and staged readings, running seven days a week in the main auditorium and in the newly constructed studios.

Films ran seven nights a week in the eighty-five-seat film center on the third floor of the annex. The film center was equipped with an early video-display system that projected a video image onto a four-by-six-foot screen,

fig. 33 Vivian Reed starred in the pre-Broadway tryout of *Bubbling Brown Sugar* at the Walnut.

where local filmmakers could exhibit their films at monthly screenings. There were series of screwball comedies, Dada and surrealism, novels into film, opera on film, first films by major directors, politically or artistically explosive movies, and ten films starring Judy Garland. Several combination screening-discussion evenings were held, with such speakers as director Robert Downey and documentarian Marcel Ophüls.

In October 1975 Al Stites introduced a Writers on Stage series, which brought authors and poets for readings and discussions. Bernard Malamud opened the semimonthly series on October 6 in the main auditorium. Subsequent readings were held in the fourth-floor speaker's forum. Among the writers appearing that season were novelist E. L. Doctorow and poets Richard Wilbur and Marge Piercy.

The fifth floor held a sixty-five-seat theatre referred to as Theatre 5. The first company to perform in the new space was a Canadian comedy troupe, CODCO, that performed sketch comedy as part of a special Canada week, held in late October. On November 7 the Avante Theatre Company of Germantown, Pennsylvania, presented Edward Albee's *The Death of Bessie Smith*. The Philadelphia Dance Alliance took over the sixth-floor dance studio for master classes and demonstrations for its members, doubling as rehearsal space for the company.

THE PHILADELPHIA COMPANY

In December the Philadelphia Company took up residence at Theatre 5. The company, which was committed to new scripts, preferably by local playwrights, had been formed the previous year by Robert Hedley, formerly the head of the Theatre Department at Villanova. Determined to find actors within the community, the Philadelphia Company also operated a school, whose students numbered 140. The company also organized a playwrights' cooperative, which sponsored staged readings of plays by local playwrights.

The Philadelphia Company presented *Marlowe*, a speculative drama on the life of playwright Christopher Marlowe, written by local playwright John Tinger. It was followed by a revival of Somerset Maugham's *Rain*. Carla Belver starred as Sadie Thompson, the prostitute trying to escape her past in Pago-Pago. An evening of one-act plays was presented, which featured David Rabe's *The Crossing* and Leslie Lee's *As I Lay Dying* and *A Victim of Spring*. The season concluded with *The Three Daughters of M. Dupont*, a new translation of Eugene Brieux's 1897 play.

ON THE MAINSTAGE

The Chelsea Theatre opened the mainstage season with its production of Isaac Bashevis Singer's *Yentl*, which was on its way to Broadway. Tovah Feldshuh starred as the teenage girl who passes herself off as a boy so she can attend the yeshiva to study the Torah. The show was produced by Philadelphia impresario Moe Septee, Cheryl Crawford, and, as a silent partner, Barbra Streisand, who optioned the movie rights for the 1983 film, which she both directed and starred in.

The Drama Guild continued to dominate the mainstage, opening its own season on November 4 with *The Royal Family*, George S. Kaufman and Edna

Ferber's comedy. Robert Gerringer, Louise Troy, and John Glover played the characters, based loosely on Lionel, Ethel, and John Barrymore. Ethel Barrymore Colt was on hand for the opening to speak about her illustrious family. Philip Klein unveiled the theatre's fire curtain featuring the Liberty Bell; the fire curtain had undergone a $10,000 restoration. Geraldine Fitzgerald and Edward Albert starred in Tennessee Williams's *The Glass Menagerie,* which played the first three weeks of December, Leonard Frey starred in Harold Pinter's *The Birthday Party,* and Roberta Maxwell played the title role in a revival of Ibsen's *Hedda Gabler.* Robert Gerringer took on the role of Harpagon in a hammed-up version of Moliere's *The Miser,* which closed out the 1975–76 season.

Divisions were developing within the Drama Guild, and they exploded in the press in the spring of 1976, when Dr. Sidney Bloom fired James B. Freydberg as managing director, citing "policy differences," and announced a search for a replacement. Freydberg remained on the Drama Guild's board, however, and in the news. "Sidney wants a managing director and an artistic director for funding purposes. But he wants veto power over them," Freydberg told the *Evening Bulletin.*[6] The Guild's artistic director, Douglas Seale, openly supported Freydberg, and a month later he was reinstated. The episode marked the end of Dr. Bloom's involvement with the Drama Guild—shortly after the 1976–77 season opened, Bloom resigned from the organization he had founded.

The dance series continued to play before sold-out houses. The series no longer focused exclusively on American dance but brought in international dance companies. Israeli dancer Margalit performed her combination of drama, mime, rhythm, and movement on October 16–17, 1975. French choreographer Maurice Béjart and his ballet company played to sold-out houses on December 26 and 27. The Murray Louis Dance Company performed abstract ballet in late January, and the Lar Lubovitch Dance Company appeared in late February. George Faison, who had recently received a Tony for his choreography in *The Wiz,* brought his twelve-member Universal Dance Experience to the Walnut in early April.

That season the Walnut added a jazz series, with performances by Buddy DeFranco, Zoot Sims and Urbie Green, the Heritage Hall Jazz Band, and Stan Kenton. The Mostovoy Soloists of Philadelphia offered chamber music with internationally known guest artists, including flamenco guitar great Carlos Montoya. The piano soloist series offered several up-and-coming piano virtuosos. The Curtis Chamber Music series presented a series of recitals by alumni and faculty members of the famed music school. Among the groups performing was the Guarneri String Quartet. On a more populist note, a *Grand Ole Opry Night at the Walnut* brought in country music stars.

As the American bicentennial approached, nearly every cultural organization in Philadelphia readied patriotic productions. The anniversary was kicked off on January 1 with a balloon ascension from Independence Mall. The Mummers' Parade that year featured a bicentennial theme. "Throughout the rest of the year, every week, almost every day had its special event, and the patriotic motif was visually extended to the smallest details; even many fire hydrants were painted red, white and blue," Philadelphia historian Stephanie G. Wolf noted.[7]

The Walnut celebrated its own anniversary on February 1, 1976, bringing in the Emmett Kelly Jr. Circus, which played to a nearly sold-out house. When the performance concluded, there was a 168th birthday party in the art gallery, with ice cream, soft pretzels, and beer. In March the Walnut opened its doors to a series of theatre tours, which included the stage, dressing rooms, and backstage areas. There was a special one-night performance of *The Wait* on February 29, 1976, a surrealistic drama by local playwright Robert Hightower that examined the experience of black women in America. It was an official bicentennial project presented by the Black Actors and Designers Guild of Philadelphia.

On April 16 and 17, the Philadanco presented a special bicentennial performance, *Roots: Two Hundred Years of Black American Dance*, which traced the development of African American dance from the sacred dances of Africa to more contemporary dances like the cake walk and black bottom. Beginning on April 20, Dana Andrews, Howard Duff, and Monte Markham appeared in *Together Tonight! Jefferson, Hamilton, and Burr*, Norman Corwin's dramatic salute to America's two hundredth birthday in which the three political figures come together for a dramatic exchange of opinions. One critic called it a bicentennial *Meet the Press*.

Bicentennial excitement climaxed that summer. The Walnut prepared patriotic productions for the estimated 20 million visitors who would visit the city that summer. Amervision, Inc. rented the Walnut during the day to screen *The Secret of '76*, a thirty-minute film designed to introduce youngsters to the history of Philadelphia. Attendance was disappointing, and the film closed after a short run.

Television star Hugh O'Brian appeared as George Washington in a bicentennial epic drama titled *The Decision*, which depicted Washington's celebrated crossing of the Delaware to attack British forces at Trenton. The play was written by Bucks County historian Ann Hawkes Hutton. Scheduled to run for eight to ten weeks that summer, it closed after five performances, when the critics savaged the play for its stilted dialogue, bland musical interludes, and two-dimensional characters.

The number of visitors failed to meet expectations, and the theatre lost $30,000 in anticipated revenues when productions were forced to close early. In August Al Stites presented the board with the profit and loss figures for the previous season, which showed more than $200,000 in losses. Board president William Kohler asked for his resignation, and Joseph Carlin became the de facto manager of the theatre, while Kohler took charge as chief executive officer.

PRESIDENTIAL DEBATE

On September 23, 1976, Jimmy Carter and Gerald Ford held their first presidential debate at the Walnut under the sponsorship of the League of Women Voters, the first time presidential candidates had debated since the Kennedy-Nixon debates in 1960. Because the debates were sponsored by the League of Women Voters, not the networks, the FCC ruled that two-sided presidential debates were permissible. Board member Frank McGlinn was a heavy contributor to Republican causes, and his daughter was working in the White House at the time. She suggested the Walnut as an appropriate venue for the debate. Given the bicentennial importance of Philadelphia, and the fact that Independence Hall was too small for such an occasion, the candidates agreed on the Walnut.

Strict security was enforced. The Secret Service looked over the theatre in advance, and on the night of the debate, they cordoned off a four-block area around the building. Several hundred protestors assembled in the streets outside, most of them prochoice advocates, joined by members of the Socialist Workers Party, who were protesting because their candidate was not invited to debate. Only the media and invited guests were allowed past police barricades. Although the theatre held more than a thousand people, only 480 people were allowed in—200 members of the media and 280 invited guests, mostly officials with the League of Women Voters. They were seated in the balcony, while the orchestra was taken over by camera equipment.

The candidates sat in two high, padded swivel chairs on a simple, blue-carpeted platform. The backdrop was a white canvas trimmed in blue. They answered questions posed by a three-person panel of journalists—ABC news correspondent Frank Reynolds, *New Yorker* magazine writer Elizabeth Drew, and *Wall Street Journal* reporter James Gannon. Edwin Newman of NBC News moderated. The bulk of the debate dealt with economic matters, and the most heated exchanges concerned unemployment. Shortly before the candidates were to make their closing remarks, the power unexpectedly went out, and it was twenty-eight minutes before the sound was restored, after which Ford and Carter gave their closing statements.

CUTBACKS

Activities were to be cut back for the 1976–77 season. The board decided that the Walnut would run an eight-month season, closing down during the summer, when it usually lost money. The theatre would limit its presentations to dance, piano recitals, and travel film series, all of which were proven moneymakers. Pornographic film star Harry Reems was the guest speaker at the opening of the 1976–77 film series. There were two movie marathons that season—a twenty-four-hour horror marathon during Halloween weekend, and a laugh marathon in early December. There were series featuring French cinema, opera and dance, Yiddish movies, and Monday night football. The dance series consisted mostly of returning groups, including the Elliot Feld Ballet, the Pilobolus Dance Theatre, the Nikolais Dance Theatre, the Erick Hawkins Dance Company, and the Paul Taylor Dance Company.

Theatrical productions were handled by outside companies. The Drama Guild produced George Bernard Shaw's *Heartbreak House* in early November. Tom Stoppard's *Enter a Free Man* played in December, Peter Shaffer's *Five Finger Exercise* in January, and Noël Coward's *Blithe Spirit* in February, while *Hamlet* finished out the season. There was growing discontent in the Drama Guild about the Walnut as a venue. The March production of *Hamlet*, with John Glover in the title role, proved to be a big hit, and the Guild wanted to extend the run. But the Walnut was already booked for other events.

STUDIO PRODUCTIONS

In Theatre 5, the Philadelphia Company presented Joe Orazi's *The Lion and the Lamb*, which depicted the life of Bert Lahr; *Future Tense*, which looked at life after a world war; *The Keeper*, a portrait of Lord Byron; and Oliver Goldsmith's eighteenth-century comedy *She Stoops to Conquer*, which was included "because our acting company needed the discipline of a revival every year," as artistic director Robert Hedley put it.[8] The company also arranged for stage readings of several original plays, including John Sevcik's *Farewell Nevada*, Clay Goss's *Workshop*, and Thomas Gibbons's *Elephant Man*.

A number of outside groups also booked Theatre 5. The Asparagus Valley Cultural Society played four weeks in January and February 1977. The company featured Penn Jillette and Teller, along with straight man Wier Chrisemer. The group had formed in the Massachusetts region of Asparagus Valley, and the company performed a mélange of magic, music, mime, and acrobatics. The Collaboratory Theatre presented *Kaspar Hauser* in March and

fig. 34 On September 23, 1976, President Gerald R. Ford (*right*) and his Democratic challenger, Jimmy Carter, came to the Walnut Street Theatre, now renamed the Philadelphia Center for the Performing Arts, for the first of their three debates that fall.

April, and the Wilma Project presented Charles Ludlam and his Ridiculous Theatre Company for two performances in June.

In the summer of 1977 Lily Tomlin brought her one-woman show *Appearing Nightly* to the Walnut for two weeks. It was quite successful, grossing nearly $280,000 and setting a record for box office receipts.[9] A touring production of *Little Willie Jr.'s Resurrection* opened the 1977–78 mainstage season. The play detailed the journeys of a young black man from a southern plantation to a big city ghetto. Hal Prince brought in *Some of My Best Friends* for a pre-Broadway tryout the week of October 11. It starred Ted Knight, best known for playing newscaster Ted Baxter on *The Mary Tyler Moore Show.* It lasted only seven performances on Broadway.

FRANK C. P. MCGLINN

Frank McGlinn, banker, theatre historian, and longtime member of the Walnut's board of directors, took over as president of the board from William Kohler in November 1977. Since the Walnut was a presenting, not a producing, house, the board saw no need to hire an artistic director, and McGlinn became the de facto head of the organization. Joe Carlin continued to supervise the day-to-day running of the theatre.

The Drama Guild continued to fill most of the Walnut's season. To open its 1977–78 season it revived Philadelphia playwright George Kelly's *The Show-Off*. Princess Grace of Monaco attended her uncle's play, accompanied by her brother, Councilman John B. Kelly Jr. The remainder of the repertoire consisted mostly of British plays: Tom Stoppard's *Travesties* in December; *Saint Joan*, by Bernard Shaw, in January; and *Hobson's Choice*, a turn-of-the-century English comedy by Harold Brighouse, in February. The season finished in March with Chekhov's *Uncle Vanya*. None of the productions was particularly spectacular, Ernest Schier noted in the *Evening Bulletin*, despite the high quality of the acting company, which now included Louise Troy, Domini Blythe, David Rounds, and Tony van Bridge.[10]

That season, the Drama Guild inaugurated its "Second Stage" series, which brought small musicals, one-person shows, experimental theatre, and staged readings to the Walnut on Monday nights, when the mainstage was normally dark. Its first offering was a revue titled *Starting Here, Starting Now*, which played the Walnut's Theatre 5 for four weeks in the fall, then revived it in mid-January for a six-week run. The studio was generally rented to outside troupes. The Asparagus Valley Cultural Society returned for a five-week engagement in the studio theatre in October and November. Theatre Arts for Youth presented *Black Noël* in early December, and the Wilma Project rented out the studio theatre for two weekends, presenting *Mime Musica* and the Ridiculous Theatre's Charles Ludlam in a pair of one-man shows for children.

The contract for the Drama Guild's artistic director, Douglas Seale, was up for renewal in the spring of 1978, and local critics turned their guns on him. William B. Collins, drama critic for the *Inquirer*, was particularly vitriolic in his criticism. "Neither Seale nor the Drama Guild has lived up to [its] responsibilities. In Seale's four seasons, there has not been one premiere of any playwright's work. Only four of the 19 plays have been by American authors, and only one of those authors (Tennessee Williams) is still alive."[11] Despite the criticisms, Seale's contract was renewed for another two years.

EUBIE!

The musical *Eubie!* broke box office records at the Walnut, where it had a pre-Broadway tryout in the summer of 1978. Moe Septee produced the show, which was based on the music of composer Eubie Blake. The cast featured tap-dancing greats Gregory and Maurice Hines; the production propelled them to stardom. The musical "played a major role in clarifying Eubie Blake's contribution to the history of black musical theatre," Allen Woll reported in *Black Musical Theatre.* The ninety-five-year-old composer had faded from public view, and the musical restored his reputation. "*Eubie!* finally returned the hero of the 1920s to the Broadway stage, and introduced new audiences to the songs and piano work of a master."[12]

The musical was the first to make use of a new computerized lighting system, which was installed that summer. The new system had a memory potential for 220 light cues, with additional cues on memory disk. At the time the Walnut was the only theatre in Philadelphia with a fully computerized lighting system.

MORE TURNOVERS AT THE DRAMA GUILD

At the start of the 1978–79 season, the Drama Guild's managing director, James B. Freydberg, announced his resignation, citing his growing frustration over the organization's failure to expand its program. "We should be doing eight major productions for a season of 40 weeks in a plant of our own," Freydberg told the *Inquirer.* "We should be doing Second Stage productions. We should have a theater school. Those are things that other major regional theaters have done."[13] But the Drama Guild was severely hampered by its deficits. According to the *Inquirer,* the company had losses of $90,000 in 1977 and was expected to run a much larger deficit in 1978. The company was regularly late in paying rent to the Walnut, seriously straining the relationship between the two groups.

Productions remained predictable and safe. Douglas Seale continued to rely on British and American classics like *The Au Pair Man,* by Irish playwright Hugh Leonard, Bernard Shaw's *Arms and the Man,* Noël Coward's *Private Lives, The Blood Knot,* by South African playwright Athol Fugard, and Tennessee Williams's *The Night of the Iguana.* "Under Seale's direction, the PDG is vastly disinterested in breaking new trails with new plays. It has an honest bias in favor of the known quantity: Shakespeare, Shaw and the proven American playwrights," Ernest Schier observed in the *Evening Bulletin.* "It is easy to sneer at the timidity of PDG's programs but it attracts the largest theater subscription in Philadelphia. It is an audience that does not care for surprises in the form of untested work. It prefers what it knows."[14]

In May 1979 Gregory Poggi was named to take Freydberg's place as managing director. Poggi came from Canada's Manitoba Theater Center, where he had been director and general manager. Poggi began to emphasize American plays. There were already rumors that the Drama Guild would be moving, with the McCarter Theater at Princeton mentioned as a possible venue.

MUSIC AT THE WALNUT

Jazz great Dexter Gordon played a one-night concert on October 10, 1978. Rock promoters Steve Apple and Bob Chipetz presented the best of the new wave groups that were revitalizing rock music, including such groups as the Ramones, the Talking Heads, and Blondie. Among the rock groups who appeared that spring were Spirit, Peter Tosh, the Police, Robert Hunter, and Steve Goodman. A jazz series brought in Lionel Hampton, the Charlie Mingus Band, and Sonny Rollins.

Music from Marlboro continued to present its chamber music series, beginning November 12. The Academy of Vocal Arts Opera Company presented *The Marriage of Figaro* for two nights in October, offering Rossini's *Otello* and Benjamin Britten's *Albert Herring* in the spring. The Philadelphia Singers and Concerto Soloists also appeared. The Opera Company of Philadelphia offered the first professional production of the opera *Rumpelstiltskin*, at the Walnut on December 26, 1978. Elwood Thornton had the lead role, and Paulette Haupt-Nolen conducted. The production, aimed at a family audience, featured dancing bears, fiery dragons, and flying birds. John Gardner did the libretto and Joseph Baber provided the music.

Five choreographers discussed the modern dance boom and how dances were created at a colloquium on October 3 at which Stella Moore, the Walnut's dance advisor, moderated. The participants were all affiliated with the companies scheduled to perform at the Walnut that season. Chiang Ching and Company performed classic Chinese and regional ethnic dance later in October; the Laura Dean Dancers performed a modern dance piece the following month. In the spring, the Kathryn Posin Dance Foundation performed "motion-poems," while Annabelle Gamson and the Theatre Dance Collection performed ballet, modern dance, jazz, and rock.

On Sunday, February 11, 1979, the Walnut hosted a conference on men's liberation. More than seven hundred people showed up to hear such celebrity speakers as Jerry Rubin, the former Yippie leader, who was active in the human potential movement. The audience, which was evenly divided between men and women, played a role-reversal game, in which women were instructed to lie about their salaries and job status when approaching men, while the men stood by coyly, deciding whether to accept or reject the women's advances. The event kicked off a five-part series of presentations, which included guest speakers, film presentations, and a book fair. Held over three weekends, it explored such topics as the relationship of fathers and sons, couples, aging, sexual relations, and stress.

THE DRAMA GUILD DEPARTS

Criticism that the Drama Guild was producing only safe work prompted Douglas Seale to offer more original works for the 1979–80 season. *The Last Few Days of Willie Calendar*, a play about the civil rights struggle of the 1960s, had its world premiere in October. During the run, it was announced that Seale's contract would not be renewed at the end of the season. December saw a production of Bernard Shaw's *You Can Never Tell*. In January Seale directed *Summer*, which followed three couples during a picnic on a hillside outside Dublin. The following month, the company presented Shakespeare's *Twelfth Night*. The season finished with *Thark*, a 1928 farce by British playwright Ben Travers set in a haunted house. Paxton Whitehead and Anna Russell starred. At the end of the season, Greg Poggi took over as artistic director of the company.

In January 1980 the Drama Guild informed the Walnut's board that it would be leaving for the Annenberg Center on the campus of the University of Pennsylvania. The Guild's departure left the Walnut in a tenuous position for the fall season. Board president Frank McGlinn tried to put the best face on it. "The Drama Guild was always late in renewing its lease," he told the *Evening Bulletin*. "Last year they didn't let us know they would be back until June. This year they told us in January they wouldn't be back. Each time they had us over a barrel waiting because it was almost too late for us to fill the 20 weeks of time assigned to them at the Walnut. Maybe they thought we'd be under so much pressure we'd reduce the rent."[15]

With the Drama Guild gone, the Walnut had twenty weeks to fill. The board briefly considered producing their own subscription series, but decided to "rent out the house as a four-wall house" for successful Broadway and regional shows. The board began searching for other companies that could present at the Walnut, contacting other important regional theatres. By June, Joe Carlin, the Walnut's general manager, and board members were able to secure promises from the Goodspeed Opera House and other companies to rent the house the following season.

THE GOODSPEED OPERA COMPANY

The Goodspeed Opera Company brought in George M. Cohan's 1904 musical *Little Johnny Jones*, which opened on October 7, 1980, with Eric Weitz in the title role. The show was entirely rewritten to reduce its running time from four hours to a more reasonable two hours and fifteen minutes. Since much of the original score was lost, holes in the script had to be reconstructed from other Cohan shows. Singer Donny Osmond attended a performance during the show's closing week, scouting it as a possible vehicle for himself. When the show opened on Broadway in 1982, Osmond had replaced Weitz.

The People's Light and Theatre Company, a troupe based in Malvern, Pennsylvania, presented *Holy Ghosts,* a drama about Pentecostal snake handlers that looks at the power of faith to transform people's lives. Actual snakes (nonpoisonous, of course) were used for the snake-handling scenes. The Trinity Square Repertory Company of Providence, Rhode Island, returned to the Walnut with *Sea Marks,* a love story about an Irish fisherman and a divorced English woman.

On January 1, 1981, the Goodspeed Opera Company returned with a revival of the 1927 Kalmar and Ruby musical *The Five O'clock Girl.* The producers had added several additional Kalmar and Ruby tunes to fill out the show. "Silly book, great songs, loveable cast," the *Inquirer* concluded. In February Emlyn Williams brought in his one-man performance as Charles Dickens. The Welsh actor had created the role in 1951, reading excerpts from the author's works. June Havoc starred as an aging star trying to make a comeback in *Jitters,* a new comedy of backstage life at a regional theatre that had a three-week tryout beginning March 18 but canceled its final week. There was friction between the playwright and director and the producer and star, and the production never made it to Broadway. George C. Scott was scheduled to play the title role in *Sly Fox,* which closed prior to its engagement at the Walnut. Instead, New York City's Roundabout Theatre presented Terrence Rattigan's *The Winslow Boy* to finish the season. Despite good reviews, the production never attracted an audience.

The subscription series was disappointing. Only thirty-nine hundred subscribers signed up—fewer than half the number hoped for. *Charles Dickens* and *Little Johnny Jones* were the only shows to recover their costs. Joe Carlin told the *Evening Bulletin* that the theatre's losses were "substantially more than we bargained for," and the company decided to drop the subscription series altogether.[16]

MUSIC AND DANCE

The Walnut did better with its established music and dance series. The Concerto Soloists offered a series of five baroque and classical concerts that season with various guest artists. In January 1981 they added a series titled Learning Through Listening aimed at children. Marlboro Music offered three concerts.

The AVA Opera Theatre staged two obscure operas—Rossini's *The Turk in Italy* and Mozart's *Idomeneo*—both of which drew well. The Opera Company of Philadelphia brought back the "family opera" *Rumpelstiltskin* during Christmas week.

The Pilobolus Dance Theatre opened the Walnut's dance series. The company, which had been founded by Dartmouth College students ten years earlier, performed an athletic, theatrical form of dance, with the dancers creating structural forms with their combined bodies. Jane Goldberg brought her Changing Times Tap Dancing Revue in for two nights, which featured two tap-dancing legends, Charles "Cookie" Cook and Leslie "Bubba" Gaines. The eight-member Murray Louis Dance Company presented three performances of modern dance in early March. One-third of the audience walked out of the Andrew DeGroat and Dancers' performance at the Walnut because of the dissonant music used in an avant-garde dance piece titled "(GRAVY) a medicine of spaces." Twyla Tharp and her dance company returned to close out the 1980–81 season in May.

Several pop musicians performed that season. Grammy Award–winning singer-songwriter Peter Allen brought his music to the Walnut for two shows on January 24. Guitarist Leo Kottke and Leon Redbone also appeared. Carole Bayer Sager and Burt Bacharach performed together on June 5.

HIGHLIGHTS OF THE WALNUT

The 1980–81 series was a financial disaster, and by the spring of 1981 the Walnut was in real danger of having to close. The William Penn Foundation wanted to cut back on its support. Its outgoing president, Richard Bennett, informed the Walnut's board that it could not continue to rely on subsidies from the foundation and urged that expert advice be sought on how to make the Walnut self-sufficient.

The theatre organized a fund-raiser called *Highlights of the Walnut* on May 3, 1981. Helen Hayes hosted the event, assisted by Cliff Robertson and Kim Hunter. The presentation was full of lore about the Walnut. Margaret Hamilton, best known as the Wicked Witch of the West in *The Wizard of Oz*, performed a pantomime from a 1943 comedy *Three's a Family*. Moses Gunn and Roberta Maxwell reenacted the strangulation scene from Shakespeare's *Othello*. Mildred Natwick re-created the séance scene from *Blithe Spirit*. The Pilobolus Dance Theatre performed, and there were songs by Louise Troy, Roderick Cook, and Andrea McArdle. Helen Hayes concluded the evening by performing the curtain scene from *Victoria Regina*, wearing the same costume she had worn in the 1935 production, which had been borrowed for the occasion from the Museum of the City of New York.

The fund-raiser failed to make much of a dent in the theatre's debts, grossing only $12,500, of which $5,500 went to pay the stagehands. In the meantime, the board had to decide whether to keep the theatre open or go dark for the season. The board calculated that, because of existing contracts with the stagehands' union, it would cost $189,000 just to keep the theatre dark for six months. The William Penn Foundation offered to finance the theatre to a maximum of $190,000, with any income the theatre received being deducted from that amount. That summer, the Walnut laid off most of its staff, maintaining only a skeleton crew.

CANCELLATIONS

Without a presold audience, not many producers were looking for a small venue in which to book their shows. A touring company came in with *I'm Getting My Act Together and Taking It on the Road* for what was to be an eight-week run. Despite unanimously favorable reviews, the show never caught on with the public. There were no other shows to take up the slack. Several that were scheduled to come to the Walnut that year canceled because of the lack of a subscription audience. That fall, Frank McGlinn stepped down as head of the Walnut Street Theatre after four a half years in office. Day-to-day operations of the theatre were taken over by Karen Horn, a board member with an extensive background in finance and management. She increasingly sought private-sector support for the theatre.

The mainstage remained dark for most of the fall, except for concerts by such reliable companies as Marlboro Music, the Philadelphia Civic Ballet, and Concerto Soloists. Then, on December 11, 1981, a modest show about Catholic school opened that turned the Walnut's fortunes around. *Do Black Patent Leather Shoes Really Reflect Up?* arrived at the Walnut after a three-year run in Chicago. Although it was an "admittedly thin and corny show" that followed several students from first grade through high school, it captured the hearts of the public. The musical played from December through May, becoming the longest-running show in the Walnut's history. The play closed to move to a Broadway theatre, but New York audiences did not take to the show, and it closed within a week.

THE AMPERSAND STUDY

Board president Karen Horn resigned in April, leaving the Walnut without leadership. Consultants were brought in to review the financial situation and prospects, and they recommended that the Walnut continue to expand its role as a performing arts center, broaden its base of support by appealing to the larger community, and become an umbrella organization for local music, drama, and dance groups. The William Penn Foundation continued to support the theatre through the transition by providing funds to develop a long-range plan.

Ampersand, Inc., a consulting firm based in Winston-Salem, North Carolina, was hired to conduct a survey of the Walnut Street Theatre. The survey concluded that its financial problems were based on "the lack of a defined purpose and programming, no 'sustained' fund-raising effort, vacancies in the chairs of executive director and board president, and a board composition which is heavily weighted with founder-members who have served for over 10 years," the *Inquirer* reported.[17] The survey also found too heavy a dependence on the William Penn Foundation, which had supported the theatre to the tune of $9 million since its conversion to a performing arts center.

The report recommended that the Walnut begin searching for additional sources of unearned income, build a board that viewed its primary responsibilities as fund-raising and policymaking, and develop "reliable and consistent programming supported by marketing at a level to generate a sufficient percentage of earned income from ticket sales." The most immediate need was to hire a new managing director to institute these changes. A transition committee, headed by Ed Rome, a founding member of the Walnut's board, began a nationwide search for a new leader.

A SUBSCRIPTION HOUSE, 1982–1999

The person tapped to lead the Walnut was the forty-one-year-old managing director of Atlanta's Alliance Theatre, Bernard Havard, who was hired as executive director, a highly unusual arrangement for a regional theatre. Normally, executive responsibilities would be split between an artistic director, who made the artistic decisions, and a managing director, who handled the business end. But Havard combined the two areas of responsibility. His appointment would cause some controversy, but it ultimately led to the success of the new venture.

Havard belonged to an old English theatrical family and had grown up in Canada, where he became a naturalized citizen. He trained at the University of Alberta and the Banff School of Fine Arts and worked as an actor in England before moving into theatre management. He toured Australia for several years as a company manager and stage manager for several shows before returning to Canada to work as a production and business manager at several regional theatres.

While working at the St. Lawrence Centre for the Arts in Toronto, Havard came under the influence of Danny Newman, whose theories—developed as a marketing consultant with the Canada Council and set forth in his 1977 book *Subscribe Now!*—revolutionized the marketing of nonprofit theatre. Havard was able to put Newman's theories into practice when he became managing director of the Alliance Theatre in Atlanta 1977. In his five years at the Alliance, Havard built it into the third-largest subscription house in the United States.

While the Walnut's board envisioned the Walnut simply as a showcase for local and out-of-town dramatic productions, Havard had very specific ideas about the kind of organization he wished to run. "If you want to have a building with heart," he told the board, "you have to produce." He announced that he would take the position only if the Walnut became a producing organization. This was a much bigger commitment than some board members were comfortable with, but Ed Rome, who had taken over as board president, saw the soundness of Havard's vision and lined up board members who were ready to work toward it. Havard was named executive director of the Walnut in November 1982.

BERNARD HAVARD TAKES THE HELM

The Walnut was dark for most of the 1982–83 season, as Havard worked to get things on a better financial footing. One of the problems he faced was that the management had never renegotiated its contracts with the actors' and stagehands' unions, which continued to treat the Walnut like a for-profit house. Havard brought them more in line with other nonprofit producing organizations. Among the concessions the unions made was relinquishing jurisdiction over Studio 5. Havard replaced paid ushers with volunteers, saving the theatre $20,000 annually.

Several independent producers rented out the theatre that year. The Shady Grove Music Fair brought in *Mass Appeal* for a monthlong run in October. Milo O'Shea re-created his Broadway role as a worldly priest challenged by an idealistic young seminarian. In April, Richard Dreyfuss appeared in *Total Abandon*, which had a two-week pre-Broadway tryout. The Philadelphia critics savaged the play, a depressing drama about a man who beats his two-year-old son into a coma. The New York critics were no kinder, and the play closed after a single performance. In July, Havard brought in the Negro Ensemble Company's production of *A Soldier's Play*, a mystery about the fatal shooting of a black sergeant at an army base in the deep South during World War II. The play won a Pulitzer Prize for its playwright, Philadelphia's own Charles Fuller. The show starred Benjamin Epps and Adolph Caesar. The cast also included Samuel L. Jackson, who would go on to movie stardom. There were also one-night concerts by the Stylistics, Marlboro Music, and Concerto Soloists. In May, Waylan and Madame, the ventriloquist act, appeared for three nights, followed by the Swiss mime troupe Mummenschanz.

The long-term financial health of the Walnut depended on two things: building a subscriber base and attracting contributed income. Since 1970 the Walnut had relied exclusively on the William Penn Foundation to cover its deficits. Havard brought in a full-time fund-raising director, Frances Bourne, who had worked with the Pennsylvania Ballet and had good local

fig. 35 This photo of Bernard Havard, executive director, was taken in 1988.

contacts. Bourne attracted corporate and foundation support to augment regular contributions from the Penn Foundation and the chemical firm of Rohm and Haas.

Just as critical was increasing earned income, which meant attracting a subscription audience. Terry Lorden was hired as marketing director. Like Havard, Lorden was a disciple of Danny Newman and had an excellent track record building subscriptions for New Jersey's Paper Mill Playhouse. Lorden put together a mailing of two hundred thousand brochures targeted to potential patrons in the hope of generating 7,500 subscribers for the first season. Havard integrated telemarketing into the direct-marketing mail campaign, and as a result they nearly doubled the goal, signing up 14,500 subscribers for the first season. With the funds generated through the fund-raising efforts and advance ticket sales, Havard was able to put together a $2 million budget for the 1983–84 season.

VOX POPULI

When it came to programming, Havard was an unabashed populist. "The point of theatre is lost if the attitude of a production is superior to the point of arrogance," he asserted. "Nobody wants to pay for a seat and feel he has entirely missed the show." But Havard understood that neither could the theatre underestimate theatergoers, who are generally better educated and more affluent than the general public. "Theatre audiences consist of intelligent people who disdain condescension as much as they do arrogance. There is definitely a point between the two that fulfills a theatergoer's expectation, which is to be entertained and enlightened."[1] Havard felt that it was important to listen to the *vox populi,* the voice of the people.

Havard brought in an old colleague, Bill Duncan, as production manager and began negotiating with a number of experienced directors about productions for the 1983–84 season. "I wanted someone who was wedded to an artistic vision of a given play," Havard told the *Inquirer.* "Most free-lance directors will do any play that comes their way because they're starving to death. They don't necessarily have an artistic vision of the play. I much prefer asking a director, 'What are the six plays you've always wanted to do?' or 'What would you like to do again that you found rewarding the first time?'"[2]

Five plays were to be presented each season—a mixture of musical, classic, and contemporary plays. The productions that season were selected with entertainment value in mind. Paxton Whitehead, a longtime favorite with Philadelphia audiences, proposed the classic French farce *A Flea in Her Ear.* When other commitments got in Whitehead's way, Donald Ewer took over directing. Charles Abbott directed *Oliver!*—a family-oriented musical based on Dickens's *Oliver Twist* that played during the Christmas season. Malcolm Black brought in *Morning's at Seven,* a 1939 comedy that had been successfully revived on Broadway several years earlier. Tom Marcus directed *A Perfect Gentleman,* an original comedy of manners that depicted the life of Lord Chesterfield and his son, which was co-produced with the Virginia Museum Theatre. Co-production made sense both artistically and economically. The Walnut reduced production costs by sharing preproduction expenses, and guaranteed a well-rehearsed production when it came into the Walnut. The closing play, *The Taming of the Shrew,* was directed by David Chambers. Malcolm Black and Charles Abbott returned regularly to direct at the Walnut, and Donald Ewer appeared frequently in both mainstage and studio shows.

THE CASE AGAINST COMMERCIALISM

The subscription plan put the Walnut back on its feet financially. Shows played for two weeks, and houses averaged 83 percent capacity. Three-quarters of the seats were occupied by season ticketholders, and the theatre finished its first season of 128 performances with a surplus of $80,000. The very success of the subscription program, however, raised the ire of the *Philadelphia Inquirer*'s influential drama critic, William B. Collins. Collins felt that business considerations were driving the Walnut's programming, to the detriment of theatrical art. "The major contribution of [the Walnut] has been to make theater a selling proposition rather than an artistic enterprise," he wrote, dismissing the Walnut's offerings as "a pastime, a business, a diversion, but not serious in any meaningful sense."[3]

In Collins's view, a not-for-profit theatre had one and only one purpose. "The only excuse for a regional theater is to serve the art," he told an interviewer. "That's why they're subsidized, that's why they were created, because of the feeling that Broadway wasn't doing it." Subscriptions, Collins felt, were strangling the art and creativity out of the theatre. He dismissed the Walnut's audience as "sheep in the mainstage and goats in the studio." Subscribers were "people who get their plays out of anthologies . . . people who don't like bad language, sex, and nudity in their plays. . . . These were nuns, high school English teachers, and people from South Jersey who just never thought of going to the theatre."[4]

Bernard Havard countered that, quite the opposite, subscriptions allowed the Walnut to take more chances artistically. By providing the theatre with a guaranteed income, subscriptions reduced the speculative nature of nonprofit arts programming, so that the theatre did not have to produce a consistent string of hits. Productions with built-in box office appeal made it possible to take chances on more experimental and more serious productions. Given the financial difficulties of recent years, Ed Rome and the board of directors stood firmly behind Havard and his vision for the Walnut.

COMMUNITY OUTREACH

While financial considerations had to drive a theatre the size of the Walnut, Havard was mindful of the role the theatre could, and should, play in the community. He tried to cast Philadelphia actors, looking for local talent before opening auditions to actors from New York and Los Angeles. He searched for other ways to involve the local theatre community. "I wanted more artists to be associated with the Walnut," Havard explained. "For me, what defines a theatre are the artists. We need the support staff—the accountants, stage hands, administrative personnel—but it is the collective voice of the artists that defines our mission."[5]

One of the ways to serve local actors was to hire them to teach. In the summer of 1984, the Walnut opened a theatre school. Andrew Lichtenberg, who had directed theatre programs at Bryn Mawr and Haverford colleges, was appointed its director. The school offered instruction to both children and adults on beginner, intermediate, and advanced levels. Tuition was kept low: the cost for the four-week children's sessions was only $40, while the cost of the eight-week sessions for high school students and adults ranged from $75 to $125. Students could audition for understudy and youth roles in the mainstage productions. The Walnut's outreach program extended into the schools with a program called *Shakespeare Alive!* in which actors from the Walnut performed scenes from *Hamlet, Othello, Macbeth,* and *Twelfth Night* before high school students and guided discussions of the plays.

SHARED-RISK PLAN

During the summer recess the mainstage was made available to local theatre companies. In June 1984 the American Music Theater Festival brought in *Strike Up the Band,* a groundbreaking musical from 1930. It was the first production of the new company, which had been organized to produce new works as well as "important works of the past that are crying to be done."[6] *Strike Up the Band,* which brought together the music of George and Ira Gershwin and the satire of George S. Kaufman and Morrie Ryskind, had not been performed since the original Broadway run. Eric Salzman, artistic director of the American Music Theater Festival, reconstructed the show from several versions of the script he located in various archives. The show featured Bill Irwin, who came to national prominence that month when he received the prestigious MacArthur "genius" award for his clowning. Despite the merits of the musical, houses were only one-third full.

To make the Walnut a more attractive place to present, Havard offered outside producers a shared-risk plan. This meant that the visiting group would not face financial disaster if attendance was low, while the theatre would profit from a hit. In August, *Do Black Patent Leather Shoes Really Reflect Up?* was remounted by an outside producer. The original production had grossed nearly $3 million, but the Walnut had received only a rental fee. The remounted production was a success, running for eleven weeks, and under the shared-risk partnership arrangement, the Walnut netted nearly $150,000. Other companies took advantage of the shared-risk plan, including a jazz dance concert called *Waves V,* the Swiss mime troupe Mummenschanz, and Concerto Soloists.

SPONSORSHIP

The Walnut opened its second season in November 1984 with *Chekhov in Yalta,* an original comedy by John Driver and Jeffrey Haddow about the Moscow

Art Theatre. The sets were built in the Walnut's new scene shop, located at an off-site facility on Front Street. There was some talk of moving the show to Broadway, but a devastating review by William Collins in the *Inquirer* made it impossible to raise the needed funds. Charles Abbott returned to direct Meredith Willson's musical *The Music Man*. The production was underwritten by the PMA Insurance Group, which began a twenty-year tradition of sponsoring the holiday musical.

In January the Walnut revived Lillian Hellman's *Another Part of the Forest*. The original production had premiered at the Walnut in 1947 on its way to Broadway. Fred Chappell, the artistic director of the Alliance Theatre, was brought in to direct. The show was videotaped by the cable network Showtime and became one of five finalists for its award for artistic excellence. Malcolm Black returned to direct *Quartermaine's Terms*, a comedy by Simon Gray about a teacher in a British school. Philadelphia-based actor Douglas Wing received rave reviews for his performance as the lonely teacher, although the play reportedly left much of the audience confused. Finishing out the year was a production of *A Midsummer Night's Dream*, directed by Gregory Hurst of the Pennsylvania Stage Company. The Walnut instituted a week of special matinees for school students, with more than five thousand students from area schools attending. The Junior League of Philadelphia paid for two thousand of these students to attend for free.

Audience surveys determined that Philadelphia's theatergoers had a strong preference for musicals and recent comedies, and the 1985–86 season reflected this. The runs were increased from two to three weeks and a second musical was added. The season opened up with Wendy Wasserstein's comedy *Isn't It Romantic*. *Gypsy* followed in December; once again Charles Abbott directed the holiday musical. Lillian Hellman's *The Little Foxes* opened in January. Josie Abady directed, the first time a woman had directed on the Walnut's stage since Lillian Hellman staged *Another Part of the Forest* in 1947. *Tomfoolery*, a musical revue based on the songs of satirist Tom Lehrer, opened in February, and the season finished up in early April with Shakespeare's *As You Like It*. Playing the minor role of Phebe was Laura San Giacomo, who went on to stardom in the 1989 film *Sex, Lies, and Videotape* and in the sitcom *Just Shoot Me*.

UNION NEGOTIATIONS

The Walnut had been saddled with union contracts left over from its days as a Shubert House. Several of these contracts came up for renewal in the 1985–86 season. At the end of the season, Ed Rome stepped down as president of the board of directors. He was replaced by John D. Graham, a marketing executive who was a founding partner of the Keystone Financial Group. Management prepared a long-range plan that set out goals for the theatre. There would be five mainstage productions and one original play each year. There would be five productions in the studio theatre. The goal was to expand the subscription base to thirty thousand over the next five years and to develop a core company of actors for the Walnut.

The Walnut was designated a LORT A house under the contracts set up by the League of Resident Theatres, the national association of nonprofit theatres. LORT served as a bargaining agent for its members with actors' and crafts' unions. With the weekly income the theatre generated, the Walnut should not have been designated a LORT A, for it limited the theatre's flexibility and increased its budget. But the Walnut had been grandfathered into this old category from its days as a for-profit house. Havard wanted the Walnut to be designated a LORT B+, which would allow it to hire nonunion actors as understudies or in walk-on roles without paying them union scale. When LORT refused to take a strike on behalf of the Walnut, Havard withdrew from the organization and began negotiating independently with the unions, obtaining the necessary concessions. The Walnut continues to negotiate on its own today.

STUDIO 3

In the fall of 1985 the third-floor film center was remodeled into a second studio theatre, seating ninety. This allowed the Walnut to mount smaller, more challenging plays where profitability was not the main concern. The first production opened in January 1986, a story about a family living with a gifted but autistic child called *A Lunacy of Moons*. Subscribers paid as little as $24 for the four-play season, which included *She Also Dances*, *Salt Water Moon*, a love story set in Newfoundland, and a one-man show by John Maxwell titled *Oh, Mr. Faulkner, Do You Write?*

Studio 3 was a place to explore controversial subjects that might have trouble drawing an audience. *She Also Dances* portrayed a romance between a young man and a paraplegic accident victim. The most successful production of the 1986–87 season was *The Normal Heart*, a powerful indictment of the government's tepid response to the AIDS epidemic by activist Larry Kramer. The smaller space made Studio 3 appropriate for one-person shows. The following season, Owen Rackleff played the great French chef in *Escoffier*. In the 1989–90 season, Conrad Bishop appeared in his own one-man show, *Mark Twain Revealed*.

fig. 36 Hugh Panaro and Jennifer Lee Andrews starred in the 1986 production of Stephen Sondheim's *A Little Night Music.*

Studio 3 saw a number of world premieres, two in 1987—*Eb and Flo* by Blake Walton and Amy Whitman, and *Nasty Little Secrets* by Lanie Robertson. Kim Hunter starred in the 1988 world premiere of *A Cup of Change,* a new drama by Robert Perring. Local playwrights were given an opportunity to have their plays produced. *Sins of the Father* was a psychological drama by Lezley Steele. Donald Drake's *Clear and Present Danger* was brought to the stage in 1990. Other productions had their American premieres in Studio 3, including *Waiting for the Parade,* by Canadian playwright John Murrell, and *The Petition,* by British playwright Brian Clark.

Outside companies also made use of the Walnut, playing in the fifth-floor studio during the regular season and taking over the mainstage during the summer months. The American Music Theater Festival returned during the summers of 1985 and 1986 with challenging musical productions. The first summer, it premiered an original opera—titled simply *X*—based on the life of Malcolm X, which was nominated for a Pulitzer Prize that year. The following year it presented *The Juniper Tree,* a collaboration between Philip Glass and Philadelphia composer Robert Moran, based on a tale by the Brothers Grimm. Other opera companies made use of the Walnut during the summer season as well. The Pennsylvania Opera Theatre presented *Threepenny Opera* and *Cosi Fan Tutti* in 1984 and returned for several summers with *Rigoletto, Tales of Hoffman, Cinderella, The Magic Flute,* and *Turn of the Screw.* The Academy of Vocal Arts Opera Company presented *La Traviata* in 1985, *Don Giovanni* in 1986, *The Merry Widow* in 1988, and *Falstaff* in 1989.

A number of summer offerings were directed at the African American community. A touring production of *Diary of a Black Man* had a brief run in May 1986. That summer, Moe Septee revived *Bubbling Brown Sugar,* which played for more than two months before moving to Atlantic City. Billy Daniels starred, and Billy Wilson directed. A gospel revue titled *Don't Get God Started* played to nearly sold-out houses in the summer of 1987 before moving to Broadway. *Diary of a Black Man* returned in the summer of 1988, which also saw a production of *Moms*—a one-woman show about comedienne Moms Mabley—and Alfred Uhry's *Driving Miss Daisy,* which starred Brock Peters and Julie Harris.

Smaller theatre companies presented in Theatre 5. The most notable of these was the Arden Theatre Company, which played its first two seasons at the Walnut. Founded in 1988 by a pair of young graduates of Northwestern University, Aaron Posner and Terry Nolen, the company specialized in adapting literary works for the stage. Posner and Nolen presented a business plan , as requested, and it was agreed there would be a revenue sharing plan. For their first season, they adapted three stories by Kurt Vonnegut, titling it *Who Am I This Time?* They followed this up with *The Good War,* based on oral histories of World War II collected by Studs Terkel. The following season, they presented original adaptations of P. G. Wodehouse's *What Ho, Jeeves!* and John Cheever's *A Love of Light,* and returned in 1989–90 with *The Sneeze* and *As You Like It* in the fall, H. G. Wells's classic *The Invisible Man* in February, and *Philly Phiction*—a series of vignettes by and about Philadelphians—in March. The following season the Arden Theatre Company moved into its own space at St. Stephen's Alley, where it remained a mainstay of the Philadelphia theatre scene.

In 1995 the Arden built its own theatre in Old City, becoming one of the most successful companies in Philadelphia.

MAINSTAGE ATTRACTIONS

The mainstage audience grew steadily throughout the 1980s. In 1986 subscriptions topped twenty thousand for the first time, giving the Walnut the largest subscription base of any theatre in Pennsylvania and the sixth-largest in the country. With a guaranteed audience, Havard was able to try more difficult pieces, balancing surefire audience pleasers like Neil Simon's *Prisoner of Second Avenue* and Stephen Sondheim's *A Little Night Music* with riskier fare. January 1987 saw a revival of a 1949 Clifford Odets play, *The Big Knife*, set in Hollywood in the 1930s. Set designer Paul Wonsek created the interior of a Hollywood mansion onstage. The play was a favorite with most of those involved with the production, but its tragic ending limited its appeal. In February the Walnut premiered *Dumas*, a rollicking play by John MacNicholas about novelist Alexandre Dumas. Much of the audience was surprised to discover that the author of *The Count of Monte Cristo* was a mulatto. Roger Robinson was cast as Dumas *père*, and the role of Dumas *fils* went to actor Geoffrey Owens, who took time off from television's *The Cosby Show* to appear. The season concluded with another musical, *Tintypes*, which featured popular songs from the turn of the twentieth century.

There were two world premieres on the Walnut's mainstage during the 1987–88 season. *Dusky Sally* was an original play about the love affair between Thomas Jefferson and his slave Sally Hemmings. It was written by Granville Burgess, who also headed the Walnut's theatre school. There was talk about moving it to Broadway, until the author of a biography of Sally Hemmings sued the playwright for copyright infringement. Robert Morse starred in a new musical titled *Mike*, about legendary producer Mike Todd, which had its world premiere at the Walnut. It featured an extravagant set, with automated scenery and a treadmill. Producer Cyma Rubin provided half a million dollars in enhancement money with the goal of taking the show to Broadway, and later took the Walnut to arbitration over financial issues. (The arbitrators ruled in favor of the Walnut.) The show was taken to Broadway by another producer some years later under the title *Ain't Broadway Grand*. Other productions that year included Michael Frayn's hilarious backstage farce *Noises Off*, the musical *Funny Girl*, and Tennessee Williams's *Cat on a Hot Tin Roof*.

While Havard could afford some experimentation, the seasonal offerings were becoming formulaic. The season opened with a comedy. A family-oriented musical followed during the holiday season. The first few months of the new year always featured a comedy and a drama, and the season would typically finish off with an established musical. The 1988–89 season, for example, opened with *Social Security,* a comedy about a pair of art dealers who must care for a cantankerous mother. It was written by Andrew Bergman, best known as the screenwriter of the Mel Brooks comedy *Blazing Saddles.* The holiday musical that season was *Guys and Dolls,* followed by J. B. Priestley's 1938 comedy *When We Are Married,* which centers around three couples celebrating their silver wedding anniversaries who discover they are not legally married. Shakespeare's *Twelfth Night* filled the fourth spot, and *Fame: The Musical* finished out the season. The stage adaptation of the award-winning film was co-produced with Baltimore's Morris Mechanic Theatre.

KEN WESLER

Eager for new challenges, Bernard Havard took on the added responsibility of managing the Gretna Theatre, a historic summer stock theatre outside Lebanon, Pennsylvania. There he worked with a young production manager, Ken Wesler, and the two theatre enthusiasts hit it off. When the general manager position opened up at the Walnut in the spring of 1989, Havard brought Wesler aboard. In this new position Wesler had the responsibility of day-to-day operations, negotiating contracts with designers and actors, and managing the theatre. The 1989–90 season was already set. It opened with Alan Ayckbourn's comedy *How the Other Half Loves.* Andrew Lloyd Webber's *Joseph and the Amazing Technicolor Dreamcoat* played during the holiday season. The production was a triumph for its star, Philadelphia-based actress Laurie Beechman, who re-created her Broadway role as the Narrator, with Sal Viviano cast in the title role. *Sherlock Holmes and the Speckled Band,* the only play Arthur Conan Doyle wrote about his renowned detective, opened in early January, breaking box office records for a straight play. It was followed by *Sly Fox,* Larry Gelbart's 1976 adaptation of Ben Jonson's *Volpone.* A British musical, *The Hired Man,* which depicted family life in a coal-mining town, had its American premiere to finish out the season.

By 1990 the subscription audience had grown to nearly thirty thousand, double the size of its first season. The annual operating budget topped $4.6 million. Nearly a quarter-million people attended performances at the Walnut that season. The season had been expanded to twenty-five weeks, and mainstage shows played to 80 percent capacity. Earned income—from ticket sales, theatre rentals, school admissions, concessions, and miscellaneous sources—accounted for 80 percent of the Walnut's income, an unusually high ratio for a nonprofit theatre. The remaining 20 percent was provided through donations from individuals, foundations, corporations, and government sources.

One of the more popular fund-raising events was the annual gala, a black-tie event held in the spring. At the 1990 birthday gala, the Walnut introduced the Edwin Forrest Award, which honored a person for his or her outstanding contribution to theatre. Former board president Frank McGlinn was the first recipient. Teller, of the comedy-magic team Penn and Teller, presented the award. The following year, another former board president, F. Otto Haas, received the honor. In 1992 it was decided to offer two awards each year, one to a businessperson who had helped the Walnut, the other to an actor or actress. The husband-and-wife team of Anne Jackson and Eli Wallach received the artist award in 1993, while Fred Anton, president and CEO of the PMA Insurance Group, received the business honor.

While the day-to-day operations were generally provided for, the Walnut's physical plant continued to offer problems. It had been more than twenty years since the theatre had had any major renovations. The roof needed to be replaced, the heating and cooling system needed to be upgraded, and there were leaking pipes and drains. Havard was eager to make some improvements, including adding a café on the lower lobby level that could serve drinks and light refreshments. In February 1990 the Walnut announced a three-year $3 million capital campaign aimed at renovating the facilities. That summer, the sidewalk in front of the building was torn up and a new heating and cooling system was installed. Ken Wesler supervised the renovations, which also included a makeover of office space.

THE RUSSIAN SEASON

The 1990–91 season saw the first downturn in the Walnut's fortunes since Bernard Havard had taken over, the result of a combination of artistic missteps and unforeseen outside events. The decline of the Communist Party in the Soviet Union produced a flowering of art and drama there. In February 1990 Havard traveled to Moscow and Leningrad to explore the possibility of a theatre exchange. Eugene Lazarev of Moscow's Mossoviet Theatre was invited to direct the season opener, a comedy by the nineteenth-century Russian playwright Alexander Ostrovsky titled *A Family Affair.* The play did not do well with the public. In addition, Iraqi dictator Saddam Hussein invaded the neighboring kingdom of Kuwait shortly before the fall season opened, which temporarily depressed theatre attendance.

Audience numbers were off for most of the shows that season. *Big River,* a musical retelling of Mark Twain's *Huckleberry Finn,* did well, but a revival of George Kelly's 1924 comedy *The Show-Off* never found an audience. Business recovered after Operation Desert Storm drove Saddam Hussein's forces out of Kuwait in February 1991. Robert Harling's comedy *Steel Magnolias* drew good audiences, in part because of the success of the 1989 film. The season finished up with another Russian piece, *How It Was Done in Odessa*, a musical about Jewish gangsters in Odessa on the eve of the Russian Revolution. Houses were only half-full much of the time; only the dependability of the subscription audience prevented the season from becoming a financial disaster.

A Yiddish musical called *Those Were the Days* came in for a weeklong run in late May, but the theatre was shut down for much of the summer of 1991, while badly needed renovations were made to the roof. The house remained dark until early August, when Avery Brooks appeared as the title character in *Paul Robeson*. Houses for both shows were poor. In late August the mainstage was rented out to Carsey-Werner Productions for shooting the pilot for Bill Cosby's remake of Groucho Marx's 1950s game show *You Bet Your Life*. Cosby, a Philadelphia native, wanted to produce the series in the theatre where the Marx Brothers had gotten their start, and there was some anticipation that this hope would be realized. Ultimately, Cosby was unable to get the theatre for the whole series, which was taped at the studios of WHYY.

SOUL SEARCHING

The problems of the 1990–91 season prompted a lot of reevaluation. Subscription renewals were hit hard, declining from 80 to 63 percent. This meant that the marketing department had to find twelve thousand *new* subscribers to equal the attendance of the previous year. It was a bad time for the performing arts in general. The economy had taken a hit after the Gulf War, and conservative members of Congress, objecting to some controversial projects that the National Endowment for the Arts had funded, were trying to eliminate *all* federal funding for the arts. While the Walnut received very little government funding, the repercussions were already being felt in the theatre community—the Walnut's board minutes in November 1991 noted that the number of professional companies in Philadelphia declined precipitously, from twenty-three in 1987 to ten in 1991.[7]

The Walnut's strength lay in attracting a paying audience, and the problems of the 1990–91 season reaffirmed Bernard Havard's commitment to focusing on the audience's wants and needs. A study commissioned by the Pew Charitable Trusts in 1989 found that the Walnut's audience was essentially conservative. Most were not regular theatergoers. For many, the initial visit to the Walnut was their first experience with live theatre. The study concluded that the Walnut functioned as "an entry point for a large Prospect market interested in attending the theatre in Philadelphia."[8] The audience, which was 96 percent white, was generally affluent and lived in the suburbs. Sixty percent came from households with incomes of more than $50,000 a year. The majority were either Catholic or Jewish. According to the Pew study, they were interested in entertainment, liked the familiar, and had little interest in being challenged. They were not interested in new socially or politically relevant pieces, classics, Shakespeare, or works by minority artists. They wanted stories they could relate to and preferred musicals, comedies, and family fare.

Ultimately, Havard decided that the Walnut's goal should be to attract a broad audience to the theatre with the mainstage productions, and then lead them to works that were more challenging and innovative. To encourage the audience to explore and experiment, he actively promoted the Studio Series, which had been playing to half-empty houses. A new marketing program stressed the sense of adventure and excitement in the program. Attendance immediately increased, from 47 percent in 1991 to 74 percent in 1992. The highlight of the 1992 season was Will Stutts's one-man show *Walt Whitman*, which drew sold-out audiences. Stutts became a regular over the next several years, doing impersonations of Tallulah Bankhead, Noël Coward, Frank Lloyd Wright, and John Barrymore in pieces commissioned by the Walnut. Three productions that season all had local premieres: Elizabeth Forsythe Hailey's *Joanna's Husband, David's Wife*, Lee Blessing's *Down the Road*, and Sharman Macdonald's *When I Was a Girl, I Used to Scream and Shout*.

The following year, the Studio Series opened with *The Sum of Us*, by David Stevens, followed by *Mrs. Klein*, by Nicholas Wright. *Cries in the Night*, a family drama by Philadelphia newsman Michael Elkin, had a world premiere. *Brilliant Traces* was an eccentric piece about a runaway bride who takes refuge in an Alaska cabin. Will Stutts appeared in drag to play his cousin, Tallulah Bankhead, in his latest one-man show, *Tallulah*.

MAINSTAGE PRODUCTIONS

The 1991–92 season relied more on big-name performers than usual. Generally, Bernard Havard had avoided hiring stars, feeling that famous names detracted from the production itself. "Stars can destroy the integrity of the play and the sense of ensemble, while making excessive demands on the institution," he stated. But this season, several opportunities presented themselves. The first production was a one-woman show, *Shirley Valentine*, about a Liverpool matron who has a fling with a Greek fisherman during a vacation and decides to forsake her dreary life in Britain. With only a single salary to pay, he was able to secure veteran Broadway actress Millicent Martin for the role. The fortunes of the theatre really rebounded with the holiday musical, *Jesus Christ Superstar.* Early sales were so strong that the run was extended by a week. Attendees were encouraged to "stubscribe," using their ticket stubs as a discount on a season subscription. With aggressive promotion like this, subscriptions came close to matching the previous year's level.

In January 1992 George Peppard and Susan Clark appeared in *The Lion in Winter.* Both were returning to the stage after successful television careers—Peppard as the star of *The A-Team* and Clark in the sitcom *Webster.* Peppard provided enhancement money for the production, which he planned to tour after the run at the Walnut. A Neil Simon farce, *Rumors,* also did well at the box office. The season concluded with *Another Kind of Hero,* an original musical underwritten by board member Matt Garfield and written by Lezley Steele and E. A. Alexander that celebrated Raoul Wallenberg's action in saving thousands of Jews from the Nazi genocide.

A farce called *Lend Me a Tenor* opened the 1992–93 mainstage season in November. *Into the Woods,* a Stephen Sondheim musical based on several Brothers Grimm fairy tales, followed. Director Charles Abbott staged it in the style of English pantomime, with a man, James Rocco, playing the witch, and an African American actress, Sherry Boone, cast as Jack, the male lead. British director Toby Robertson was brought in to direct *The Old Devils,* a dark comedy set in a small Welsh village, based on a 1986 novel by Kingsley Amis. It was followed by *Henceforward,* an Alan Ayckbourn comedy about a composer who turns to a malfunctioning robot to act as nanny to his child. Frank Ferrante played the title role in *Groucho: A Life in Revue* to finish up the season. Subscriptions increased by seventeen hundred over the previous year, reaching a total of 34,500.

During the summer, *Twist,* an R&B version of *Oliver Twist,* had its world premiere at the Walnut. It featured a mostly black cast. Andrea McArdle, Broadway's original Annie, had a guest spot as Oliver's mother. Another black-oriented show, *Good Black Don't Crack,* played for two weeks in July.

OUTSIDE COMPANIES

Concerto Soloists board members approached Bernard Havard about taking on the accounting, marketing, and administrative functions of Marc Mostovoy's chamber orchestra. Mostovoy had been affiliated with the Walnut for nearly twenty years. There was some question whether the Walnut was spreading its resources too thin, but Wesler and Havard ultimately agreed to manage the company, in addition to their respective responsibilities at the Walnut.

The Red Heel Theatre began presenting at the Walnut in the fall of 1991. The company had been formed in New York in 1989 to "restore neglected masterpieces of classical theatre" and relocated to Philadelphia the following year. In the fall of 1991 it presented *The Mandrake* and *The Cenci*, returning the following season with *Fair Maid of the West* and *Life Is a Dream*, and, in the fall of 1993, *The Two Noble Kinsmen*, *La Bête*, and *The Changeling*. In 1994–95 the Red Heel offered *The Second Shepherd's Play* and *Medea*, and in 1996 produced *Deirdre of the Sorrows* and *The Butterfingers Angel*. Later that year, the company became the Philadelphia Shakespeare Festival.

Several other theatre groups presented acts at the Walnut's Theatre 5. Philip Roger Roy Productions had a successful five-month run of the comedy *Greater Tuna* during the 1990–91 season. The Vox Theatre presented *Lloyd's Prayer*, *The Madman and the Nun*, and *The Rose of Contention* in 1991–92, and returned with *Kvetch* the following fall. Theatre Ariel—a company specializing in Jewish dramas—presented *All That Our Eyes Have Witnessed*, *Punch Me in the Stomach*, and *10 x 10: A Minyan of Women*. Among the other small theatre companies that performed at the Walnut in the early 1990s were Shadowcast Theatre Works, DQD Theatre Company, Laughing Stock Theatre Company, Doorways to Lint, A Buncha Actors, Lantern Theatre Company, and Theatre International Exchange.

EDUCATIONAL INITIATIVES

The Walnut continued to expand its outreach activities. Under the leadership of Granville Burgess, the theatre school expanded its curriculum, offering training in commercial acting, screenwriting, and film acting. In 1991 the school introduced a lunchtime theatre series, which played on Tuesdays and Thursdays from January 19 through February 11 in the Filbert Courtyard of the Reading Terminal Market. Students from the Walnut theatre school performed scenes from Shakespeare's *As You Like It* and *Hamlet*, and Edgar Allan Poe's works "The Cask of Amontillado" and "The Raven."

The Walnut expanded its community outreach further with a program for elementary and middle school students called American Anthology, which dramatized the works of Edgar Allan Poe and Mark Twain. Some twenty-six thousand students watched the in-school productions, up from fourteen hundred only three years before. The Walnut's theatre school had an enrollment of more than a thousand students and offered day and evening classes, a summer camp, and a teen workshop.

BARRYMORE'S

The 1993–94 season marked the Walnut's tenth season as a producing house. Patrons could now visit Barrymore's, a new, polished wood and brass bar located in the lower lobby. Barrymore's was built in the tradition of British theatre bars, with an engraved mirror above the bar and walls adorned with theatre memorabilia depicting the influential Philadelphia acting family. The bar opened an hour before showtime and served sandwiches, pastries, and coffee drinks. Barrymore's was just one of the many improvements made possible by the $3 million capital campaign.

The opening production that season was *Jake's Women*, an autobiographical comedy by Neil Simon. It was followed by the musical *Me and My Girl*, a 1930s British comedy that had been successfully revived on Broadway in 1990. Susan Clark returned to the Walnut to star opposite Douglas Wing in *The Vortex*, an early dramatic work by Noël Coward. *Cyrano de Bergerac* followed in mid-March, with Alan Scarfe playing the legendary swordsman, philosopher, and wit. When it turned out that the Wilma Theater was also planning to mount the play, Havard invited the Wilma to co-produce with the Walnut, and the Wilma's artistic director, Jiri Zizka, directed the play. Finishing out the season was the musical *Pageant*, a satire of beauty contests featuring a cast of men playing the female contestants. Audience members selected the winner each night.

The studio season opened on January 4, 1994, with the world premiere of Paul Minx's *A Worm in the Heart*, a study of racism in the early years of the civil rights movement. Louis Fantasia played an orchestral musician in a one-man comedy, *The Double Bass*. Bernard Havard directed his first Walnut production, *Someone Who'll Watch over Me*, a drama about three hostages being held by terrorists in Lebanon. *About Time* featured veteran actors Jenny Turner and Donald Ewer. Will Stutts presented another one-man show, *Noël Coward at the Café de Paris*.

MARK SYLVESTER

In 1994 the Walnut acquired a talented young marketing director in the person of Mark Sylvester, whom Havard hired away from the Coconut Grove Playhouse in Miami. Sylvester had experience in both for-profit and nonprofit theatre, and he improved the Walnut's marketing. Under his direction the telemarketing department was streamlined, and he instituted a more cohesive marketing plan that emphasized selling the theatre itself, rather than just individual productions. He improved the artwork for the posters and brochures, giving the theatre an identifiable image in all its communications. Ticket sales increased dramatically. The seats for the mainstage productions grew from 73 percent of capacity in 1993–94 to 80 percent the following year, while attendance for studio shows jumped from 71 to 90 percent of capacity. The biggest increase came from single-ticket sales.

The season opener was a production of *Dracula*. Havard commissioned Granville Burgess to prepare a new stage adaptation of Bram Stoker's novel. When the resulting script proved too sexually charged with lesbian overtones, Havard went back to a 1971 version by Ted Tiller. Malcolm Black's direction emphasized the comic aspects of the melodrama. Karen K. Edissi got good reviews for the title role in *Mame*, the holiday musical. The January production, an original drama titled *Italian Funerals and Other Festive Occasions*, was heavily publicized in the Italian American community and generated one of the Walnut's top single-ticket sales of all time. The following production, *Conversations with My Father*, was promoted in the Jewish community and also did well. Alan Feinstein played a Russian-Jewish bar owner in the 1930s who tries to hide his heritage. *Lust*, a musical version of William Wycherly's Restoration comedy *The Country Wife*, had its American premiere at the Walnut before moving to New York for an off-Broadway run. It was written by the Heather Brothers, a team of four brothers who had been writing together for more than twenty years.

The Studio Series celebrated its tenth anniversary in 1995. Every production was sold out in subscriptions even before the season opened. Productions included *Shooting Simone*, which depicted the relationship between French philosophers Simone de Beauvoir and Jean-Paul Sartre. Harold Pinter's *The Caretaker* proved to be an acting triumph for Greg Wood, Michael Toner, and Donald Ewer. Jack Heifner's comedy *Vanities* followed a trio of 1960s cheerleaders from high school to adulthood. Will Stutts returned in another one-man show, *Barrymore! The Old Wicked Songs* explored the relationship between a Jewish piano prodigy and his anti-Semitic vocal coach, and won a Pulitzer Prize nomination for its playwright, Jon Marans. Frank Ferrante directed this world premiere. Before the season was over, Ken Wesler left the Walnut to manage the Grand Theatre in Wilmington, Delaware.

BARRYMORE AWARDS

In the fall of 1995 the first annual Barrymore Awards for Excellence in Theatre were announced by the Theatre Alliance of Greater Philadelphia. Ken Wesler and Bernard Havard had been heavily involved in organizing the awards, along with Aaron Posner, artistic director of the Arden Theatre Company. Philadelphia's theatrical community gathered at the Annenberg

Center to honor their own. The F. Otto Haas Award was a $10,000 cash prize given to an emerging Philadelphia theatre artist. *Lust* was nominated for best musical, as was its director, Bob Carlton, and star, Denis Lawson. Lawson won the Barrymore Award as Best Actor in a Musical for his portrayal of the rascally Horner.

Surpluses from the previous season were funneled back into the production budget to improve production values. Inventive stage effects and gore were the appeal of *Blood Money*, a British thriller by the Heather Brothers that opened the 1995–96 season. The play, which had its American premiere at the Walnut, was about a game show host and his actress wife who are terrorized in their home. Originally produced at England's Derby Playhouse, the play was reset in Bucks County. The Derby's artistic director, Mark Clements, directed Alan Feinstein and Kathleen Doyle. The holiday production was *The Wizard of Oz*, adapted from the motion picture screenplay and featuring the familiar songs of Harold Arlen and Yip Harburg. Kelli Rabke played Dorothy and Charles Antalosky played the wizard. Dozens of local youngsters were hired to play Munchkins. *Philadelphia, Here I Come* returned in January and February. The original production had had its American debut at the Walnut thirty years earlier during a Broadway tryout. Oliver Goldsmith's eighteenth-century comedy *She Stoops to Conquer* followed. The *Inquirer* dismissed it as a period artifact, and attendance was disappointing.

The highlight of the 1995–96 season was the season closer, *Cabaret*. Charles Abbott took time away from directing to give a "bravura performance as the smarmy Emcee," in the words of the *Inquirer*'s reviewer, Clifford A. Ridley.[9] The production received eight Barrymore nominations and won the award for Outstanding Production of a Musical. Barrymore Awards also went to director Bruce Lumpkin, star Charles Abbott, supporting actress Taina Elg, and costume designers Michael Bottari and Ronald Case.

In Studio 3, Susan Miller starred in *My Left Breast*, a one-woman show about a cancer survivor. Donald Ewer played an old actor planning a comeback in *The Return of Herbert Bracewell*. Kathleen Doyle garnered rave reviews as the whiskey-voiced, chain-smoking single mother in Paul Zindel's 1965 Pulitzer Prize–winning *The Effect of Gamma Rays on Man-in-the-Moon Marigolds*. She won a Barrymore for Leading Actress in a Play for her role, while the play received a nomination for Best Play. Tom Teti and Tom McCarthy portrayed the friendship between the late baseball commissioner Bart Giamatti and his assistant and successor, former Columbia Pictures chairman Fay Vincent, in *Bart and Fay*, which had its world premiere. Will Stutts closed out the studio season with his latest one-man show, *Frank Lloyd Wright*, which Havard commissioned.

A third musical was added to the lineup for the 1996–97 season. Musicals cost nearly twice as much as straight plays to produce, but Havard and his senior staff determined that they were financially able to do so. Audiences grew from 81 percent capacity the previous year to 89 percent, with visitors topping a quarter-million that year, and the surplus was plowed back into more elaborate stage productions. The opening show was *Paper Moon,* a musical adaptation of the 1973 film. It was a co-production with Goodspeed Opera House. The musical had previously premiered at New Jersey's Paper Mill Playhouse but was completely reworked for the run at the Walnut. Shortly after it opened, the Walnut was honored by the dedication of the official state marker honoring the Walnut Street Theatre, which identified its place in American theatre history.

Camelot, starring James Brennan as King Arthur, played during the Christmas season and set box office records. It was followed by Neil Simon's *Laughter on the 23rd Floor* in January. Frank Ferrante directed this comedy about television comedy writers and starred as Max Prince, Simon's alter ego. During the run, Ferrante reprised his role as Groucho Marx for a one-night performance. Sheridan's eighteenth-century comedy *The Rivals* was reset in the roaring 1920s, in a co-production with England's Derby Playhouse. The Derby's artistic director, Mark Clements, directed a half-British and half-American cast. It was the first time British and American Equity actors had collaborated on a non-Shakespearean production. Most of the actors in the season-closer, *1776,* were from Philadelphia. James Brennan starred as John Adams, with Charles Antalosky as Ben Franklin and David Hess as Thomas Jefferson. The Walnut's longtime stage manager, Frank Anzalone, directed his first mainstage show. The set was a replica of Independence Hall.

The Walnut studio season opened with Josslyn Luckett in her one-woman show *Chronicles of a Comic Mulatta.* David Ogden Stiers, best known for his role as Major Winchester on the sitcom *M*A*S*H,* directed the next production, *Autumn Canticle,* which explored a relationship between two gay musicians, based on composer Benjamin Britten and his lover, tenor Peter Pears. David Mamet's *Oleanna* depicted a college professor who is accused of sexual harassment when he attempts to help a failing co-ed. William Roudebush received a Barrymore nomination for his direction, as did Greg Wood and Maggie Siff for their performances. *Faith Healer* followed a traveling preacher through Wales and Scotland. William Leach received a Barrymore nomination for his portrayal of the faith healer. Will Stutts wrote and directed *Kemble vs. Butler,* a historical drama commissioned by the Walnut about Fanny Kemble and her husband, which closed the season.

The Barrymore Awards were held at the Walnut that year. Bruno Kirby and Karen Hinton hosted the awards ceremony, held on October 20, 1997. James Brennan was nominated for his roles in both *Camelot* and *1776,* and took home the award for Best Actor in a Musical for his role as John Adams in the latter. Charles Antalosky received a Barrymore for Best Supporting Actor in a Musical for his performance as Benjamin Franklin in *1776.* The Lifetime Achievement Award that year went to Walnut regular Doug Wing. Sadly, Wing had passed away from cancer only a few days earlier. He had worked as an actor in the Philadelphia area for more than forty years, and was featured in productions on the Walnut's mainstage and in Studio 3. Later that year, Philadelphia also lost Laurie Beechman, who had been battling ovarian cancer.

CAPITAL CAMPAIGN, ACT II

In the fall of 1997 the Walnut announced a new capital campaign to raise $1 million for new seats and carpeting in the auditorium, and to expand the ladies' restrooms. Women gave especially generously to this campaign. Tony Award winner Donna McKechnie, known for her role as Cassie in the original production of *A Chorus Line,* played the title role in the 1997–98 season opener, the Neil Simon/Marvin Hamlisch musical *The Goodbye Girl.* The holiday musical, *Crazy for You,* featured the songs of George and Ira Gershwin, which were integrated into a new story by playwright Ken Ludwig. Ludwig also penned *Moon over Buffalo,* a backstage farce about a second-rate theatre troupe stuck in Buffalo, which opened in January.

The most significant play of the season was a stage adaptation of Harper Lee's Pulitzer Prize–winning novel *To Kill a Mockingbird,* which played through March and April. It was produced in collaboration with New Jersey's George Street Playhouse and Florida's Coconut Grove Playhouse. The play proved to be extraordinarily popular: single-ticket sales were the highest ever for a drama at the Walnut. Will Stutts played the lawyer Atticus Finch, while upstairs in the Walnut's studio theatre, Stutts's original play *The Gift* examined the writing of *To Kill a Mockingbird.* Without directly referring to Harper Lee or her novel, the play suggested that Lee's novel was actually rewritten by her close friend, Truman Capote. Closing out the mainstage season was a British musical, *Blood Brothers,* about fraternal twins separated at birth and raised in different social classes. It was nominated for several Barrymore Awards, including Best Musical. Susan Dawn Carson received a Barrymore for Best Leading Actress in a Musical.

In the studio theatre, William Leach did a one-man performance of *A Christmas Carol,* acting out all the roles in the Charles Dickens classic. The third-floor studio received a new name, Independence Studio, on 3. Sonja Robson and Pearce Bunting co-starred in Harold Pinter's one-act play *The Lover*, and Sally Mercer starred as a woman who wakes up after twenty-nine years in *A Kind of Alaska*. *Shylock* explored the issues of playing Shakespeare's most problematic character. William Leach played both the character and the actor. Kim Hunter headed up the cast in *Greytop in Love*, which included her husband, Bob Emmett. Frank Ferrante finished out the season as playwright George S. Kaufman in his one-man show *By George!*

The Barrymore Award ceremonies returned to the Walnut in the fall of 1998. David Ogden Stiers and Jilline Ringle hosted the event. Walnut productions received thirteen nominations. Susan Dawn Carson won the award for Leading Actress in a Musical for her role in *Blood Brothers*, and Mary Jane Houdina won for her choreography for *Crazy for You*. Former board president Frank C. P. McGlinn was recognized for his many contributions to the theatre with a Lifetime Achievement Award.

A SEASON OF DRAMA

The contract with the stagehands' union was up again in 1998, and the Walnut entered into negotiations with the union with the idea of putting the contract in line with other nonprofit theatres. Havard and the board decided to go for broke and sustain a strike if they had to. Mayor Ed Rendell and his deputy mayor for labor became involved in the negotiations, which were tied to an agreement with the City at the Convention Center. The Walnut was successful in removing departmentalization. The theatre's first official Web site also came online.

Triumph of Love opened the 1998–99 mainstage season. It was a musical version of an eighteenth-century comedy by the French playwright Marivaux. Despite good songs and strong performances by Jennifer Lee Andrews and James Brennan, the show was hampered by a somewhat dated plot. Cole Porter's score was the reason to see the holiday musical *Anything Goes*, a lightweight 1934 comedy set aboard an ocean liner. It featured a collection of Porter classics, including "You're the Top" and "I Get a Kick Out of You" from the original production, and several others from other Cole Porter musicals.

Marina Sirtis, best known as Counselor Troi on *Star Trek: The Next Generation*, was featured in Neil Simon's *Hotel Suite*, which opened the new year. The play was a selection of scenes from Simon's previous hotel plays—*Plaza Suite*, *California Suite*, and *London Suite*. Malcolm Black directed Edward Albee's Pulitzer Prize–winning drama *Three Tall Women*, with outstanding performances by M'el Dowd, Grace Gonglewski, and Alice White. The season finished with a musical production of *Grand Hotel*, best remembered from the 1932 MGM film version starring Greta Garbo and Lionel Barrymore. Set in Germany just before World War I, the production featured period costumes designed by Santo Loquasto and a magnificent set by John Ferrell depicting the lobby of Berlin's poshest hotel. The set, props, and costumes were later toured to the Pittsburgh Civic Light Opera, the Theatre Under the Stars in Houston, and the Fifth Avenue Theatre in Seattle. Most of the principals performed at each venue.

Will Stutts starred in *Holiday Memories*, which played in the Independence Studio on 3 from Thanksgiving through Christmas. He was named director of the Walnut's theatre school. The regular studio season opened in January with a production of Jean Genet's *The Maids*. Two African American men—Forrest McClendon and Kirk Wendell Brown—played the maids, while E. Ashley Izard played their mistress. *Portrait of a Nude*, by Laura Shamas, and *Orphans*, a 1985 play by Lyle Kessler set in North Philadelphia, followed. Will Stutts penned *Oscar Wilde's Lover*, which starred Dan Olmstead as Wilde and Paul Soileau as his lover, Lord Alfred Douglas. Bernard Havard directed William Leach and Karen Hinton in David Hare's London hit *Skylight*.

MAXIMIZING OUT

The Walnut was now a $7 million annual operation. A full 91 percent of its operating budget was generated from ticket sales and theatre rentals—an extraordinary figure in the nonprofit world, where many theatres depend on donations for more than half their income. Subscriptions reached fifty thousand in the 1998–99 season.

The Walnut had experienced tremendous growth since becoming a producing theatre in 1983. No other theatre in the United States could match the size of its subscription audience, and few could match the total attendance of 280,000. Mainstage and studio shows played to nearly 90 percent capacity. That figure had remained static, but the number of performances had been increased. Mainstage shows played for seven weeks, with the holiday musical playing an additional two weeks to accommodate single-ticket buyers. The season had been extended as long as it could be—from Labor Day to the Fourth of July. It would be extremely difficult to increase the audience much more.

In January 1998 Bernard Havard tapped Mark Sylvester to be the Walnut's general manager. Sylvester had had considerable success improving the theatre's marketing efforts. Now he would be responsible for the business side of the operation, and he turned his attention to controlling costs and streamlining operations, to make the best use of the resources they had.

The managers realized that the period of extraordinary growth was over. The facilities were already strained. There was very little room for classes, which often had to be held in hallways and executive offices. As they began to plan for the new millennium, they recognized that their focus needed to change. They needed to find a way to bring in new income and audiences while continuing to serve the fifty thousand people who supported the theatre through subscriptions. In January 1999 the Walnut organized a board retreat to consider the options.

One possibility was to expand the physical plant. The lot directly east of the theatre was a parking lot. The land was owned by two different owners: one portion was held by a consortium of real estate developers, while the other was owned by the Catholic Church. Havard and incoming board chairman Lou Fryman began looking into the possibility of buying the property and building a new wing. Havard envisioned a three- to four-hundred-seat theatre-in-the-round, a multistory parking structure, and retail space. Such a building would provide more office space for the staff, classroom facilities for the school, and adequate rehearsal space.

The other option was to increase donated income. Havard's emphasis on producing popular plays that would appeal to a broad audience limited its appeal to foundation and government funders, which tended to support more "groundbreaking" and "cutting-edge" work. The Walnut's most reliable funders, the William Penn Foundation and the Pew Charitable Trusts, had cut back on their support. The Walnut's new director of development, Rebekah Sassi, wanted to get board members more involved. They had been very successful in helping to bring in corporate and individual donations for capital improvements. As the second capital campaign was winding down, it was time to enlist the board's help in raising funds for day-to-day operations—to share ideas on fund-raising possibilities, to articulate fund-raising goals and strategies, and to make fund-raising more fun and interesting.

THE RETURN OF EDWIN FORREST

In the spring of 1999, Edwin Forrest returned to the theatre where he had gotten his start. The great statue of Forrest as Coriolanus, which had been commissioned by fans of the great tragedian in 1863, was held by the Historical Society of Pennsylvania. The Historical Society rethought its mission and decided to deaccess its collection of paintings and statuary. It offered the statue to the Freedom Theatre, which occupied Forrest's former home on Broad and Master streets, but the cost of reinforcing the floor to support the 5.5-ton statue was too great, and the Freedom Theatre declined the gift. Bernard Havard fought very hard to bring the statue to the Walnut, petitioning the Orphan's Court, which had jurisdiction over Pennsylvania nonprofits. Judge Arlin Mc-

Adams determined that the statue should be offered to the Walnut and further ruled that the Historical Society, which had been provided funds from the Edwin Forrest Trust for its upkeep, had to give up part of the money to have the statue moved and installed in the Walnut. The lobby floor was reinforced, and the statue was officially unveiled on Edwin Forrest's birthday, March 9, 1999, following the annual laying of a wreath on Forrest's grave at St. Paul's churchyard. The great tragedian would have been 193 years old. There was a lavish buffet in the Walnut's lobby for the hundred or so officials and guests who attended the wreath-laying ceremony.

Three months later, on June 8, 1999, the Pennsylvania House of Representatives recognized the Walnut's historic significance by passing a resolution declaring it the official State Theatre of Pennsylvania. That summer, the Walnut underwent a major facelift. In his new position as general manager, Mark Sylvester spearheaded the renovations. New seats were installed in the auditorium, which provided more legroom. New carpeting was put in place. Lighting and sound equipment was upgraded. Throughout the house, several improvements made the theatre more accessible, including special seating and a handicap-accessible restroom on the main floor. The ladies' restroom facilities were more than doubled. The exterior façade was thoroughly cleaned, sealed, and repainted. The backstage area was also renovated—dressing rooms received new carpeting, paint, and lighting. The lighting booth was moved from the back of the orchestra to the balcony, and the empty booth was converted into a luxury box for corporate donors. The colors of the auditorium were changed from brown to a more appealing purple and gray, with maroon seats and a deep blue floor. In the offices, new computers were installed and networked together. The entire renovation was completed in six weeks during the summer of 1999. The Walnut was ready for its new role as the State Theatre of Pennsylvania.

THE STATE THEATRE OF PENNSYLVANIA, 2000 AND BEYOND

It was the opening night of the 1999–2000 season. Members of the Walnut's board of trustees arrived shortly before four in the afternoon for the first board meeting of the season. Meetings were timed to coincide with the opening night of each mainstage production, and once business was taken care of, board members enjoyed cocktails and a buffet dinner before attending the show. There were some important issues to discuss that afternoon, and most of the thirty-six board members were present. They were joined in the fourth-floor rehearsal studio by the Walnut's senior staff—producing artistic director Bernard Havard, general manager Mark Sylvester, director of development Rebekah Sassi, and the Walnut's controller, Len Karabell.

Board chairman Lou Fryman called the meeting to order, and Havard led off with the financial reports. Single-ticket sales for that night's production, *Buddy*, were strong, helped along by a new radio ad campaign. Subscriptions were ahead of the previous year, and Havard expected to break the fifty thousand mark for the second time. The 1998–99 season had been a good one. Preliminary results from the annual audit showed a $572,000 surplus on a total budget of $11 million.

Various committee chairs gave their reports. Marty Spector, head of the Membership Committee, introduced two new board members—Lisa Binder, president of the Retail Division of Mellon Bank, and Dr. Fred Balduini, an orthopedic surgeon specializing in sports medicine. Al Giagnacova, chair of the Education Committee, reported on the search for a new education director. The responsibilities of the director of the theatre school were being expanded, and the committee was looking for someone with experience in community outreach. Susan Nicodemus Quinn, a former acting apprentice at the Walnut who had gone on to manage a children's theatre company, would soon join the Walnut's staff in this position. There were updates from Terry Loscalzo on the Gala Committee's preparations for the silent auction and the spring gala.

The major order of business of this meeting was the expansion plan. Fryman and Havard had been in touch with one of the primary owners of the property next door. They had contacted a developer, and plans were being drafted for a primarily residential building, which would also meet the theatre's needs for a second stage, rehearsal space, housing for actors, and possibly some retail space. Havard had a theatre architect, Barton Myers, with whom he had worked before, advising on the project. The Pennsylvania Assembly had appropriated $5 million toward construction of a new building, on the condition that the Walnut come up with a match. There were obstacles, however. Fryman had contacted the Catholic archdiocese about selling its half of the property and learned that the decision had to be approved by the Vatican. Income from the property supported St. Edmund's Home, which cared for physically and mentally handicapped children, and the church was not eager to give up its income from the parking lot.

Havard concluded the meeting with the plans for the upcoming season. The studio was celebrating its fifteenth season, and he had made the final selections. Will Stutts was reviving his one-man show, *Noël Coward in the Café de Paris,* to commemorate the hundredth anniversary of Coward's birth. Havard had also commissioned Stutts to create a one-man show about Edwin Forrest, which would go up in February. Among the other plays that would be presented was a two-character drama by Donald Margulies, *Collected Stories,* which Richard Parison, Havard's assistant in the Artistic Office, would direct. Ellen Tobie, one of the board members present, would play the lead. Frank Anzalone, the Walnut's production stage manager, would direct Donald Ewer in a new comedy, *Visiting Mr. Green.*

Havard announced a new children's theatre series that would begin in December. TheatreWorks USA, a nationally known children's theatre troupe, would present *Sundiata: The Lion King of Mali* for three matinee performances on Saturday, December 11. Two other shows, *Ramona Quimby* and *The Frog Prince,* were scheduled later in the season. The series was made economically viable by an agreement concluded with the stagehands' union the previous winter. Union rules were changed so that Havard could bring in a separate stage crew to work during the day. A daytime children's series could be produced without sending the regular crew into costly overtime.

The Walnut was developing an original musical, *Camila,* about a woman from a prominent Argentine family who falls in love with a Jesuit priest. The author-composer, Lori McKelvey, would be in town in October for two weeks of workshops. If the show proved to be good, it would be slotted into the 2001–2 season.

That concluded the formal part of the meeting. The rest of the time was given over to an enrichment session. Frank Anzalone gave a slideshow charting the productions in the seventeen years since the Walnut became a producing theatre. Anzalone was in a position to know—he had worked as stage manager on every mainstage show since 1983. At half past five the meeting concluded, and the trustees went down to the Langworthy Lounge for drinks and dinner before the evening's performance.

A SEASON TO CELEBRATE

The show that night was *Buddy*, a musical tribute to rock-and-roll legend Buddy Holly. Christopher Sutton starred as the bespectacled singer-songwriter. Nick Anselmo and William Laney played Ritchie Valens and the Big Bopper—the two musicians who died with Holly when their small plane crashed after a concert. The musical featured all the big Buddy Holly hits—"That'll Be the Day," "Peggy Sue," and "Rave On"—as well as Valens's "La Bamba" and the Big Bopper's "Chantilly Lace." The actors played their own instruments and had people dancing in the aisles. Despite *Buddy*'s tragic ending, the audience was on its feet at the curtain demanding an encore, which the actors happily provided.

The holiday musical was *Phantom*—not the familiar Andrew Lloyd Webber musical but a lesser-known work by playwright Arthur Kopit and composer Maury Yeston. Many considered it a finer piece—wittier and more intelligent, with a stronger musical score. Nat Chandler played the horribly disfigured Phantom, with Kristin Carbone as the young soprano he abducts from the Paris Opera House. The show received standing ovations at every preview. When *Phantom* failed to be nominated for any Barrymore Award, Havard withdrew the Walnut from consideration, challenging the process by which productions were selected. "They don't have many qualified nominators," Havard told the *Inquirer*, noting, "It's been a problem for several years, and it's only gotten worse."[1] Actors, directors, and designers complained that their work at the Walnut was unjustifiably neglected, and Havard felt that the nominators were prejudiced against the populist works the Walnut was producing. The issue was resolved within a few weeks, when the Philadelphia Theatre Alliance agreed to review its nominating process and to set up new procedures for appeals. *Phantom* was nominated in several categories, including Best Overall Production of a Musical.

The other mainstage shows that season included *The Last Night of Ballyhoo*, the Tony Award–winning comedy-drama about a highly assimilated

Jewish family living in Atlanta just before World War II who are preparing for "Ballyhoo," a lavish cotillion sponsored by their country club. The play was a co-production with Totem Pole Playhouse, a summer theatre in Fayetteville, Pennsylvania. The show's playwright, Alfred Uhry, received the Edwin Forrest Award that year, along with Paul Beideman of Mellon Bank. *The Heiress* was a 1947 dramatization of Henry James's novel *Washington Square,* which had recently been revived on Broadway. Grace Gonglewski played an awkward spinster who is wooed by a dashing fortune hunter. The season finished with the musical *La Cage aux Folles.* Jeffrey Coon played a young man who brings his fiancée and her parents to meet his father—who happens to be gay. Dan Schiff played the father, the owner of a gay nightclub, and Jamie Torcellini was the father's flamboyant cross-dressing lover. The season was successful both artistically and financially, and the theatre projected a surplus of more than half a million dollars.

THE ROLE OF NONPROFIT THEATRE

There is a common misconception that nonprofit theatres should not show a profit. This stems from a basic misunderstanding of the role of nonprofit organizations. Nonprofits are entitled to make a profit; they just cannot distribute that profit to shareholders. Any profits the Walnut made were plowed back into the theatre, either as capital improvements to the property or as part of the endowment. While for-profit theatres exist to make money for investors, nonprofits serve a higher purpose. The stated mission of the Walnut was "to sustain the tradition of professional theatre and contribute to its future viability and vitality." The Walnut fulfilled its mission in four ways: through the production and presentation of professional theatre; through the encouragement, training, and development of artists; through the development of diverse audiences; and through the preservation and chronicling of its theatre building.

The board of trustees existed to ensure that the Walnut's mission was being carried out, while meeting its fiduciary responsibilities. A theatre cannot continue to fulfill its mission unless it remains financially sound. Keeping a theatre operating in the black is no easy task, as this history has certainly shown. Competitive pressure on the theatre has rarely been greater than it is in the early twenty-first century. The Walnut was not simply competing against other theatres but against an entire array of amusement options—movies, live sporting events, television, concerts, the Internet, travel, dining out, and so on. When consumers have a choice of so many leisure activities, theatres must be able to offer the public something entertaining and exciting.

The cost of operating a 1,076-seat theatre in a historic structure with seven unions, including the cast and crew, required that management be prudent about the level of risk to which the theatre was exposed. Risk was incurred each time the performance schedule was expanded, a show was extended, the productions grew more ambitious, or the Walnut took on a new educational initiative. By becoming a producing house, not just a theatre that presented touring shows, the Walnut embraced risk, but it did so in a financially responsible manner.

Like other theatres of its size, the Walnut has had to adopt the outlook and methods of the for-profit sector. Populism was essential to the Walnut's ability to operate in a fiscally sound manner. For Havard, the challenge was to plan seasons that were both exciting to the audience and challenging to the artists—to produce work that had broad general appeal and real entertainment value at the highest standards possible. Studies have shown that less than 5 percent of the American public attends the theatre in any given year. Havard saw the Walnut's role as introducing live theatre to the other 95 percent.

As the Walnut's annual budget had grown to more than $10 million, Havard needed to rely more and more on his senior staff. All areas of the theatre had to be working effectively to the same end. Putting up a show was just the beginning. The operation also required professional marketing, with well-produced promotional materials, careful list building, a targeted advertising campaign, and relentless telemarketing efforts to drive subscription sales. Earned revenue had to be supplemented with contributed income, particularly in the areas of corporate and individual fund-raising. The Walnut's development staff had to make a clear and compelling case why subscribers needed to contribute. Some of this came from the community and educational programming the theatre provided—its Touring Outreach Program, its Adopt-a-School Program—as well as the activities designed to nurture and develop local theatre artists—the theatre school and the professional apprenticeship program. Another part of the picture was the ongoing effort to emphasize the Walnut's historic significance by supporting the writing of its history and acquiring important pieces of memorabilia related to its past.

Havard delegated much of the day-to-day running of the theatre to Mark Sylvester, who was promoted to the position of managing director. In this position, Sylvester oversaw all of the daily operations of the theatre, including finance, personnel, operations, and maintenance, and worked with the various department heads to keep the organization running efficiently. He negotiated the actors' and directors' contracts, letting Havard concentrate on the artistic decisions, board relations, and long-range planning.

Havard made the decisions on programming both the mainstage and studio shows. The format for the mainstage season evolved over the years. The season opener was always a musical—usually a lesser-known or more experimental one. This was Havard's one opportunity, apart from the Independence Studio on 3, to be challenging and experimental, and he tried to uncover and present overlooked classics. The 2000–2001 season opened with *Rags,* a collaboration between Stephen Schwartz, the lyricist of *Godspell* and *Pippin,* and Charles Strouse, the composer of *Annie.* The book by Joseph Stein followed Rebecca Hershkowitz, a Jewish immigrant from Russia (played by Betsi Morrison), as she struggles to make a place for herself in New York City at the turn of the twentieth century. *Rags* had had only a short run on Broadway in 1986, but it had gained many fans in the intervening years from its cast album and numerous regional productions.

The holiday musical was always a family-oriented show, designed to bring a broad audience into the theatre. December was a time when parents took their kids to the theatre, and Havard looked for something that would appeal to all ages. Because the holiday show ran two weeks longer than other productions, Havard counted on single-ticket sales to fill those extra weeks. In 2000, *Singin' in the Rain* filled the holiday slot. Christopher Sutton had the Gene Kelly role in this stage adaptation of the famed MGM movie musical, with Jennifer Piech in the role identified with Debbie Reynolds and Michael Tapley in the Donald O'Connor part. The highlight of the production was the onstage rainstorm—two, actually: one for the close of the first act, in which Sutton performed the famous "singin' and dancin' in the rain" sequence, and a larger downpour for the finale. Approximately five hundred gallons of heated water were used for each show, covering an area as wide as the stage, thirty-two by fourteen feet.

The third and fourth selections were straight plays. Neil Simon plays had proved popular over the years, and for the 2000–2001 season Havard elected to go with *The Sunshine Boys.* Seventy-eight-year-old Irwin Charone and eighty-two-year-old Michael Marcus played Willie Clark and Al Lewis, two retired vaudeville comics brought together by Willie's nephew Ben, played by Frank Ferrante, who also directed the show. The drama opened in March. Havard would often go with a period piece, something that required elaborate sets and costumes. In 2001 he selected *Gaslight,* the 1938 thriller by British playwright Patrick Hamilton, most familiar from the 1944 George Cukor film starring Ingrid Bergman and Charles Boyer. Sally Mercer played Mrs. Manningham, whose husband, played by John Bourgeois, conspires to drive her insane. Set in nineteenth-century London, the production showed off the design and construction skills of the Walnut's technical crew, with elaborate period costumes designed by Hilary Corbett and Victorian interiors designed by Paul Wonsek and lit by Jerold Forsyth.

The mainstage season concluded with a third musical—something with built-in audience appeal that could be extended into the summer and would encourage people to look forward to the fall season. The choice needed to be as recognizable as the holiday musical, but with more mature content. Closing out the 2000–2001 mainstage season was *A Chorus Line*, the 1975 Tony Award–winning musical about Broadway chorus dancers. Director Mitzi Hamilton re-created Michael Bennett's original choreography, and the production used the original set and costume designs of Robin Wagner and Theoni Aldredge.

THE STUDIO SEASON AND THREE-MUSICAL PACKAGE

With the fall season in place, Bernard Havard spent July and August reviewing the selections for the winter's studio season. When it came to programming the studio theatre, Havard could be more daring. Scripts came from a variety of sources. Havard might be intrigued by a review in *Backstage*, *Variety*, or *London Stage*. Some scripts were submitted by actors who were interested in playing a specific role or by directors interested in a specific project. Havard solicited new plays from playwrights he had worked with before. The theatre got its fair share of unsolicited manuscripts as well. Occasionally Havard would commission new works, indulging his interest in history while supporting local playwrights.

Havard and his assistant reviewed studio productions during the spring and had a slate of possible titles by the beginning of summer, firming up the lineup by September. The 2001 studio season opened with a pair of Eugene O'Neill one-acts, *Before Breakfast* and *Hughie*. These were followed by Tennessee Williams's *Two-Character Play*, which featured Will Stutts and Gale Zoë Garnett, and A. R. Gurney's family drama *Children*. Stutts also premiered a new work, *Eye of the Storm*, a biography of Judge Frank Johnson Jr., an important figure in the civil rights movement. The season finished off with the Tom Jones and Harvey Schmidt musical *I Do! I Do!*—which was marketed in conjunction with the last two mainstage musicals as a "Three-Musical Sampler." The run was extended to five weeks to accommodate the larger audience that the money-saving sampler drew to the smaller venue.

The Walnut tried to support the rest of the theatrical community by renting out its fifth-floor studio. Studio 5 was a fifty-two-seat black box theatre, rented between the last week of August and the first week of July to local theatre companies that did not have a home of their own. The cost was $500 per week, and they had to rent it for two consecutive weeks. Several troupes made regular use of the studio theatre, among them Luna Theatre Company, Exclamation Theatre, Hunger Theatre, Vox Theatre Company, Intrepid Theatre, and 1812 Productions.

A SEASON OF PASSION

Another way that the Walnut supported the theatrical community was by developing works by new playwrights and composers, like *Camila*, which opened the 2001–2 season. It was the first major production for the show's composer, lyricist, and librettist, Lori McKelvey. Elizabeth Sastre played a historical figure, Camila O'Gorman, an aristocratic woman who falls in love with a young priest, played by Michael Hayden. The show opened on September 12, the night following the terrorist attacks on the World Trade Center in New York. Havard was determined to keep the show going despite the tragedy. "I was born in London during the 1941 Blitz," he told a columnist from the *Philadelphia Daily News*. "During the Second World War, a theater only closed when it got bombed. My parents' attitude was: Don't let the bastards win. I am determined not to let the bastards win."[2] During a curtain speech before the show, board president Lou Fryman dedicated the world premiere performance to the men and women who had lost their lives in the attacks.

The audience needed a pick-me-up after the events of 9/11, and the Walnut was fortunate in having chosen Lerner and Loewe's classic *My Fair Lady* as the holiday show. James Brennan played Professor Henry Higgins and Jessica Boevers played Eliza Doolittle, the Cockney girl he trains to speak and act like a high-born lady. More than 73,000 people saw the show, a record attendance for the Walnut. That year, the Walnut began a tradition of offering Charles Dickens's *A Christmas Carol* for several matinee performances in December. In 2001 the production played within the sets that were already onstage for *My Fair Lady*.

Bernard Havard made his mainstage directorial debut in January with *Art*, a French comedy about three art connoisseurs—played by Carl Schurr, Robert Ari, and Ben Lipitz—whose friendship is tested when one of them pays an exorbitant amount of money for an abstract painting that appears to be a plain white canvas. Havard had seen the play in London the previous year and was determined to bring it to the Walnut. The drama that year was *Great Expectations*, a co-production with England's Derby Playhouse. The Derby's artistic director, Mark Clements, adapted the Dickens novel for the stage and directed the international cast. *Damn Yankees*, the classic Adler and Ross musical adaptation of the Faust legend, closed out the season. Dan Schiff and Erik Lautier both played Joe Hardy, an aging fan of the Washington Senators who is transformed into a star outfielder when he sells his soul to the devil. Jamie Torcellini played the sinister Mr. Applegate (the devil), with Darcie Roberts as the seductive Lola, the devil's temptress.

The 2002 studio season featured *Elegy,* a story about a Holocaust survivor who struggles to forget his past; *Brief Lives,* a biography of the English author John Aubrey; a pair of Noël Coward one-acts titled *A Suite in Two Keys;* a drama, *Wenceslas Square,* about a professor who returns to Czechoslovakia during the artistic flowering of the 1970s; and the musical *Forever Plaid,* about members of a doo-wop group who are killed in a car accident but return to earth to perform a concert they were always meant to do.

During the Barrymore Awards ceremony in 2002, the Walnut failed to receive any awards, although it received several nominations in the acting category. When the following year's nominations were announced, *My Fair Lady* failed to garner any, and Bernard Havard recommended to the Walnut's Executive Committee that the Walnut withdraw from consideration for the Barrymores. The problem, as he saw it, was that the number of productions being considered had grown significantly, demanding a considerable time commitment from nominators and judges. Havard questioned the quality of the judges, feeling that the Theatre Alliance was selecting judges on the basis of their availability, not because they had the requisite experience. Moreover, the Theatre Alliance, which gave out the awards, had abandoned its appeals process, which was instituted in response to the Walnut's complaint two years earlier. Havard argued that if funders and subscribers saw that the Walnut participated in the award process but was not receiving any awards, they might conclude that the quality of the programming was somehow lacking. The board concurred, and at the end of the season the Walnut withdrew from the Barrymore Awards, although it remained involved in the Theatre Alliance.

A SEASON TO CHERISH

The Walnut continued to offer world-class productions of overlooked or forgotten gems. *She Loves Me,* an early work by Jerry Bock and Sheldon Harnick, the team that created *Fiddler on the Roof,* occupied the first slot of the 2002–3 season. It was a co-production with Maine State Music Theatre. Brigid Brady played a lonely sales clerk who carries on a romantic correspondence with a man who turns out to be her fellow-employee, whom she despises. James Brennan directed the show, then returned to play the part of Captain von Trapp in the holiday musical, Rodgers and Hammerstein's *The Sound of*

fig. 37 Harley Granville-Barker's drama of manners and morals, *The Voysey Inheritance,* was part of the Walnut's 2002–3 season. The cast included Sara Pauley and Paxton Whitehead, shown here.

Music. Luann Aronson co-starred as Maria, the former nun hired to take care of the von Trapp children, who falls in love with the captain.

Neil Simon's *Brighton Beach Memoirs* was the comedy, the first of a semi-autobiographical trilogy recalling his childhood. Jesse Bernstein played fourteen-year-old Eugene Jerome, Simon's alter ego. Bernstein would return the following two seasons to reprise the role in *Biloxi Blues* and *Broadway Bound,* the last two shows in the trilogy. Frank Ferrante directed the cast, which was made up entirely of local actors, a first for a Walnut mainstage show.

The Voysey Inheritance occupied the drama spot that season. Few people had heard of the 1905 drama by British playwright Harley Granville-Barker, but it was a play that Bernard Havard had wanted to do for a long time. The recent scandal involving the energy firm Enron made this play about financial improprieties timely. Paxton Whitehead returned to the Walnut for the first time since 1979 to play Mr. Voysey, the head of a British investment firm trying to stave off bankruptcy, with Canadian actor Blair Williams playing his conscience-ridden son, who is drawn into his father's financial improprieties.

Evita, the Andrew Lloyd Webber–Tim Rice musical about Eva Peron, the charismatic wife of Argentine strongman Juan Peron, closed out the

fig. 38 Philadelphia actor Jeffrey Coon portrayed Pablo Picasso, and Broadway star Jessica Boevers played his lover, Eva Humbert, in the 2003 American premiere of *La Vie en Bleu.*

season. Ana Maria Andricain played the title role, with *As the World Turns* star Scott Holmes cast as her husband and Jeffrey Coon as the show's narrator, Che Guevara.

The opening production in the studio theatre was *The Last Flapper.* Grace Gonglewski held the stage as Zelda Fitzgerald in this one-woman play by William Luce. A romantic comedy by Norm Foster, *Wrong for Each Other,* followed. Then came two world premieres—Robert Caisley's *The Lake,* and *Summons to Sheffield,* a new play by Will Stutts. The season finished off with *Jacques Brel Is Alive and Well and Living in Paris,* a cabaret-style show featuring songs by the Belgian singer-songwriter.

Another show developed at the Walnut opened the 2003–4 season. *La Vie en Bleu* was a French musical about the early career of Pablo Picasso. Jeffrey Coon starred as Picasso. The play was first produced in Monte Carlo in 1997 and was commissioned by the Monaco royal family to celebrate their seven hundredth year of rule. The play was first literally translated from the French, then adapted for the American stage and considerably shortened from its original four-hour running time. Director Bruce Lumpkin and co-writer Bill Van Horn created the English book, while Elaine Rowan set English lyrics to Pascal Stive's score. There had been two workshop performances at the Walnut the previous season.

Charles Kading's sets for *Annie* gave the holiday musical the look of a comic strip panel. Two teams of children were hired to play the chorus of orphans, and the part of Little Orphan Annie was also double-cast, with Ashlee Keating playing the title role on weeknights and Arianna Claire Vogel on weekends. Deborah Jean Templin played Miss Hannigan, the autocratic ruler of the orphanage, and Patrick Quinn played Daddy Warbucks, the billionaire who tries to adopt Annie. The show was a box office smash. Single-ticket sales outgrossed subscription sales on this show for the first time in the Walnut's history.

Biloxi Blues, the second installment of Neil Simon's autobiographical trilogy, opened the new year. Jesse Bernstein returned as Eugene Jerome, who is sent to basic training in Mississippi during World War II. Philip Barry's society comedy *The Philadelphia Story* followed. Jessica Boevers played Tracy Lord, the role written for Katharine Hepburn, who played the role on Broadway and in the 1940 film. *Hello, Dolly* finished out the season. Deborah Jean Templin returned to sing the title role.

Templin was busy at the Walnut that season, for she was also featured in a one-woman show, *Unsinkable Women,* which opened the 2004 studio season, playing nine different women who had survived the sinking of the *Titanic.* Templin, who conceived the show and researched the lives of these women, had performed the show across the United States and Europe for nearly four years before bringing it to the Walnut. *Here on the Flight Path,* a romantic comedy by Norm Foster, followed in February. Tony-nominated songwriter David Rogers performed his one-man show *Naked on Broadway,* in which he reflected on his years writing lyrics for Broadway musicals. Drucie McDaniel played the title role in *Moll,* John B. Kean's comedy, set in Ireland, about a housekeeper who moves in to help three parish priests and proceeds to dominate their lives. *Pump Boys and Dinettes,* a musical set in a gas station in rural North Carolina, finished out the season.

STRATEGIC PLANNING

During the summer of 2004, the Walnut finally concluded a deal with the Catholic archdiocese for the purchase of its portion of the adjacent parking lot. The Walnut had already negotiated for the other part of the property with Al Gilbert, who acquired the property directly beside the Walnut when the real estate consortium (of which he was a member) broke up. The purchase price was $2.45 million. Negotiations for the other portion of the lot had taken longer. The Vatican authorized the Philadelphia archdiocese to sell its portion of the parking lot, but rather than accept the Walnut's offer, the archdiocese began shopping the property around to various developers. Nevertheless,

Havard and Lou Fryman were able to finalize the purchase from the archdiocese for $3.5 million. Havard hoped to have a new facility up and ready to go by the bicentennial year—or at least under way. The theatre-in-the round he envisioned for the space would be a suitable commemoration for a theatre originally used as a circus ring.

In the fall of 2004 a strategic planning committee was organized to develop a new strategic plan for the Walnut, one that would take the theatre through the two-hundredth anniversary season. The committee included board members and members of the Walnut's senior staff. The committee met a half a dozen times during the 2004–5 season to review the previous plan and reorganize and strengthen the document to better suit the needs of the organization. On November 3, 2005, it presented the document to the rest of the board for feedback and suggestions, and produced a finished document early the following year.

A SEASON TO EXPERIENCE

Annie Warbucks, the sequel to *Annie,* opened the Walnut's 2004–5 mainstage season. Several cast members returned to reprise their roles, including Patrick Quinn as Daddy Warbucks, Amy Bodnar as Grace Farrell, and John-Charles Kelly as FDR. Two new girls, Andie Belkoff and Christiana Anbri, shared the title role of Little Orphan Annie, while the two young actresses who had played Annie the previous season alternated in the supporting role of Pepper. Director Chuck Abbott and choreographer Mary Jane Houdina were also back, as was some of the scenery.

Andrew Lloyd Webber's musical *Cats* was the holiday show that year, and the Walnut's stage was transformed into an oversize rubbish dump. The skyline of Philadelphia could be seen in the background. The production included a rarely heard song, "The Ballad of Billy McCaw," which had been cut from the original London production but was put back in at the request of the composer. Richard Stafford, who had choreographed a number of Walnut musicals, made his directorial debut for this dance-heavy production.

Broadway Bound, the concluding installment of Neil Simon's autobiographical trilogy, brought Eugene Jerome back to his home in Brighton Beach following World War II. Jesse Bernstein was back as Eugene, Ellen Tobie and Tom McCarthy reprised their roles as Eugene's mother and father, and Scott Greer returned as Eugene's older brother, Stan, who entices Eugene into the comedy-writing business.

W. Somerset Maugham's drama *The Constant Wife* occupied the fourth spot in the season. Malcolm Black directed this co-production with Miami's

Coconut Grove Playhouse. Alicia Roper played Constance Middleton, the wife of a wealthy London surgeon who is fully aware of her husband's infidelity, which her friends try to hide from her. Broadway and television star Nancy Dussault, best known as Ted Knight's wife in the sitcom *Too Close for Comfort*, appeared as Constance's mother. Paul Wonsek designed the sets, which were based on sketches by Maugham's wife, Syrie, a noted interior designer who designed the sets for the original 1926 production. *West Side Story* finished out the season. Heading the cast of young singers and dancers were Christina DeCicco as Maria and Michael Gillis as Tony, the star-crossed lovers in this 1957 updating of *Romeo and Juliet*. Response was so good that the run was extended an extra week into July and the musical became the highest-grossing production in the Walnut's history as a producing organization.

In the Independence Studio on 3, Jane Ridley played Fanny Kemble in the season opener, *Mrs. Kemble's Tempest*, which depicted the famed actress near the end of her life doing a reading of Shakespeare's *The Tempest* and reflecting on her own tumultuous life. David Jackson performed his autobiographical one-man revue *Flight*, in which he described how a black kid from West Philadelphia fell in love with the Broadway musical and went on to have a successful career singing and dancing on Broadway. Benjamin Lloyd and Rich Orlow played multiple roles in *Stones in His Pocket*, an Olivier Award–winning comedy that explores what happens when a Hollywood film crew invades a rural village in Ireland. Anne Meara's comedy *After-Play* followed, while *The Fantasticks* closed out the studio season.

A SEASON OF MAGIC

The Walnut kicked off its 2005–6 "magical season" with *Finian's Rainbow*, a musical fable by lyricist Yip Harburg, composer Burton Lane, and playwright Fred Saidy. Ian D. Clark and Jennifer Hope Wills played an Irish immigrant and his daughter, who travel to a mythical town in the Old South. When a magical leprechaun, played by Christopher Sutton, follows them to reclaim his stolen pot of gold, the community is turned upside down. The musical, originally produced in 1947, tackled the issue of racial prejudice in the Old South and was the first musical to feature a fully racially integrated cast.

Christina DeCicco, who had recently appeared as Maria in *West Side Story*, played Belle in Disney's *Beauty and the Beast*, opposite Rob Richardson as the prince trapped in a monster's body. Peter Barbieri designed the extravagant sets, which depicted a gothic castle, a gloomy forest, and a fairy tale village. Miguel Angel Huidor and Colleen McMillan were responsible for the costumes, which included dancing teapots, twirling platters, and a talking candelabra. It proved very popular with the family audience and became the second-highest-grossing holiday show, after *Annie*.

Neil Simon's Pulitzer Prize–winning comedy *Lost in Yonkers* was another co-production with Miami's Coconut Grove Playhouse. It followed a pair of boys who are sent to Yonkers to live with their cruel grandmother and her simple-minded daughter. The drama *Trying* had its Philadelphia premiere that season. The play depicted the life of Philadelphia's Francis Biddle. Judge Biddle, the scion of a renowned Philadelphia family, had been attorney general under Franklin Roosevelt and the chief American judge at the Nuremburg trials. The play focused on his later years, as the esteemed member of the bench confronted his own mortality. The play was written by Joanna Glass, who had been Biddle's secretary during the last years of his life. John Horton portrayed Judge Biddle and Jody Stevens was Sarah Schoor, the stand-in for the playwright.

Godspell concluded the season. This musical retelling of the Gospel of Matthew was set under the Ben Franklin Bridge, and the cast was a colorful group of homeless musicians. Originally written as a master's thesis project at Carnegie Mellon in 1970, *Godspell* had been a hit on and off Broadway and an often-revived show. Michael Gruber played Jesus. It was to be the last show for the Walnut's longtime stage manager, Frank Anzalone, who retired after twenty-three years and 115 shows at the Walnut to devote himself full time to directing and teaching.

The year 2006 was the two-hundredth anniversary of Edwin Forrest's birth, and theatres around the city honored Philadelphia's native son. The Walnut mounted an exhibition of Forrest memorabilia in the lobby. The featured production in Independence Studio on 3 was *Forrest: A Riot of Dreams*, the winning submission for a playwrighting competition held the previous year. Armen Pandola, a Philadelphia-based lawyer, won with a play that centered on Forrest's sensational divorce trial from his wife, Catherine Sinclair. Dan Olmstead played the renowned actor, and Emma O'Donnell played his wife. As usual, on the actual birthday, March 9, members of the Edwin Forrest Trust laid a wreath on Forrest's tomb, then assembled in the lobby of the Walnut to honor the first American theatrical star. Actress Zoe Caldwell came down from New York to participate.

The other studio productions were all being seen in Philadelphia for the first time that year. Eric Emmanuel Schmitt's *Enigma Variations* was inspired by Edward Elgar's 1898 musical masterpiece. Stage manager Debi Marcucci directed Jeffrey Coon in *Lobby Hero*, where the search for a murderer brings neighbors together in the lobby of their apartment building. *Natural History* was a set of four loosely linked stories set in different rooms in the New York Museum of Natural History. Mark Clements directed the closing musical, *The*

Thing About Men, a comedy about a two-timing advertising executive who leaves his wife and becomes the roommate of a down-on-his-luck artist, with whom she is having an affair.

WEB-BASED MARKETING AND AUDIENCE DEVELOPMENT

Major changes were taking place in the way shows could be marketed. The Internet was the important technological advance of the millennium. While no one could predict the full impact of the World Wide Web, people were increasingly doing their shopping from home, purchasing all manner of goods and services via their personal computers. The Walnut had had a Web presence since 1998, when the first Web site opened at wstonline.org. Most work stations were computerized in 1999, and the building was rewired so that all stations were networked together. Six years later, however, the system was showing its age and needed to be upgraded.

Rather than invest immediately in the latest technology, the Walnut's management studied other companies' best practices and waited for new systems to prove themselves. The box office was operated manually, with paper tickets, until 2006, when the theatre adopted Archtics, a state-of-the-art computer system for ticketing and database management. The system, created by Ticketmaster, the nation's leading sports and entertainment ticketing agency, had recently been adapted for performing arts organizations. The new system allowed the Walnut to consolidate information from ticket sales, mailing lists, and fund-raising records.

The new system made it possible for theatergoers to renew subscriptions, buy tickets online, and e-mail tickets to friends if they could not use them. Customers could access all of this through the Walnut's newly expanded Web site at walnutstreettheatre.org. Soon, a third of all tickets were being sold online, with another third sold over the phone and the remaining third purchased directly at the box office. People also used the Internet to sign up for classes and make their annual donations to the theatre or to read the latest press releases. The theatre could reach its entire audience—or any targeted segment—with a simple e-mail announcement.

Although the subscription audience had maxed out at fifty-five thousand, the new system allowed the theatre to be more efficient in its exchange policy, and provided a better resale opportunity for exchanged tickets. Subscribers could pass their tickets on to friends with a simple e-mail. If they chose not to attend, they could print out tickets for another performance from home, at any time of the day or night. Or they could donate unused tickets back to the theatre. Any unused or exchanged tickets could be immediately placed on sale. The theatre saw a substantial increase in income as a result.

In 2006–7 the Walnut returned to the Barrymore Awards, receiving twenty-two nominations, more than any other theatre in the city. The season opened with *Windy City*, a musical version of Ben Hecht and Charles MacArthur's 1928 newspaper comedy, *The Front Page*. David Elder played Hildy Johnson, who is trying to get out of the newspaper business. Paul Schoeffler played his editor, Walter Burns, who schemes to keep his top reporter on the job. Composer Tony Macaulay and writer-lyricist Dick Vosburgh collaborated on the musical, which had premiered in London's West End in 1982. Tony Macaulay updated the script and added three new songs for the Walnut's production.

Another stage adaptation of a popular film, Busby Berkeley's 1933 backstage drama *42nd Street*, filled the holiday slot. Cara Cooper played Peggy Sawyer, the chorus girl who gets her big break and must fill in for the show's star on opening night. The musical featured such familiar Harry Warren–Al Dubin songs as "We're in the Money," "Lullaby of Broadway," and "42nd Street." Charles Abbott received a Barrymore Award for Outstanding Direction of a Musical.

Anthony Lawton and Scott Greer played George and Lenny, two lonely migrant workers struggling to get by in Depression-era America in John Steinbeck's drama *Of Mice and Men*. The production received rave reviews and went on to win a Barrymore Award for Outstanding Overall Production of a Play, and a second for the show's director, Mark Clements. *Enchanted April* followed in March. Alicia Roper and Maureen Garrett played two British housewives who vacation at a luxurious Italian villa. This 2003 play by Matthew Barber was based on a 1922 novel by Elizabeth von Armin.

Rodgers and Hammerstein's 1945 musical *Carousel* closed out the season. Jeffrey Coon played Billy Bigelow, a rough carnival barker who falls in love with a young millworker, played by Julie Hanson, and marries her. To provide for his baby daughter, he foolishly gets involved in a robbery attempt, which goes sour, and he kills himself rather than be caught by the police. Unable to enter heaven, he must return to earth to redeem himself. Bernard Havard's son, Brandon, followed his father into the family trade, taking a small part in the production.

In the Independence Studio on 3, Jamie Torcellini directed and co-starred in Charles Ludlam's gender-bending send-up of Gothic melodramas, *The Mystery of Irma Vep*, which opened the studio season. Torcellini and co-star Madi Distefano played multiple cross-dressed characters. The show, which was expected to do well, could not be extended at the end of its run, so it opened early, on November 30, 2006. It was followed by *Bookends*, a new play by Michael J. Feely about the effect of McCarthyism on a successful Holly-

fig. 39 The 2007 production of *Of Mice and Men* starred Scott Greer (*left*) as Lennie and Anthony Lawton as George.

wood writer-director team. The play had its world premiere at the Walnut as part of the Philadelphia New Play Festival. David Schulner's romantic comedy *An Infinite Ache* followed, providing an opportunity for two young actors, Steven Klein and Eunice Wong. *The Dishwashers,* a humorous look behind the scenes in a restaurant, filled the fourth spot. The four-person cast included Lee Golden—who performed in the first season in 1983—Jared Michael Delaney, Evan Jonigkeit, and Bill Van Horn, who also directed. Rounding out the season was *Side by Side by Sondheim,* a musical revue featuring the early work of Stephen Sondheim, with songs from *West Side Story, Gypsy, A Funny Thing Happened on the Way to the Forum,* and other hit shows.

THE NEW ADDITION

At the time of this writing, as the Walnut's bicentennial approaches, it has become clear that construction on the new theatre will have to be put off until

fig. 40 The interior of the Walnut Street Theatre as it appears today.

sometime after the 2008–9 season. There are permits to get and neighborhood groups to talk to. All of the plans are conditional on putting together the financing for the project. Walnut trustee Rick Mitchell, the general counsel of CMS Companies, a privately held real estate firm, chaired a property development committee, which included board members with legal, real estate, and property development experience. They have explored various options for developing the property.

It has become clear that this will require some kind of private-public partnership. The theatre needs to raise upward of $25 million just to build the new facility, and a capital campaign committee has been put together to identify individual, foundation, and government sources for this funding, to advise on staffing, and to coordinate with the Property Development Committee, which is assessing different plans for the project.

In 2006 the committee sent a request for proposals to developers. They wanted to partner with a commercial concern to develop a multiuse facility, the revenues from which could subsidize expanded theatrical activities. A dozen companies responded, and two were invited to make formal presentations. The committee finally settled on Roskamp, a property management and development company that specialized in senior living communities. Roskamp proposed building a forty-five-story continuing care retirement community. The presence of the Walnut and other cultural activities would make it an attractive location for the affluent, fifty-five-plus age group targeted for the building.

The Walnut would expand into a thirty-thousand-square-foot area connected to the lobby of the existing facility. There would be a café in the expanded lobby open to the general public. The facility would also include rehearsal space, classroom facilities, and offices for support staff. The theatre's staff decided to work with the developer's architects to advise on designing needs. The project would include a four-hundred-seat permanent theatre-in-the-round, with audience seating on two levels—six to eight rows of seats on the orchestra level on all four sides of a central playing area, and a balcony above it with two rows of seating.

A SEASON OF ADVENTURE

While the bicentennial season was looming, there was still the 2007–8 season to put together. Bernard Havard made the selections for all mainstage and studio shows, while Mark Sylvester negotiated with the royalty holders. Sometimes getting the rights to a play was easy. At other times, the negotiations could drag on for years. The Walnut is limited by its proximity to New York City, for when a show is bound for Broadway or a national tour, the Walnut cannot get the rights in Philadelphia. Sylvester did online research on which theatres had run a given show in recent years, and then contacted the theatres to find out what kind of royalties they paid (often 10 percent of the gross). Because the Walnut had unusually large grosses, Sylvester could often secure the rights for less. The Walnut might hold on to the rights for several years before mounting the production.

Havard announced the mainstage season to the trustees in December and to the public in January. The 2007–8 season, dubbed "a season of adventure," would open with *Man of La Mancha*, the musical adaptation of Miguel de Cervantes's *Don Quixote*. Bruce Lumpkin would direct. *Peter Pan* would occupy the holiday slot. Marc Robin, who had previously directed *Windy City*, would stage this flying-heavy musical. Once again, Havard went with a drama for the third production of the year—Arthur Miller's *The Price*. The production featured Robert Prosky and his two sons, Andy and John. Michael Carleton, a newcomer to the Walnut, would direct this drama, about two estranged brothers who meet each other in the attic of their childhood home following the death of their father. The play had debuted at the Walnut prior to its Broadway premiere in 1968. Carleton had previously directed the play for New Jersey's Cape May Stage, where he was also the artistic director. In the fourth slot, Havard returned to a Neil Simon comedy, *The Odd Couple*, which Bill Van Horn would direct. Finishing out the season would be *Les Misérables*, the musical adaptation of Victor Hugo's classic novel. The Walnut was one of only eight theatres in the country chosen to present an originally produced version of the world's most popular musical. Mark Clements would be brought over from England to direct.

Marketing for the new season began in January, when a letter went out to subscribers announcing the shows featured in the upcoming season and inviting them to renew their subscriptions. The Walnut took special care of its subscribers, for they were its lifeblood, providing the financial stability it required. The best seats in the house were held by season ticket holders, who got the same seats for every performance they attended. Those who did not immediately respond to the renewal letter received follow-up letters. If they still failed to respond, they received a courtesy call from the telephone sales department. Then their seats were made available to other subscribers who had expressed interest in changing their seat locations. Roughly 80 percent of subscribers renewed each year, with more than 90 percent of those who had subscribed for more than one season renewing.

Once the plays for the new season were announced, Rebekah Sassi lined up a corporate sponsor for each. It cost $27,500 to sponsor one of the main-stage productions, $35,000 for the holiday show. Sponsors got their logo on every piece of promotional material that went out. This included posters, newspaper advertisements, bus shelter ads, banners, flyers, and brochures. With half a million brochures mailed out each year, this offered sponsors a large public presence. The company also received five "patron night" dinners at the theatre at any time during the season. Ten people enjoyed a private gourmet dinner in the Langworthy Lounge, prepared by a master chef. The dinner guests then sat in the luxury box for the evening's show. The sponsors of the 2006–7 season would all be returning—the law firm of Stradley Ronon Stevens & Young would sponsor *Man of La Mancha;* Citizens Bank would sponsor *Peter Pan;* Harmelin Media would sponsor *The Price;* another law firm, Blank Rome LLP, would sponsor *The Odd Couple;* and Progressive Business Publications would sponsor the season closer, *Les Misérables.*

BUDGETING AND NEGOTIATIONS

Once the new season was announced, the budget had to be worked out. Havard and Sylvester worked with the production manager, the controller, and the various department heads to work out a budget for each show. The holiday musical was budgeted at half a million dollars. That covered all the materials and labor for the sets, the cost of renting or building costumes, hiring stage crew and dressers for the run of the production, and running costs for the nine-week run. The other musicals were budgeted at between $430,000 and $450,000, depending on the complexity of the set. Straight plays cost quite a bit less, since they required fewer sets, but production costs still averaged $300,000.

Sylvester also negotiated artists' salaries, figuring what made sense and was fair while controlling costs. Actors and directors negotiated as individuals, usually through their agents. Salaries were not based simply on the size of the role but on considerations of the actors' life situations and previous service to the theatre. It was another way that Sylvester and Havard tried to support local actors so that they could stay in Philadelphia and earn a living. Thus, you could find an actor like Jeffrey Coon playing the lead in one production and performing as a member of an ensemble in the next.

Budgets from the various departments went to the Walnut's controller, Len Karabell. Karabell had been the theatre's chief financial officer for most of his working life. He was only two years out of college, with a degree in accounting from Drexel University, when he came to the Walnut in 1973. The Walnut was a relatively small operation then, with an annual budget of less than $1 million. By 2007 the budget had grown to more than $13 million. Karabell and a part-time assistant did all the accounting for the theatre, inputting sales figures into the computer and generating monthly financial reports, which Karabell submitted to the producing artistic director and managing director. Between February and April the budget would go through several drafts, as Karabell, Sylvester, and Havard coordinated the budget with the various departments. By mid-April the budget for the next fiscal year was generally in place, and the various departments knew what the year would be like. The final budget then went to the Finance Committee, and finally to the full board for approval.

CASTING

With the budget in place and directors chosen, casting could begin. Bernard Havard's assistant, Kate Galvin, was the casting director for both mainstage and studio theatre productions. Her responsibility was to choose performers for consideration by the director, musical director (in the case of musicals), and producing artistic director. Casting typically began two to six months before the first rehearsal, but sometimes as much as a year ahead. The first production for the fall season was cast in May and the holiday musical in June. Casting sessions took place in Philadelphia and New York, with the Walnut giving preference to local actors. The audition process could be simple or complicated, depending on how many parts were precast and the director's concept of the show. Equity rules required that the Walnut hold auditions in New York City. These took place two or three months after the Philadelphia auditions. Auditions could last from two to five days. For a simple show, there was a day of auditions for the chorus and another for principals. For a musical, there were separate days for an Equity chorus call, an open chorus call, auditions for invited dancers, for invited singers, and a day of callbacks.

Often the director would have a particular actor in mind for a role. For the role of Captain Hook, Havard and director Marc Robin had their eye on Paul Schoeffler, who had played the role of Walter Burns in the 2006 production of *Windy City*, which Robin had directed. Schoeffler played Captain Hook in the 1998–99 Broadway revival and on the national tour opposite gymnast Cathy Rigby, and was featured in a telecast of the show on the A&E network. Cary Michele Miller, who was playing Carrie Pipperidge in *Carousel*, impressed Havard and Robin as a great Peter Pan, a role she had always wanted to play. A number of children in the Walnut's theatre school won roles as some of the Lost Boys in the production. Director Bruce Lumpkin also tapped Paul Schoeffler for the title role in *Man of La Mancha*. Jamie Torcellini, a frequent player at the Walnut, got the comic role of Sancho Panza, Don Quixote's long-suffering servant.

The studio season was announced in mid-May. *Greater Tuna*, an off-Broadway hit comedy about small-town life in Texas in 1982, was set to open on November 30. *Vivien*, a one-woman show about Vivien Leigh, was to follow. Janis Stevens, who would play the title role, had won numerous awards for her portrayal of the legendary actress. *Mr. Bailey's Minder* was a drama by Australian playwright Debra Oswald, which would receive its American premiere at the Walnut. The fourth production of the studio season would be *Quartet*, a touching comedy by Academy Award–winning writer Ron Harwood, about a pair of elderly opera singers living in an old-age home. The season would finish off with *The Irish . . . and How They Got That Way*, a salute to Irish music and culture by Pulitzer Prize–winning author Frank McCourt.

MARKETING

The big advertising push took place in the late spring and early summer, when the Walnut sent out a four-color brochure announcing the upcoming season to roughly half a million households in the Delaware Valley, people who had purchased tickets to a single show as well as lists from other local arts organizations. Ralph Weeks headed up the Marketing Department. Weeks had come to the Walnut in 2003, having held a similar position at California's famed Pasadena Playhouse. But the Walnut was a much bigger operation.

In selecting plays and musicals for the mainstage, Bernard Havard looked for shows that were already "branded," or recognizable to the general public. The major musicals of the day were just those kinds of events. Although musicals were more expensive to produce than straight plays—requiring larger casts, more luxurious costumes, and multiple sets—they brought a quality of spectacle that made the production more than a theatrical show; it became an *event* not to be missed. In designing their posters and display ads, the Walnut used artwork for which the show was best known but incorporated it in a format that was unmistakably the Walnut's. The same image appeared on bus shelter ads, direct-mail pieces, and window cards, reinforcing the brand.

Over the summer, the telemarketers followed up with as many potential patrons as possible. Even with an 80 percent renewal rate, the Walnut had to come up with ten thousand new subscribers each year. The telemarketers needed to generate enthusiasm for the upcoming season, and to encourage single-ticket buyers and those who were sent a brochure to sign up for the entire season. Weeks saw this as an educational function. By the end of the summer, the marketing department was expected to have met its goal of fifty thousand subscribers for the mainstage season.

Publicity for the fall season began in June, when announcements went out about the new season, and subscription ads and guide listings went into local newspapers and magazines. During the summer, the communications manager, Tom Miller, began pitching stories with local writers that would run in early September. Most magazines had a three-month lead time. He went on to book and place display ads. Ads announcing the entire season appeared in the *Inquirer* and various suburban papers in July.

CAMP WALNUT AND THE EDUCATION DEPARTMENT

Summer was also the time when kids took over the theatre, as Camp Walnut was in session. One hundred twenty children ages eight to eighteen were admitted to the intensive acting program, which lasted from nine in the morning until 4:30 in the afternoon. The advanced students in the master's division worked on an actual show during the course of the six-week program, either a straight play or a musical, which they showcased in the Independence Theatre on 3 in early August. The less experienced students in the discovery and development divisions took classes in voice and speech, character development, acting for the camera, and other subjects. Admission to the master's and development divisions was based on auditions. Camp Walnut was operated by the Walnut's Education Department, which was also responsible for the regular theatre school, the apprentice program, community outreach, and student matinees.

Once Camp Walnut concluded in early August, the Education Department prepared for the arrival of the apprentices. The Walnut hired twenty-five apprentices each year, college students with a background in some aspect of theatre. Each apprentice was hired for thirty to forty-five weeks and received a stipend of $285 a week, plus health insurance. There were apprentices in general management, literary management, and stage management. Others were employed in the costume and set shops. Susan Nicodemus Quinn, the Walnut's education director, worked most closely with the four acting apprentices, who spearheaded the Walnut's outreach program. The Touring Outreach Company traveled to schools up and down the Delaware Valley, presenting a variety of one-hour programs tailored to specific age groups. They would perform before more than a hundred thousand schoolchildren before the school year was done.

PRODUCTION AND REHEARSALS

In the offices of the Walnut's scene and prop shop in North Philadelphia, preparations for the fall season began shortly after the previous season ended. Roy Backes was the Walnut's production manager. Chris Hanes and Glen Sears served as technical director and prop master, respectively. Hanes was responsible for building all the scenery for the Walnut's shows, both mainstage and studio. He drew up plans, based on the set designer's drawings, showing how the scenery was to be built so that it could be loaded into a truck and set up at the theatre. He hired the carpenters and painters and supervised the building of the set. Sears was responsible for all the furniture, set dressing, and hand props that the actors would use.

Colleen Grady was the third key member of the production team. She was the Walnut's costume shop supervisor and had been with the Walnut since 1997. If outside designers were called in to do the costumes for the show, Grady would assist them. More typically, some costumes—usually the principals'—would be designed and built in-house, while those of the ensemble were rented. Grady worked with a full-time assistant and two apprentices, who stayed for a season at a time. If the costuming was complex, she would bring in from two to four extra people to assist. A separate wardrobe staff was employed as backstage dressers during the run of the show.

Production activity geared up in the middle of August, when actors arrived to rehearse *Man of La Mancha*. Each mainstage production needed three to four weeks of rehearsals. The Walnut employed two full-time stage managers for the mainstage and one for the studio theatre. Debi Marcucci and Lori Aghazarian worked the mainstage production. They arrived a week before rehearsals began, to do prep work and to orient the two stage management apprentices who were hired for the season. The stage managers worked out the rehearsal schedule in collaboration with the director. One or the other would attend every rehearsal, assisting the director, tracking the props, and recording the blocking and technical cues. Rehearsals lasted from ten in the morning until six at night, with a one-hour lunch break. During the rehearsal process, the stage managers communicated with the actors, scheduling rehearsal times and reporting on the progress to senior management.

Rehearsals took place on the fourth and sixth floors. While the director was working with the principals in the fourth-floor studio, the choreographer could be working with the chorus on the sixth floor. Rehearsals for a major musical were complicated, and it was up to the stage managers and their apprentices to schedule the rehearsal spaces and inform the actors of their call times. On the second day of rehearsals, there was a photo shoot with the principals, which was used for the advance press. The publicist also set up newspaper and broadcast interviews with the actors.

LOAD IN AND TECH

Two weeks before previews were set to begin, the production staff "loaded in" the show. The set was trucked in from the scene shop and installed on the stage. Roy Backes would hire as many as thirty stagehands for load in. It took a week and a half to load in the set for *Man of La Mancha*. Stagehands put in between seventy-five and eighty hours a week during this period. The set needed to be in place and fully operational by the Wednesday before Labor Day. That was when the actors had their first run-through on the stage. In many cases the playing area on stage was larger than that in the rehearsal hall, so the actors and director needed time to make spacing adjustments. Tech rehearsals began the following day and ran through the Sunday of Labor Day weekend.

The Walnut employed a five-person "house crew" of union stagehands who were required to be at every show. Each was in charge of a department—one was an electrician, one a carpenter, one a prop woman (for the first time in the history of the theatre), one a soundman, and one a flyman. Depending on the complexity of the show, the Walnut would hire up to twelve additional stagehands. At this point the stage crew knew nothing about the blocking or the sound and light cues. The Thursday rehearsal onstage was a tech run-through, where the stagehands learned the blocking and the various lighting and sound cues. During tech run-throughs and for the run of the show, the stage manager was in charge. Lori Aghazarian "called the show." Sitting in a control booth at the rear of the mezzanine, she communicated with the stagehands via headset microphones, giving them cues for a lighting change, a piece of recorded music or sound effect, or when a piece of scenery needed to be flown in or out. Meanwhile, Debi Marcucci "worked the deck," standing backstage and making sure the actors made their entrances and exits and had their props. Marcucci also supervised the two stage management apprentices until they were comfortable enough running the show that they could take over.

Saturday night was the first dress rehearsal, the first time the actors worked with the costumes. The Walnut employed two full-time dressers to work the show. Their responsibility was to make sure that the costumes were where they should be—either in the actors' dressing rooms or in the wings, when an actor had to make a quick costume change. On a large musical, there might be as many as six dressers working backstage. Problems inevitably arose—a snap might not work or a sleeve not fit, so the costumers were present to make any last-minute adjustments in the costumes.

On Sunday night the actors had a final dress rehearsal, and it was photographed and clips were videotaped, so that local television stations could have footage of the show. On Labor Day, the cast and crew had a day off, preparing for the first preview, which took place the following night. The previews were treated as full-fledged productions, with a subscription audience attending. The actors rehearsed during the day.

OPENING A NEW SEASON

The opening night of the 2007–8 season took place on September 12, the Wednesday after Labor Day. Opening night was always an exciting affair. The press was in attendance. Reviewers from the *Inquirer*, the *Daily News*, *Philadelphia Weekly*, and various suburban papers would be there. The Walnut's communications manager, Tom Miller, could be found sitting behind a table ready to check in the critics and give them their press kits. A number of seats were set aside for the Walnut's administrative staff, which numbered roughly fifty. Everyone who worked at the Walnut was invited to attend. Members of the Walnut's board attended with their families, guests, and prospective board members. Representatives from the company sponsoring the show had special seats, front row center.

The curtain went up shortly after 7:00 P.M. Before the show began, Richard Woosnam, chairman of the Walnut's board of trustees, took the stage to thank the audience and the show's sponsor, the law firm of Stradley Ronon. Up in the control booth at the rear of the mezzanine, Lori Aghazarian called for the houselights to dim, and the curtain came up on a cathedral-like dungeon set lit by burning torches, where Miguel Cervantes was awaiting trial and almost certain death by the Spanish Inquisition. The entire musical was played against the backdrop of the dungeon, as the prisoners conducted a mock trial to determine whether Cervantes would be allowed to keep the manuscript he had written about a self-proclaimed knight errant, Don Quixote. The prisoners became the characters in the story, using props and costume pieces taken from a theatrical trunk. Torture devices were transformed into set pieces for the story—an interrogation chair became a throne in one scene and the wheel that turned the torture rack was transformed into a windmill in another. The dark and gritty realism of the dungeon contrasted sharply with the show's soaring message of hope, expressed in its most familiar song, "The Impossible Dream."

When the curtain went down that night and the audience had departed, there was a reception for the cast, crew, and entire staff. Members of the Walnut's board of trustees usually attended. It was a brief breather, for by the next day most of them would be turning their attention to the next production. Roy Backes's production team would go to work building the sets for the holiday show, *Peter Pan*. Three weeks after the premiere, Debi Marcucci was pulled off *Man of La Mancha* to begin prepping the next show. The full-time stage managers alternated in calling the productions. One was always preparing for the next show.

Reviews came out in the *Inquirer* and other daily papers two days after the premiere. Suburban papers and weeklies ran reviews in the following week or so. The communications manager clipped the reviews for the Walnut's archives. In the telemarketing department, the emphasis shifted to filling the remaining seats for the holiday show. Because the holiday musical ran for two weeks longer than the other shows, the marketing staff had to sell more than $1 million worth of single tickets.

The Education Department got busy as the fall semester began. Fall classes started the last week in September, and the school was signing up students for both adult and teen workshops. The four acting apprentices spent the month of September rehearsing the shows they would take to local schools beginning in October—*The Frog Prince and Other Enchantments*, *Mufaro's Beautiful Daughters*, and *The Boy Who Cried Bully*, all aimed at elementary school children; *Mean Girlz R Bullies 2* for middle schools; and *No Easy Road to Freedom* for middle school and high school students.

In the Development Office, Rebekah Sassi was preparing for the first fund-raising event of the season, an auction that took place in late October. She would coordinate with board members to ensure that there would be items available for the bidding. Proceeds would help support the Walnut's education programs, and they were experimenting with online bidding. In November, Sassi would begin gearing up for the Angels Campaign, reaching out to subscribers for an end-of-the-year donation to the theatre. At that time, telemarketers would be shifted from selling subscriptions to soliciting donations. Raising money was an ongoing activity, and deadlines for grant applications were always coming up. Preliminary planning was getting under way for the spring gala. They were submitting names for the artistic and business honorees for the Edwin Forrest Awards.

PETER PAN

Rehearsals began for the holiday musical, *Peter Pan*, four weeks after *Man of La Mancha* opened. Paul Schoeffler had to pull double duty, rehearsing the role of Captain Hook in the afternoons and performing as Cervantes/Don Quixote in the evenings. He knew the part of Hook well enough, however, for he had played it nightly for several years on the national tour. The script was the 1954 version, which starred Mary Martin as Peter Pan opposite Cyril Ritchard as Captain Hook. Baby boomers recalled the annual telecast of the show in the 1950s and 1960s. It was one of the rare Broadway shows of the time that was recorded from beginning to end. Though Mary Martin had a long and illustrious career on Broadway, it was as "the boy who never grew up" that she was most fondly remembered. Philadelphia native Mark "Moose" Charlap and Carolyn Leigh created the music and lyrics of several of the show's most memorable songs, including "I Won't Grow Up" and "I Gotta Crow." The show was originally produced as a play with incidental music, but composer Jules Styne and lyricists Betty Comden and Adolph Green were brought in to provide additional songs and make it a full-fledged musical.

Local children filled out the cast, and the fortunate ones got to fly, after Peter Pan sprinkled fairy dust on them and took them off to Neverland. Kristen Paulicelli, from Flemington, New Jersey, played Wendy, and Griffin Back, of Cherry Hill, played John, the older Darling boy. The younger boy, Michael, was double cast, with Havertown's Dante Mignucci and Bala Cynwyd's Conor O'Brien alternating in the role. There were two teams of Lost Boys, one for weekdays and one for weekends.

The equipment and know-how for the production were provided by Flying by Foy, which used a counterweight system. A sandbag the same weight as each actor was connected by a line over a pulley system, which allowed the flying operator to raise or lower the actor with ease. Tim Mackay of Flying by Foy spent two days training the Walnut's stagehands, who handled the flying during the run of the show. Flying required delicate coordination between the actors and the operator backstage. Actors needed to know how to propel themselves into the air, while the flying operator had to pull on the line at the right moment to make the flying seem smooth and effortless.

The most impressive piece of flying came at the curtain call, when Peter Pan walked to the edge of the stage, then leapt out over the audience and flew within a few feet of the mezzanine, sprinkling green fairy dust on the audience below. Cary Michele Miller enjoyed the audible gasp that came from the audience every night she did it.

LOOKING FORWARD

Peter Pan became the most profitable holiday production on record, with *West Side Story* still holding the title for all-time highest box office sales. Both were sure to be overtaken by *Les Misérables*, which was to close out the 2007–8 season. Billed as the world's most popular musical, it would run for a total of fifteen weeks—three weeks longer than any other show—ending in early August. Paul Schoeffler would be back for a third featured role on the Walnut's mainstage that season, this time in the role of Javert, the police inspector whose relentless pursuit of the hero, Jean Valjean, provides the central story line for the musical staging of Victor Hugo's sprawling novel. Hugh Panaro was cast as Jean Valjean. A Philadelphia native, Panaro got his Actor's Equity card in 1986, when he was cast in the Walnut's production of *A Little Night Music*. He had since gone on to a successful Broadway career.

The plans for the bicentennial were taking shape. The exterior of the theatre was due for a facelift. Over the summer, the stucco would be sandblasted and then repainted. For the entire bicentennial season, the theatre would be decorated in red, white, and blue bunting. All the marketing materials would be branded with a bicentennial logo, which would also appear on various souvenirs and commemorative items. Historic displays were to be installed throughout the building, and a pair of books would be published. Other projects under discussion included an expanded gala and a documentary on the theatre.

Havard had made his final selections for the season, and on January 1, 2008, the Walnut issued a press release announcing the mainstage schedule for the bicentennial anniversary. In keeping with the Walnut's role as the oldest theatre in the United States, the season would feature "all-American

fig. 41 The street marker that now sits in front of the theatre along Walnut Street.

stories." Rodgers and Hammerstein's *State Fair* would kick off the season, with Bruce Lumpkin directing this story about a family's visit to the Iowa State Fair. Originally produced as a film, it was adapted for the stage in 1996. The holiday musical would be *Hairspray*, another stage adaptation of a popular film. Chuck Abbott was slated to direct this John Waters comedy about racial integration through dance in 1960s Baltimore. Malcolm Black would direct Tennessee Williams's *A Streetcar Named Desire*—an appropriate choice for the bicentennial year, given the play's significance in the history of the Walnut. It would be followed by *Born Yesterday*, a 1946 comedy by Garson Kanin about corrupt business dealings in Washington. No director had been settled on, and Havard was hoping to co-produce with another theatre. Marc

Robin would direct the season finale, *The Producers,* Mel Brooks's wildly popular musical adaptation of his 1968 film comedy.

The actual anniversary night, February 2, 2009, would land on a Monday, a night when the theatre would normally be dark. A gala evening was in the works, one that would recall and reflect on the Walnut's historic significance and its continuing commitment to American musical theatre. The theatre's bicentennial is, of course, not the end of the story but another milestone in the ongoing history of a remarkable performance space. While it marks the end of this narrative, the history of the Walnut will continue to unfold. The future is certain to hold both promise and problems, as public tastes and attitudes change, as new genres take shape, and as new technology becomes available that will shape the direction of live theatre in unimagined ways. The managers who are charged with the stewardship of this historic facility are optimistic about the future, so long as they—and those who follow in their footsteps—continue to be centered on the audience and to respond to *vox populi,* the voice of the people.

PROLOGUE

1. Scharf and Westcott, *History of Philadelphia*, 1:980.

CHAPTER 1

1. Quoted in Kelley, *Life and Times in Colonial Philadelphia*, 103.

2. Ibid.; Houchin, "Struggle for Virtue," 170.

3. Pollock, *Philadelphia Theatre in the Eighteenth Century*, 4.

4. Wilson, *Three Hundred Years of American Drama*, 8.

5. Odell, *Annals of the New York Stage*, 1:144.

6. Vail, *Random Notes on the History of the Circus*, 13–14.

7. Odell, *Annals of the New York Stage*, 1:222.

8. J. Durang, *Memoir of John Durang*, 5.

9. Kelley, *Life and Times in Colonial Philadelphia*, 103–4.

10. McNamara, "Scenography of Popular Entertainment," 17.

11. Dye, "Pennsylvania Versus the Theatre," 352.

12. Pollock, *Philadelphia Theatre in the Eighteenth Century*, 6.

13. Hewitt, *Theatre U.S.A.*, 3.

14. Ibid., 8–9.

15. Stine, "Philadelphia Theatre, 1682–1829," 22.

16. C. Durang, *Philadelphia Stage*, 1:2–5. This work originally appeared as a series of articles in the *Philadelphia Sunday Dispatch;* Thompson Westcott arranged these articles into seven volumes, divided into two parts. Citations are to part number and page number(s). See also Hewitt, *Theatre U.S.A.*, 8.

17. Crawford, *Romance of the American Theatre*, 27.

18. Pollock, *Philadelphia Theatre in the Eighteenth Century*, 13.

19. Glazer, *Philadelphia Theatres, A–Z*, 210.

20. Hughes, *History of the American Theatre*, 35.

21. Stine, "Philadelphia Theatre, 1682–1829," 39.

22. Ibid., 43.

23. Pollock, *Philadelphia Theatre in the Eighteenth Century*, 33.

24. Hughes, *History of the American Theatre*, 35.

25. Scharf and Westcott, *History of Philadelphia*, 1:966.

26. Quoted in Chindahl, *History of the Circus in America*, 6.

27. Crawford, *Romance of the American Theatre*, 89–90, quoting C. Durang, *Philadelphia Stage*.

28. See ibid., 90.

29. Durang, J. *Memoir of John Durang*, 27.

30. Ibid., 37.

31. Glazer, *Philadelphia Theatres, A–Z*, 84.

32. J. Durang, *Memoir of John Durang*, 106.

33. From an account by Moreau de Saint-Méry, *Voyage aux Etats-Unis de l'Amerique, 1793–1798*, quoted in Hewitt, *Theatre U.S.A.*, 39.

34. Quoted in Odell, *Annals of the New York Stage*, 1:157.

35. Chindahl, *History of the Circus in America*, 6–7.

36. Thayer, *Annals of the American Circus*, 1:5.

37. Ibid., 1:8.

38. Pollock, *Philadelphia Theatre in the Eighteenth Century*, 61–62.

39. J. Durang, *Memoir of John Durang*, 95.

40. Ibid., 103.

41. James, *Cradle of Culture*, 26–28.

42. See Hewitt, *Theatre U.S.A.*, 43.

43. James, *Cradle of Culture*, 30.

CHAPTER 2

1. Most early histories of Philadelphia say that Victor Pepin was born in Philadelphia. However, in his *Random Notes on the History of the Early*

American Circus, R. W. G. Vail cites circus acrobat George Stone as saying that "Pepin was born in Albany, at the corner of North Market Street and the Colony" (81). In an 1860 interview with the *Albany Morning Express*, Stone asserted that he received this information directly from Pepin in New Orleans (clipping, Joel Munsell scrapbook, American Antiquarian Society Library, Worcester, Massachusetts). The most detailed biography of Pepin is Ferguson, *Victor Pepin, Circus Career.*

2. Thayer, *Annals of the American Circus,* 1:131 (quoting a *New York Clipper* article of June 1875).

3. C. Durang, *Philadelphia Stage* 1:98.

4. Thayer, *Annals of the American Circus,* 1:38, 41.

5. C. Durang, *Philadelphia Stage,* 1:98.

6. Ibid.

7. Thayer, *Annals of the American Circus,* 1:46–47.

8. *Philadelphia Aurora General Advertiser,* February 2, 1809.

9. Ibid., February 21, 1809.

10. Ibid., April 28, 1809.

11. Pepin and Breschard's tours are detailed in Thayer, *Annals of the American Circus,* vol. 1.

12. Ibid., 1:136.

13. Odell, *Annals of the New York Stage,* 2:375.

14. Mease, *Picture of Philadelphia for 1824,* 331.

15. C. Durang, *Philadelphia Stage,* 1:99.

16. Ibid., 1:96.

17. Wood, *Personal Recollections of the Stage,* 142–43.

18. James, *Old Drury of Philadelphia,* 19.

19. Written by Matthew Gregory "Monk" Lewis, *Timour the Tartar* was an immediate success when it premiered in London in 1811.

20. Thayer, *Annals of the American Circus,* 1:58.

21. A mortgage document dated February 22, 1812, is in the Theatre Arts Collection of the Harry Ransom Humanities Research Center at the University of Texas at Austin.

22. Thayer, *Annals of the American Circus,* 1:69.

23. Stine, "Philadelphia Theater, 1682–1829," 149.

24. James, *Old Drury of Philadelphia,* 21–22.

25. Brede, *German Drama in English on the Philadelphia Stage,* 200.

26. C. Durang, *Philadelphia Stage,* 1:113–14.

27. Saxon, *Enter Foot and Horse,* 7.

28. C. Durang, *Philadelphia Stage,* 1:113.

29. Quoted in ibid., 1:118.

30. Ibid., 1:120.

31. Ibid., 1:127.

32. Thayer, *Annals of the American Circus,* 1:102–3, 128–32.

33. Thayer, "Victor Pepin's Genealogy," 31.

34. Thayer, *Annals of the American Circus,* 1:142–43.

35. C. Durang, *Philadelphia Stage,* 2:57.

36. Thayer, "Victor Pepin's Genealogy," 31.

CHAPTER 3

1. Wood, *Personal Recollections of the Stage,* 326.

2. Ibid., 237.

3. Ibid., 249.

4. C. Durang, *Philadelphia Stage,* 1:139.

5. Quoted in Alger, *Life of Edwin Forrest,* 66.

6. Moody, *Edwin Forrest,* 18.

7. C. Durang, *Philadelphia Stage,* 1:138.

8. Alger, *Life of Edwin Forrest,* 143.

9. C. Durang, *Philadelphia Stage,* 1:151.

10. Wood, *Personal Recollections of the Stage,* 260.

11. Ibid., 262.

12. C. Durang, *Philadelphia Stage,* 1:154.

13. Quoted in ibid.

14. Wood, *Personal Recollections of the Stage,* 275.

15. Wood says in his autobiography that it was William Forrest, Edwin's brother, who had the part. A letter published in Alger, *Life of Edwin Forrest,* however, has Edwin writing to William about his triumph on the stage that night (72).

16. See James, *Old Drury of Philadelphia,* 344.

17. Stuart Thayer says that Hunter made his American debut in Baltimore on December 9, 1822 (1:112), while Charles Durang has him joining the show the following season. Announcements in the *Franklin Gazette* support Durang's date.

18. C. Durang, *Philadelphia Stage,* 1:190–91.

19. Ibid., 1:213.

20. Ibid., 1:202.

21. Wood, *Personal Recollections of the Stage,* 331.

22. C. Durang, *Philadelphia Stage,* 1:238.

23. Ibid., 1:253.

24. Cowell, *Thirty Years Passed Among the Players,* 83.

25. C. Durang, *Philadelphia Stage,* 1:259.

26. Wemyss, *Theatrical Biography,* 144.

27. Wilson, *Three Hundred Years of American Drama,* 83.

28. See Morris, *Curtain Time,* 86.

29. Forrest had played in Philadelphia twice since then. In January 1828 he appeared at the Chestnut in *Brutus, Damon and Pythias, William Tell,* and *Virginius,* and he returned in late April with Thomas Cooper in *Othello* and *Venice Preserved.* They played two performances of *Othello.* In the first, on April 30, Forrest played Iago to Cooper's Othello. At the second performance of the play, on May 5, they switched roles.

30. C. Durang, *Philadelphia Stage,* 1:261.

31. Wood, *Personal Recollections of the Stage,* 353.

CHAPTER 4

1. C. Durang, *Philadelphia Stage*, 2:274.

2. Cowell, *Thirty Years Passed Among the Players*, 80.

3. Wemyss, *Theatrical Biography*, 160.

4. The Chapmans' career on riverboats is detailed in Graham, *Showboats*, 9–21.

5. C. Durang, *Philadelphia Stage*, 2:40.

6. Ibid., 2:40, 63.

7. Ibid., 2:75.

8. Wemyss, *Theatrical Biography*, 182.

9. Ibid., 178.

10. C. Durang, *Philadelphia Stage*, 2:71.

11. Ibid., 2:172.

12. Wemyss, *Theatrical Biography*, 200–201.

13. C. Durang, *Philadelphia Stage*, 2:118, 120–21.

14. Ibid., 2:118.

15. Wilson, *History of the Philadelphia Theatre*, 94.

16. C. Durang, *Philadelphia Stage*, 2:120.

17. Wemyss, *Theatrical Biography*, 212.

18. C. Durang, *Philadelphia Stage*, 2:121.

19. Wemyss, *Theatrical Biography*, 208.

20. C. Durang, *Philadelphia Stage*, 2:119.

21. Ibid., 2:130.

22. Ibid., 2:137.

23. This and the quotations in the following section are from ibid., 2:154, 115, and 157, respectively.

24. Ibid., 2:164.

25. Wemyss, *Theatrical Biography*, 256.

26. C. Durang, *Philadelphia Stage*, 2:165.

27. Wemyss, *Theatrical Biography*, 258.

28. Wilson, *History of the Philadelphia Theatre*, 13, 16.

29. Wemyss, *Theatrical Biography*, 271.

30. Ibid., 272–73.

CHAPTER 5

1. Ireland, *Records of the New York Stage*, 2:318.

2. C. Durang, *Philadelphia Stage*, 2:186.

3. Quoted in ibid., 2:198.

4. Wemyss, *Theatrical Biography*, 301.

5. C. Durang, *Philadelphia Stage*, 2:199.

6. Ibid., 2:173.

7. Thayer, *Annals of the American Circus*, 2:86–87.

8. Vandenhoff, *Leaves from an Actor's Note-Book*, 195.

9. Ibid., 196.

10. C. Durang, *Philadelphia Stage*, 2:215.

11. Ibid., 2:235.

12. Ibid., 2:251.

13. Ibid., 2:258, 260, 261.

14. Ibid., 2:273.

15. Ibid., 2:292.

16. Ireland, *Records of the New York Stage*, 2:528.

17. C. Durang, *Philadelphia Stage*, 2:299.

18. Ibid., 2:300.

19. *Philadelphia Public Ledger*, June 4, 1849.

20. C. Durang, *Philadelphia Stage*, 2:355.

CHAPTER 6

1. Thomas Baldwin and J. Thomas, *New Gazetteer of the United States, 1854*, quoted in Weigley, *Philadelphia*, 310.

2. Williams, "Guy Mannering and Charlotte Cushman's Meg Merrilies," 34.

3. Leach, *Bright Particular Star*, 223.

4. C. Durang, *Philadelphia Stage*, 2:303.

5. Leach, *Bright Particular Star*, 233.

6. *Philadelphia Public Ledger*, January 20, 1852.

7. Ibid., June 4, 1852.

8. C. Durang, *Philadelphia Stage*, 2:378.

9. Ibid., 2:392.

10. Ibid., 2:408.

11. Morris, *Curtain Time*, 177.

12. Beauvallet, *Rachel and the New World*, 149, 152–53.

13. Scharf and Westcott, *History of Philadelphia*, 1:726.

14. *Philadelphia Daily News*, December 21, 1857, quoted in Curry, *Nineteenth-Century Women Theatre Managers*, 78.

15. Coder, "History of the Philadelphia Theatre," 72.

16. *Philadelphia Press*, August 23, 1858.

17. Ibid., September 27, 1858.

18. *New York Dramatic Mirror*, August 1, 1903, 14.

19. *Philadelphia Public Ledger*, October 1, 1859.

CHAPTER 7

1. Coder, "History of the Philadelphia Theatre," 162.

2. "The Last of a Triad of Great Comedians," *Brooklyn Daily Eagle*, November 15, 1885, John Sleeper Clarke file, Harvard Theatre Collection, Harvard University.

3. Coder, "History of the Philadelphia Theatre," 90.

4. Catton, *Reflections on the Civil War*, 87.

5. *Spirit of the Times*, October 4, 1862, quoted in Curry, *Nineteenth-Century Women Theatre Managers*, 83.

6. Coder, "History of the Philadelphia Theatre," 93.

7. Ibid., 31.

8. Ibid., 170.

9. Quoted in Bordman, *Oxford Companion to the Theatre*, 93.

10. Clarke, *John Wilkes Booth*, 91.

11. Coder, "History of the Philadelphia Theatre," 100.

12. Scharf and Westcott, *History of Philadelphia*, 1:824.

13. Kimmel, *Mad Booths of Maryland*, 271.

14. Quoted in Morris, *Curtain Time*, 25.

CHAPTER 8

1. Pitou, *Masters of the Show*, 22, 25.

2. Ibid., 21.

3. Coder, "History of the Philadelphia Theatre," 37.

4. Pitou, *Masters of the Show*, 21.

5. Review by William Winter in the *New York Tribune*, quoted in Williams, *Our Moonlight Revels*, 124.

6. Pitou, *Masters of the Show*, 21–22.

7. Quoted in Morris, *Curtain Time*, 206.

8. Pitou, *Masters of the Show*, 21.

9. Coder, "History of the Philadelphia Theatre," 107.

10. Pitou, *Masters of the Show*, 18.

11. Forrest remained the biggest draw at the Walnut. His first week there, he was paid $2,806.90—presumably half the total receipts. The following week he earned $2,676.99, and the third week $2,234.84. Only Joseph Jefferson and Mr. and Mrs. Barney Williams came close to matching Forrest that season. Neither of them brought in more than $2,000 a week. These figures are based on Thomas Hemphill's account books, quoted in Coder, "History of the Philadelphia Theatre," 40.

12. Pitou, *Masters of the Show*, 16–17, 20.

13. Quoted in Durham, *American Theatre Companies*, 61.

14. Ibid., 215.

15. *Brooklyn Daily Eagle*, November 15, 1885.

16. Bordman, *American Theatre, 1869–1914*, 60.

17. *Philadelphia Press*, May 17, 1873.

18. Ruggles, *Prince of Players*, 238.

19. See Rees, *Life of Edwin Forrest*, 502.

20. Coder, "History of the Philadelphia Theatre," 52, 130.

21. "Walnut-Street Theatre," *Philadelphia Press*, November 24, 1873.

22. Ruggles, *Prince of Players*, 235.

23. Bordman, *American Theatre, 1869–1914*, 89.

24. Weigley, *Philadelphia*, 466.

25. Marshall, "History of the Philadelphia Theatre," 4–5.

26. Skinner, *Footlights and Spotlights*, 60, 57, 75, 59.

27. Ibid., 80.

CHAPTER 9

1. Marshall, "History of the Philadelphia Theatre," 19–20.

2. Pitou, *Masters of the Show*, 131.

3. Marshall, "History of the Philadelphia Theatre," 24.

4. Kiralfy, *Bolossy Kiralfy*, 109.

5. Marshall, "History of the Philadelphia Theatre," 42.

6. *Philadelphia Public Ledger*, February 3, 1880.

7. Smith, *Musical Comedy in America*, 60.

8. Bordman, *American Theatre, 1869–1914*, 153.

9. *Philadelphia Public Ledger*, October 25, 1881.

10. Marshall, "History of the Philadelphia Theatre," 61–62.

11. For more on Frank Bush, see Erdman, *Staging the Jew*, 75–83.

12. Bordman, *American Theatre, 1869–1914*, 123.

13. Marshall, "History of the Philadelphia Theatre," 89.

14. Bordman, *American Theatre, 1869–1914*, 228.

15. Marshall, "History of the Philadelphia Theatre," 102, 103, 120, 122.

16. Bordman, *American Theatre, 1869–1914*, 238, 249.

17. Potts, "History of the Philadelphia Theatre," chapter 1, p. 11. The page numbering of this doctoral dissertation starts over at 1 in each chapter, hence the provision of chapter as well as page numbers in citations of this source.

18. Ibid., chapter 1, pp. 1, 3.

19. Brown, *History of the American Stage*, 306.

20. Quoted in Dill, *Mathew Dill Genealogy*, 2:67.

21. Perry, *James A. Herne*, 167. Perry states that the play was staged at the Chestnut Street Theatre. In fact, it opened at the Walnut.

22. Potts, "History of the Philadelphia Theatre," chapter 2, p. 3.

23. *Philadelphia Public Ledger*, September 6, 1892.

24. Potts, "History of the Philadelphia Theatre," chapter 1, p. 13.

25. See Carroll, *Matinee Idols*, 61.

26. *Philadelphia Public Ledger*, November 19, 1895.

27. Ibid., December 3, 1895.

28. Ibid., December 7, 1895.

29. Bordman, *American Theatre, 1869–1914*, 383.

CHAPTER 10

1. Poggi, *Theater in America*, 14.

2. Potts, "History of the Philadelphia Theatre," chapter 7, pp. 5–6.

3. *Philadelphia Public Ledger,* October 5, 1898.

4. Wilstach, *Richard Mansfield,* 328.

5. Meconnahey, "History of the Philadelphia Theatre," 3–4.

6. Slide, *Encyclopedia of Vaudeville,* 494.

7. Ibid., 488.

8. Lippman, "History of the Theatrical Syndicate," 93.

9. Bordman, *American Theatre, 1869–1914,* 468.

10. Bordman, *Oxford Companion to the Theatre,* 36.

11. Ibid., 483.

12. Meconnahey, "History of the Philadelphia Theatre," 23.

13. Hirsch, *Boys from Syracuse,* 45.

14. Poggi, *Theater in America,* 17.

15. Green and Laurie, *Show Biz,* 50.

16. Da Ponte, "Greatest Play of the South," 17.

17. Meconnahey, "History of the Philadelphia Theatre," 36–37.

18. Da Ponte, "Greatest Play of the South," 22.

19. Poggi, *Theater in America,* 30.

20. Bordman, *American Theatre, 1869–1914,* 675.

21. Glazer, *Philadelphia Theatres, A–Z,* 23.

22. Lippman, "History of the Theatrical Syndicate," 158.

23. Bernheim, *Business of the Theatre,* 71.

24. *Philadelphia Public Ledger,* March 30, 1915.

25. Hill, *Shakespeare in Sable,* 92–95.

26. Green and Laurie, *Show Biz,* 113.

27. Crosby, *America's Forgotten Pandemic,* 60–61.

28. *Philadelphia Public Ledger,* December 18, 1920.

CHAPTER 11

1. "Rededicating the Ancient and Honorable Walnut," *Philadelphia Public Ledger,* December 26, 1920.

2. "Walnut Opens with 'The Green Goddess,'" ibid., December 28, 1920.

3. *Philadelphia Inquirer,* December 28, 1920.

4. Alexander Woollcott, quoted in Bordman, *American Theatre, 1914–1930,* 145.

5. "Walnut Opens with 'The Green Goddess.'"

6. Quoted in Bordman, *Oxford Companion to the Theatre,* 293.

7. "'The Emperor Jones' a Study in Atavism," *Philadelphia Public Ledger,* November 22, 1921.

8. C. H. Bonte, "Anna and Her Ancestors," ibid., December 10, 1922.

9. Arthur B. Waters, "Where to Go and Why," ibid., December 28, 1924.

10. "Otis Skinner Stars in 'Captain Fury,'" ibid., March 2, 1926.

11. Green and Laurie, *Show Biz,* 269–70.

12. Crichton, *Marx Brothers,* 245.

13. "'I'll Say She Is' Has Propitious Opening," *Philadelphia Public Ledger,* June 5, 1923.

14. Bordman, *American Musical Theatre,* 365–66.

15. Arthur P. Dudden, "The City Embraces 'Normalcy,' 1919–1929," quoted in Weigley, *Philadelphia,* 572.

16. Arthur B. Waters, "Youth Is Served Again," *Philadelphia Public Ledger,* November 21, 1926.

17. Hayes, *My Life in Three Acts,* 119.

18. Hayes, *Gift of Joy,* 127.

19. Poggi, *Theater in America,* 84.

20. "Wiles of Feminine Slayers Satirized in Play at Walnut," *Philadelphia Public Ledger,* February 7, 1928.

21. "Mirthful Comedy from Ancient Greece to Launch New Theatre Group's Season," ibid., April 20, 1930.

22. "'As You Desire Me,' Pirandello Drama, Given at Walnut," ibid., December 2, 1930.

23. "'Hamlet' Cloaked in New Grandeur by Geddes' Craft," ibid., October 21, 1931.

24. Bailey and Kennedy, *American Pageant,* 807.

25. "Program at Walnut," *Philadelphia Public Ledger,* February 23, 1933.

26. "Walnut Reopens with Films, Vaudeville," ibid., February 23, 1934.

27. Sidney B. Whipple, undated clipping, Brothers Ashkenazi file, Free Library of Philadelphia.

28. "'Third of a Nation' Adapted to Phila.," *Philadelphia Inquirer,* October 18, 1938.

29. "'Prologue to Glory' at Walnut," ibid., December 20, 1938.

30. "'Spirochete' at Walnut," ibid., February 21, 1939.

31. Flanagan, *Arena,* 252.

32. Oderman, *Lillian Gish,* 245.

CHAPTER 12

1. Hirsch, *Boys from Syracuse,* 216.

2. Stagg, *Brothers Shubert,* 342.

3. Ibid., 357.

4. Hirsch, *Boys from Syracuse,* 199.

5. *Philadelphia Inquirer,* February 24, 1942.

6. Sidney B. Whipple, "Native Son Stark Drama Stamped with Genius," undated clipping, *Native Son* clippings file, Free Library of Philadelphia.

7. Quoted in Edwards, *Remarkable Woman,* 226–27.

8. Langner, *Magic Curtain,* 336.

9. Hughes, *History of the American Theatre*, 448.

10. Linton Martin, "'Blithe Spirit' Opens Here at Walnut," *Philadelphia Inquirer*, October 5, 1943.

11. Linton Martin, "Gestapo Play at Walnut," ibid., December 21, 1943.

12. Linton Martin, "'Man Who Had All the Luck' Opens on Walnut Stage," ibid., November 14, 1944.

13. Linton Martin, "Eva Le Gallienne Brings 'Cherry Orchard' Here," ibid., November 21, 1944.

14. Langner, *Magic Curtain*, 261.

15. Stagg, *Brothers Shubert*, 357.

16. Laurents, *Original Story By*, 76, 75.

17. Linton Martin, "'Heartsong' Makes Bow at the Walnut," *Philadelphia Inquirer*, March 18, 1947.

18. Laurents, *Original Story By*, 77, 74–75.

19. "Blackstone's Magic at Walnut," *Philadelphia Inquirer*, November 12, 1946.

20. Jerry Gaghan, "'The Iceman Cometh'—O'Neill Drama at Walnut," *Philadelphia Daily News*, April 8, 1947.

21. *Philadelphia Inquirer*, September 25, 1947.

22. Linton Martin, "'Streetcar Named Desire' Is Strong Dramatic Meat," *Philadelphia Inquirer*, November 23, 1947.

23. Edwin H. Schloss, "'Streetcar Named Desire' Opens at the Walnut," ibid., November 18, 1947.

24. R. E. P. Sensenderfer, "A Streetcar Named Desire," *Philadelphia Evening Bulletin*, November 18, 1947.

25. Bob Franci, "Mr. Roberts," *Billboard*, February 28, 1948.

26. Linton Martin, "'Mr. Roberts' Hailed as Best of War Comedies," *Philadelphia Inquirer*, January 28, 1948.

27. Green and Laurie, *Show Biz*, 532.

28. Londré and Watermeier, *History of American Theater*, 361.

29. Green and Laurie, *Show Biz*, 541.

30. Edwin H. Schloss, "'Life with Mother' Opens on Walnut Stage," *Philadelphia Inquirer*, October 5, 1948.

31. Nadel, *Pictorial History of the Theatre Guild*, 219.

32. Edwin H. Schloss, "Schwartz Star of 'Hershel' at Walnut," *Philadelphia Inquirer*, February 22, 1949.

33. Henry T. Murdock, "'Riverside Dr.' Brought Here by Schwartz," ibid., December 20, 1950.

34. Hirsch, *Boys from Syracuse*, 219, 217.

35. R. E. P. Sensenderfer, "Gigi," undated clipping, *Gigi* file, Free Library of Philadelphia.

36. Laura Lee, "Continental Actress Makes U.S. Stage Debut in 'Gigi,'" *Philadelphia Sunday Bulletin*, November 11, 1951.

37. Bordman, *American Theatre, 1930–1969*, 303.

38. Laurents, *Original Story By*, 193.

CHAPTER 13

1. Stagg, *Brothers Shubert*, 384.

2. Atkinson, *Broadway*, 426.

3. Hirsch, *Boys from Syracuse*, 229.

4. Henry T. Murdock, "'The Diary of Anne Frank' Opens at Walnut Theatre," *Philadelphia Inquirer*, September 16, 1955.

5. Strasberg, *Bittersweet*, 52.

6. Schildkraut, *My Father and I*, 237.

7. Barbara Wilson, "Marceau, Pantomimist, at Walnut," *Philadelphia Inquirer*, November 22, 1955.

8. Hirsch, *Boys from Syracuse*, 229.

9. Frank Brookhouser, "Man About Town," *Philadelphia Evening Bulletin*, February 5, 1959.

10. Quoted in Hansberry, *To Be Young, Gifted, and Black*, 128.

11. Quoted in Carter, *Hansberry's Drama*, 25.

12. Wapshott, *Rex Harrison*, 215.

13. Henry T. Murdock, "'Face of a Hero' Stars Jack Lemmon," *Philadelphia Inquirer*, September 15, 1960.

14. Henry T. Murdock, "Merry Marionettes," ibid., December 25, 1960.

15. Henry T. Murdock, "'Blow Your Horn' Plays Laugh Tone," ibid., February 3, 1961.

16. Simon, *Rewrites*, 69–70.

17. Walter Kerr quoted in "B'Way Likes 'Horn,'" *Philadelphia Inquirer*, February 26, 1961.

18. Edelman and Kupferberg, *Matthau*, 131.

19. Henry T. Murdock, "Old Play Gets New Outlook," *Philadelphia Inquirer*, March 21, 1962.

20. Henry T. Murdock, "Eva Le Gallienne Reaches Peak as 'Elizabeth,'" ibid., November 29, 1961.

21. Sheehy, *Eva Le Gallienne*, 345, 361.

22. Hirsch, *Boys from Syracuse*, 253.

23. Ibid., 256.

24. Evans, *All This and Evans, Too*, 288.

25. Henry T. Murdock, "'Two Players' Provides Rich Gallery of Bard," *Philadelphia Inquirer*, February 26, 1963.

26. Henry T. Murdock, "Road to a Man's Destruction in Osborne's 'Inadmissible Evidence,'" ibid., November 11, 1965.

27. Quoted in Lax, *On Being Funny*, 214, 211.

28. Devlin, *Conversations with Tennessee Williams*, 204.

29. Henry T. Murdock, "'Seven Descents of Myrtle' Is Newest Williams Play," *Philadelphia Inquirer*, March 12, 1968.

30. Henry T. Murdock, "Flanders, Swann Open in 'Drop of Another Hat,'" ibid., November 8, 1966.

CHAPTER 14

1. Loving, "Restoration of the Walnut Street Theatre," 31.

2. Minutes of the meeting of the board of directors, August 15, 1972, Walnut Street Theatre archives.

3. William J. Nazzarro, "Walnut Theatre Names Duprey Artistic Director," *Philadelphia Bulletin*, undated clipping in Walnut Street Theatre scrapbook, "Press Releases 1971–74," ibid.

4. William B. Collins, "Drama Guild Needs Money, and Lots More Imagination," *Philadelphia Inquirer*, April 21, 1974.

5. *Philadelphia Inquirer*, August 31, 1975.

6. *Philadelphia Evening Bulletin*, May 16, 1976.

7. Wolf, "The Bicentennial City, 1968–1982," quoted in Weigley, *Philadelphia*, 731.

8. *Philadelphia Evening Bulletin*, September 10, 1976.

9. Minutes of the meeting of the board of directors, September 20, 1977, Walnut Street Theatre archives.

10. Ernest Schier, "What's a Stage Without the Players?" *Philadelphia Evening Bulletin*, February 12, 1978.

11. William B. Collins, "The 'Chef' Is Fine; It's Just His Menu," *Philadelphia Inquirer*, March 19, 1978.

12. Woll, *Black Musical Theatre*, 270–71.

13. *Philadelphia Inquirer*, September 11, 1978.

14. Ernest Schier, "Seale's Seal on the Guild," *Philadelphia Evening Bulletin*, April 1, 1979.

15. Ernest Schier, "Walnut Won't Miss the Drama Guild," ibid., June 2, 1980.

16. John R. Cochran, "Belt-Tightening at the Walnut: No More Subscription Series," ibid., April 28, 1981.

17. William B. Collins, "His Mission: Restore the Walnut St. Theatre to Glory," *Philadelphia Inquirer*, December 5, 982.

CHAPTER 15

1. Press release, "Bernard Havard Named Executive Director of Philadelphia's Walnut Street Theatre," October 11, 1982, Walnut Street Theatre archives.

2. William B. Collins, "Walnut Will Undertake a New Role," *Philadelphia Inquirer*, October 14, 1982.

3. William B. Collins, "There's Plenty on the Stage Here, But Is It Theatre?" ibid., May 13, 1984.

4. Quoted in Gleklen, "The Times They Are a Changin'," 9, 6.

5. *Walnut Street News*, vol. 5, no. 1, 1993–94, Walnut Street Theatre archives.

6. *New York Times*, June 24, 1984.

7. Long Range Planning Committee meeting minutes, November 26, 1991, Walnut Street Theatre archives.

8. Pew Charitable Trusts, "Philadelphia Arts Market Study: The Walnut Street Theatre," September 7, 1989, prepared by Ziff Marketing, Inc., New York, xxvi, ibid.

9. Clifford A. Ridley, "'Cabaret' with the Show's Heart Out of Balance," *Philadelphia Inquirer*, May 3, 1996.

CHAPTER 16

1. *Philadelphia Inquirer*, December 9, 1999.

2. Quoted in Dan Geringer, "My Hometown," *Philadelphia Daily News*, October 1, 2001.

Alger, William Rounseville. *Life of Edwin Forrest, the American Tragedian*. 1877. Reprint, New York: Benjamin Blom, 1972.

Alpert, Hollis. *The Barrymores*. New York: Dial Press, 1964.

Archer, Stephen M. *Junius Brutus Booth, Theatrical Prometheus*. Carbondale: Southern Illinois University Press, 1992.

Armstrong, W. G. *A Record of the Opera in Philadelphia*. 1884. Reprint, New York: AMS Press, 1976.

Atkinson, Brooks. *Broadway*. New York: Macmillan, 1974.

Baigell, Matthew Eli. "John Haviland." PhD diss., University of Pennsylvania, 1965.

Bailey, Thomas A., and David M. Kennedy. *The American Pageant*. 9th ed. Lexington, Mass.: D. C. Heath, 1991.

Bank, Rosemary K. "A Reconsideration of the Death of Nineteenth-Century American Repertory Companies and the Rise of the Combination." *Essays in Theatre* 5, no. 1 (1986): 61–75.

Barnum, P. T. *Barnum's Own Story*. Ed. Waldo R. Browne. 1927. Reprint, Gloucester, Mass.: Peter Smith, 1972.

Baumol, William J., and William G. Bowen. *Performing Arts: The Economic Dilemma*. New York: Twentieth Century Fund, 1966.

Beauvallet, Léon. *Rachel and the New World: Tragedienne in America*. New York: Abelard-Schuman, 1967.

Bernheim, Alfred L. *The Business of the Theatre*. New York: Actors' Equity Association, 1932.

Binns, Archie. *Mrs. Fiske and the American Theatre*. New York: Crown, 1955.

Bloom, Arthur. *Joseph Jefferson, Dean of the American Theatre*. Savannah, Ga.: Frederic C. Beil, 2000.

Bordman, Gerald. *American Musical Comedy: From Adonis to Dreamgirls*. New York: Oxford University Press, 1982.

———. *American Musical Theatre: A Chronicle*. New York: Oxford University Press, 1978.

———. *American Theatre: A Chronicle of Comedy and Drama, 1869–1914*. New York: Oxford University Press, 1994.

———. *American Theatre: A Chronicle of Comedy and Drama, 1914–1930*. New York: Oxford University Press, 1995.

———. *American Theatre: A Chronicle of Comedy and Drama, 1930–1969*. New York: Oxford University Press, 1996.

———. *The Oxford Companion to the Theatre*. New York: Oxford University Press, 1984.

Brede, Charles Frederic. *The German Drama in English on the Philadelphia Stage from 1794 to 1830*. Philadelphia: Americana Germanica Press, 1918.

Bridenbaugh, Carl, and Jessica Bridenbaugh. *Rebels and Gentlemen: Philadelphia in the Age of Franklin*. New York: Reynal & Hitchcock, 1942.

Brown, T. Allston. *History of the American Stage*. 1870. Reprint, New York: Benjamin Blom, 1969.

Bryan, Vernanne. *Laura Keene: A British Actress on the American Stage, 1826–1873*. Jefferson, N.C.: McFarland, 1993.

Burge, James C. *Lines of Business: Casting Practice and Policy in the American Theatre, 1752–1899*. New York: Peter Lang, 1986.

Butsch, Richard. *The Making of American Audiences: From Stage to Television, 1750–1990*. New York: Cambridge University Press, 2000.

Buttitta, Tony, and Barry Witham. *Uncle Sam Presents: A Memoir of the Federal Theatre, 1935–1939*. Philadelphia: University of Pennsylvania Press, 1982.

Carey, Gary. *All the Stars in Heaven: Louis B. Mayer's M-G-M.* New York: E. P. Dutton, 1981.

———. *Katharine Hepburn: A Hollywood Yankee.* New York: St. Martin's Press, 1983.

Carlyon, David. *Dan Rice: The Most Famous Man You've Never Heard Of.* New York: Public Affairs, 2001.

Carroll, David. *The Matinee Idols.* New York: Galahad Books, 1972.

Carter, Steven R. *Hansberry's Drama: Commitment and Complexity.* Urbana: University of Illinois Press, 1991.

Catton, Bruce. *Reflections on the Civil War.* Ed. John Leekley. New York: Berkley Books, 1981.

Chandler, Charlotte. *Hello, I Must Be Going: Groucho and His Friends.* Garden City, N.Y.: Doubleday, 1978.

Chindahl, George L. *A History of the Circus in America.* Caldwell, Idaho: Caxton Printers, 1959.

Christy, Jim. *Theatre in Philadelphia.* Philadelphia: Pew Charitable Trusts, 2001.

Clark, Susie C. *John McCullough as Man, Actor, and Spirit.* New York: Broadway Publishing, 1914.

Clarke, Asia Booth. *John Wilkes Booth: A Sister's Memoir.* Ed. Terry Alford. Jackson: University Press of Mississippi, 1996.

Coad, Oral Sumner, and Edwin Mims Jr. *The American Stage.* Pageant of America 14. New Haven: Yale University Press, 1929.

Cockrell, Dale. *Demons of Disorder: Early Blackface Minstrels and Their World.* New York: Cambridge University Press, 1997.

Coder, William Dickey. "A History of the Philadelphia Theatre, 1856–1878." PhD diss., University of Pennsylvania, 1936.

Cowell, Joe. *Thirty Years Passed Among the Players in England and America.* New York: Harper & Brothers, 1844.

Crawford, Mary Caroline. *The Romance of the American Theatre.* New York: Halcyon House, 1913.

Crichton, Kyle. *The Marx Brothers.* Garden City, N.Y.: Doubleday, 1950.

Crosby, Alfred W. *America's Forgotten Pandemic: The Influenza of 1918.* New York: Cambridge University Press, 1989.

Crowther, Bosley. *Hollywood Rajah: The Life and Times of Louis B. Mayer.* New York: Holt, Rinehart and Winston, 1960.

Curry, Jane Kathleen. *Nineteenth-Century American Women Theatre Managers.* Westport, Conn.: Greenwood Press, 1994.

Da Ponte, Durant. "The Greatest Play of the South." *Tennessee Studies in Literature* 2 (1957): 15–24.

Davis, Peter A. "From Stock to Combination: The Panic of 1873 and Its Effects on the American Theatre Industry." *Theatre History Studies* 8 (1988): 1–9.

Devlin, Albert J., ed. *Conversations with Tennessee Williams.* Jackson: University Press of Mississippi, 1986.

Dickey, John M. "The Restoration of the Walnut Street Theatre—the Exterior." *Bulletin of the Philadelphia Old Town Historical Society* 1, no. 2 (1971): 27–30.

Dieck, Herman L. "Centenary of America's Oldest Playhouse." *Theatre Magazine,* April 1908, 96–100.

Dill, Rosalie Jones. *Mathew Dill Genealogy: A Study of the Dill Family of Dillsburg, York County, Pennsylvania, 1698–1935.* 2 vols. Spokane, Wash., 1935.

Disher, Maurice Willson. *Blood and Thunder: Mid-Victorian Melodrama and Its Origins.* London: Frederick Muller, 1949.

Dizikes, John. *Opera in America: A Cultural History.* New Haven: Yale University Press, 1993.

Donohue, Joseph W., Jr., ed. *The Theatrical Manager in England and America: Player of a Perilous Game.* Princeton: Princeton University Press, 1971.

Douglas, Ann. *The Feminization of American Culture.* 2nd ed. New York: Knopf, 1977.

Duclow, Geraldine A. "Now Presenting America's Oldest Playhouse: The Walnut Street Theatre." *Pennsylvania Heritage* (Winter 1998): 32–38.

Dudden, Faye. *Women in the American Theatre: Actresses and Audiences.* New Haven: Yale University Press, 1994.

Dunlap, William. *History of the American Theatre and Anecdotes of the Principal Actors.* New York: Burt Franklin, 1963.

Durang, Charles. *History of the Philadelphia Stage Between the Years 1749 and 1855.* 1856. Arranged and illustrated by Thompson Westcott. 7 vols. in 2 parts. Source Materials in the Field of Theatre 36, reels 6–9. Ann Arbor: University Microfilms, 1956.

Durang, John. *The Memoir of John Durang.* Ed. Alan S. Downer. Pittsburgh: University of Pittsburgh Press, 1966.

Durant, John, and Alice Durant. *Pictorial History of the American Circus.* New York: A. S. Barnes, 1957.

Durham, Weldon B., ed. *American Theatre Companies, 1749–1887.* Westport, Conn.: Greenwood Press, 1986.

Dye, William S. "Pennsylvania Versus the Theatre." *Pennsylvania Magazine of*

History and Biography 55 (October 1931): 332–72.
Edelman, Rob, and Audrey Kupferberg. *Matthau: A Life*. New York: Taylor Trade, 2002.
Edgett, Edwin F. *Edwin Loomis Davenport*. New York: Dunlap Society, 1901.
Edwards, Anne. *A Remarkable Woman: A Biography of Katharine Hepburn*. New York: William Morrow, 1985.
Emery, George M. "Passing of America's Oldest Playhouse." *Theatre Magazine*, June 1920, 506–8, 572.
Erdman, Harley. *Staging the Jew: The Performance of an American Ethnicity, 1860–1920*. New Brunswick: Rutgers University Press, 1997.
Evans, Maurice. *All This and Evans, Too: A Memoir*. Columbia: University of South Carolina Press, 1987.
Fawkes, Richard. *Dion Boucicault: A Biography*. New York: Quartet Books, 1979.
Felheim, Marvin. *The Theater of Augustin Daly: An Account of the Late Nineteenth-Century American Stage*. Cambridge: Harvard University Press, 1956.
Ferguson, Delane Cobb. *Victor Pepin, Circus Career: Descendants and Ancestors, 1760–1900*. Decorah, Iowa: Anundsen, 1992.
Field, Kate. *Charles Albert Fechter*. 1882. Reprint, New York: Benjamin Blom, 1969.
Fielder, Mari Kathleen. "Chauncey Olcott: Irish-American Mother-Love, Romance, and Nationalism." *Eire-Ireland* 22, no. 2 (1987): 4–26.
Fields, Armond. *Eddie Foy: A Biography*. Jefferson, N.C.: McFarland, 1999.
Fisher, Judith L., and Stephen Watt, eds. *When They Weren't Doing Shakespeare: Essays on Nineteenth-Century British and American Theatre*. Athens: University of Georgia Press, 1989.
Flanagan, Hallie. *Arena: The Story of the Federal Theatre*. 1940. Reprint, New York: Limelight Editions, 1985.
Fox, Charles Philip. *A Pictorial History of Performing Horses*. New York: Bramhall House, 1960.
Gallman, J. Matthew. *Mastering Wartime: A Social History of Philadelphia During the Civil War*. Philadelphia: University of Pennsylvania Press, 2000.
Geib, George W. "Playhouses and Politics: Lewis Hallam and the Confederation Theater." *Journal of Popular Culture* 5 (1971): 324–39.
Glazer, Irvin R. *Philadelphia Theatres, A–Z*. Westport, Conn.: Greenwood Press, 1986.
Gleklen, Jonathan Ian. "The Times They Are a Changin': Changes in Philadelphia's Walnut Street Theater as a Model for the Recent Changes in American Theater." Paper, April 2, 1985, Walnut Street Theatre archives.
Graham, Philip. *Showboats: The History of an American Institution*. Austin: University of Texas Press, 1951.
Graver, Lawrence. *An Obsession with Anne Frank: Meyer Levin and the Diary*. Berkeley and Los Angeles: University of California Press, 1995.
Green, Abel, and Joe Laurie Jr. *Show Biz: From Vaude to Video*. New York: Henry Holt, 1951.
Grimsted, David. *Melodrama Unveiled: American Theatre and Culture, 1800–1850*. Chicago: University of Chicago Press, 1968.
Hall, Roger A. *Performing the American Frontier, 1870–1906*. New York: Cambridge University Press, 2001.
Halttunen, Karen. *Confidence Men and Painted Women: A Study of Middle-Class Culture in America, 1830–1870*. New Haven: Yale University Press, 1982.
Hansberry, Lorraine. *To Be Young, Gifted, and Black*. New York: New American Library, 1969.
Hayes, Helen. *A Gift of Joy*. New York: J. B. Lippincott, 1965.
Hayes, Helen, with Katherine Hatch. *My Life in Three Acts*. New York: Touchstone, 1990.
Henneke, Ben Graf. *Laura Keene: A Biography*. Tulsa, Okla.: Council Oak Books, 1990.
Hewitt, Barnard. "'King Stephen' of the Park and Drury Lane." In *The Theatrical Manager in England and America: Player of a Perilous Game*, ed. Joseph W. Donohue Jr., 87–141. Princeton: Princeton University Press, 1971.
———. *Theatre U.S.A., 1665 to 1957*. New York: McGraw-Hill, 1959.
Higham, Charles. *Merchant of Dreams: Louis B. Mayer, M-G-M, and the Secret Hollywood*. New York: Donald L. Fine, 1993.
Hill, Errol. *Shakespeare in Sable: A History of Black Shakespearean Actors*. Amherst: University of Massachusetts Press, 1984.
Hillebrand, Harold Newcomb. *Edmund Kean*. 1933. Reprint, New York: AMS Press, 1966.
Hirsch, Foster. *The Boys from Syracuse: The Shuberts' Theatrical Empire*. Carbondale: Southern Illinois University Press, 1998.
Hischak, Thomas S. *American Theatre: A Chronicle of Comedy and Drama, 1969–2000*.

New York: Oxford University Press, 2001.

Hodge, Francis. *Yankee Theatre: The Image of America on the Stage, 1825–1850.* Austin: University of Texas Press, 1964.

Houchin, John H. "The Struggle for Virtue: Professional Theatre in Eighteenth-Century Philadelphia." *Theatre History Studies* 19 (1999): 167–88.

Hughes, Glenn. *A History of the American Theatre, 1700–1950.* New York: Samuel French, 1951.

Inscoe, John C. "*The Clansman* on Stage and Screen: North Carolina Reacts." *North Carolina Historical Review* 64 (1987): 139–61.

Ireland, Joseph N. *Records of the New York Stage from 1750 to 1860.* 2 vols. 1866–67. Reprint, New York: Burt Franklin, 1968.

James, Reese David. *Cradle of Culture, 1800–1810: The Philadelphia Stage.* Philadelphia: University of Pennsylvania Press, 1957.

———. *Old Drury of Philadelphia: A History of the Philadelphia Stage, 1800–1835.* 1932. Reprint, New York: Greenwood Press, 1968.

Jefferson, Joseph. *The Autobiography of Joseph Jefferson.* Ed. Alan S. Downer. Cambridge: Belknap Press of Harvard University Press, 1964.

Jones, Charles K., and Lorenzo K. Greenwich II, eds. *A Choice Collection of the Works of Francis Johnson.* New York: Point Two Publications, 1983.

Jones, John Bush. *Our Musicals, Ourselves: A Social History of the American Musical Theatre.* Hanover, N.H.: Brandeis University Press, 2003.

Kasson, Joy S. *Buffalo Bill's Wild West: Celebrity, Memory, and Popular History.* New York: Hill & Wang, 2000.

Keese, William Linn. *William E. Burton, Actor, Author, Manager.* New York: G. P. Putnam's Sons, 1885.

Kelley, Joseph J., Jr. *Life and Times in Colonial Philadelphia.* Harrisburg, Pa.: Stackpole Books, 1973.

Kelley, Paul B. "Portrait of a Playhouse: The 'Troc' of Philadelphia, 1870–1978." PhD diss., New York University, 1982.

Kimmel, Stanley. *The Mad Booths of Maryland.* Indianapolis: Bobbs-Merrill, 1940.

Kiralfy, Bolossy. *Bolossy Kiralfy, Creator of Great Musical Spectacles, an Autobiography.* Ed. Barbara M. Barker. Ann Arbor: UMI Research Press, 1988.

Koster, Donald Nelson. "The Theme of Divorce in American Drama, 1871–1939." PhD diss., University of Pennsylvania, 1942.

Kotler, Philip, and Joanne Scheff. *Standing Room Only: Strategies for Marketing the Performing Arts.* Boston: Harvard Business School Press, 1997.

Lacy, Robin Thurlow. *A Biographical Dictionary of Scenographers, 500 B.C. to 1900 A.D.* New York: Greenwood Press, 1990.

Langner, Lawrence. *The Magic Curtain.* New York: E. P. Dutton, 1951.

Laurents, Arthur. *Original Story By: A Memoir of Broadway and Hollywood.* New York: Knopf, 2000.

Laurie, Bruce. *Working People of Philadelphia, 1800–1850.* Philadelphia: Temple University Press, 1980.

Lax, Eric. *On Being Funny: Woody Allen and Comedy.* New York: Charterhouse, 1975.

Leach, Joseph. *Bright Particular Star: The Life and Times of Charlotte Cushman.* New Haven: Yale University Press, 1970.

Lifson, Davis S. *The Yiddish Theater in America.* Cranbury, N.J.: A. S. Barnes, 1965.

Lippman, Monroe. "History of the Theatrical Syndicate: Its Effect on the Theatre in America." PhD diss., University of Michigan, 1937.

Loackridge, Richard. *Darling of Misfortune: Edwin Booth, 1833–1893.* New York: Century, 1932.

Londré, Felicia Hardison, and Daniel J. Watermeier. *The History of American Theater: The United States, Canada, and Mexico from Pre-Columbian Times to the Present.* New York: Continuum International, 2000.

Loney, Glenn N. "Before and After: The Renovation and Reconstruction of Philadelphia's Walnut Street Theatre." *Theatre Design and Technology* 31 (December 1972): 7–15.

Loving, F. Bryan. "The Restoration of the Walnut Street Theatre—the Exterior." *Bulletin of the Philadelphia Old Town Historical Society* 1, no. 2 (1971): 30–32.

MacArthur, David Edward. "A Study of the Theatrical Career of Winthrop Ames from 1904 to 1929." PhD diss., Ohio State University, 1962.

MacCan, Richard Dyer. *The Silent Comedians.* Metuchen, N.J.: Scarecrow Press, 1993.

MacKay, Winnifred K. "Philadelphia During the Civil War, 1861–1865." *Pennsylvania Magazine of History and Biography* 70 (January 1946): 3–51.

Mammen, Edward William. *The Old Stock Company School of Acting: A Story of the Boston Museum.* Boston: Trustees of the Public Library, 1945.

Marion, John Francis. *Within These Walls: A History of the Academy of Music in Philadelphia*. Philadelphia: Academy of Music, 1984.

Marker, Lise-Lone. *David Belasco: Naturalism in the American Theatre*. Princeton: Princeton University Press, 1975.

Marshall, Thomas F. "A History of the Philadelphia Theatre, 1878–1890." PhD diss., University of Pennsylvania, 1941.

———. *A History of the Philadelphia Theatre for 1878, 1879, and a Checklist of Plays, 1878–1890*. Philadelphia: College Offset Press, 1943.

Mason, Jeffrey D. *Melodrama and the Myth of America*. Bloomington: Indiana University Press, 1993.

Mates, Julian. *The American Musical Stage Before 1800*. 1962. Reprint, Westport, Conn.: Greenwood Press, 1986.

Mathews, Brander, and Laurence Hutton, eds. *Actors and Actresses of Great Britain and the United States, from the Days of David Garrick to the Present Time*. 5 vols. New York: Cossell & Co., c. 1886.

Mayorga, Margaret G. *A Short History of the American Drama: Commentaries on Plays Prior to 1920*. New York: Dodd, Mead, 1932.

McConachie, Bruce A. "American Theatre in Context, from the Beginnings to 1870." In *The Cambridge History of American Theatre*, ed. Don B. Wilmeth and Christopher Bigsby, vol. 1, *Beginnings to 1870*, 111–81. New York: Cambridge University Press, 1998.

———. *Melodramatic Formations: American Theatre and Society, 1820–1870*. Iowa City: University of Iowa Press, 1992.

McGlinn, Alice A. "A Chronology of the Walnut Street Theatre, 1900–1920." Paper, January 1972. Walnut Street Theatre file, Theatre Collection, Free Library of Philadelphia.

McNamara, Brooks. "The Scenography of Popular Entertainment." *Drama Review* T-61 (March 1974): 16–24.

———. *The Shuberts of Broadway: A History Drawn from the Collections of the Shubert Archive*. New York: Oxford University Press, 1990.

Mease, James. *Picture of Philadelphia for 1824*. Philadelphia: Thomas Town, 1823.

Meconnahey, Joseph H. "The History of the Philadelphia Theatre from 1900–1910." PhD diss., University of Pennsylvania, 1937.

Melnick, Ralph. *The Stolen Legacy of Anne Frank: Meyer Levin, Lillian Hellman, and the Staging of the Diary*. New Haven: Yale University Press, 1997.

Merrill, Lisa. *When Romeo Was a Woman: Charlotte Cushman and Her Circle of Female Spectators*. Ann Arbor: University of Michigan Press, 1999.

Meserve, Walter J. *An Emerging Entertainment: The Drama of the American People to 1828*. Bloomington: Indiana University Press, 1977.

———. *Heralds of Promise: The Drama of the American People in the Age of Jackson, 1829–1849*. New York: Greenwood Press, 1986.

Miller, Arthur. *Timebends: A Life*. New York: Grove Press, 1987.

Miller, Jordan Y., and Winifred L. Frazer. *American Drama Between the Wars: A Critical History*. Boston: Twayne, 1991.

Moody, Richard. *The Astor Place Riot*. Bloomington: Indiana University Press, 1958.

———. *Edwin Forrest: First Star of the American Stage*. New York: Knopf, 1960.

Morris, Lloyd. *Curtain Time: The Story of the American Theater*. New York: Random House, 1953.

Moses, Montrose J. *The Fabulous Forrest: The Record of an American Actor*. 1929. Reprint, New York: Benjamin Blom, 1969.

Moy, James S. "John B. Ricketts' Circus, 1793–1800." PhD diss., University of Illinois at Urbana-Champaign, 1977.

Mullenix, Elizabeth Reitz. *Wearing the Breeches: Gender on the Antebellum Stage*. New York: St. Martin's Press, 2000.

Naabe, Derek. "Philadelphia's Theatre Heritage: The Walnut Street Theatre." *Germantown Crier* (Winter 1970): 14–18.

Nadel, Norman. *A Pictorial History of the Theatre Guild*. New York: Crown, 1969.

Nevins, Thomas F. "History of the Walnut Street Theatre in Philadelphia." Master's thesis, Villanova University, 1962.

Newman, Danny. *Subscribe Now! Building Arts Audiences Through Dynamic Subscription Promotion*. New York: Theatre Communications Group, 1983.

Oberholtzer, Ellis Paxton. *Philadelphia: A History of the City and Its People*. 2 vols. Philadelphia: S. J. Clarke, 1912.

Odell, George. *Annals of the New York Stage*. 15 vols. New York: Columbia University Press, 1927–49.

Oggel, L. Terry. *Edwin Booth: A Bio-Bibliography*. New York: Greenwood Press, 1992.

Olcott, Rita O'Donovan. *A Song in His Heart*. New York: House of Field, 1939.

Oderman, Stuart. *Lillian Gish: A Life on Stage and Screen*. Jefferson, N.C.:McFarland, 2002.

Pauly, Thomas H. *An American Odyssey: Elia Kazan and American Culture*. Philadelphia: Temple University Press, 1983.
Perry, John. *James A. Herne: The American Ibsen*. Chicago: Nelson-Hall, 1978.
Peterson, Bernard L., Jr. *Profiles of African American Stage Performers and Theater People, 1816–1960*. Westport, Conn.: Greenwood Press, 2001.
Pitou, Augustus. *Masters of the Show*. New York: Neale, 1914.
Playfair, Giles. *The Flash of Lightning: A Portrait of Edmund Kean*. London: William Kimber, 1983.
Poggi, Jack. *Theater in America: The Impact of Economic Forces, 1870–1967*. Ithaca: Cornell University Press, 1968.
Poitier, Sidney. *This Life*. New York: Knopf, 1980.
Pollock, Thomas Clark. *The Philadelphia Theatre in the Eighteenth Century*. New York: Greenwood Press, 1968.
Potts, Edgar Leroy. "A History of the Philadelphia Theatre, 1890–1900." PhD diss., University of Pennsylvania, 1932. Typescript, Annenberg Rare Book and Manuscript Library, University of Pennsylvania.
Quinn, Arthur Hobson. *A History of the American Drama from the Beginning to the Civil War*. New York: Harper & Brothers, 1923.
———. *A History of the American Drama from the Civil War to the Present Day*. 2 vols. New York: Harper & Brothers, 1927.
Rees, James. *The Life of Edwin Forrest*. Philadelphia: T. B. Peterson & Brothers, 1874.
Rice, Edward Le Roy. *Monarchs of Minstrelsy: From "Daddy" Rice to Date*. New York: Kenny, 1911.
Richardson, Gary A. *American Drama from the Colonial Period Through World War I: A Critical History*. New York: Twayne, 1993.
Riis, Thomas. "Musical Theatre." In *The Cambridge History of American Theatre*, ed. Don B. Wilmeth and Christopher Bigsby, vol. 2, *1870–1845*, 411–45. New York: Cambridge University Press, 1999.
Rourke, Constance. *Troupers of the Gold Coast, or the Rise of Lotta Crabtree*. New York: Harcourt Brace, 1928.
Rowell, George. *The Victorian Theatre: A Survey*. London: Oxford University Press, 1956.
Ruggles, Eleanor. *Prince of Players: Edwin Booth*. New York: W. W. Norton, 1953.
Sagala, Sandra K. *Buffalo Bill, Actor: A Chronicle of Cody's Theatrical Career*. Bowie, Md.: Heritage Books, 2002.
Salmon, Eric, ed. *Bernhardt and the Theatre of Her Time*. Westport, Conn.: Greenwood Press, 1984.
Sandrow, Nahma. *Vagabond Stars: A World of Yiddish Theater*. New York: Limelight Editions, 1977.
Saxon, A. H. *Enter Foot and Horse: A History of Hippodrama in England and France*. New Haven: Yale University Press, 1968.
Scharf, J. Thomas, and Thompson Westcott. *History of Philadelphia, 1609–1884*. 2 vols. Philadelphia: L. J. Everts, 1884.
Schildkraut, Joseph. *My Father and I*. New York: Viking Press, 1959.
Seymour, Bruce. *Lola Montez: A Life*. New Haven: Yale University Press, 1996.
Shafer, Yvonne. *American Women Playwrights, 1900–1950*. New York: Peter Lang, 1995.
Shattuck, Charles H. *Shakespeare on the American Stage: From the Hallams to Edwin Booth*. Washington, D.C.: Folger Shakespeare Library, 1976.
———. "The Theatrical Management of Edwin Booth." In *The Theatrical Manager in England and America: Player of a Perilous Game*, ed. Joseph W. Donohue Jr., 143–88. Princeton: Princeton University Press, 1971.
Sheehy, Helen. *Eva Le Gallienne: A Biography*. New York: Knopf, 1996.
Shelton, Suzanne. *Divine Dancer: A Biography of Ruth St. Denis*. Garden City, N.Y.: Doubleday, 1981.
Shockley, Martin Staples. *The Richmond Stage, 1784–1812*. Charlottesville: University Press of Virginia, 1977.
Simon, Neil. *Rewrites: A Memoir*. New York: Simon & Schuster, 1996.
Skinner, Otis. *Footlights and Spotlights: Recollections of My Life on the Stage*. Indianapolis: Bobbs-Merrill, 1924.
Slide, Anthony. *The Encyclopedia of Vaudeville*. Westport, Conn.: Greenwood Press, 1994.
Slout, William L. *Clowns and Cannons: The American Circus During the Civil War*. San Bernardino, Calif.: Borgo Press, 1997.
———. *Olympians of the Sawdust Circle: A Biographical Dictionary of the Nineteenth-Century American Circus*. Clipper Studies in the Theatre 18. San Bernardino, Calif.: Borgo Press, 1998.
Smith, Cecil. *Musical Comedy in America*. New York: Theatre Arts Books, 1950.
Smith, Geddeth. *Thomas Abthorpe Cooper: America's Premier Tragedian*. Madison: Fairleigh Dickinson University Press, 1996.

Smith, Sol. *Theatrical Management in the West and South for Thirty Years*. New York: Harper & Brothers, 1868.
Stagg, Jerry. *The Brothers Shubert*. New York: Random House, 1968.
Stevens, Sylvester K. *Pennsylvania: Birthplace of a Nation*. New York: Random House, 1965.
Stine, Richard D. "The Philadelphia Theater, 1682–1829: Its Growth as a Cultural Institution." PhD diss., University of Pennsylvania, 1951.
Strasberg, Susan. *Bittersweet*. New York: G. P. Putnam's Sons, 1980.
Sturtevant, C. G. "The Circus in Philadelphia." *White Tops*, November–December 1949, 3–10.
Thayer, Stuart. *Annals of the American Circus*. Vol. 1, *1793–1829*. Manchester, Mich.: Rymack Printing, 1976. Vol. 2, *1830–1847*. Seattle: Peanut Butter Publishing, 1986.
———. "Victor Pepin's Genealogy." *Bandwagon*, May–June 1992, 31.
Toll, Robert C. *Blacking Up: The Minstrel Show in Nineteenth-Century America*. New York: Oxford University Press, 1974.
Traubner, Richard. *Operetta: A Theatrical History*. New York: Doubleday, 1983.
Trussler, Simon. *The Cambridge Illustrated History of British Theatre*. New York: Cambridge University Press, 1994.
Turner, Mary M. *Forgotten Leading Ladies of the American Theatre*. Jefferson, N.C.: McFarland, 1990.
Vail, R. W. G. *Random Notes on the History of the Early American Circus*. Worcester, Mass.: American Antiquarian Society, 1934.
Vandenhoff, George. *Leaves from an Actor's Note-Book*. New York: D. Appleton, 1860.
Wapshott, Nicholas. *Rex Harrison: A Biography*. London: Chatto and Windus, 1987.
Weigley, Russell F., ed. *Philadelphia: A Three-Hundred-Year History*. New York: W. W. Norton, 1982.
Wemyss, Francis Courtney. *Theatrical Biography, or The Life of an Actor and Manager*. Glasgow: R. Griffin, 1858.
———. *Wemyss' Chronology of the American Stage from 1752 to 1852*. 1852. Reprint, New York: Benjamin Blom, 1968.
Williams, Gary Jay. "Guy Mannering and Charlotte Cushman's Meg Merrilies." In *When They Weren't Doing Shakespeare: Essays on Nineteenth-Century British and American Theatre*, ed. Judith L. Fisher and Stephen Watt, 19–38. Athens: University of Georgia Press, 1989.
———. *Our Moonlight Revels: A Midsummer Night's Dream in the Theatre*. Iowa City: University of Iowa Press, 1997.
Williams, Simon. "European Actors and the Star System in the American Theatre, 1752–1870." In *The Cambridge History of American Theatre*, ed. Don B. Wilmeth and Christopher Bigsby, vol. 1, *Beginnings to 1870*, 303–37. New York: Cambridge University Press, 1998.
Williams, William H. A. *'Twas Only an Irishman's Dream: The Image of Ireland and the Irish in American Popular Song Lyrics, 1800–1920*. Urbana: University of Illinois Press, 1996.
Wilmeth, Don B., and Christopher Bigsby, eds. *The Cambridge History of American Theatre*. 3 vols. New York: Cambridge University Press, 1998–2000.
Wilson, Arthur Herman. *A History of the Philadelphia Theatre, 1835 to 1855*. Philadelphia: University of Pennsylvania Press, 1935.
Wilson, Garff B. *A History of American Acting*. Bloomington: Indiana University Press, 1966.
———. *Three Hundred Years of American Drama and Theatre: From "Ye Bear and Ye Cubb" to "Hair."* Englewood Cliffs, N.J.: Prentice Hall, 1973.
Wilstach, Paul. *Richard Mansfield: The Man and the Actor*. New York: Charles Scribner's Sons, 1909.
Winter, Marian Hannah. *The Theatre of Marvels*. Trans. Charles Meldon. New York: Benjamin Blom, 1964.
Winter, William. *The Wallet of Time*. New York: Moffat, Yard, 1915.
Witham, Barry B., ed. *Theatre in the United States: A Documentary History*. Vol. 1, *1750–1915, Theatre in the Colonies and the United States*. New York: Cambridge University Press, 1996.
Wittke, Carl. *Tambo and Bones: A History of the American Minstrel Stage*. Durham: Duke University Press, 1930.
Woll, Allen. *Black Musical Theatre: From Coontown to Dreamgirls*. New York: Da Capo Press, 1989.
Wood, William B. *Personal Recollections of the Stage*. Philadelphia: Henry Carey Baird, 1855.
Woods, Alan. "Mademoiselle Rhea—an American Bernhardt?" In *Bernhardt and the Theatre of Her Time*, ed. Eric Salmon, 183–201. Westport, Conn.: Greenwood Press, 1984.
Wright, Richardson. *Hawkers and Walkers in Early America*. 1927. Reprint, New York: Frederick Ungar, 1965.

Italicized page references indicate illustrations and "cap" indicates references to captions.